A Cultural History of
Japanese Buddhism

A Cultural History of
Japanese Buddhism

William E. Deal and Brian Ruppert

WILEY Blackwell

This edition first published 2015
© 2015 William E. Deal and Brian Ruppert

Registered Office
John Wiley & Sons, Ltd, The Atrium, Southern Gate, Chichester, West Sussex, PO19 8SQ, UK

Editorial Offices
350 Main Street, Malden, MA 02148-5020, USA
9600 Garsington Road, Oxford, OX4 2DQ, UK
The Atrium, Southern Gate, Chichester, West Sussex, PO19 8SQ, UK

For details of our global editorial offices, for customer services, and for information about how
to apply for permission to reuse the copyright material in this book please see our website at
www.wiley.com/wiley-blackwell.

Library of Congress Cataloging-in-Publication Data

Deal, William E.
A cultural history of Japanese Buddhism / William E. Deal and Brian Ruppert.
      pages   cm. – (Wiley-blackwell guides to Buddhism ; 1)
   Includes bibliographical references and index.
   ISBN 978-1-4051-6700-0 (hardback) – ISBN 978-1-4051-6701-7 (paper)
1. Buddhism–Japan–History.   2. Buddhism and culture–Japan–History.   I. Ruppert,
Brian Douglas, 1962–   II. Title.
   BQ678.D43 2015
   294.30952–dc23

                                        2015004073

A catalogue record for this book is available from the British Library.

Cover image: Bodhisattva, from Descent of the 25 Blessed, Fujiwara period (1069–1155) Japanese
(detail). The Art Archive / Lucien Biton Collection Paris / © Gianni Dagli Orti / Picture-desk
Cover design by Design Deluxe

Set in 10/13pt Dante by SPi Publisher Services, Pondicherry, India
Printed and bound in Malaysia by Vivar Printing Sdn Bhd

1   2015

Contents

List of Illustrations   vii

Acknowledgments   ix

Introduction   1

1 Early Historical Contexts (Protohistory to 645)   13

2 Ancient Buddhism (645–950)   45

3 Early Medieval Buddhism (950–1300): The Dawn of Medieval Society and Related Changes in Japanese Buddhist Culture   87

4 Late Medieval Buddhism (1300–1467): New Buddhisms, Buddhist Learning, Dissemination and the Fall into Chaos   135

5 Buddhism and the Transition to the Modern Era (1467–1800)   171

6 Modern Buddhism (1800–1945)   209

7 Buddhism Since 1945   231

Character Glossary   255

Index   287

List of Illustrations

Figure 1.1   China Sea interaction sphere   15

Figure 1.2   Shaka Triad, Hōryūji Kondō, Nara Prefecture   35

Figure 3.1   Jizō Bodhisattva image, circa Edo period, Sanzen'in
temple, Ōhara   94

Figure 3.2   Nachi Falls, with Torii gate in foreground, Kumano   97

Figure 3.3   Entrance to traditional monastic cloister called Sonshō'in
(Seigantoji temple) at Nachi, Kumano, currently also used
for visitor lodging   104

Figure 3.4   Major Sites of the High Medieval Japanese Buddhist world   116

Figure 3.5   Scene from *Yūzū nenbutsu e-maki*, artist unknown, early
fourteenth century, handscroll   121

Figure 4.1   Grave of Hōnen, Chion'in Temple, Higashiyama, Kyoto   138

Figure 4.2   Medieval Buddhist Centers and Networking Sites   155

Figure 4.3   Esoteric Buddhist altar, Daikakuji temple, Kyoto   157

Figure 5.1   Ichiji Kinrin rite divinities (Sanskrit and Japanese), copy
of Daigoji sacred work *Genpi shō* made by monk Taijō (n.d.),
Hagaji temple (Wakasa, now Fukui Prefecture)   182

Figure 5.2   Illustrated guidebook mixing (top) non-iconic list of
33-Kannon of Kyoto (*Rakuyō sanjūsan ban fudasho*)
with visual depictions and descriptions (bottom) of
the 33-Kannon of the Kansai region (*Saigoku sanjūsan sho*),
attached to rear of *Kannongyō hayayomi e shō*, Osaka
and Kyoto   193

Figure 5.3   *Kannongyō hayayomi e shō* illustrations of Kannon saving
a man, respectively, from fire (Figure 5.3a) and from dragons,
fish, and demons (Figure 5.3b); kundoku reading together
with scriptural text below, and Japanese exegesis above   195

Figure 5.4   Prayer petition of Koike Iemon of Kazurashima village,
Shinshū (Kantō), Meiwa 5.3 (1768), signed by Dharma
Seal master Jitsujō, on behalf of the monthly-death-anniversary
rites of two departed spirits, memorial hall (*shidō*), Miroku'in
cloister, Kōyasan Kongōbuji monastery   196

Acknowledgments

There are many individuals and institutions to thank. Michael Jamentz offered invaluable advice with regard to both editing and content of major portions of the manuscript. Discussions with fellow scholars has also been of great importance, and we would like to especially mention Jacqueline Stone, Ryuichi Abé, Abe Yasurō, Nagamura Makoto, Matsuo Kōichi, Kikuchi Hiroki, Uejima Susumu, Kamikawa Michio, Sakamoto Masahito, Taira Masayuki, Abe Mika, Martin Collcutt, Hank Glassman, Barbara Ambros, Matthew Stavros, Chikamoto Kensuke, Takahashi Shin'ichirō, Hayashi Yuzuru, Atsuya Kazuo, Naitō Sakae, Sueki Fumihiko, Imai Masaharu, Helen Hardacre, Haruko Wakabayashi, James Baskind, Mikael Adolphson, Mikael Bauer, Elizabeth Tinsley, Asuka Sango, Iyanaga Nobumi, Fabio Rambelli, Lori Meeks and Paul Swanson. Thanks are also in order to the Historiographical Institute of the University of Tokyo, the International Center of Japanese Studies (Nichibunken), the National Museum of Japanese History (Rekihaku), Ninnaji, Hōryūji, Nara National Museum, Daigoji, Kanazawa Bunko Prefectural Museum, and the Art Institute of Chicago for their cooperation, support and, in some cases, permissions for use of materials. We would especially like to thank Matthew Stavros for his expert advice and production of the maps.

William E. Deal thanks the Baker-Nord Center for the Humanities at Case Western Reserve University for a visiting scholar grant that brought Brian to campus and, as a result, sparked the idea for writing this book. I thank Religious Studies colleagues Tim Beal and Peter Haas for their ongoing support and friendship – it means a lot! I am indebted to Lisa Robertson for her thoughtful editing and indexing expertise on this project. Lee Zickel and Allison Schifani, Baker-Nord Center colleagues, have provided much-needed editing and chapter structure advice, and, despite my protests, were right in insisting I take some breaks with them at several of Cleveland's excellent bars and restaurants. My close friends, Jim Butler and Ron Goggans, have been wonderful and supportive, and I am grateful to have them as my friends. And the girls: Yuki, Sumi, and Miso were always cute and distracting when I needed encouragement. And kudos to Sumi for adding some thoughtful, if incomprehensible, phrasing as I worked on the manuscript. It turns out that you don't need fingers to type – paws work, too. As always, my brothers, Bruce Deal and Robert Deal, have nurtured me with their love, kindness, and support. I am especially grateful to Renée Sentilles for her patience, support, and encouragement. She transformed the last months of the work on this book into a much more pleasant experience and was always available when I needed a muse.

Brian Ruppert would particularly like to thank Junko and Shō for their support, advice, and patience. If it were not for your love and understanding, this project would have never been completed. I would also like to thank my mother Rose for still living – gracing us with her presence – for me and all of my siblings and our children. The friendship and advice of Mike Jamentz and his wife Tomiko, Alexander Mayer, and Robert McKim (and his wife Norma) have been greatly appreciated, as has been the support throughout of the Department of East Asian Languages and Cultures and of the Department of Religion at the University of Illinois, especially my colleagues in Japanese studies, Elizabeth Oyler, Bob Tierney, and Misumi Sadler. Steve Haney and Roger Holt are two dear friends, and the late professor Willis Stoesz was a wonderful mentor.

Remarks from the two anonymous readers were also of great help to our formulation of the book in its early stages. We are also deeply grateful to Wiley-Blackwell and to Religion publisher Rebecca Harkin, Project editors Ben Thatcher and Georgina Coleby, Project manager Gunalan Lakshmipathy and Copy-editor Anna Oxbury for their respective patience and expertise throughout this project.

Introduction

The notion that "Buddhism" is a "world religion" is an idea derived from nineteenth-century Western scholars. Moreover, the discourse of "world religions" is alive and well in the twenty-first century, as world religions courses have, if anything, proliferated at North American and European colleges and universities. Despite revisionist views within the history of religion that call into question the unitary character of any of the great "isms," Buddhism frequently continues to be described as a singular and stable tradition. The result is the obfuscation of manifold "Buddhisms" displaying complex, multiple religious practices and ideas.

On campuses and in college towns throughout the world, Zen centers and Tibetan monks confront us with the fact there are those among us who continue to enter Buddhist lineages and follow these religious paths. The appetite for books on Buddhism in English has similarly grown in recent decades, and while Buddhist paths are better understood in the West currently than at any time in the past, they are typically represented as emanations of a mostly "outsider" religion, a faith both monolithic and the obverse of Western monotheisms. Buddhism, such representations often suggest, is impersonal, lacks any notion of sin or hell, and is realized through a direct experience that, presumably, transcends the limitations of institutions or customs.

Unfortunately, the appearance that there is an essential core to Buddhism is also inadvertently suggested by the many books on the history of Buddhism that treat Japanese Buddhism as either an afterthought or as a not-fully-orthodox version of Indian Buddhism. Many histories of Buddhism provide but scant coverage of its Japanese traditions and often end coverage at the beginning of the seventeenth century, when lineages of Japanese Buddhism faced increasing ideological competition from neo-Confucian and Shintō adherents. Rarely do these volumes cover contemporary Japanese Buddhism.

This study offers an in-depth, nuanced account of the history of Japanese "Buddhisms" that attempts to rectify the many lacunae of scope and content evident in books that only cursorily deal with Japanese Buddhist traditions. Incorporating scholarship not represented sufficiently in the coverage of introductory volumes on

A Cultural History of Japanese Buddhism, First Edition. William E. Deal and Brian Ruppert.
© 2015 William E. Deal and Brian Ruppert. Published 2015 by John Wiley & Sons, Ltd.

Buddhism, we attempt to break new ground by taking advantage of the many insights of scholarship from Japan and the West. The vast majority of authors of Buddhist histories are scholars of Indian or Indo-Tibetan Buddhism, which has contributed to confusion about Japanese Buddhism, including profound ignorance about features as basic as the identity of major Buddhist institutions and the sheer volume of cultural production in Japanese Buddhist traditions. (A recently published and prominent dictionary of Buddhism failed to include any discussion of Daigoji, an institution that has played a major role in Japanese Buddhist and secular history and which holds what may be the largest manuscript collection in all of Japanese Buddhism.)

We include coverage of Japanese Buddhism(s) beginning with the introduction in sixth-century Japan of continental monks, Buddhist images and texts, and related ritual paraphernalia, and continue to the present. In doing so, we use a periodization scheme that follows moments of significant transition within Buddhist organizations and in their relationship to the larger society rather than one based solely on political regime change. For example, we place "medieval" Japanese Buddhists in a period beginning in the tenth century because it was in this era that cultural practices such as writing and inheritance took on features very different from those of earlier eras but were clearly distinct from those practiced after the tumultuous events associated with the Ōnin war (1467–77), the appearance of Westerners and their religion, and the consolidation of power under the Tokugawa shogunate. We also attempt to highlight local variations in Japanese Buddhism by drawing attention to mountain-related traditions (e.g., beliefs and practices of mountain ascetics) as well as the increased physical movement of figures such as networking monks who carried Buddhist beliefs and practices between geographical and cultural centers and peripheries.

Our rationale for this approach is to engage upper-level undergraduate and graduate students as well as scholars in more detailed discussion of issues of discourse and material culture current in the eras under study. In doing so, we explore how Japanese Buddhists of varying contexts drew upon Buddhist ideas and practices to make sense of their lives, to solve problems, and to create a meaningful world – a cosmos – out of chaos. In drawing attention to figures like networking monks as well as to physical mobility and landscape, we also want to underscore that Japanese Buddhist paths included local traditions that were often very different from those, for example, of the royal court (including aristocrats) and the warrior class, particularly in the commonly studied settings of the shogunate's headquarters and the royal capital. Our attention to material culture such as visual media centers attention on the exchange and appropriation of material objects in the practices of Japanese Buddhism. As with Buddhist paths in other cultural milieux, those of Japanese Buddhists were complex traditions with broad philosophical and ritual implications, and it is ultimately impossible to disentangle practices we associate with the "material" from others since, for example, writing in and of itself was often undertaken as a religious act and, clearly, an extension of the religious practitioner's identity – an expression of religious modes of performative interaction with his or her environs.

Finally, readers can see that we maintain a focus throughout on Japanese Buddhist discourse, which provides a means of exploring with greater depth the multiple interpretations that people in the Japanese isles made of Buddhist texts and ideas. Japanese Buddhist thought and language are sometimes treated as if they were part of a unitary and, implicitly, unchanging cognitive complex. In fact, Japanese Buddhists appropriated Buddhist discourses to justify multiple and often competing perspectives. In sum, Japanese Buddhists "performed" Japanese Buddhism(s) at both the state and local levels, utilized material objects as a means of ritual exchange and enactment, and undertook multiple interpretations that utilized Buddhist language – all toward different and sometimes competing religious, social, and political ends.

Overview of the Book

Chapter 1: Early Historical Contexts (Protohistory to 645)

This chapter explores the multiple contexts that made possible the introduction of Buddhist texts, images, and ritual objects into sixth-century Japan, and the conditions for its development over the subsequent two centuries. We begin with a discussion of the narrative in the mytho-history *Nihon shoki* (720) of the introduction of Buddhist images and implements to the Japanese royal court. Through this discussion, the chapter considers the continental Asian influences, the struggle between the Soga and Mononobe families over the advisability of embracing Buddhist rituals, the representations of Prince Shōtoku's support of Buddhist practices, Buddhism in the late seventh-century Yamato Court, the early construction of Buddhist temples, and the relationship between Buddhas, bodhisattvas, and the indigenous *kami*. Particular attention is given to the early Buddhist images such as those in the Shaka Triad at Hōryūji, which were an important focus of devotional practice.

Chapter 2: Ancient Buddhism (645–950)

This chapter focuses on the development and flourishing of Buddhist institutions in the Nara and early Heian eras. Of note is the significance of the ruling family's support of Buddhist monastics and temples as well as the spread and propagation of Buddhism beyond the immediate circle of court families. This chapter includes coverage of the nationwide temple system inaugurated during the Nara period, the six

Nara Buddhist lineages, the construction of such temples as the Tōdaiji, the ritual significance of sutra-copying bureaus, the monastic hierarchy, the relationship between court families and Buddhist clerics, the increasing prominence of Buddhist rituals performed for the protection of the ruling class, the establishment of the Shingon and Tendai lineages, and the use of Buddhist rituals at court. It concludes with a discussion of women in ancient Japanese Buddhism.

Chapter 3: Early Medieval Buddhism (950–1300): The Dawn of Medieval Society and Related Changes in Japanese Buddhist Culture

This chapter explores the discursive and ritual dominance of Buddhist lineages in the lives of Japanese aristocrats as well as the former's increasing influence in the lives of wider segments of the Japanese population. The chapter includes coverage of the relationship between dominant court families – such as the Fujiwara – and Buddhist practices, annual Buddhist ceremonies at court, temple-shrine patronage, the marked growth of esoteric Buddhist rituals to the Heian court, the increasing importance of Pure Land Buddhist practices and discourses, important temples and pilgrimage sites, the role of Buddhas and bodhisattvas in Japanese religious lives, new interactions with continental East Asia, the popularization of Buddhist lineages and the seminal beginnings of "New Kamakura Buddhisms" (e.g., Zen, Pure Land, and Nichiren), the role of older lineages in the Kamakura era, and the changing relationship between Buddhism and *kami* worship (Shintō) in this time period.

Starting with the Japanese royal court, about which there is a substantial historical record, we especially focus on how Buddhist practices informed the life of nobles and those close to them. Then we turn to the Tendai lineages because these Buddhist groups were arguably the closest institutionally to the mid-Heian court and gave rise to important changes in Buddhist belief and practice. From there, we explore the increase in prominence of Pure Land discourses and practices and turn as well to the evolving relationship between *kami* and Buddhist divinities in sacred sites. After addressing the question of the relationship between Buddhism and the development of the arts, we consider the rising prominence of esoteric Buddhism in early medieval Japan, which introduced new ways of gathering ritual knowledge and played an integral role in the development of artistic lineages.

Meanwhile, court relations with continental East Asia resumed following a short period of virtual non-engagement. From the mid-tenth century onward, great architectural activity was regularly undertaken at the royal court, accompanied soon after or preceded by conflagration (Uejima 2010: 293–302). Aristocrats gradually made efforts to integrate the arts into Buddhist practice. Interaction increased between lay believers and monastic practitioners, including the development of monastic cloisters (*monzeki*) inhabited and operated by leading nobles or princes. Over time, the numbers of Buddhist ascetic practitioners (e.g., *hijiri, jikyōja*) who were semi-independent of the monasteries burgeoned. *Kami*–Buddha combinatory relations came to be elaborated in a variety of court rites in the capital region and, eventually, rites patronized by aristocrats, warriors, and members of the populace throughout the isles.

Chapter 4: Late Medieval Buddhism (1300–1467): New Buddhisms, Buddhist Learning, Dissemination and the Fall into Chaos

This chapter focuses on changes that Japanese Buddhists undertook or otherwise experienced during the concluding period of the medieval era. From the latter period of the Kamakura shogunate onward, the circumstances of life in the Japanese isles changed fundamentally. It was an era that began with the temporary disintegration of the royal family. The splintering of the royal family into northern and southern courts and establishment of the Ashikaga shogunate in the Muromachi area of northern Kyoto (1336) were indeed accompanied by important changes in the cultural life of the aristocracy and leading warriors. The medieval era would eventually culminate with the devastating Ōnin/Bunmei war in Kyoto, entering into a transitional period marked by the decentralization of power, the landing of Europeans, and the destruction of the greatest temple complex in Japanese history, Enryakuji (Mount Hiei).

Moreover, the chaos that began the period may have contributed to the ease with which monks of assorted Buddhist lineages continued their travel throughout the land; sometimes studying under multiple masters of lineages of both older forms of Buddhism and of newer Buddhist movements. They founded temples in locations throughout eastern and western Japan. We draw attention to the Buddhist culture of learning, which thrived on new levels in the fourteenth century and permeated virtually all of the major lineages of Japanese Buddhism. What we call here networking monks, active in varied peripatetic traditions, were often intimately linked with this culture, and the temples they founded or frequented contributed to its flourishing. These included figures such as practitioners of mountain asceticism, related "holy ones"(*hijiri, shōnin*), and what would come to be called student-visitor monks (*kyakusō*), all of whom were much more active throughout the land than similar figures in the previous era, and many of them closely tied to the major Buddhist institutions. Meanwhile, monks of warrior background, especially those close to the shogunate, took on an increasingly prominent role within Buddhist culture. Zen monks began to specialize in performing funerals for parishioners, which contributed to the wider dissemination of Buddhism to the populace. Major Buddhist institutions increasingly engaged in trade with others across the sea, and they also increasingly used block-print as a medium for reproducing sacred works which they distributed.

During the same period, some Buddhists began to increasingly conceive of the Japanese isles as not simply a realm at the edge of the world of Jambudvīpa but a unique polity distinct from continental traditions. A series of arts informed by Buddhist themes and practices became increasingly prominent among warriors, aristocrats, and, in some cases, the larger populace. Often, in this connection, preaching and related liturgical practices developed across the vast array of lineages of Japanese Buddhism, and increasingly made use of visual imagery. Taken as a whole, these varied developments contributed to the geographical and social dissemination of Buddhist beliefs and practices (although they would be propelled to new levels of prominence after the establishment of the Tokugawa shogunate).

The chapter concludes with an extensive treatment of the position and activities of women. Recognizing that women's capacity for Buddhahood was variously conceived in continental Buddhism as well as in Japanese Buddhism, we draw a connection between such topoi and developments in Japanese Buddhist lineages between the ancient and early modern periods. We also consider the relationship between the social status of women, religious practice, and religious communities of premodern Japan.

Chapter 5: Buddhism and the Transition to the Modern Era (1467–1800)

This chapter considers issues around the popularization of Buddhist lineages in this time period, their increasing interaction with the population throughout the Japanese isles, and the evolving positions of Buddhists as well their learning and ritual within an increasingly *national* society. Drawing upon recent arguments that "new" Kamakura Buddhism became prominent in roughly the latter half of the fifteenth century and that the period of the late fifteenth century marked a kind of gateway to the modern – for example, the case of the "True Pure Land" school master Rennyo's (1415–1499) ascendance – we note the devastation wrought by the Ōnin war (1467–1477) and the subsequent period of near-constant war as a veritable charnel ground of the epoch commonly called medieval Japan. Admittedly, a number of features of medieval Japanese Buddhism would continue but only do so almost invariably in muted forms given the onset of novel beliefs, practices, and social organization cast within a world newly cognizant of Ming China and the West. Printing, which had always taken a backseat to handwriting as a cultural practice – and a general emphasis on rarefaction of religious knowledge by means of esoteric transmission – now enabled a novel mode and level of dissemination of Buddhist texts. Even so-called "sacred works" (*shōgyō*) of Japanese Buddhist traditions came to be commonly purchased, a practice virtually unimaginable prior to this period.

Tracing prominent cultural developments such as the appearance of new modes of tea practice fostered by Buddhist monks and others, the chapter turns to outline the character of the ascendance of the "new" lineages of so-called "Kamakura Buddhism." It focuses on Rennyo in his efforts to disseminate his lineage of Jōdo Shinshū, and proceeds to highlight his coordinated emphasis on vernacular writing and ritual practice, worship of Shinran, and the increase of local meetings. We follow the lead of Ōkuwa Hitoshi and other recent scholars in their interpretation of the warrior provinces period as the historical era in which the shift to the "early modern" became apparent, manifested in a broad series of changes in Japanese religion and society.

We call attention to the fact that, from the fifteenth century onward, itinerant practitioners peopled the landscape, including figures such as mountain ascetics, who had already been organized and governed for some time by major Buddhist institutions and whose status was lower ranking within the monastic system. They are comparable to the so-called temple assistants (*dōshu*, also referred to as *zenshu*, *gyōnin*, *gesu*). Meanwhile, leading monks of the traditional Buddhist monastic institutions were more interactive than ever before with those in the rural temples, such as in the case of the Daigoji Hōon'in abbot Chō'e (1432–1516), who initiated rural monks into the Hōon'in and Muryōju'in lineages in distant Kantō areas. He, along with successors at Daigoji, attempted to convert such rural institutions into branch temples.

Our discussion of Buddhism in the Edo period focuses initially on the effects of the Tokugawa regime, partially represented by the deluge of manuscript and printing production enabled – at least in part – by the newly stable political and financial situation. Moreover, this thriving Edo culture of learning benefited from the support of the shogunate. Monks and lay believers were fascinated by commentaries and other works by Japanese as well as continental Buddhist masters, and even in seemingly "sectarian" lineages like those of True Pure Land some studied teachings of multiple masters – and often went to study the teachings of the traditional schools in Nara.

We will see that although the head–branch system (*honmatsu seido*) and the temple affiliation system (*jidan*; alt. *danka seido*) seem to have initially developed prior to the Edo shogunate and partially in reaction to local needs, it was the shogunate that consolidated these trends. It was the shogunate that especially promoted reclassification of lineages to promote clearer social categories among Buddhists, including application of Kogi and Shingi Shingon as modes of Shingon organization, increased use of the "Tendai" sectarian label for both Enryakuji (Hiei)-affiliated and Onjōji (Miidera)-affiliated lineages, and undertook novel policies designed generally to weaken the authority of traditional kenmitsu monasteries over organizations of itinerant religious practitioners. The shogunate also eyed the broad array of itinerant

groups, treating a few groups – such as the komusō entertainers – as officially designated organizations but subjecting most others – such as Yin-yang practitioners – to
a marginal position.

Despite images to the contrary, Buddhists on the whole experienced a revival and,
arguably, a renaissance of learning in the Edo period. The strict regulations (*hatto*)
undertaken by the regime actually helped promote vital interest in Buddhist studies.
The major Buddhist lineages developed so-called *danrin* seminaries. The Zen lineages, for example, undertook reforms that respectfully focused on newly institutionalized *kōan* examination system and on Dōgen's writings – features that have
continued into current Japan. At the same time, preaching performances and literatures flourished and further contributed to Edo Buddhist culture. Royal convents
developed what might be called a kind of "cultural salon" in their broad and deep
engagement of Buddhist and non-Buddhist writings. Meanwhile, a prominent effort
was undertaken to revive adherence to the precepts, resulting in a precepts movement that became increasingly prominent over the course of the Edo period and
into high modernity.

Chapter 6: Modern Buddhism (1800–1945)

This chapter explores the role and treatment of Buddhist lineages and institutions in
the period of Japan's modernization and emergence as a world power. We first turn
to the transition to the modern period, and draw attention to the fact that much
historical scholarship has ignored the continuing place of Buddhist institutions,
beliefs, and practices in Japanese life in the nineteenth century and their connection
with modern cultural and historical trends. In some ways the transition to what we
now call the "modern" begins at the beginning of the nineteenth century and is
peculiarly marked by movements of religious belief and practice distinct from what
came before – and often antagonistic toward Buddhists. Figures such as Motoori
Norinaga and Hirata Atsutane played pivotal roles in these movements and greatly
contributed to the development of modern nativism.

The chapter goes on to include coverage of the government's anti-Buddhist policies, the "separation of *kami* and Buddhas," the destruction of Buddhist temples and
images, the international spread of Zen and other Buddhist lineages by such notable
figures as D. T. Suzuki, the evolving custom of clerical marriage, the varied reactions
to the changing times of prominent monks (e.g., Shaku Unshō, Fukuda Gyōkai,
former priest Inoue Enryō, and Shimaji Mokurai), the related rise of Buddhist missions overseas, the role of Buddhist lineages in the Pacific War, and the development
of new Buddhist movements like Seishin-shugi. (Although the work of Jason Ānanda
Josephson [2012] is an essential contribution to our understanding of the production
of the concept of "religion" in the modern period, its focus is specifically on the

construction of that concept rather than Buddhisms and their cultural-historical constitution, so we do not directly address that work in this study, instead only referring to it parenthetically where relevant.)

Chapter 7: Buddhism Since 1945

This chapter details Buddhist thought and practice from 1945 to the present. It foregrounds legal changes that occurred following the catastrophic defeat of the Japanese nation in the war, which radically changed the environs within which Buddhist and other groups developed and otherwise appeared. Moreover, given the reduction of the population centers to "burnt fields" (*yake nohara*) following the firebombings (*kūshū*) and the atomic bombs, the cultural and topographical landscape of Japanese society changed as significantly as any time since the Ōnin war of the late fifteenth century. (The cultural environs following the development of the modern nation-state and the "Meiji Restoration" were as radically new, but not marked by comparable destruction of population hubs.)

Given the legal and other changes, of particular note are the rising prominence of new Buddhist lineages and lay organizations, such as Sōka Gakkai, and the status of the traditional Buddhist lineages in contemporary Japan. This chapter includes coverage of various new Buddhist movements, as well as the ostensibly Buddhist movement known as Aum Shinrikyō, infamous for the deadly 1995 sarin gas attack in the Tokyo subway system. This chapter also examines the status of institutional Buddhism in contemporary Japan, paying particular attention to charges of class and gender discrimination leveled at some Buddhist groups, as well as the use of Buddhist rituals to assuage – after, sometimes, engendering – the guilt of women who have had abortions. Also considered is the place of traditional Buddhist rituals in the lives of contemporary Japanese. We also turn to academe itself, where the "Critical Buddhism" movement has left an indelible mark, attempting to find an authentic Buddhism – a questionable task – while also offering solutions to problems such as conferral of discriminatory precept-names (*sabetsu kaimyō*). Finally, this chapter examines Buddhist-themed *manga* (comics), performance art, and the utilization of media by both new and traditional Buddhist groups.

On Translation

We have attempted to maintain historical accuracy wherever possible in our translation. For example, we avoid use of the term "emperor" as a translation for *tennō* ("heavenly thearch") before the Meiji period, bearing in mind that the original Daoist meaning may also have held cosmological implications. Instead, we have variously referred to the Japanese political ruler as "king", "heavenly sovereign," and "sovereign" and his court as a "royal" court prior to the modern era because the Japanese polity did not constitute an empire until modern times.

Another translation practice is our use of "lineage" rather than "school" for the term *shūha*, because the term school is associated with thought traditions ("school of thought") and because the terms school as well as sect imply exclusive affiliation to particular religious traditions. Although there were a few major monasteries identified almost exclusively with a single *shūha*, major temple complexes often included study of multiple scholastic and ritual traditions of *shūha*. For example, Tōdaiji is well known for having included multiple *shūha* (e.g., Kegon, Shingon, Ritsu, Sanron, etc.), but the same can be said – in varying degrees – for Daigoji (including Shingon but also Sanron), Kōzanji (Shingon and Kegon), Saidaiji (Shingon and Ritsu), Shōmyōji (Shingon, Ritsu, Zen, etc.), Kōfukuji (Hossō, Shingon), Tōfukuji (Rinzai Zen, Shingon) and other monastic centers historically.

Nevertheless, for stylistic purposes, we occasionally use "school" to refer to *shūha*, but otherwise we use the term lineage to refer to both *shūha* and *ryū* (*ryūha*), the larger traditions as well as their individual sub-lineages. The term *ryū* refers to all sub-lineages, including sub-sub-lineages in Japanese, so the Japanese language is in many ways ambiguous in this regard; indeed, there are sets of sub-lineages that constitute a major tradition within *shūha* such as the case of the several sub-lineages referred to in Shingon as being either of the Ono-ryū or of the Hirosawa-ryū, respectively associated with the monasteries of the Ono area to the southeast of Kyoto and those associated with the traditions emanating from Ninnaji in north Kyoto. Premodern texts, moreover, use these terms in multiple ways, so that Ono-ryū sometimes refers to the multiple lineages traced to the Ono-area monasteries and sometimes *specifically* to the sub-lineage of the founder Ningai (951–1046) originating at Zuishin'in (Mandaraji). Similar distinctions are sometimes made in texts concerning what is now generally referred to as the Hirosawa-ryū set of sub-lineages in Shingon. For Ono-ryū and Hirosawa-ryū, on those occasions when they refer to the respective sets of sub-lineages in Shingon, we use the term "branch." Such editorial and translation decisions do not offer perfect answers, but they do offer increased readability without unduly sacrificing accuracy.

Conventions

In the main, we have followed the guidelines of *The Chicago Manual of Style*. Citations are given in the text with full details in the References section at the end of each chapter.

There are so many Japanese terms in the text that we have avoided placing any kanji within the main text, instead providing them in a glossary at the end of the book. The terms listed in the glossary are limited to prominent words in the main text. Roman transliterations of these terms are italicized in the text and in the glossary, except for proper nouns, which are capitalized and lack italics. Titles of works, however, are capitalized and italicized. We have incorporated related terms to refer to etymologically connected terms, which are placed next to the most prominent related term, to preserve brevity (e.g., *shū* (rel. *shūha*)). Characters for geographical terms have been limited to regions (e.g., Kantō) and important sites (e.g., Kamakura).

We have romanized terms using the following systems: Pinyin for Chinese, Revised Hepburn for Japanese, and McCune-Reischauer for Korean.

The following abbreviations are used:

alt.	*alternative*
Ch.	Chinese
J.	Japanese
K.	Korean
mod.	modern
rel.	related
Skt.	Sanskrit

References

Uejima Susumu. 2010. *Nihon chūsei shakai no keisei to Ōken*. Nagoya: Nagoya Daigaku Shuppankai.

Early Historical Contexts (Protohistory to 645)

Buddhism's Transmission to Yamato: The *Nihon shoki* Narrative

The *Nihon shoki* (Chronicles of Japan) is the primary textual source for narrative details about the transmission of Buddhist texts, images, and ritual objects to the Japanese islands, and for Buddhism's early development. Compiled by imperial command and completed in 720 CE, it narrates the history of Japan from its mythic origins to 697 CE. According to the *Nihon shoki*, Buddha's Dharma (i.e., teaching) was introduced to Japan in 552 CE:

> 552 CE. Winter, 10th Month: King Sŏngmyŏng of the Korean kingdom of Paekche [J. Kudara] – also known as King Sŏng – dispatched Norisach'igye [J. Nurishichikei] and other retainers to Japan. They offered as tribute a gold and copper statue of Śākyamuni Buddha, ritual banners and canopies, and several volumes of sūtras and commentaries. In a separate declaration, King Sŏng praised the merit of propagating and worshipping the Dharma, stating, "This Dharma is superior to all the others. It is difficult to understand and difficult to attain. Neither the Duke of Chou nor Confucius was able to comprehend it. This Dharma can produce immeasurable, limitless meritorious karmic consequence, leading to the attainment of supreme wisdom. It is like a person who has a wish-fulfilling gem whose every desire is granted. The jewel of this wonderful Dharma is also like this. Every prayer is answered and not a need goes unfulfilled. Moreover, from distant India (Tenjiku) all the way to the three Korean kingdoms this teaching has been followed and upheld. There is no one who does not revere it. Accordingly, I, King Sŏngmyŏng, your vassal, have humbly dispatched my retainer Norisach'igye to the Imperial Country [that is, Yamato] to transmit and propagate this teaching throughout the land, thereby effecting what the Buddha foretold, "my Dharma will spread to the east." (adapted from Inoue 1987: 2.474–5 and Deal 1995: 218)

The Buddha may have foretold the eastward transmission of the Dharma, but this did not mean that its acceptance in Japan did not merit discussion among the

A Cultural History of Japanese Buddhism, First Edition. William E. Deal and Brian Ruppert.
© 2015 William E. Deal and Brian Ruppert. Published 2015 by John Wiley & Sons, Ltd.

Heavenly Sovereign's (*tennō*) most powerful advisors. The same *Nihon shoki* entry continues by recounting the manner in which Buddhism was received as a result of the Paekche king's urging.

> This very day the Heavenly Sovereign [that is, Kinmei] heard this declaration and leapt with joy. He declared to the envoys, "From ancient times to the present we have not heard of such a fine Dharma as this. Nevertheless, we cannot ourselves decide whether to accept this teaching." Thereupon he inquired of his assembled officials, "The Buddha presented to us from the country to our west has a face of extreme solemnity. We have never known such a thing before. Should we worship it or not?"
>
> Soga no Iname humbly responded: "The many countries to the west all worship this Buddha. Is it only Japan [Nihon] that will reject this teaching?"
>
> Mononobe no Okoshi and Nakatomi no Kamako together humbly responded: "The rulers of our country have always worshipped throughout the four seasons the 180 deities of heaven and earth. If they now change this and worship the deity of a foreign country [*adashikuni no kami*], we fear that the deities of our country [*kuni tsu kami*] will become angry."
>
> The Heavenly Sovereign declared, "I grant to Soga no Iname the worship of this Buddha image in order to test its efficacy."
>
> Soga no Iname knelt down and received the statue. With great joy, he enshrined it in his home at Owarida and devotedly performed the rituals of a world renouncer [that is, a practicing Buddhist]. He also purified his home at Mukuhara and made it into a temple. (adapted from Inoue 1987: 2.475 and Deal 1995: 219)

The *Nihon shoki* account of Buddhism's introduction to Japan raises a number of historical and conceptual issues. Historically, there is a wider East Asian context for Buddhism's transmission: Buddhism was received in China from Central Asia by way of India, and from China to the Korean peninsula and the Japanese archipelago. Once transmitted to the Japanese islands, there are issues regarding Buddhism's reception and its cultural impact. Conceptually, what did the Heavenly Sovereign and his courtiers understand Buddhism to be? Or, put another way, what did they assume they were adopting or rejecting? Though there may be no definitive answer to this question, we can explore Japanese responses to Buddhism in this formative period following its transmission to the Japanese islands. We will consider these issues from both the larger East Asian perspective and from the specific context of Japan.

Buddhism in the China Sea interaction sphere

Joan Piggott's (1997) notion of the China Sea interaction sphere (or China Sea sphere)[1] offers one way to frame East Asian relations in the era of Buddhist transmission. This term refers to the shared material and intellectual culture that flowed

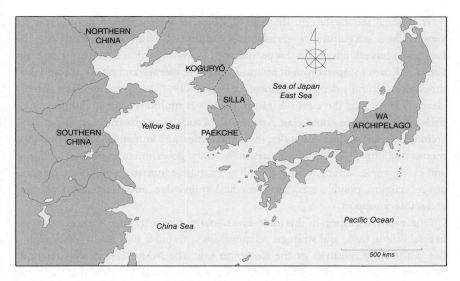

Figure 1.1   China Sea Interaction Sphere. Map by Matthew Stavros.

between parts of the Chinese mainland, the Korean peninsula, and the Japanese archipelago by way of the China Sea during the third through eighth centuries (see Figure 1.1). Exchange in the China Sea sphere impacted emerging notions about Japanese kingship and, ultimately, the formation of the state known as "Nihon," a term in use by the late 670s. Piggott stresses that China Sea sphere cultural transmission was multidirectional, and not simply Chinese culture radiating unidirectionally out to other parts of East Asia, as has sometimes been assumed. Ko, Haboush, and Piggott (2003: 9–10) argue that the China Sea sphere shared, to some extent, "compatibility in written language, institutions, law, religions, and aesthetics. Confucian texts, along with Buddhist sutras, gave elites a common vocabulary that transcended ethnic and national boundaries." They go on to note that despite these shared elements, each East Asian region maintained its own distinctive cultural and intellectual perspectives.

The transmission of Buddhism to Japan, then, constitutes one aspect of a larger process of the selective adaptation and use of East Asian mainland culture. Examples of material and intellectual culture exchanged included – in addition to Buddhism, Confucian, and Daoist ideas – the Chinese language and writing system, artistic techniques, medical knowledge, political structures, and social configurations. These cultural influences flowed into the Japanese archipelago at the same time as powerful extended families or clans (*uji*)[2] were competing for political ascendancy over Yamato. The transmission of Buddhism to the Japanese islands was thus intimately connected with struggles over the consolidation of political power.

Traditional scholarship on the role of China in ancient East Asia has typically viewed China as a cultural juggernaut that transmitted culture and civilization to the East Asian hinterlands. From this perspective, a one-way cultural transmission from China to Korea to Japan brought political, religious, literary, and artistic traditions to otherwise culturally deprived regions. As Piggott (1997) suggests, however, there is clear evidence that the cultural transmission was multidirectional. Cultural flows back and forth throughout East Asia included such things as trade goods, art and architectural techniques and styles, texts, medicines, and human resources (Buddhist monks and nuns, Confucian scholars, merchants, government emissaries, artisans, and craftspeople, among others) as well as intangible human resources such as language, religion, political structures, medical knowledge, and promises of political and military support.

One important aspect of this multidirectional cultural exchange was its usefulness in establishing trade and strategic relationships with other East Asian political entities in the early centuries of the Common Era. The *Nihon shoki* depicts relations between the Japanese archipelago and the Korean peninsula. It is clear that there was much maneuvering on the part of the kings of Yamato and the Korean Three Kingdoms (Koguryŏ, Paekche, and Silla) to secure support, threaten retaliation, and otherwise jockey for position. In Japan's case, its relations with the Korean peninsula and the Chinese mainland reinforced the growing power of the Yamato Great Kings.[3] Importantly, this relationship was also one of tribute. Besides the establishment of trade relations and military alliances, "Buddhism" was one of the many things that were exchanged as tribute. In the *Nihon shoki* example, Paekche's King Sŏngmyŏng sent his envoys to the Japanese archipelago seeking Yamato military support for its war against Silla and China, offering Buddhism in exchange. In this way, Buddhist material culture, because it was a part of the tribute-paying process, was implicated in the creation of alliances across East Asia.

An additional historical fact is important to understanding the dissemination of Buddhism across East Asia. In the fourth to sixth centuries, the East Asia we now think of as comprising the national entities called "China," "Korea," and "Japan" did not yet exist – these were later appellations. Rather, our use of the terms "China," "Korea," and "Japan" in reference to this time period refers to descriptions of geographical locations corresponding to the Chinese mainland, the Korean peninsula, and the Japanese archipelago.

In this time period, the Chinese mainland was undergoing a period of disunion, with multiple political regimes struggling against each other for supremacy. Similarly, the Korean peninsula was divided into three kingdoms, with an additional weaker federation. Political power in the Japanese archipelago was concentrated in a relatively small area of central Honshū known as the kingdom of Yamato[4] and was contested by extended clan (*uji*) lineages vying for hegemony.[5] It was within such unsettled political spheres that Buddhism was introduced and transmitted within East Asia.

Although Buddhism was officially introduced to China in the first century CE – and likely earlier – it was not until the late fourth century that Buddhist ideas and practices became significant and were, in turn, transmitted to the kingdoms of the Korean peninsula and to the islands of Japan. Further, it was, in part, because of political intrigue and the need for alliances that the Korean kingdom of Paekche sent envoys, accompanied by gifts of Buddhist imagery and texts, to Japan in the sixth century. Buddhism, then, played a significant role in the transformation of the political and religious landscapes of China, Korea, and Japan. Thus, the transmission of Buddhism to Japan needs to be understood within the context of relations between the Japanese archipelago, the Korean peninsula, and the Chinese mainland.

Buddhist transmission routes: imperial narratives and private receptions

While the *Nihon shoki* is by no means the only official document to narrate the transmission of Buddhism to the Japanese archipelago, it is the one most often cited in such discussions. This account has become – historically and often in scholarly discussions – canonical shorthand for Buddhism's transmission to Japan. In isolation from similar Buddhism transmission narratives in other parts of East Asia, it is easy to assume that the *Nihon shoki* account is somehow peculiarly Japanese, or represents a reception story unlike those in other East Asian cultural contexts. However, similar narratives attended the transmission of Buddhism to China and Korea as well as variant records of its movement into Japan. Thus, we need to understand that the transmission of continental Buddhist traditions to Japan by the sixth century CE occurred within the broader religious and political landscapes of contemporaneous East Asia.

Although official imperial narratives – like the one expressed in the *Nihon shoki* – have often been cited as defining the moment when Buddhism made the leap from one cultural context to the next, there were in fact official and unofficial versions of Buddhism's transmission in each country. The official story marks Buddhism as an entity embraced or accepted by the formal imperial bureaucracy. The unofficial story concerns the Buddhist faith of immigrants, merchants, and others who enacted their religion in new regions. The latter is often a difficult story to tell because the evidence is mostly diffused in archaeological remains.

There are, then, two models for the transmission of Buddhism to East Asian cultural contexts in general and to the Japanese islands in particular. The first model is of Buddhism as transmitted from the ruler of one country to another. Buddhism then comes to be officially supported and patronized by the ruling classes and only later spreads to the larger population. In the second model, and the one often ignored, Buddhism is seen as transmitted from person to person within the general population. Buddhism in this instance usually meets with at least some initial antipathy from the ruling classes.

Japanese scholars, like Tamura Enchō, describe two primary routes of transmission that Buddhism followed through the China Sea interaction sphere: an imperial/royal route and a route of individual travelers (Tamura 1996: 6–8). Tamura refers to the imperial/royal route by the term "temple Buddhism" (*garan bukkyō*) in recognition of the fact that the acceptance of Buddhism in a particular kingdom was typically followed quickly by imperial patronage of temple-building projects and the creation of a rudimentary monastic system to run the temple and conduct rituals – rituals often directed toward the well-being of the kingdom and its ruling class. Buddhist transmission stories – like the *Nihon shoki* narrative – describe this route. The imperial route is also conspicuous for financial resources needed to finance temple construction projects and human resources, especially skilled craftspeople, necessary to build these temples. Imperial transmission routes and the narratives compiled to describe them were especially implicated in displays of ruling power and expressions of legitimate authority.

In contrast to "temple Buddhism," Tamura describes the other mode of transmission as "household Buddhism" (*shitaku bukkyō*). This form of Buddhism was centered on private Buddhist practices that often revolved around Buddhist images, such as sculpture or paintings, which depicted particular Buddhas and bodhisattvas. This form of Buddhism was transmitted in an informal way, but was often the result of interactions between immigrants, merchants, and others who traversed the China Sea interaction sphere and were also Buddhists. Evidence for this form of Buddhist dissemination typically predates official transmission stories and their ideological need to control the story of Buddhism's spread lest this powerful religious tradition be placed in the hands of those outside the ruling class. There had been significant contact between the Japanese islands and the Asian mainland prior to the middle of the sixth century, and Buddhist ideas and material culture would have been exchanged as a result of those contacts.[6]

This story of Buddhism's transmission recounted in texts like the *Nihon shoki* is the official one. But Buddhism – as a private or household practice – was introduced to Japan prior to this time through Chinese and Korean immigrants who were Buddhists and who settled in Japan. Immigrants from the Korean peninsula, for instance, brought Buddhist practices to Japan earlier than the official date. From around 400 CE, immigrants from the Asian mainland – especially from the Korean peninsula – came to Yamato and settled within fixed kinship groups. They brought with them the worship of Buddhism as a private faith practiced within the kinship group. As a result, it is more than likely that Buddhist texts and images were brought to Japan, prior to the official sixth-century introduction of Buddhism to Japan, by such notable figures as Shiba Tatto (grandfather of Tori Busshi), thought to have arrived in Japan in 522 CE. According to the late eleventh century *Fusō ryakki* (Abridged Annals of Japan), Buddhist images were enshrined in the Yamato region and worshipped as the *kami* of the Great Tang.

Conflicting dates for the transmission of Buddhism to the Japanese archipelago

The transmission of Buddhism to Japan is a notion that is both factually and conceptually problematic. Factually, there are two competing dates given in early texts for the moment Buddhism "arrived" in Japan. While the *Nihon shoki* provides the date of transmission as 552 CE, another text, a temple legend called the *Gangōji garan engi narabi ni ruki shizai chō* (Circumstances Leading to the Founding of the Monastery Complex of Gangōji and a List of Its Accumulated Treasures),[7] gives the date 538 CE, as does the *Jōgū shōtoku hōō teisetsu* (The Imperial Record of Shōtoku, Dharma King of the Upper Palace). The reason for this discrepancy is unclear and various theories have been asserted to account for it. Because all three texts have compilation dates well after the events they describe, it is impossible to use any of them to provide a reliably exact date for when King Sŏng sent his envoys to Japan. The *Nihon shoki* was compiled by order of the Yamato Court in 720 CE, while *Gangōji garan engi* was compiled, according to its own postscript, in 747 CE, but the text we have today was probably a Heian-period (794–1185 CE) compilation, itself based on an earlier eighth-century – and no longer extant – text called *Gangōji engi*. The main section of the Imperial Record dates to the eighth or ninth century.

There are additional, and more specific, problems that make these dates factually suspect. For instance, with regard to the *Nihon shoki* transmission, it has long been pointed out that the statement uttered by King Sŏng in praise of the Dharma he is offering in tribute to King Kinmei – and quoted in the transmission passage for 552 – is partly a quotation from the *Konkōmyō-saishō-ō-kyō* (*Sovereign Kings of the Golden Light Sūtra*; Skt. *Suvarṇa-prabhāsattama-rāja Sūtra*). This particular translation of the *Sovereign Kings Sūtra* was not produced until 703 by the Chinese priest Yijing (J. Gijō; 635–713), who was working at the time in the Tang capital of Chang'an. Given this fact, at least parts of the 552 account were written post-703 by the compilers of the *Nihon shoki* and do not reflect older records. One widely held speculation is that the famous Nara-period monk Dōji was responsible for this addition. Dōji studied Buddhism in China from 701 to 718 so he may have been the one to import this translation into Japan. It may also have been Dōji who located the transmission of Buddhism to Japan to the year 552 because he would have been knowledgeable of the fact that the so-called Period of the End of the Dharma (*mappō*) was said to begin in that year.[8]

Buddhism as an object and Buddhism as its objects

Conceptually, the idea that Buddhism arrived in Japan in a certain year on a particular day assumes an overly simplistic model of cultural transmission. Further, when we speak of the transmission of Buddhism to Japan what are we saying was transmitted? Buddhism is not a singular "thing" that can be carried to a new place in a single instant. Even conceding that material objects significant to Buddhist practice and thought – such as Buddha images and sūtras – were brought to Japan in a certain year, the broader conceptual and performative meanings of Buddhist doctrines and ritual prescriptions were learned and transformed over a much longer period of time.

Regardless of which date, if either, is correct, it is sufficient to note that Buddhism was likely "officially" transmitted to the Japanese islands during the first half of the sixth century, and was present prior to this transmission in the guise of individuals who had taken up some minimal form of Buddhist practice. Dating aside, there is another issue that is arguably more important for understanding early Japanese Buddhism. This is the dual notion of Buddhism as an object and Buddhism as its objects. Put another way, the *Nihon shoki* account, like other East Asian Buddhism transmission narratives, treats Buddhism in two basic ways: (1) Buddhism as an object that can be contained, transmitted, and handed over from one king to another; and (2) Buddhism as its objects: sutras, images, and other ritual paraphernalia and aspects of Buddhist material culture. The *Nihon shoki* effectively treats Buddhism as a commodity, tangible tribute to purchase the support of the Yamato Great King. As a concrete object, the commodity Buddhism can be accepted or rejected as occurs in the *Nihon shoki* narrative.

The ideology of official transmission narratives

Embedded in Buddhist transmission narratives in general, and in the *Nihon shoki* story in particular, is the significant issue of who controls Buddhism. The control of Buddhist knowledge and ritual power has important ideological and social implications. The *Nihon shoki* narrative presents a story about the transmission of Buddhism that is part of a larger construct that the imperial family and its supporters were trying to craft in order to legitimate their power. Historians have long discussed ways in which texts like the *Nihon shoki* sought the ideological high ground over other competing claims to power and authority. Just as the *Nihon shoki* was, in general, attempting to legitimate the power and authority of the ruling and aristocratic families, so it was also claiming Buddhism as an imperial prerogative. Much of the language justifying these positions – whether political or religious – was retrodictive. Politically, terms like *Nihon* ("Japan") or *tennō* ("Heavenly Sovereign" or, sometimes, "Emperor/Empress") would not likely have been used in the middle of the sixth century.

Religiously, it would make no sense for the Heavenly Sovereign to have understood what was meant by terms like Buddha or Dharma without some explanation. Such explanation is not forthcoming in the *Nihon shoki*.

Similarly, as we have already suggested, the idea that Buddhism "entered" Japan on a particular day and year is more ideologically plausible than factual. Scholars like Tsuda Sōkichi (1950) long ago pointed out that texts like the *Nihon shoki* include fabrications introduced by its compilers for ideological reasons. The *Nihon shoki* narrates a history of the newly emergent country of Japan from the perspective of the imperial family. Starting with the origins of Japan in the age of the gods, the narrative concludes in 697 CE with the abdication of Heavenly Sovereign Jitō. The text was compiled at imperial command and narrates events from a court-friendly perspective.

As we have noted, despite the dates given in the official narratives, it is evident from other data, such as archaeological remains, that Buddhist objects and practices already existed in Japan by the middle of the sixth century, brought to various locations in the Japanese archipelago by traders and envoys. The narratives are best seen as a story for control over what must have been perceived to be a powerful, ideologically significant force: the path of the Buddha (*butsudō*) and its world of ritually powerful objects. In the *Nihon shoki*, Buddhism stands outside of competing clans – Buddhism is portrayed as the possession of the imperial family and the central government.

Foreign gods vs. indigenous gods

We have already noted the role of immigrants in bringing Buddhism to the Japanese islands and of promoting its practice, whether privately or publicly. The importance of immigrant kinship groups to the spread and development of Japanese Buddhism was apparent early in the transmission process. The *Fusō ryakki* (Abridged Annals of Japan), a history of Japan to 1094 that focuses on the history of Japanese Buddhism and that cites much older sources,[9] reports that in the early sixth century southern Chinese immigrants – apparently practicing Buddhists – made their new home in the Yamato region and established a temple. This is the same region occupied by the Soga family and may be one of the sources for Soga interest in Buddhism. This account also suggests that Buddhism arrived in Japan prior to its official transmission.

According to the *Nihon shoki*, the official transmission of Buddhism to Japan precipitated a crisis within the Yamato court over whether it was good or bad to accept and worship foreign deities. As we saw in the passage above, King Kinmei is confronted with a decision to accept or reject the gift of Buddhism. The transmission of Buddhism to Yamato becomes an ideological conflict between competing court ministers and their factions. The *Nihon shoki* describes a conflict between indigenous *kami* as opposed to foreign *kami* as a way to frame the issue of whether Buddhism should be accepted or not. Concern is expressed over the "feelings" that the indigenous gods have toward a foreign *kami* – in this instance, the Buddha.

The Soga kinship group – led by court minister Soga no Iname (?–570) – represented the faction that embraced what the *Nihon shoki* terms "foreign gods" (*adashikuni no kami*), that is, the Buddha. The Soga family, likely immigrants themselves, was deeply connected with immigrant kinship groups active in the Yamato plain. The Soga, through a number of political machinations, such as marriage into the ruling line, became one of the most powerful families at the Yamato court. In part because of their immigrant connections, the Soga became strong proponents of continental culture, especially Buddhism, and urged the acceptance of Buddhism by the court. They, along with powerful immigrant kinship groups such as the Hata, built temples, sponsored the education of Buddhist clerics, and engaged in other pro-Buddhist activities.[10]

The Mononobe kinship group – led by court minister Mononobe no Okoshi (dates unknown) – and the Nakatomi kinship group – led by court minister Nakatomi no Kamako (dates unknown) – represented the faction that rejected the foreign deity, Buddha, in favor of the Yamato gods (*kuni tsu kami*). The Mononobe were professional soldiers, while the Nakatomi family were associated with *kami* worship and other ritual matters.

As we saw above, Kinmei, in the end, grants Soga no Iname custody of the Buddha image for the purpose of ascertaining whether its worship is efficacious. But the matter does not end there. The same 552 entry continues:

> Later, an epidemic afflicted the country and cut short the lives of many people. With the passing of time, more and more people died of this incurable disease. Mononobe no Okoshi and Nakatomi no Kamako together humbly addressed the Heavenly Sovereign: "Previously, the counsel we offered went unheeded. As a result, this epidemic has occurred. Now, before it is too late, this situation must be rectified. Throw away the statue of the Buddha at once and diligently seek future blessings."
>
> The Heavenly Sovereign responded: "We will do as you have counseled."
>
> Officials took the Buddha statue and threw it into the waters of the Naniwa canal. They then set fire to the temple in which it was enshrined and burned it to the ground. At this time, although the winds were calm and the sky cloudless, suddenly a fire broke out in the Great Hall [of the Heavenly Sovereign's palace]. (adapted from Inoue 1987: 2.475 and Deal 1995: 219)

Despite the attempt to locate the cause of the epidemic in the worship of the Buddha image, the resulting fire in the Great Hall suggests otherwise. But the discussion of Buddhism in this entry ends here, leaving the matter unresolved. In 553, however, there is an entry that recounts the discovery of a camphor wood log emitting a bright light as it floated on the sea. The log is recovered and given to Heavenly Sovereign Kinmei, who has two Buddha images made from it. Although nothing else about these images is conveyed, it seems that Buddhist practice has been given another chance.

The next sustained entries concerning Buddhism in the *Nihon shoki* do not occur until the reign of King Bidatsu (r. 572–585). It is at this point in the text – starting in the year 577 – that Buddhist-related entries become prominent, and the conflict over the reception of Buddhism is finally decided in favor of the Soga family. In a story reminiscent of the events that occurred some 30 years earlier, Soga no Umako (Iname's son) is given possession, in 584, of two stone Buddha statues that had been brought to Yamato by Japanese envoys returning from Paekche. Seeking to further promote the Dharma, Umako builds a family temple (*ujidera*) called Hōkōji (known originally as Asukadera; it is located in modern Nara Prefecture); oversees the renunciation and patronage of Yamato's first monastics, three young women; and puts a Buddha relic through a number of tests meant to destroy it. When the relic remains unscathed, his faith in the Buddha's Dharma is secured. That same year, Umako becomes sick and, at King Bidatsu's urging, he prays to the Buddhia image to be cured. Shortly after, an epidemic breaks out and many people die.

As a result of the epidemic, Mononobe no Moriya and Nakatomi no Katsumi convince King Bidatsu that the cause of the disease was the fact that Soga no Umako was worshipping the Buddha. King Bidatsu issues an order that worship of the Buddha cease immediately. Umako's nuns are flogged and returned to secular life, his temple is burned down, and the Buddha statue enshrined there is destroyed. However, another epidemic occurs and the supposition this time is that this is retribution for destroying the Buddha image. Umako himself remains ill, and at his request, King Bidatsu allows Umako alone to continue the private practice of Buddhist rituals in order to cure his disease. The three nuns are returned to him, and he rebuilds his temple.

In 587 the Soga family gained control over the court. Soga no Umako, then, eventually wins the religious conflict. Besides the ideological Buddhist victory, Umako also effects a political resolution: he seizes power in 592 by arranging for the assassination of his political rivals and placing in power a ruler amenable to his ideas. There is another political consideration. The Soga extended family realized a need for a new system of government to unify clans around the central authority of the imperial line; Buddhism was one of the tools used to accomplish significant aspects of this process.

We conclude this discussion with two historical notes. First, the *Nihon shoki* represents the bad things that happen to those who would oppose the acceptance of Buddhism as a punishment meted out by the result of karmic consequence, suggesting that Buddhist supporters wrote this *Nihon shoki* narrative. In this case, King

Bidatsu dies of the epidemic, apparently the price he played for denigrating Buddhism. Yoshida Kazuhiko argues that certain *Nihon shoki* entries are patterned on Chinese antecedents that discuss the recompense meted out to rulers who denigrate Buddhism. For this reason, Yoshida believes that a Buddhist priest wrote such sections of the *Nihon shoki*. He conjectures that this was the monk Dōji. These narratives also follow a pattern whereby the idea of the End of the Dharma (*mappō*) is invoked to explain the suppression of Buddhism. This, in turn, gives way to a struggle against this oppression, and the result is that Buddhism is restored. For these reasons, Yoshida questions whether there really was opposition to Buddhism in the Asuka period (Yoshida 2006: 15–16).

Second, the struggle between the Soga and Mononobe has often been described as a struggle between Buddhism and Shintō, but this is a problematic perspective because Shintō as a systematic, organized religion did not exist in this time period (Kuroda 1981; Yoshida 2003: 2). It appears that the early Japanese conception of Buddhism was to see the Buddha as a foreign *kami* rather than as something completely different from indigenous cults and cultic practices. Seen in this light, we can understand this struggle as one over who would control the rituals and cultic centers that were seen as so important to holding and maintaining power and prosperity. This was played out in terms of the comparative efficaciousness of indigenous *kami* over foreign *kami*, and of continental symbols of power versus indigenous ones. Changes in cultic practices and centers meant changes in who held the symbolic reigns of power. In the end, this struggle did establish Buddhism as central to the task of nation-building as its patronage by the royal family in subsequent decades attests. However, Buddhism did not replace the various indigenous *kami* cults, but rather took on a ritually important role alongside them.

Queen Suiko and Senior Prince Shōtoku

By the late sixth century, Buddhism – already strongly supported by the Soga aristocratic family – was becoming a significant ideological presence in the development of a nascent centralized court bureaucracy. According to the *Nihon shoki*, it was during the reign of Queen Suiko and her chief minister, Senior Prince Shōtoku, that Buddhism became a formal aspect of royal rule, inscribed, for instance, in the Seventeen Article Constitution.

Queen Suiko was of direct royal lineage: she was the daughter of King Kinmei, her brother was King Yōmei, and she was the widow of King Bidatsu. However, her connections to the Soga family were also strong. Her mother was from the Soga family and she was Soga no Umako's niece. Given her Soga connections, it is not surprising that Buddhist rituals and other practices were depicted as central to her reign. It is also likely that at least some of the interest in Buddhism that texts like the

Nihon shoki attribute to Suiko and other members of the royal family was a way to write into the official record royal support for Buddhism, especially in a period in which Buddhism was mostly promoted by the Soga and related immigrant extended families.

Some scholars, therefore, have questioned the commitment that Suiko had to Buddhism. While the Soga extended family and others were deeply concerned with promoting Buddhist practice, it is less certain how the Great Kings thought about this potentially disruptive new ideology. Some have claimed that Queen Suiko was anti-Buddhist because of the rebuke she apparently makes to Soga no Umako regarding Buddhist worship. In 607, Suiko issued this edict:

> We hear that Our Imperial ancestors, in their government of the world, bending lowly under the sky and treading delicately on the ground, paid deep reverence to the Gods of Heaven and Earth. They everywhere dedicated temples to the mountains and rivers, and held mysteroius communion with the powers of Nature. Hence the male and female elements became harmoniously developed, and civilizing influences blended together. And now in Our reign, shall there be any remissness in the worship of the Gods of Heaven and Earth? Therefore let Our Ministers with their whole hearts do reverence to the Gods of Heaven and Earth. (Aston 1972: 2.135)

In this passage, she appears to be saying that worship of *kami* is central to the successful administration of government and for a peaceful land. Scholars such as Sonoda Kōyū have argued that this royal edict was a rebuke to Soga no Umako and his support of Buddhism (Sonoda 1993: 378–9). The *Nihon shoki* goes on to report that six days after the edict was issued, Soga no Umako and Senior Prince Shōtoku worshipped the "Gods of Heaven and Earth" (Aston 1972: 2.136). Beyond this one statement of compliance with the edict – an edict that does not forbid the worship of Buddhism – there is no other specific evidence that Suiko was anti-Buddhist. If the *Nihon shoki* accounts are to be trusted, however, there is evidence that Suiko was a Buddhist supporter. She did, after all, request that Senior Prince Shōtoku lecture on Buddhist sutras. Suiko, despite Sonoda's objection, seems to have been pro-Buddhist even as she also had responsibility for the worship of *kami*. She was Great Queen when there was increasing Buddhist activity, and if she had truly tried to abolish Buddhist practices, it seems odd that there would not have been more written to suggest this. One other bit of information further belies Sonoda's interpretation: in 623, the *Nihon shoki* records that Yamato was home to 46 temples, 816 monks, and 569 nuns (Aston 1972: 2.154).

If Queen Suiko was only a tentative Buddhist, her nephew and chief minister, Senior Prince Shōtoku was apparently an ardent Buddhist. The *Nihon shoki* depicts him as a strong advocate for Chinese modes of government and religion in general, and as a devout Buddhist in particular. The history of early Japanese Buddhism used to revolve around the figure of Senior Prince Shōtoku (Shōtoku Taishi; also known, more correctly, as Umayado no miko). The long held view of the prince was of a brilliant statesman and erudite Buddhist, the first Japanese Buddhist to fully understand the profundity of the Buddha's Dharma. In the case of Shōtoku, old views linger on, but they are changing.

The advent of both new historical data and persuasive alternative textual interpretations provide good reasons to be suspicious of the traditional accounts of the role that Shōtoku Taishi played in the development of early Japanese Buddhism. Senior Prince Shōtoku has become a flashpoint for radical reinterpretations of early Japanese Buddhism. Much of what had long been assumed to be true about Asuka Buddhism has turned out to be highly problematic and Shōtoku is at the center of these interpretive debates. As a result, our discussion is divided into two parts: the first outlines the traditional view of Shōtoku; the second discusses recent scholarship that questions much of the veracity of the received view.

The traditional view of Shōtoku derives from texts dating to the early eighth century and later, such as the *Nihon shoki* (or *Nihongi*; Chronicles of Japan, 720 CE) and the *Jōgū Shōtoku hōō teisetsu* (The Imperial Record of Shōtoku, Dharma King of the Upper Palace).[11] These and similar narratives tell us that Shōtoku Taishi (Prince Shōtoku; 574–622) was the son of Emperor Yōmei. He became crown prince during the reign of his aunt, Queen Suiko (r. 592–628), overseeing the affairs of state from 593 until his death in 622. These texts represent Shōtoku as a devout Buddhist, a sagacious ruler, and, increasingly over time, as having Buddha- and bodhisattva-like spiritual acumen and superhuman abilities. The cult of Shōtoku Taishi that developed after the Prince's death was primarily focused on the hagiographical features of his biography. The notion that Shōtoku is the founder of Japanese Buddhism and father of the Japanese nation is one that started in these early texts and continues to the present day. Most recently, some Japanese scholars have begun to question whether Shōtoku was even an historical person. Rather, it is argued, he was a social construction that served the political purposes of those who inscribed these legends in texts like the *Nihon shoki* and the *Jōgū Shōtoku hōō teisetsu*. In short, myth and history collide head on in the personage of Senior Prince Shōtoku.

According to these early texts, Shōtoku was a highly capable statesman who exhibited extraordinary political acumen. Shōtoku served as regent (*sesshō*) to his aunt, Queen Suiko. In this capacity, Shōtoku was noted for his ability in dealing with both domestic affairs and foreign diplomacy. He is said to have written the Seventeen Article Constitution (*Jūshichijō kenpō*), established a hierarchical 12-rank court system (*kan'i jūnikai*), dispatched envoys to Sui dynasty (581–619) China (*kenzuishi*) starting in 607, and utilized Confucian values of loyalty and harmony as the foundation for the administration of government. In sum, Shōtoku is represented as having mastered the complexities of Chinese political thought and selectively applied it to the emerging Japanese state.

These same early texts valorize Shōtoku as a devout Buddhist with a profound comprehension of the Dharma; it is this kind of representation of Shōtoku that was the foundation for his status as the father of Japanese Buddhism. It is recorded that Senior Prince Shōtoku studied Buddhism – especially sutras – with a Koguryŏ priest named Hyeja (J. Eji; resident in Japan from 595 to 615). It is also recorded that he wrote commentaries on three Buddhist sutras (known collectively as the Three Commentaries, or *Sangyō gisho*). These three sutras developed key Mahayana Buddhist ideas: the *Queen Shrimala Sūtra* (J. *Shōman-gyō*) recounts the story of Shrimala, an Indian queen, whose Buddhist practice leads to enlightenment; the *Lotus Sūtra* (J. *Hoke-kyō*) teaches, among other things, that all sentient beings will one day attain enlightenment; and the *Vimalakirti Sūtra* (J. *Yuima-gyō*), narrates the story of a lay Buddhist named Vimalakirti whose understanding of the Dharma exceeded that of Manjushri (J. Monju), the bodhisattva of wisdom. While others in his day were chanting sutras for their salvific efficacy, we are told that Shōtoku was reading sutras for their Buddhist meaning and writing commentaries on them. The *Nihon shoki* also states that Shōtoku lectured to Empress Suiko on the *Queen Shrimala Sutra*; such an entry is presumably meant to directly associate Suiko with Queen Shrimala.

Despite the importance of the image of Shōtoku in Japanese Buddhist history, our understanding of him is almost entirely hagiographical. Some Japanese scholars have questioned the factuality of the Shōtoku accounts found in the *Nihon shoki* and other texts. Others have argued that Shōtoku did not actually exist, but is rather the invention of the earliest texts about him that constructed his existence for religio-political purposes.[12]

Traditional interpretations of Shōtoku's Buddhist erudition rested largely on the acceptance of the assertion in early texts that he wrote the *Sangyō gisho*. It has long been speculated that, given the very short time between the introduction of Buddhism to the Japanese islands and the time that Shōtoku supposedly wrote the three commentaries, it would not have been possible for him to have mastered the language and complex understanding to write sophisticated Buddhist commentaries by himself. For this reason, more cautious scholars have contended that Shōtoku wrote the commentaries, but with the assistance of monastics from the Korean peninsula, such as the Koguryŏ monk Hyeja mentioned above. More recently, however, evidence has emerged revealing that the *Sangyō gisho* was brought back to Japan by envoys sent to Sui dynasty China and, thus, was not the work of Shōtoku. Further evidence is found in the Dunhuang caves. In the Mogao Caves (J. Bokkō-kutsu), Cave 17, a large number of scrolls were discovered. Among these was a text titled the *Shōmangyō Commentary* (*Shōmangyō gisho*) that is the source for the *Shōmangyō* commentary attributed to Shōtoku.[13] It is likely that his two other sutra commentaries also have Chinese origins. It appears that the three commentaries were only later attributed to Shōtoku.

Others have also expressed doubt about Shōtoku's historicity or about the factualness of the early stories about him. For instance, Tsuda Sōkichi (1950) argued that Shōtoku could not have been the author of the Seventeen Article Constitution on the grounds that the *Nihon shoki* was the product of a later time, produced by a group of editors with a particular ideological agenda to promote. More recently, Ōyama Seiichi has argued that the political and religious erudition of Senior Prince Shōtoku is largely a fiction constructed by the editors of the *Nihon shoki*. He claims that there is little about Shōtoku that we can be confident is historically accurate. Ōyama does acknowledge the existence of a figure named Prince Umayado (Umayado no miko) – presumably the historical figure behind the Shōtoku story – but that what we know of him is extremely limited historically, such as that he was King Yōmei's son, that his actual name was Umayado, that he was born in 574, that he lived in the Ikaruga Palace, and that he built the temple known as Ikarugadera, later renamed Hōryūji.[14] If we accept Ōyama's claims, there is little choice but to accept that the Senior Prince Shōtoku who has come down to us through history was in fact an historical fiction meant, in part, to associate the ruling family with the powerful ideology of Buddhism at a time when it was largely in the hands of the Soga and other likeminded extended families. Even making the case for downsizing Shōtoku's historical reputation, it still stands that he has powerfully represented many different things to different Japanese Buddhists.

Asuka Buddhism (552–645)

The forms of Buddhist practice and thought that developed after 552 are usually referred to collectively as Asuka-period Buddhism (*Asuka bukkyō*). The Asuka period (552–645) is named for an area in the southeastern Nara Basin and surrounded by the Yoshino mountains. This region was particularly associated with the Soga extended family. One of the most important characteristics of this period is the fact that there were powerful extended families active in court government and politics – most notably the Soga extended family – that were also major promoters of Buddhist practice. Notable, too, were those powerful extended families that represented indigenous *kami* cultic practices that were opposed to Buddhist practice.

Another important characteristic of this period is that the promotion of Buddhism was not just the effort of the Soga family, but also the result of immigrants to the Japanese archipelago who brought the Buddhist faith with them. Extended families, such as the Hata, were actively Buddhist and, like the Soga, were responsible for some of the earliest Buddhist temples constructed in the Japanese islands.

In discussing Asuka Buddhism, there are four aspects that particularly frame the contours of Buddhism in this era: (1) the importance of immigrants to the development of Asuka Buddhism, (2) aristocratic family patronage of Buddhism (*ujizoku bukkyō*), (3) the centrality of Buddhist material culture, and (4) the decided emphasis on ritual over doctrine. We will explicate each one of these aspects in turn, utilizing the example of the Soga family and their patronage of temples and a fledgling monastic community as a way to further illuminate the significance of these four aspects of Asuka Buddhism.

Immigrants and the development of Asuka-period Buddhism

Immigrants and immigrant kinship groups were crucial to the development of Asuka culture in general and Asuka Buddhism in particular. We have already touched on the fact that Buddhism arrived in Japan prior to its official introduction, as recounted in texts like the *Nihon shoki*, by means of immigrants – some of whom were Buddhists – to the Japanese islands from the Asian mainland. The *Nihon shoki* refers to immigrants and their immediate descendants by the term *kikajin*, "people who have come from other regions." This discussion, however, adopts Michael Como's (2003) terminology replacing the term "immigrants" with "immigrant kinship group" as a way to more clearly "refer to any kinship group that claimed as a founding ancestor a figure that arrived in the Japanese islands from across the sea."[15] Immigrant kinship groups were important to the development of ancient Japan because they were the bearers of Chinese culture – including Buddhism – and its material artifacts such as texts, art, and technologies. These groups were responsible for the introduction to Japan of such things as pottery techniques, silkworm cultivation, horse breeding, and other technologies. They also brought to Japan expertise in government administration and economic systems, as well as Buddhist, Confucian, Daoist, and other Chinese intellectual ideas. Over time, the distinction between immigrant kinship groups and native Japanese evaporated because of intermarriage and their importance to crafting Yamato culture.

King Sŏngmyŏng's gift in 552 was by no means a unique interaction between the Asian mainland and the Japanese islands. The following year, the *Nihon shoki* recorded that Paekche sent scholars of medicine, divination, and calendars to Yamato in exchange for Yamato arms and troops. In subsequent years, Yamato was the recipient of additional human resources, notably Buddhist sculptors, architects, and artisans. In this way, immigrants from China and the Korean peninsula – whether extended kinship groups or individual experts in a particular area of knowledge – played a central role in the transmission of Buddhism, political and social ideas, and other cultural forms that were crucial to early Japanese nation-building.

Textual and other evidence strongly suggests that early Japanese Buddhists relied on and were guided by Buddhists who arrived in the Japanese islands from the Chinese continent. The *Nihon shoki* depicts Senior Prince Shōtoku as an ardent

Buddhist believer and patron, and states that he studied with monks from the Korean peninsula. Reading between the lines of early texts that recount Shōtoku's Buddhist erudition, the fact that Shōtoku studied with Korean Buddhist monks suggests that those Japanese who wanted to study Buddhism required the tutelage of Korean monks in order to understand Buddhist sutras and images, and to learn proper ritual procedures. As we have seen, the earliest Buddhist objects to arrive in Japan came mostly from the Korean peninsula. Additionally, Korean monks, artisans of Buddhist ritual objects, and ritual specialists also accompanied envoys to Japan. In these ways, Korean Buddhists were central to the early development of Japanese Buddhism.

Besides expertise in Buddhist thought, ritual, art, and architecture, Korean Buddhists were sometimes appointed to administer monastic institutions and to assist with writing ecclesial regulations. In 625 CE, for instance, the *Nihon shoki* records the appointment of Ekan (his Japanese name; dates unknown) a Koguryŏ Buddhist priest, to the highest monastic rank of primary prelate (*sōjō*). Apparently, there were not yet Japanese monks sufficiently qualified to fill such a position. Regardless, Ekan was very accomplished. He studied Sanron (Three-Treatise) Buddhist thought (see Chapter 2) in Sui dynasty China with the famous monk Jizang (J. Kichizō; 549–623). The *Nihon shoki* tells us that in 625 he was sent to Yamato as tribute by the Koguryŏ king and appointed primary prelate by Queen Suiko.

There are numerous other mentions of Korean peninsula monks and nuns traveling to the Japanese archipelago bringing both Buddhist material culture and knowledge of Buddhist thought and practice. For instance, in 577, the *Nihon shoki* recounts that a Japanese envoy in Paekche was given both human and material Buddhist resources to take back with him to Yamato. Among these resources were sutras and sutra commentaries, and six experts in things Buddhist: "a precept master (*risshi*), a meditation master (*zenji*), a nun, a *dhāraṇī* (J. *darani*; ritual incantations) master (*jugonshi*), a Buddhist statue-maker, and a temple architect" (adapted from Inoue 1987: 2.475 and Deal 1995: 219). Without question, then, Asuka-period Buddhism was largely shaped by continental influences and especially by Korean monastics.

Aristocratic family Buddhist patronage

From *Nihon shoki* accounts and other evidence, both textual and archaeological, it is evident that early Japanese Buddhism was largely the purview of aristocratic extended kinship groups, especially the Soga, and that their Buddhism focused largely on the creation and use of Buddhist material culture and the rituals performed in conjunction with these objects, and not on something primarily doctrinal. This early form of Soga family Buddhism is sometimes referred to as *ujizoku bukkyō* – Buddhism of the great families. Emblematic of the Soga family patronage of

Buddhism was their family temple (*ujidera*) called Asukadera, and later referred to as Hōkōji or Gangōji.

The transmission of Buddhism across East Asia in the early centuries of the Common Era was marked, in part, by the construction of temples, symbolic of the power and prestige afforded by the religion. Patronage of temples and having them constructed may have been an expression of the power of Buddhist ritual practices, but it was also a way to align one's ruling authority with this powerful ideology. In short, temples were conspicuous symbols of the power associated with Buddhism. Once a ruler decided to adopt Buddhism, temples were typically constructed. East Asian imperial capitals, which became centers of interest in Buddhism, also included the construction of Buddhist temples. These sites included Luoyang and Chang'an in China, Hwando (J. Ganto) and Pyongyang (J. Heijō) in Koguryŏ, Ungjin (J. Yūshin) and Sabi (J. Shihi) in Paekche, and Gyeongju (J. Keishū) in Silla. Moreover, with the exception of Yamato, the first Buddhist temples were built in the capitals of these various countries by order of the particular ruler. For instance, King Pŏp (r. 599–600) of Paekche ordered the construction of Wanghŭngsa temple in the capital city of Sabi. The temple was built as a result of court patronage of Buddhism, and was part of the practice of building temples for the protection of the kingdom. At the same time, and perhaps as importantly, such temples also represented the power of the king and asserted the legitimacy of the ruling elite (Tamura 1996: 6).[16]

The absence of royal patronage by the Yamato Great Kings in the late sixth and early seventh centuries is perhaps explained by the ambivalence with which the court received the Buddhist gifts from Paekche and the fact that it was Soga and related aristocratic families that were the early champions of Buddhist ritual practices. Although royal patronage of Buddhism, and the building of Buddhist temples, became fully developed in the Nara period, temples were nevertheless important to the development of Asuka Buddhism. The patronage, though, came from the Soga and not the royal family. Asukadera and similar Asuka-period temples were powerful symbols of the political and cultural influence wielded by the Soga extended family in this era.[17]

The Soga's major temple-building project, overseen by Soga no Umako, was the Asukadera.[18] The *Gangōji garan engi*, introduced above, recounts the early history of this temple.[19] Unlike the official temples found in other parts of East Asia, this temple was an *ujidera*, or clan temple, utilizing a Chinese continental style typical of all Asuka-period temples. A *Nihon shoki* entry for 624 reports that there were 46 temples in Yamato, home to the Soga and similar immigrant extended families. There is little evidence that any of these were specifically built through the patronage of the royal family. Temples associated with Senior Prince Shōtoku and the royal family – such as Hōryūji (originally, Ikarugadera) – have unclear origins and hence unclear connections with royal patronage.[20] While there were temples other than Asukadera built, its provenance, for such an early temple, is relatively well known, and archaeological findings have revealed that Asukadera was a large and imposing temple.[21]

Asukadera was constructed by Umako as fulfillment of a vow made in 587 that he would construct a temple if he were victorious in battle against his anti-Buddhist foes, the Mononobe and Nakatomi. This particular struggle over the foreign deities of Buddhism is the result of a plague that strikes Yamato. The Mononobe and Nakatomi declare that the plague is the result of the Soga family's worship of and support for Buddhism. After much struggle, the Soga are victorious, Buddhist worship is vindicated, and, in return, Umako starts construction on Asukadera, completed in 596.

Soga no Umako had other temples built, constituting the earliest known patronage of a nascent Buddhist monastic system. According to the *Nihon shoki*, Yamato's first Buddhist monastic renunciants were women. In 584, Soga no Umako appointed the former Koguryŏ monk Hyep'yon (J. Eben or Ebin; dates unknown) as his Dharma teacher.[22] Umako then built a temple to house the first three renunciants, where they were instructed by Hyep'yon: Shima (574–?) the 11-year-old daughter of Shiba Tatto (or, Shiba Tachito; dates unknown), whose Buddhist name was Zenshinni; Toyome, the daughter of Ayahito no Yabo, whose Buddhist name was Zenzō-ni (dates unknown); and Ishime, the daughter of Nishigori no Tsubu, whose Buddhist name was Ezen-ni (dates unknown). The latter two nuns were Shima's servants. The renunciation of these three nuns facilitated by a powerful aristocrat became the model for the later system of "official nuns" (*kan'ni*) appointed and recognized by the royal ruler. Of significance is that all three women were descended from immigrant kinship groups, again underscoring the importance of such groups to the promotion of Asuka-period Buddhism.

Soga no Umako was a staunch supporter of these women renunciates. It is reported that he built temples for them and otherwise provided them with the means to live a monastic life. He also charged them with carrying out Buddhist rituals. The nuns traveled to Paekche in 588 to study Buddhism. They returned in 590, having received formal Buddhist ordination while there. It should be noted that they were permitted to travel to the Korean peninsula by Umako, not by the Yamato government. These three nuns had the dubious distinction of being the first Yamato Buddhists to suffer persecution during one of the skirmishes between the Soga and Nakatomi over the fate of Yamato Buddhist practice.

Asuka-period Buddhist material culture and ritual practices

In the decades immediately following the sixth-century Paekche gift of Buddhist objects to Yamato, the development of Asuka-period Buddhist ritual practice was largely centered on material culture – especially images and temples – and the artisans capable of producing it. These two aspects of Asuka Buddhism – material culture and ritual – were really two sides of the same phenomenon. Buddhist material culture was not created as works of art; nor was it meant to go unused. For this reason, we eschew the term "art" in favor of the notion of "material culture" for the primary reason that Buddhist objects, aesthetically pleasing as they may have been, were prized as ritual objects and not as art in any contemporary sense. The emphasis was on ritual practice rather than abstract doctrine. Buddhist doctrines were slowly disseminated, but formal, systematic doctrine, as would develop by the eighth century, was in little, if any, evidence during the Asuka period, although Senior Prince Shōtoku was retroactively, and no doubt erroneously, described as having prodigious doctrinal erudition.

Not surprisingly, then, the Soga and other pro-Buddhist families were primarily concerned with Buddhist practice rather than Buddhist thought, and with magico-religious efficacy rather than the abstraction of enlightenment. Asuka-period rituals were typically concerned with immediate problems and personal concerns. We find in this earliest Japanese Buddhist context a penchant for what has come to be referred to as "this-worldly benefits," or *genze riyaku*. This notion, still current today in contemporary Japanese religions, refers to real, tangible benefits that are the result of proper ritual actions.[23] In the Asuka period, rituals were performed for a number of situations, such as to cure an illness, or, failing that, to speed the spirit of the deceased to a better rebirth, particularly in a Buddhist paradise. Similarly, rituals were directed at relief from drought and famine, protection of one's family, and victory over one's enemies. Such practices as chanting sutras and commissioning the construction of Buddhist images and temples were believed to be particularly efficacious for achieving these ends. Rites were part of a ritual economy in which the chanted sutra or crafted image served as the currency with which the believer purchased the efficacy of the enacted ritual.

Asuka-period Buddhist images: The Shaka Triad

Yamato Buddhists regarded Buddhas and bodhisattvas as protectors and benefactors, if approached in a ritually prescribed way. The Asuka period marks the beginnings of a long tradition of Buddhist image-making, especially sculptures executed in bronze or wood. As a result, Buddhist sculpture, and the temples in which such images were enshrined, became the focal point for the rituals practiced by Asuka-period aristocrats.

Asuka-period Buddhist sculpture exemplifies, among other things, stylistic qualities shared with images from the Chinese mainland and Korean peninsula. Some of these images were made in Yamato, but others were produced on the Korean peninsula. It is not always easy to determine which is which, underscoring the pan-East Asian nature of Asuka Buddhism. Aside from extant images, the other source for the images produced in the Asuka period – or brought to the Japanese islands at this time – derive from textual sources that we have already cited for their importance to our understanding of Asuka Buddhism in general. Such texts as the *Nihon shoki*, *Jōgū shōtoku hōō teisetsu*, and *Gangōji garan engi narabi ni ruki shizai chō* describe the crafting and use of Buddhist images. The other significant textual source is images that include an inscription, typically on the mandorla, stating the name of the patron or patrons, the artisan, and the reason for creating the image.

One way to consider the early production of Buddhist images in Yamato is to think in terms of a network of interconnected nodes consisting, especially, of patrons, artisans, images, ritual requests, and temples. In brief, patrons – such as the Soga, Hata, and other aristocratic families, and later, the royal rulers – would engage an artisan to craft a Buddhist image with the express purpose of seeking some specific ritual benefit such as to cure an illness, to ensure birth in a Buddhist paradise for the deceased, or for victory over one's enemies. Thus, temples where these images were enshrined became a focal point for Buddhist ritual praxis.

In the late sixth and early seventh centuries, Yamato Buddhist image-making was dominated by an artisan, Tori Busshi, or the school of sculptural style he oversaw, referred to as Tori style. Tori, whose family name was Kuratsukuri no Tori, was active in the early seventh century. He was descended from an immigrant family lineage, most likely from the Korean peninsula, who were saddle-makers (*kuratsukuri*). Tori's grandfather was Shiba Tatto, a supporter of Buddhism, and his father, Shiba's son, was Kuratsukuri no Tasuna, also a maker of Buddhist images. Tori was later given the honorific title *busshi* (Buddhist master sculptor). What little detail is known about Tori Busshi's life and activities derives from some *Nihon shoki* passages about his image-making, and from an inscription on one of his most famous images, the Shaka Triad, which we discuss in detail below.

There are a number of extant Buddhist images dating from the seventh century that bear significantly similar stylistic characteristics to the so-called Tori-style, which are considered the work of the same artisan or school. Donald McCallum (2004: 19) lists nine such images, including such well-known images as the Asukadera Daibutsu, Shaka Triad, and Yumedono Kannon. The attribution of this style to Tori derives mostly from the Shaka Triad mandorla that includes an incised inscription that states that Tori Busshi was its crafter. On this basis, all stylistically similar images from this time period (early seventh century) are assigned to Tori or his stylistic school. This style, in turn, borrows the Buddhist sculptural style of Northern Wei dynasty (386–534) China that was imported to Yamato from the Korean peninsula.

Asuka-period Buddhist images are taken from the pantheon of Mahayana Buddhas and bodhisattvas such as Shaka (the historical Buddha; Skt. Śākyamuni), Yakushi Nyorai (Healing Buddha; Skt. Bhaiṣajyaguru), Kannon (bodhisattva of compassion; Skt. Avalokiteśvara), and Miroku (bodhisattva and future Buddha; Skt. Maitreya). In canonical fashion, these figures are represented in specific poses and hand gestures (mudras) that are used across Buddhist traditions. Stylistic issues aside, Asuka-period

Buddhist images were made for ritual purposes. A famous example is the Yakushi Nyorai sculpture located in the Hōryūji *kondō*. The original idea for this image came at the request of King Yōmei in 586. According to the *Jōgū Shōtoku hōō teisetsu*, which cites the mandorla inscription on the back of a Yakushi image, King Yōmei became ill and requested that Prince Shōtoku and Queen Suiko construct an image of Yakushi and a temple to enshrine it, in order that he might be cured. Yōmei died before work on the temple and image began. In 607, Shōtoku and Suiko sought to fulfill the king's command so they commissioned the construction of the temple and image, presumably, too, as a ritual to ensure Yōmei's happy rebirth (Deal 1999: 331–332; Mizuno 1974: 32–33).

Of all the Tori-style images, analysis of the Shaka Triad (Shaka *sanzonzō*) presents a number of interpretive problems that attend any discussion of Asuka-period Buddhism. The Shaka Triad is a gilt bronze image enshrined in the main hall (*kondō*) of Hōryūji. It consists of an image of a seated Shaka attended by two standing bodhisattvas: Yakuō and Yakujō (see Figure 1.2). The Shaka image is 86.5 centimeters

Figure 1.2   Shaka Triad, Hōryūji Kondō, Nara Prefecture. Asuka period (623), gilt bronze, height of Shaka image: 86.5 cm. Courtesy of Hōryūji temple, Nara. Photograph by Asuka-en.

high; the bodhisattvas are 91 centimeters high, and the entire image, including pedestal and mandorla (kōhai), is 382 centimeters high. The Shaka image is depicted with some of the classic symbols used to materially represent a Buddha (Mizuno 1974: 34–38): he is seated in meditation with legs crossed, he has elongated ears – a sign that Shaka was a wealthy prince prior to enlightenment, who would have worn heavy jewelry that would have stretched his earlobes – and his hands are depicted in the gestures known as *mudras* (J. *in*). His right hand is in the gesture of resassurances (*semui-in*; Skt. *abhaya mudrā*) and his left hand is in the gesture of wish-granting (*yogan-in*; Skt. *vara mudrā*). Further, he is represented with some of the 32 physical marks of a Buddha (*sanjūni sō*), including gilding (though little remains) symbolizing the golden glow of the Buddha's skin (*konjikisō*); snail-shell-curl hair (*rahotsu*); the tuft of hair between the eyebrows (*byakugo*; Skt. *ūrṇā*; missing on the Shaka image though the spike which it was attached to remains); and the protuberance on the top of the Buddha's head (*nikkei*; Skt. *uṣṇīṣa*).

The bodhisattva on Shaka's left is Yakuō (Bodhisattva Medicine King; Skt. Bhaiṣajya-rāja); to his right is Yakujō (Bodhisattva Superior Medicine; Skt. Bhaiṣajya-samudgata). This was a standard grouping – Shaka attended by Yakuō and Yakujō – in this era (Washizuka *et al.* 1997: 15). Both of these standing images are holding jewels in their hands, which symbolize the ability to heal those who are sick. They are depicted wearing jewelry, representing the royal status of a bodhisattva prior to attaining enlightenment and becoming a Buddha.

The provenance of this image is made clear – or apparently so – by the inscription incised on the back of its mandorla. The 196-character inscription indicates that the image is the work of Tori Busshi and that it was commissioned in 622 and dedicated in 623. The 622 commission was an attempt to cure an ailing Senior Prince Shōtoku; when he died, the commission was rededicated to securing his rebirth – and the rebirth of his mother and consort who had also recently died – in a Buddhist Pure Land (McCallum 2004: 24–25; Mizuno 1974: 32; Tamura 2000: 31).

McCallum (2004) studied this image and argues that the mandorla inscription was incised considerably later than the image itself. Historical analysis, he says, "indicates that the text was written after 670, as one component of the campaign to enhance the reputation of the prince" (McCallum 2004: 25). He also notes that the inscription was inscribed on the surface of the mandorla and is not a part of the original casting of the images. Thus, the inscription could have been easily incised at a later date (2004: 23) There is one other piece of evidence that strongly suggests that the man-dorla inscription is a later addition to the Shaka Triad. This involves the honorific term *busshi* – master of Buddhist sculpture – that is ascribed to Tori. As McCallum notes, the "term *busshi* is not found elsewhere with reference to Tori, nor does it seem to have been employed as early as the Asuka period. Consequently, the occur-rence here of *busshi* appears to be one more piece of evidence suggesting that the inscription was written later" (McCallum 2004: 25).

For McCallum, the significance of these facts is another retrodictive moment. The inscription, probably inscribed after 670, attempts to rewrite the historical record in order to "shift credit for the patronage of Buddhism from the Soga clan to the 'imperial' line" (McCallum 2004: 33–34). In so doing, the Soga have been pre-empted and credit for the promotion and patronage of Buddhism is now made to reside with the ruling family and its exemplar, Senior Prince Shōtoku. The result of this analysis is further evidence that the hagiographical treatment of Senior Prince Shōtoku is a revisionist construction meant to legitimate the ruling family's political power and authority by means of Buddhist symbols. This is significant because if we can no longer take the historical data at face value – whether the *Nihon shoki* or the Shaka Triad mandorla inscription – then traditional interpretations of early Japanese Buddhism, such as the depth of Shōtoku's Buddhist knowledge and the rapidity with which at least some Japanese grasped the profundity of the Buddha's Dharma, must be re-evaluated.

Notes

1 See also Barnes 1993, who refers to this as the Yellow Sea interaction sphere.
2 The meaning of the concept *uji*, and how this term should be translated into English – if at all – has been much debated. Translating *uji* as "clan" has been common, but some argue that this suggests an extended family, when *uji* as a social entity included members from outside the bloodline and was, politically, a status given for royal service. Piggott (1997: 328) translates *uji* as "a royally recognized lineage," explaining *uji* as "an extended kinship solidarity the structure of which is thought to have resembled a conical clan. Reception of a *kabane* [noble] title in return for services rendered to the Yamato Great King established the *uji*, which continued thereafter through the generations. The unity and status of the *uji* continued to be based on service to the Yamato king, along with devotion to the ancestor who established the lineage."
3 The term "Great King" (or Queen) is the translation for the term *ōkimi* (or, its alternative pronunciation, *daiō*). This was a term typically used to describe the Yamato rulers prior to the adoption of the term *tennō* (Heavenly Sovereign, or Emperor). For simplicity's sake, we use the terms King or Queen in reference to specific monarchs.
4 The term "Yamato" refers to the region and the rulers residing in central Honshū (present-day region of Nara) in the larger region known in the Chinese mainland and the Korean peninsula as Wa. "Wa" – or "Wo" in Chinese – is the Japanese reading for the Chinese character that appears in Chinese texts, including the *Wei zhi* (Chronicles of the Wei Kingdom), compiled in the late third century CE, to refer to the land and people of the Japanese archipelago. By the late seventh or early eighth century, Yamato rulers replaced this term with the indigenously coined term "Nihon" (or, "Nippon") to refer to the Japanese islands.

5   Contemporary historians of early Japan are in general agreement that the long-held notion of a single geographical point of origin for the emergence of a unified, ethnically homogeneous, Japanese nation is no longer a tenable thesis. Our focus here is on the central Honshū region known as Yamato because this was the main location for the transmission and development of early Japanese Buddhism. There is evidence, however, that Buddhist objects and practices also made their way to other parts of ancient Japan, such as Kyūshū. According to Piggott (1997: 95), in addition to late sixth- and early seventh-century temple remains found in central Honshū, "temple remains from the turn of the seventh century have also been uncovered in Kyūshū and eastern Japan, especially at places where trade or immigrant settlement fostered Buddhist development." See also Suda 1991.

6   Queen Himiko, sovereign of Yamatai, sent envoys to Wei dynasty China on two occasions: 239 CE and 243 CE. These envoys were dispatched to the capital at Luoyang. This was a place and time where Buddhism was taking hold, sutras were being translated from Sanskrit and other languages into Chinese, and temples built. The territorial boundaries of the Wei dynasty included sections of the Silk Road and, notably, the Dunhuang Caves. It is likely that Himiko's envoys would have encountered Buddhist activities and reported on these upon their return to Yamatai. However, there are no reports of Buddhism being practiced in Japan in texts like the Wei-zhi wo-ren-chuan (History of the Kingdom of Wei: The People of Wa; J. Gishi-wajin-den).

7   For an introduction to and translation of this text, see Stevenson 1999.

8   On Dōji, see Chapter 2 of this volume. For a brief discussion and comparison of the Nihon shoki and Suvarṇaprabhāsa Sūtra passages, see Sakamoto et al. 1965: 100–101 and headnote 19 on p. 101. For a concise overview of these dating issues, see Yoshida 2006: 8–10.

9   The compilation of this text has usually been attributed to a Tendai Buddhist monk, Kōen, who died in 1169 (Imaizumi 1999: 882), but new research suggests that the text was compiled earlier, sometime between 1094 and 1107. For a brief analysis of this story, see Piggott 1997: 93.

10 For a brief overview on the Hata, see Como 2008: 171–2.

11 The main section of the Jōgū Shōtoku hōō teisetsu was composed in the eighth century by an unknown author. A subsequent section, probably dating to the tenth century, concerns the five generations after Emperor Kinmei.

12 For a brief review of Japanese scholarly critiques of the historicity of Senior Prince Shōtoku, see Yoshida 2003: 12–13; and Yoshida 2006: 70–96.

13 On this issue, see Fujieda 1975: 484–544. Fujieda compares the Sangyō gisho with texts from Dunhuang to prove that these were Chinese texts and not the work of Senior Prince Shōtoku.

14 Among Ōyama's several books, see especially Ōyama 2003.

15 Como 2003: 64, n. 4. Herman Ooms eschews the term "immigrant" as a translation of kikajin, preferring the term "allochthon" – "people generated in a different soil" – because terms like immigrant "strongly imply a modern nation and state apparatus." See Ooms 2009: xviii and 43.

16 On Northern Wei/Luoyang temples see Tsukamoto 1985: I.133–136; and Thorp and Vinograd 2001: 160–169. On Sui and Tang temples see Thorp and Vinograd 2001: 195–201.

On Three Kingdom temples see Washizuka *et al.* 2003. On Paekche and Koguryŏ temples see Best 2006: 134–137, 161–162, 179–180. On Silla temples in the Three Kingdoms period, see: Park 2003.

17 For a list of temples constructed between 590 and 670, see Hayami 1986: 52. Yoshida 2003: 3–4 comments on the archaeological evidence for these temples: "'There are about fifty temple ruins from this period known to us today; these centered around Asuka in Yamato, mostly in the Kinai (Kansai) area. It is believed that most were family temples of the *ujizoku*. For the most part, Asuka Buddhism could be described as the Buddhism of the *ujizoku*. Another characteristic of this period is that many nuns were active during the early days of Buddhism in Wa, and many temples (*amadera*) were built for nuns."

18 For a review of recent scholarship on Asukadera, see McCallum 2009: 23–82.

19 There are two temples named Gangōji. The current Gangōji temple – associated with the Nara-period Sanron school of Buddhism – is located in Nara. Construction began in 716. The Gangōji temple referred to in the *Gangōji garan engi* is in fact Umako's Hōkōji, built in the late sixth century. See Stevenson 1999 and McCallum 2009: 23–82 for additional details. Of the Gangōji, Piggott remarks: "According to the Gangōji Chronicle, Soga Umako built the Soga family temple, Hōkōji (also known as Asukadera), on the shores of the Asuka River between 588 and 596. Umako is said to have employed immigrant craftsmen from Paekche, and archaeologists have indeed demonstrated that the architectural layout – comprising three chapels around a central pagoda, with each chapel dedicated to the worship of a different Buddha – was like that used in Koguryo and Paekche temples of the time. Not surprisingly, when the Hōkōji pagoda was excavated in modem times, its foundation was found to have been stuffed with jewels, horse trappings, and gold and silver baubles similar to goods previously buried in mounded tombs. The fashioning of Hōkōji's central Buddha image represented another epochal moment in Yamato kingship. Completed in 608, the Hōkōji Buddha was a sixteen-foot-tall image of Shakyamuni into which a fortune in copper and gold was poured. It visibly represented the unstinting patronage of Great King Suiko and her senior minister for the Buddhist cult. After its completion Hōkōji was home to both nuns and monks, including immigrants and visitors from the three Korean kingdoms" (Piggott 1997: 93–5).

20 On the issue of temple patronage in early Asuka Buddhism, see McCallum 2009: 24–5.

21 On Asukadera archaeological findings see McCallum 2009: 23–82.

22 Hyep'yon was a former Buddhist priest who had returned to secular life. Such secularized monks were known as *genzokusō*.

23 For a discussion of *genze riyaku* in Japanese religions generally, see Reader and Tanabe 1998.

References

Aston, W. G., trans. 1972. *Nihongi: Chronicles of Japan From the Earliest Times to A.D. 697.* Rutland, VT and Tokyo: Charles E. Tuttle Company, Inc.

Barnes, Gina L. 1993. *China, Korea and Japan: The Rise of Civilization in East Asia.* New York: Thames and Hudson.

Best, Jonathan W. 2006. *A History of the Early Korean Kingdom of Paekche, Together with an Annotated Translation of the Paekche Annals of the Samguk Sagi.* Cambridge, MA: Harvard University Asia Center, Harvard University Press.

Como, Michael. 2003. "Ethnicity, Sagehood, and the Politics of Literacy in Asuka Japan." *Japanese Journal of Religious Studies* 30 (1–2): 61–84.

Como, Michael. 2008. *Shōtoku: Ethnicity, Ritual, and Violence in the Japanese Buddhist Tradition.* Oxford and New York: Oxford University Press.

Deal, William E. 1995. "Buddhism and the State in Early Japan." In Donald S. Lopez, Jr. (ed.), *Buddhism in Practice,* 216–227. Princeton, NJ: Princeton University Press.

Deal, William E. 1999. "Hagiography and History: The Image of Prince Shōtoku." In George J. Tanabe, Jr. (ed.), *Religions of Japan in Practice,* 316–333. Princeton, NJ: Princeton University Press.

Fujieda Akira. 1975. *Kaisetsu: Shōmangyō gisho.* In Ienaga Saburō, *et al.* (eds.), *Shōtoku Taishi shū (Nihon shisō taikei 2),* 484–544. Tokyo: Iwanami Shoten.

Hayami Tasuku. 1986. *Nihon bukkyōshi: Kōdai.* Tokyo: Yoshikawa Kōbunkan.

Imaizumi Yoshio, ed. 1999. *Nihon bukkyōshi.* Tokyo: Yoshikawa Kōbunkan.

Inoue Mitsusada, ed. 1987. *Nihon shoki.* 2 vols. Tokyo: Chūō Kōronsha.

Ko, Dorothy, JaHyun Kim Haboush, and Joan Piggott, eds. 2003. *Women and Confucian Cultures in Premodern China, Korea, and Japan.* Berkeley, CA: University of California Press.

Kuroda, Toshio. 1981. "Shinto in the History of Japanese Religion." *Journal of Japanese Studies* 7 (1): 1–21.

McCallum, Donald F. 2004. "Tori-busshi and the Production of Buddhist Icons in Asuka-Period Japan." In Melinda Takeuchi (ed.), *The Artist as Professional in Japan,* 17–37. Stanford, CA: Stanford University Press.

McCallum, Donald F. 2009. *The Four Great Temples: Buddhist Archaeology, Architecture, and Icons of Seventh-Century Japan.* Honolulu: University of Hawai'i Press.

Mizuno, Seiichi. 1974. *Asuka Buddhist Art: Horyu-ji.* Trans. Richard L. Gage. New York and Tokyo: Weatherhill / Heibonsha.

Ooms, Herman. 2009. *Imperial Politics and Symbolics in Ancient Japan: The Tenmu Dynasty, 650–800.* Honolulu: University of Hawai'i Press.

Ōyama Seiichi, ed. 2003. *Shōtoku Taishi no shinjitsu.* Tokyo: Heibonsha.

Park, Youngbok. 2003. "The Monastery Hwangnyongsa and Buddhism in the Early Silla Period." In Washizuka Hiromitsu, Youngbok Park, and Woo-bang Kang (eds.), *Transmitting the Forms of Divinity: Early Buddhist Art From Korea and Japan,* 140–153. New York: Japan Society.

Piggott, Joan R. 1997. *The Emergence of Japanese Kingship.* Stanford, CA: Stanford University Press.

Reader, Ian, and George J. Tanabe, Jr. 1998. *Practically Religious: Worldly Benefits and the Common Religion of Japan.* Honolulu: University of Hawai'i Press.

Sakamoto Taro, Ienaga Saburo, Inoue Mitsusada, and Ono Susumu, eds. 1965. *Nihon shoki,* vol. 2 (Nihon koten bungaku taikei 68). Tokyo: Iwanami Shoten.

Sonoda Kōyū, with Delmer M. Brown. 1994. "Early Buddha Worship." In John Whitney Hall, *et al.* (eds.), *The Cambridge History of Japan,* vol. 1: *Ancient Japan,* 359–414. Cambridge: Cambridge University Press.

Stevenson, Miwa, trans. 1999. "The Founding of the Monastery Gangōji and a List of Its Treasures." In George J. Tanabe, Jr. (ed.), *Religions of Japan in Practice,* 299–315. Princeton, NJ: Princeton University Press.

Suda Tsutomu. 1991. "Zōji no hirogari." *Kikan kōkogaku* 34: 26–30.

Tamura Enchō. 1996. *Zusetsu Nihon bukkyō no rekishi: Asuka, Nara jidai.* Tokyo: Kōsei Shuppansha.

Tamura, Yoshirō. 2000. *Japanese Buddhism: A Cultural History.* Tokyo: Kōsei Shuppansha.

Thorp, Robert L., and Richard Ellis Vinograd. 2001. *Chinese Art and Culture.* New York: Harry N. Abrams, Inc., Publishers.

Tsuda Sōkichi. 1950. *Nihon koten no kenkyū.* Tokyo: Iwanami Shoten.

Tsukamoto, Zenryū. 1974. "Buddhism in the Asuka-Nara Period." *Eastern Buddhist* 7 (1): 19–36.

Washizuka, Hiromitsu *et al.* 1997. *Enlightenment Embodied: The Art of the Japanese Buddhist Sculptor (7th–14th Centuries).* New York: Japan Society.

Washizuka Hiromitsu, Youngbok Park, and Woo-bang Kang, eds. 2003. *Transmitting the Forms of Divinity: Early Buddhist Art From Korea and Japan.* New York: Japan Society.

Yoshida, Kazuhiko. 2003. "Revisioning Religion in Ancient Japan." *Japanese Journal of Religious Studies* 30 (1–2): 1–26.

Yoshida Kazuhiko. 2006. *Kodai bukkyō o yominaosu.* Tokyo: Yoshikawa Kōbunkan.

Further Reading

Allen, Chizuko T. 2003. "Prince Misahun: Silla's Hostage to Wa from the Late Fourth Century." *Korean Studies* 27: 1–15.

Augustine, Jonathan Morris. 2004. *Buddhist Hagiographies in Early Japan: Images of Compassion in the Gyōki Tradition.* RoutledgeCourzon.

Barnes, Gina L. 1999. "Buddhist Landscapes of East Asia." In Wendy Ashmore and A. Bernard Knapp (eds.), *Archaeologies of Landscape: Contemporary Perspectives*, 101–123. Oxford: Blackwell.

Barnes, Gina L. 2007. *State Formation in Japan: Emergence of a 4th-Century Ruling Elite.* London and New York: Routledge.

Best, Jonathan W. 1990. "Early Korea's Role in the Stylistic Formation of the Yumedono Kannon, a Major Monument of Seventh-Century Japanese Buddhist Sculpture." *Korea Journal* 30 (10): 13–26.

Best, Jonathan W. 2003a. "Buddhism and Polity in Early Sixth-Century Paekche." *Korean Studies* 26 (2): 165–215.

Best, Jonathan W. 2003b. "The Transmission and Transformation of Early Buddhist Culture in Korea and Japan." In Washizuka Hiromitsu, Youngbok Park, and Woo-bang Kang (eds.), *Transmitting the Forms of Divinity: Early Buddhist Art From Korea and Japan*, 18–43. New York: Japan Society.

Best, Jonathan W. 2005. "Paekche and the Incipiency of Buddhism in Japan." In Robert E. Buswell Jr. (ed.), *Currents and Countercurrents: Korean Influences on the East Asian Buddhist Traditions*, 15–42. Honolulu: University of Hawai'i Press.

Bowring, Richard. 2005. *The Religious Traditions of Japan, 500–1600.* Cambridge: Cambridge University Press.

Brown, Delmer M., ed., 1993. *The Cambridge History of Japan*, vol. 1: *Ancient Japan.* Cambridge: Cambridge University Press.

Como, Michael. 2007. "Horses, Dragons, and Disease in Nara Japan." *Japanese Journal of Religious Studies* 34 (2): 393–415.

Ebersole, Gary L. 1989. *Ritual Poetry and the Politics of Death in Early Japan*. Princeton, NJ: Princeton University Press.

Farris, William Wayne. 1998. *Sacred Texts and Buried Treasures: Issues in the Historical Archaeology of Ancient Japan*. Honolulu: University of Hawai'i Press.

Grayson, James Huntley. 2002. *Korea: A Religious History*. Rev. edn. London: RoutledgeCurzon.

Hong, Wontack. 1994. *Paekche of Korea and the Origin of Yamato Japan*. Seoul: Kudara International.

Hong, Wontack. 2010. *Ancient Korea–Japan Relations: Paekche and the Origin of the Yamato Dynasty*. Seoul: Kudara International.

Holcombe, Charles. 1999. "Trade-Buddhism: Maritime Trade, Immigration, and the Buddhist Landfall in Early Japan." *Journal of the American Oriental Society* 119 (2): 280–292.

Hori, Ichirō. 1958. "On the Concept of *Hijiri* (Holy-Man)." *Numen* 5 (2) and 5 (3).

Hori, Ichirō. 1968. *Folk Religion in Japan: Continuity and Change*. Edited by Joseph M. Kitagawa and Alan A. Miller. Chicago: The University of Chicago Press.

Ienaga Saburō, ed. 1967. *Nihon bukkyōshi, 1: Kodai-hen*. Kyoto: Hōzōkan.

Inoue Mitsusada. 1971. *Nihon kodai no kokka to bukkyō*. Tokyo: Iwanami Shoten.

Itō, Kimio. 1998. "The Invention of *Wa* and the Transformation of the Image of Prince Shōtoku in Modern Japan." In Stephen Vlastos (ed.), *Mirror of Modernity: Invented Traditions of Modern Japan*, 37–47. Berkeley, CA: University of California Press.

Kakao, Takashi. 1984. "The *Lotus Sūtra* in Japan." *Eastern Buddhist* 17 (1): 132–137.

Kasahara, Kazuo, ed. 2001. *A History of Japanese Religion*. Trans. Paul McCarthy and Gaynor Sekimori. Tokyo: Kōsei Publishing Co.

Kashiwahara, Yusen, and Kōyū Sonoda, eds. 1994. *Shapers of Japanese Buddhism*. Trans. Gaynor Sekimori. Tokyo: Kōsei Publishing Co.

Katada Osamu. 1967. "Shoki no bukkyō." In Ienaga Saburō (ed.), *Nihon bukkyōshi, 1: Kodai-hen*, 46–105. Kyoto: Hōzōkan.

Katsuura Noriko. 2000. *Nihon kodai no sōni to shakai*. Tokyo: Yoshikawa Kōbunkan.

Kidder, J. Edward. 1972. *Early Buddhist Japan*. New York and Washington: Praeger Publishers.

Kitagawa, Joseph M. 1966. *Religion in Japanese History*. New York: Columbia University Press.

Kuroda, Toshio. 1981. "Shinto in the History of Japanese Religion." *Journal of Japanese Studies* 7 (1): 1–21.

Lancaster, Lewis R. Chai-shin Yu, and Kikun Suh, eds. 1996. *Buddhism in Koryŏ: A Royal Religion*. University of California, Berkeley: Institute for East Asian Studies.

Matsunaga, Daigan, and Alicia Matsunaga. 1974. *Foundation of Japanese Buddhism*, vol. 1: *The Aristocratic Age*. Los Angeles and Tokyo: Buddhist Books International.

McCallum, Donald F. 1995. "The Buddhist Triad in Three Kingdoms Sculpture." *Korean Culture* 16 (4): 18–25.

McCallum, Donald F. 2001. "The Earliest Buddhist Statues in Japan." *Artibus Asiae* 61 (2): 149–188.

Morse, Samuel C. 1987. "Japanese Sculpture in Transition: An Eighth-Century Example From the Tōdai-Ji Buddhist Sculpture Workshop." *Art Institute of Chicago Museum Studies* 13 (1): 52–69.

Ōyama Seiichi. 1999. "*Shōtoku Taishi*" no tanjō. Tokyo: Yoshikawa Kōbunkan.

Ōyama Seiichi. 2001. *Shōtoku Taishi to Nihonjin*. Nagoya: Fūbaisha.

Piggott, Joan R. 1990. "Mokkan: Wooden Documents From the Nara Period." *Monumenta Nipponica* 45 (4): 449–470.

Piggott, Joan R., ed. 2005. *Capital and Countryside in Japan, 300–1180: Japanese Historians Interpreted in English.* Ithaca, NY: East Asia Program, Cornell University.

Ruch, Barbara, ed. 2002. *Engendering Faith: Women and Buddhism in Premodern Japan.* Ann Arbor, MI: Center for Japanese Studies, University of Michigan.

Sone Masato. 2000. *Kodai Bukkyōkai to ōchō shakai.* Tokyo: Yoshikawa Kōbunkan.

Sone Masato. 2007. *Shōtoku Taishi to Asuka bukkyō.* Tokyo: Yoshikawa Kōbunkan.

Sonoda, Kōyū. 1994. "Saichō (767–822)." In Yūsen Kashiwahara and Kōyū Sonoda (eds.), *Shapers of Japanese Buddhism,* 26–38. Tokyo: Kōsei Publishing Co.

Sueki Fumihiko *et al.*, eds. 2010. *Nihon Bukkyō no kiso (Shin Ajia bukkyōshi 11, Nihon 1).* Tokyo: Kōsei Shuppansha.

Swanson, Paul L., and Clark Chilson, eds. 2006. *Nanzan Guide to Japanese Religions.* Honolulu: University of Hawai'i Press.

Tamura, Kōyū. 1984. "The Doctrinal Dispute Between the Tendai and the Hossō Sects." *Acta Asiatica* 47: 48–81.

Tanabe, George J., Jr., ed. 1999. *Religions of Japan in Practice.* Princeton, NJ: Princeton University Press.

Tanabe, George J., Jr., and Willa Jane Tanabe, eds. 1989. *The Lotus Sūtra in Japanese Culture.* Honolulu: University of Hawai'i Press.

Totman, Conrad. 2005. *A History of Japan.* 2nd ed,. Oxford: Blackwell.

Tsutsui, William M., ed. 2007. *A Companion to Japanese History.* Oxford: Blackwell.

Ushiyama Yoshiyuki. 1990. *Kodai chūsei jiin soshiki no kenkyū.* Tokyo: Yoshikawa Kōbunkan.

Visser, Marinus Willem de. W. 1935. *Ancient Buddhism in Japan: Sutras and Ceremonies in Use in the Seventh and Eighth Centuries A.D. and Their History in Later Times.* 2 vols. Leiden: Brill.

Weinstein, Lucie R. 1989. "The Yumedono Kannon: Problems in Seventh-Century Sculpture." *Archives of Asian Art* 42: 25–48.

Whitfield, Roderick. 2000. *Cave Temples of Mogao.* Los Angeles: Getty Conservation Institute and the J. Getty Museum.

Yoshida Kazuhiko. 1995. *Nihon kodai shakai to bukkyō.* Tokyo: Yoshikawa Kōbunkan.

Yoshida Kazuhiko, Katsuura Noriko, and Nishiguchi Junko. 1999. *Nihonshi no naka no josei to bukkyō.* Kyoto: Hōzōkan.

2

Ancient Buddhism (645–950)

Hakuhō-Period Buddhism (645–710)

Toward a state Buddhism

The era that began in 645 and ended when the capital was moved to Heijōkyō (present-day Nara) in 710 is sometimes referred to as the Hakuhō period, and the Buddhism of this time as Hakuhō Buddhism (Hakuhō *bukkyō*). The term Hakuhō refers to King Tenmu's (r. 672–686) unofficial reign name. Hakuhō Buddhism marks the transition from aristocratic family (*ujizoku*) sponsorship of Buddhism to a Buddhism patronized by rulers. Thus, Hakuhō Buddhism is the start of the process of making Buddhism a state religion that reaches its apex in the subsequent Nara period. Hakuhō Buddhism came increasingly under the influence of the Tang dynasty (618–907). This included art and architectural styles used to render Japanese Buddhist material culture. This was also a period in which Buddhism began its gradual diffusion outward from the Yamato area to other regions of the Japanese islands and to a broader spectrum of society. Yoshida Kazuhiko, for instance, describes a monk named Hōrin, active in Kawachi Province, who in the late seventh century established a group of lay Buddhists for the purpose of copying sutras (Yoshida 2003: 5–6).

The year 645, inaugurating the Hakuhō era, brought significant political changes that transformed not only the administration of government, but Buddhism's development over the next three centuries. In this year, Soga no Iruka, Soga scion, was assassinated as the result of a plot against him engineered by, among others, a royal prince, Naka no Ōe, and a Soga rival, Nakatomi no Kamatari. This event brought Soga control over the royal court to a violent end. The conspirators against the Soga shifted power by their actions and, as a result, became important political figures: Naka no Ōe would rule from 668 to 671 as King Tenji (or, Tenchi) and, at the end of his life, Kamatari was given the honorific family name Fujiwara, thus inaugurating

A Cultural History of Japanese Buddhism, First Edition. William E. Deal and Brian Ruppert.
© 2015 William E. Deal and Brian Ruppert. Published 2015 by John Wiley & Sons, Ltd.

the long hegemony of Fujiwara family influence at court. The defeat was also an important element in wresting the symbols of Buddhist power – especially temples and rituals – from long-held Soga patronage. In short, the advent of the *ritsuryō* state – organized around a penal code (*ritsu*) and an administrative code (*ryō*) – also marked the transition of Buddhism from Soga control to royal control (Sonoda 1993: 388).

Following the events of the assassination plot, King Kōtoku (r. 645–654) established the Taika ("Great Change") Reform (Taika *kaishin*), named for the era newly declared. These reforms represented a first attempt to establish administrative and penal codes, patterned after Tang dynasty Chinese models, intended to bring stability to political rule and a centralized government administration. Essentially, the reforms were meant to put into place the legal and political structures necessary for establishing a centralized state under an absolute monarch. There is much debate over the extent to which the *ritsuryō* reforms established, or at least moved, Yamato toward a centralized state. Piggott, for one, argues that what was created in the late seventh and early eighth centuries was not so much a centralized state as a "historical bloc" that lent its support to the ruling authority of the Yamato monarchs (Piggott 1997: 13). Although it is unclear whether all the reforms that the *Nihon shoki* records as having started in 645 were instituted at that time, it is the case that the legal reforms instituted starting with the Taika Reform would be amended on a number of occasions, and that the *ritsuryō* system it codified endured in a number of different forms and with varying degrees of effectiveness from 645 until the latter part of the twelfth century.

The Taika reform focused on four areas: (1) land reforms that reassigned aristocratic landholdings on the basis of official rank; (2) the establishment of a permanent capital and an administrative structure that divided the countryside into provinces, districts, and villages; (3) new controls and regulations concerned with agricultural land, social classes, population and land distribution, and taxation; and (4) the creation of a formal military. Enacting these reforms further consolidated the power of the ruling family and established regulations that gave them important controls over people, land, and taxation. By so doing, the ruling family suppressed the power that strong aristocratic families had previously exerted over the court, as well as some of their wealth (Inoue 1993: 184–201; Piggott 1997: 167–235; Totman 2008: 23–4). Accompanying the strategy to secure a centralized ruling authority with the Taika Reform was the appropriation of Buddhist rituals and institutions in order to put them in service and support of the state. This also enhanced the charisma of the ruler.

The effects of the newly established *ritsuryō* statutes codified, in part, the proper relationship between government administration and ritual praxis. These were, in actuality, two sides to the same performative end. Rituals for both personal well-being and for the prosperity of Yamato had been performed prior to this time. With the *ritsuryō* codes, a more formal and centralized set of rituals was established, with the rulers and other bureaucrats acting as the chief ritual agents. Rituals, both Buddhist- and *kami*-related, were performed in the palace or capital, and also in provincial districts. Contemporary notions of separate religious traditions do not apply here: These rituals were understood as collectively necessary for the peace and prosperity of the state. Additionally, this extensive ritual calendar also served the purpose of legitimating the power and authority of the ruling class, further solidifying royal control.

In 645, King Kōtoku issued an imperial edict to a gathering of monks and nuns at Asukadera (Hōkōji) (Deal 1995: 224). The edict made clear that the government was in charge of Buddhism by introducing an enhanced governance structure over the monastic community. The edict read in part:

> We [the imperial government] now wish to reiterate our desire to revere the Buddha's true teaching and to shine widely the light of this great Dharma. Therefore, we appoint the following priests Dharma teachers: The Korean Dharma masters Fukuryō, Eun, Jōan, Ryōun, and Eshi, and the temple heads Sōmin, Dōtō, Erin, and Emyō. We separately appoint Dharma teacher Emyō the head priest of the temple Kudara-dera. These Dharma teachers will thoroughly instruct the monastic community and lead them in the practice of the Buddha's teaching so the Buddha's Dharma is properly followed. From the emperor to the managerial class, we will all assist in the building of temples. We will now appoint temple head priests and lay administrators. Temples will be visited to determine the actual situation pertaining to monks and nuns, their servants, and their rice fields. All findings will be presented to the emperor. (based on Deal 1995: 224)

For ideological purposes, the *Nihon shoki* claims that the ruling family had supported Buddhism since the reign of Queen Suiko. The historical veracity of this claim aside, it is clear that during Tenmu's rule Buddhist practices became a central aspect of state administration. Tenmu (626–686; r. 672–686) became Yamato king at the end of a violent dispute – known as the Jinshin Disturbance (*Jinshin no ran*) – over the proper line of succession precipitated by the death of King Tenji in 671. In 672, the conflict was settled when Tenji's brother, Prince Ōama, became King Tenmu, ascending to power over Tenji's son (Prince Ōtomo). As king, Tenmu increased the power of the ruler through government reforms based on Tang Chinese models of a centralized bureaucracy (Toby 1985: 341). He also oversaw temple-building projects and actively promoted sutra copying and recitation and other rituals as a means of ensuring the well-being of the state (*Nihon shoki* 685.3.27; de Visser 1935: 3-26, 116–189, 431–443). In effect, just as the king was the chief *kami* ritualist, so was the ruler the chief Buddhist ritualist. Tenmu's consort and successor, Queen Jitō (645–703; r. 690–697) – the first ruler to refer to herself as *tennō* ("heavenly sovereign"), the term that is typically translated as "emperor" or "empress" – continued strong royal support of and control over Buddhism, including the implementation of monastic ordination regulations and state sponsorship of temples and rituals.

Hakuhō-period Buddhism is marked, among other things, by three interrelated developments that, by the end of the period, produced elements necessary for the formation of state Buddhism: (1) establishment of state temples, (2) state-sponsored ritual practices, and (3) state control of the monastic community. With increasing royal control of Buddhist practices and institutions, Buddhism was put into the service of promoting the idea of a unified state legitimately controlled by the royal family. As part of this process, the state became an active patron, commissioning temples and images, and sponsoring Buddhist rituals (*hō'e*).

Establishment of state temples

Temple-building, which began with the private temples of aristocratic families like the Soga and Hata, was also a feature of Hakuhō-period Buddhism. While individual extended families continued to commission temple construction, the Taika Reform brought with it the first state temples. State-established temples took the power of Buddhist symbols out of the exclusive hands of aristocratic families, and re-purposed them in order to promote state-building and the legitimation of royal authority. The *Fusō ryakki* (compiled in the late Heian period sometime after 1094) reports that in 692 there existed 545 temples (Katata 1967: 102). The *Nihon shoki* reported that in 624 there were 46 temples. If the *Fusō ryakki* is accurate, this represents a nearly twelvefold increase in the number of temples in a span of 68 years.

Hakuhō-era kings and queens were active temple-builders. Sometimes temples were built for what amounted to personal reasons, but other times there were specific attempts to brand a temple as being necessary for the needs of the state. Sometimes, too, a temple might be built for personal reasons but later reconceived as a state temple. State control of temples brought with it the added benefit of state control of the monastic community. Sonoda argues that it is impossible to tease apart the political and the religious connections that were established after the Taika reform. To this end, he associates significant Buddhist developments between 645 and 710 (the beginning of the Nara period) with two rulers: King Tenji and King Tenmu. Both promoted Buddhism as a state religion, but they also supported *kami*-related rituals, thereby carrying out the royal responsibility of serving as both ruler and priest (Sonoda 1993: 388–389).

In the Hakuhō period, the Tenji/Tenmu line of kings was especially active in promoting Buddhism. King Tenji (r. 661–672) established several temples, including Kawaradera (ca. 660; later called Gufukuji), which became one of the four

Fujiwarakyō state temples. Among other ritual purposes, Tenji intended Kawaradera to be a place to pray for the soul of Queen Saimei, his mother (Kasahara 2001: 60–62). Tenji likely modeled his behavior on that of the Chinese ruler, Tang Taizong (r. 627–649), who made a vow to build a temple for the repose of his mother's soul. That temple, Hongfusi, is written with the same Chinese characters as for Gufukuji (see the Glossary for the characters used), Kawaradera's subsequent name (McCallum 2009: 189).

King Tenmu (r. 673–686), Tenji's successor and younger brother, vowed to establish the Yakushiji (680). Like Tenji, Tenmu was motivated by his desire to seek a cure for the illness of his consort, who later became Queen Jitō (r. 686–697). Another temple, the Kudara Ōdera (alt., Kudara Daiji), originally constructed for King Jomei (r. 629–641) in 639 in an area on the Kudara River north of Asuka, was moved to Asuka in 673 by Tenmu. Tenmu issued a decree that the Kudara Ōdera be renamed Daikan Daiji, or Great Official Temple, serving effectively as a state temple and as a model for the idea of a central state temple – and a state temple system – the precursor to the Nara-period Tōdaiji temple of King Shōmu (Sonoda 1993: 392–393).

Buddhist temples also figured prominently in the new, short-lived, capital constructed at Fujiwara. Fujiwarakyō, capital from 694 to 710, was laid out in an organized grid, following the style of Chinese capitals, such as the Tang capital at Chang'an. In an entry for 702, the *Shoku Nihongi* mentions that there were four great temples (*shidaiji*). An entry the following year indicates the four temples are named Daianji (Daikan Daiji), Yakushiji, Gangōji (Hōkōji or Asukadera), and Gufukuji (Kawaradera). In 705, the *Shoku Nihongi* (*Chronicles of Japan, Continued*; covers the years 697–791) mentions that the five great temples (*godaiji*) were ordered to read the *Konkōmyōkyō* in order to relieve the people from their sufferings. The names of the temples are not cited so it is unclear which temple constituted the fifth one. It may have been Kōfukuji because, in 735, the *Shoku Nihongi* again mentions the four great temples by name with Kōfukuji listed and Gufukuji omitted (Tamura 1969: 101–112; McCallum 2009: 158–159).

The four state temples were considered significant enough to move when the capital moved, often given new names in their new locations. When Queen Genmei moved the capital to Heijōkyō, Daikan Daiji was dismantled and then moved to the new capital, where it was reconstructed in 716 with a new name: Daianji. Similarly, both Yakushiji and Asukadera were moved to Heijōkyō. Yakushiji retained its original name, but Asukadera became Gangōji. Kawaradera was not moved to Heijōkyō, but another aristocratic family temple, the Nakatomi/ Fujiwara lineage's Yamashinadera, was moved to Heijōkyō and renamed Kōfukuji (Yoshida 2006b: 147).

These temples, among others, are discussed in the *Shoku Nihongi* as important ceremonial sites for personal ritual requests and for rituals for the protection and well-being of the state. The presence of these four major temples marked the increasing significance of Buddhism as the religion of the state (Tamura 1969: 101–112). It is instructive that the *Shoku Nihongi* uses the formal Buddhist names for all of these temples, rather than their older, Japanese names based on location of the temple, suggesting that by the end of the eighth century when the *Shoku Nihongi* was compiled, the transition from family temples to state temples was complete.

It must be noted, though, that temple construction was not limited to the ruling elite and aristocracy, but also extended to regional locations. Archaeological and other research on these local temples reveals that hundreds were in existence at this time. While these were not the temples of the most powerful families, they nevertheless represent the power and prestige of local families who had the necessary wealth to commission a temple for their use (Yoshida 2003: 6). There was also a political benefit to such temples because it extended the imperial authority, through Buddhist symbols, to outlying regions. In 685, for instance, King Tenmu "decreed that every household in every province would construct a Buddhist altar to enshrine a Buddha image and sutras for the purpose of worship and making offerings" (Deal 1995: 226). According to Sonoda (1993: 393–394), "every household" refers to the domiciles of both aristocrats and provincial bureaucrats, suggesting the extension of the imperial government into the provinces.

State-sponsored Buddhist rituals

The Hakuhō period witnessed a significant expansion of state-sponsored Buddhist rituals (*hō'e*). These rituals, often lavish, were typically performed at state temples or in the imperial palace. The purpose of these rituals typically focused on either the welfare and prosperity of the state or the health and well-being of the ruling elite. When the life of an aristocrat could not be sustained by a Buddhist ritual, another ritual was performed in hopes of ensuring a happy rebirth for the deceased. However, the boundary between these two kinds of state-sponsored rituals was porous. For instance, in 671, King Tenji fell ill. According to the *Nihon shoki* (Aston 1972: 2: 297; Sakamoto *et al.* 1984: 2: 378–379), in an attempt to effect a cure, 100 Buddhist images were consecrated (*kaigen*) at the palace and valuable objects were sent as offerings to the Buddha image at Hōkōji temple. On the one hand, these were rituals meant to effect the cure of an illness, but because these rites involved the king, they were state rituals, and not simply for personal benefit. In any event, these kinds of rituals often pivoted around the Buddhist notion of merit, that is, good karmic consequence that accrues to one who engages in good behaviors. In this time period, merit was especially associated with upholding and propagating the Dharma, a notion advocated in some of the period's most revered sutras. To this end, frequent practices included chanting and copying sutras, and praying to Buddhas and bodhisattvas.

A brief overview of King Tenmu's patronage of ritual practices provides a window on state-sponsored Buddhist rituals in the latter half of the seventh century. One of his earliest Buddhist-related decrees after ascending the throne in 672 was to assemble a group of scribes at Kawaradera to begin copying the canon of Buddhist texts (*issaikyō*), considered a very meritorious endeavor (Aston 1972: 2: 322; Sakamoto *et al.* 1984: 2: 411). Additional meritorious ritual and material support of Buddhism followed.

Whether royal decrees or invitations to the palace, Tenmu displayed a strong Buddhist faith, at least as depicted in the *Nihon shoki*. Among other actions, we are told that Tenmu hosted more than 2,400 monks and nuns at the palace in order to celebrate a Buddhist vegetarian meal, or *sai-e* (Aston 1972: 2:328; Sakamoto *et al.* 1984: 2:418–419). The meal was considered an offering to the monks and nuns. He placed restrictions on when hunting could occur and what kinds of fish and animals could be eaten. Tenmu issued an edict requiring all provinces observe a ritual to liberate all captive animals (*hōjō-e*). When his consort fell ill, Tenmu vowed to build the temple Yakushiji and commanded 100 people to become Buddhist priests in order to effect a cure. Even in death Tenmu created ritual precedents. The memorial services performed for him in 687 became a ritual enacted for subsequent monarchial memorials.

Of the many different state-sponsored rituals practiced in this era, particular attention was paid to rites that centered on sutras. Copying, chanting, and lecturing on Buddhist texts was viewed as meritorious. Additionally, the increasing significance of Buddhism to the emerging Japanese state was exemplified, in part, by the appropriation of Buddhist sutra rituals for the protection of the nation. In particular, two sutras were utilized for this purpose: the *Golden Light Sūtra* and the *Humane Kings Sūtra*. It was believed that chanting or copying these sutras would actualize the salvific power available through ritual manipulation of the sacred words of the texts. These sutras were popular, in part, because they discuss the protection the sutras can provide to countries and rulers who uphold them. Rituals related to these two texts were initially performed at temples in the capital, but by the 670s these rituals were also being performed at provincial temples.

Two different translations of the *Golden Light Sūtra* were read and recited in ancient Japan. Dharmakṣema's (385–433) fifth-century Chinese translation of the Sanskrit *Suvarṇaprabhā sūtra* (J. *Konkōmyōkyō*) was the version used in Japan through the middle of the Nara period. It was later replaced by Yijing's (635–713) early eighth century translation. Yijing's version is titled *Konkōmyō-saishō-ō-kyo*, or *Sovereign Kings of the Golden Light Sūtra* (Skt. *Suvarṇa-prabhāsattama-rāja sūtra*) (see de Visser 1935: 1.14–16 and 2.431–488). The sutra recounts a time when the Buddha was preaching on Eagle Peak. The Buddha states that the four heavenly kings (*shitennō*) protect those who uphold and praise the sutra. The sutra further reveals that a ruler who upholds the Dharma will gain the protection of the country from the four heavenly kings. Conversely, a country will meet with disaster if the ruler denigrates or ignores the Dharma (Sonoda 1993: 393).

Kumārajīva (344–413) translated the *Humane Kings Sūtra* (*Ninnōkyō*; Skt. *Kāruṇikā-rāja-prajñāpāramitā sūtra*; lit. *Benevolent Kings Perfection of Wisdom Sūtra*) (see de Visser 1935: 2.116–189) into Chinese in the early fifth century. The text relates a dialogue between the historical Buddha, Śākyamuni, and Prasenajit, ruler of the Indian kingdom of Kosala. The text warns that if the true Buddhist teaching disappears, seven disasters will result. To prevent this from occurring, and, by extension, to save the nation and ensure its well-being, the sutra must be upheld. Futaba (1984: 232–233) provides a useful discussion of the significance of these two sutras in Tenmu's era.

State control of the Buddhist monastic community

The state's attempt to control monastic institutions – their size and power, as well as the conduct of monks and nuns – dates to at least as early as 623. In this year, according to the *Nihon shoki*, Queen Suiko established the first institutional structure to oversee temples and monastic activities. This was in response to an incident in which a monk murdered his grandfather with an ax. Consequently, Queen Suiko issued an edict implementing monastic codes and the creation of a three-person council to supervise the monastic community. These were the positions of *sōjō* (primary prelate), *sōzu* (secondary prelate), and *hōtō* (or, *hōzu*; head of the Dharma). This structure, or something similar to it, was probably borrowed from Chinese models by way of Paekche. The first two of these positions were held by monks who oversaw monastic life and practice; the head of the Dharma – a non-monastic position – was responsible for managing monastic financial matters (for a detailed discussion of Suiko's monastic structure, see Hayami 1986: 71–75; for the *Nihon shoki* entry, see Deal 1995: 223).

After the Taika Reform, this nascent monastic supervisory structure developed into the increasingly more complex and hierarchical Monastic Office (*sōgō*), which included a system of monastic ranks (see Piggott 1997: 94 for a chart outlining the development of the *sōgō* in ancient Japan). The intention was to try to ensure that monks and nuns received proper training, but it was also a way for the state to maintain control over the monastic community. In 689, for instance, an edict was issued requiring the permission of the ruler in order for one to take Buddhist vows and join a monastic community. Even the appearance of monastics was micromanaged by the state: the *Nihon shoki* reports a 679 edict in which King Tenmu prescribed regulations concerning the monastic garb of monks and nuns, including the color of the robes. Additionally, measures were set in place to ensure state control over Buddhist temples, especially those built by powerful aristocratic families. State control of the temples meant, in effect, control over competing aristocratic interests.

In 701, the state bureaucracy established the Taihō Code (no longer extant), which included regulations to control the monastic community. The Regulations for Monks and Nuns (*sōniryō*) was modeled on a Tang Chinese law known as the *Daosengge* (J. *Dōsōkaku*). This code established the legal maintenance of the monastic system and the proper relationship between the ruler – and by extension, the imperial court – and the Buddhist community. Our understanding of post-Taika Reform Buddhism is interpreted largely through the monastic rules and regulations of the *ritsuryō*. But as Yoshida Kazuhiko points out, although there are *sōniryō* sections in such codes as the Taihō *ritsuryō* and Yōrō *ritsuryō*, we must be careful to distinguish between what the regulations say and the actual state of Buddhism at the time, and not reconstruct Buddhism solely from the codes (Yoshida 2006a: 4).

The problem of "state Buddhism" in the Hakuhō period

Scholarly interpretation of mid-seventh through Nara-period Buddhism – dating back to at least the 1940s (see Tamamuro 1940) – often characterizes it as "state Buddhism" (*kokka bukkyō*). The question, however, is to what extent the concept of state Buddhism provides an accurate picture of Hakuhō and Nara Buddhism. The idea of *kokka bukkyō* is sometimes used to contrast Buddhism in the Asuka period from that of the Hakuhō and Nara periods. This perspective, argued by scholars such as Tamura Enchō (1982), says that Buddhism's initial interactions in Japan revolved mostly around the Buddhist interests of the *ujizoku*, or extended family lineages. It is from 645 and the Taika Reform that Buddhism becomes controlled by the state, which promotes Buddhism to further its own needs for power and political legitimation. Others, such as Inoue Mitsusada (1971), propose a view of state Buddhism not so much from the perspective of ruling-class interests, but from the perspective of monastic regulations such as the Regulations for Monks and Nuns (*sōniryō*). He argues that if we want to understand how state Buddhism operated in the Hakuhō and Nara periods, we need to pay particular attention to how Buddhism was regulated by law. This perspective is sometimes referred to as *ritsuryō teki kokka bukkyō*, or *ritsuryō*-based state Buddhism.

Regardless of how one perceives the evidence, it is clear that Buddhism and the state were closely connected in this time period, and that both the state and the Buddhist community mostly benefited from this relationship. However, there are limitations to the explanatory power of a notion of *kokka bukkyō*. Yoshida (1995: 6 and 8–10) points out, for instance, that any perspective that focuses on monastic regulations will need to account for the fact that enforcement of these rules was inconsistent and, at times, mostly disregarded. As we will discuss in the next section, Gyōki is the exemplar of a monk operating outside the *sōniryō*, who is conspicuous for his good works, and then becomes embraced by the ruling elite. As Yoshida (2006a: 27–28) argues, a more nuanced view of the notion of "state Buddhism" is needed. In short, Yoshida says that we must study not only the Buddhist practices of the imperial court, but also the Buddhist practices of aristocrats, provincial clans, and common people – and how these different forms of Buddhist expression interacted with each other (see Yoshida 1995: 2–10 for a discussion and critique of theories of state Buddhism in ancient Japan; for an abbreviated discussion in English, see Yoshida 2003: 6–7).

Nara-Period Buddhism (710–794)

Buddhism in the permanent capital of a new nation

By the end of the seventh century, the kingdom of Yamato was consolidating power across the Japanese archipelago. Textual and archaeological evidence indicates that Yamato aristocratic sponsorship and patronage of Buddhist temples coincided with the emergence of the concept of the ruler as *tennō*, literally "heavenly sovereign," but often translated by the term "emperor" or "empress." This idea, necessary for creating a unified nation, replaced the idea of multiple, competing clan heads vying for power. Each clan was ritually represented by a clan deity (*ujigami*). With the emergence of a single ruling family – the subsequent imperial line – the idea of the head of a clan was replaced with the idea of the heavenly sovereign of the nation, whose clan deity was now writ large as the country's foremost deity. It was a self-created socio-religious structure through which the aristocracy was able to legitimate the imperial line as rightful rulers of the emerging nation. In these early years after the transmission of Buddhism to Japan, Buddhas and bodhisattvas were understood as offering, through proper ritual practices, any number of material and spiritual benefits (*riyaku*), very similar to the powers of the indigenous gods (*kami*). Thus, the emerging imperial family claimed authority to rule because they were in ritual control not only of the native deities, but also of those recently arrived from the West.

By the late 670s, the end of the Hakuhō period, the Japanese archipelago was known throughout the China Sea interaction sphere as Nippon (the Japanese word for Japan; the characters for which are also pronounced as Nihon). Shortly thereafter, in the 690s, Queen Jitō declared herself *tennō*. Thus, by the early eighth century, the concepts of Yamato and Great King (*ōkimi*; alt. *daiō*) were replaced with the concepts of Nippon and *tennō*. These changes in nomenclature were rhetorically significant. Instead of a clan ruling over a region of Japan – Yamato – the new language for land and ruler articulated a nascent national polity: a *tennō* ruling over the nation of

Nippon. Although these linguistic changes attempted to set the ruling family apart from others, the reality of competing aristocratic family interests remained.

In 710, Queen Genmei had the capital permanently moved to Heijōkyō, thereby inaugurating the Nara period (710–784). This represented a significant social shift as the capital had typically been moved after the death of every ruler, likely reflecting – or at least being justified by – the indigenous notion that death was polluting and therefore deleterious to those who came in contact with it. However, as the administrative bureaucracy grew in the Hakuhō period, the human and material costs of frequently building a new capital city became prohibitive. Modeling Japan's first permanent capital on the long-permanent Tang China capital at Chang'an also likely reflected a desire to display a clear center for ruling power, as well as an assertion of the legitimacy of that power. The significant influence of Tang China on Nara-period politics, society, and culture was the result, in part, of missions dispatched to the Chinese mainland.

Continuing precedents set during the Hakuhō era, the Nara period witnessed even stronger ties forged between the state and Buddhism. Central to the advancement of this mutually beneficial relationship between politics and religion was the establishment of the *kokubunji* system of national temples in each province. Though centered at the Tōdaiji temple in Heijōkyō, this national temple system provided an effective structure for securing political authority in the provinces, becoming an integral part of the bureaucratic hierarchy needed to establish control over wide tracts of land and to assert a unified state with a centralized ruling power. The national temple system was charged with, among other things, engaging in rituals for the protection of the nation (*chingo kokka*). Despite increased state control of Buddhist institutions and practices, there were nevertheless significant stresses in the system, including: temples amassing great wealth and landholdings, monastics intruding into political affairs (exemplified by the Dōkyō affair described below), and some Buddhists operating outside the formal monastic system entirely (exemplified by the monk Gyōki, described below).

Although evidence from this period indicates an increasing degree of governmental control over Buddhism, both rulers and powerful aristocratic families continued to be devout Buddhist patrons. Both funded and supported numerous projects such as the construction of temples, the creation of images of Buddhas and bodhisattvas, material support of monastic communities, and the performance of an increasingly large assemblage of Buddhist rituals.

Nara-period state sponsorship of Buddhism meant that monastic institutions were dependent on the now centralized government to build temples, and then to provide monastic necessities such as food and robes. The Nara period was also significant for the intellectual activity of six Buddhist research groups that were important to the development of doctrinal study in Japanese Buddhism. The temples and monasteries that were home to these groups were as much places to learn

Buddhist doctrine as they were places for ritual practice and devotional activities. These doctrinal lineages also received significant support from rulers and aristocrats. The Heijōkyō monastic community was anchored by the so-called seven great temples of the Southern Capital (*Nanto shichidaiji*): Tōdaiji, Gangōji, Saidaiji, Yakushiji, Daianji, Kōfukuji, and Hōryūji. After 759, Tōshōdaiji was added to this list. Besides serving as doctrinal study centers, these state-sponsored temples were also centers for the performance of Buddhist rituals for the protection and prosperity of the nation.

In addition to state sponsorship of rituals, aristocrats often invited monastics to reside in their homes. Parts of homes were converted into private monasteries, or new monasteries were built. The Fujiwara family built the Kōfukuji for this purpose. Private-home monastics were responsible for engaging in rituals for the protection and well-being of the family, such as curing disease. In addition to state- and family-sponsored monastics, there was a movement of self-ordained monastics that operated outside the rules and regulations of official Buddhism.

The six officially recognized Buddhist research groups – known as the *Nanto rokushū* (literally, "six groups of the southern capital," i.e., Heijōkyō) – were doctrinal traditions derived from texts and lineages developed originally in India or China. Although these groups are designated by the term *shū*, usually translated as "sect," "school," or "denomination," they bore little resemblance to the Buddhist lineages that developed in the Heian period and after, which focused on a school's particular practices and teachings. The six Nara-period doctrinal traditions are better understood as assemblies of monks and nuns studying Buddhist doctrine within temple grounds that housed libraries of sutras and commentaries. They were not exclusive doctrinal traditions requiring allegiance to one school only. Although a lineage would be headquartered at a specific temple, monks and nuns could study in multiple lineages regardless of the lineage their home temple might be associated with. A better way to think of the six Nara research groups is as keepers of particular doctrinal texts and ideas, and not as formal, sectarian institutions.

The six lineages were:

- **Hossō** (Skt. Yogācāra; Ch. Faxiang; Consciousness-Only, or Dharma Characteristics). Hossō's textual focus was on Dharmapāla's *Vijñaptimātratā siddhi* (J. *Jōyuishikiron*; Treatise on the Completion of Mere Ideation), which teaches that reality is nothing but mental ideations. During the Nara period, Hossō doctrine was widely studied and several important monks of the period identified with this school. Hossō was connected with several prominent temples: Hōryūji, Yakushiji, and Kōfukuji.
- **Kegon** (Skt. Avatamsaka; Ch. Huayan; Flower Garland). Kegon was a Chinese lineage that was influential throughout East Asian Buddhism. The school is named for the text that is its focus: the *Avataṃsaka sūtra* (J. *Kegonkyō*; Flower

Garland Sūtra), which declares the mutual interpenetration – or, connectedness – of all things. Nara-period Kegon was centered at Tōdaiji.

- **Ritsu** (Skt. Vinaya; Ch. Lu; Precepts). Ritsu was mainly concerned with Mahayana rules of behavior for monastics, and Japanese interest in these regulations was especially high during the Nara period when control over the monastic community was a central concern of the state. Ritsu was important to the establishment of the official ordination platform (*kaidan*) at Tōdaiji. Ritsu was closely associated with the Heijōkyō temple Tōshōdaiji.
- **Sanron** (Skt. Madhyamaka; Ch. Sanlun; "Three Treatises"). Doctrinally, the Sanron school focuses on the idea of "emptiness" (Skt. *śūnyatā*; J. *kū*), that all existing entities are devoid of any essence because all things are interdependent. Three works are the textual foundation for this school: Nāgārjūna's *Madhyamaka Śāstra* (J. *Chūron*; Treatise on the Middle Way) and *Dvādaśadvāra* (J. *Jūnimon*; Treatise on Twelve Gates), and Āryadeva's *Śataśāstra* (J. *Hyakuron*; One Hundred Verse Treatise). Several Heijōkyō temples were centers for Sanron studies, including Gangōji and Daianji.
- **Kusha** (Skt. Abhidharmakośa; Ch. Jushe; "Dharma Essence"). Kusha doctrine is based on Vasubandhu's *Abhidharmakośa* (J. *Kusharon*; Treasury of Higher Law). Kusha thought holds that the constituent elements of existence (*dharmas*) are all conditioned, that is, interdependently caused and without independent existence. Kusha was never organized into an independent school, but was studied along with Hossō doctrine.
- **Jōjitsu** (Skt. Satyasiddhi; C. Chengshi; "Completion of Truth"). Jōjitsu's textual focus is Harivarman's *Satyasiddhi śāstra* (J. *Jōjitsuron*; Treatise on the Completion of Truth), which denies the existence of both mind and matter. Among other things, this means that neither the self nor anything else has a permanent existence or reality. Jōjitsu was never organized into an independent school, but its ideas were taught in tandem with Sanron doctrine.

A national temple system

Shōmu *tennō* (r. 724–749), his consort Kōmyō (Kōmyō *kōgō*), and their daughter Kōken were by all measures devout Buddhists. Shōmu was the first *tennō* to become an ordained monk. Soon after his ordination in 749, he abdicated and his daughter ascended the throne as Kōken *tennō*. In 764, she too abdicated and became a nun. Later, she returned to reign as Shōtoku *tennō*, becoming the only sovereign in Japanese history to rule while ordained. Kōmyō expressed her faith in a number of ways, including her strong support of the Office of Sutra Transcription (*shakyōsho*). In 740, Kōmyō made a vow (*hotsugan*) to copy the *Issaikyō* – the collection of all Buddhist sutras – for the karmic benefit of her deceased parents. We know this because

Kōmyō's vow is recorded at the end of the copy of the second volume of the *Ajātaśatru sūtra* (J. *Ajaseō-kyō*; King Ajase Sūtra). The product of this vow to copy the more than 7,000 texts that comprised the *Issaikyō* in eighth-century Japan is known as the May 1st Sutra (*gogatsu tsuitachi kyō*) because Kōmyō's vow is dated May 1, 740. The project itself began in 736 and continued for some 20 years (Sugimoto 2010: 132–5).

Shōmu and his family were also prodigious patrons of Buddhist rituals and material culture, sponsoring, among other things, temple construction, the crafting of Buddhist imagery, and the performance of Buddhist rituals, such as sutra copying and chanting. Their most prominent project, both religiously and politically, was a provincial temple system (*kokubunji*) based on a Tang Chinese model. In 741, as a way to secure the peace and prosperity of the newly emerging nation of Japan, and especially to shield the ruling family from court intrigue and rebellion that threatened an orderly succession of rulers, Shōmu, with the strong encouragement of Kōmyō, issued an edict ordering the creation of this temple system. A provincial monastery (*kokubunsōji*) and provincial convent (*kokubunniji*) were built in pairs in every province, and connected to a head temple, Tōdaiji, located in the capital at Heijōkyō.

As an offering for the success of this enterprise, Shōmu made a copy of the *Konkōmyō-saishō-ō-kyō* and ordered that every province make 10 copies each of the *Konkōmyō-saishō-ō-kyō* and *Myōhō-renge-kyō* (Lotus Sūtra; often referred to as *Hokekyō*). The choice of these two sutras is found, in part, in what the two texts say about those who uphold and expound these sutras. The *Konkōmyō-saishō-ō-kyō* teaches that in places where this sutra is taught, there will be no enemies or disease, and prosperity will flourish. The *Myōhō-renge-kyō* is connected with the notion of enlightenment or salvation for women through the story of the dragon king's daughter's attainment of Buddhahood.

These temples, whose monastics were charged with the protection, peace, and prosperity of the state through the performance of Buddhist rituals – such as sutra chanting and copying – were also linked to these two sutras. Provincial monasteries were referred to as Temples for the Protection of the Nation by the Four Heavenly Kings (Konkōmyō shitennō gokoku no tera) and were ritually connected to the *Konkōmyō-saishō-ō-kyō*. Provincial nunneries were referred to as Temples for the Expiation of Karmic Transgressions by the *Lotus Sūtra* (Hokke metsuzai no tera) and were ritually connected to the *Lotus Sūtra*. Ritual performances involving these two texts were believed to have great merit and therefore the power to right any transgressions that, if not corrected, would subject the nation to all manner of disaster and hardship.

The primary temple of the *kokubunji* system was the Tōdaiji (Great Eastern Temple), which served as its head temple (*sōkokubunji*). Tōdaiji occupied a central location in Heijōkyō, reinforcing its role as the locus of both religious and political power. It contained the main ordination platform and it supervised the provincial temples, thereby overseeing provincial monastics and controlling the dissemination of Buddhism in the provinces. Constructed in the mid-eighth century, Tōdaiji became the head temple of the Kegon lineage, but it was also a place for the study of other Buddhist doctrinal schools.

The Tōdaiji was itself an imposing complex, but the centerpiece of the temple was the large and stately cast, gilt-bronze image of Dainichi Nyorai (or, Birushana Buddha; Skt. Mahāvairocana; Great Sun Buddha). At a height of over 50 feet, the image, known as the Daibutsu (Great Buddha), was intended as an awe-inspiring presence. Dainichi, as the cosmic Buddha, represents the reality of the universe – and the interrelatedness of all things – because, according to Kegon doctrine, the universe is a manifestation of this Buddha's words, thoughts, and actions.

Building the Tōdaiji, the Daibutsu, and the entire *kokubunji* system, was a time-consuming, massive undertaking that required significant resources – both human and material – drawn from many parts of the fledgling Japanese state. Shōmu spent state funds on this project, and expected – and received – financial donations from aristocratic families across the country. A corvée labor system required peasants to serve 60 days working at these temple sites. Financial resources were also secured from the general population through private fund-raising efforts (*chishikiyui*) by monks like Gyōki, no doubt giving non-aristocrats a sense of connection to this project. Forty years after Shōmu's decree, construction on the majority of these temples was completed.

While the Tōdaiji/*kokubunji* project was significant religiously, it also had important political implications. It was, for instance, an especially powerful symbol of the power and authority of the court. The court, in turn, was closely linked to Tōdaiji and the monastic bureaucrats at provincial temples. As we have seen, provincial temple monastics served as extensions of government by enforcing laws, collecting taxes, and seeking the protection of the state beyond the capital through Buddhist ritual practices. That is, even as the state funded the increased production of Buddhist symbols, the state gained political legitimacy through those very symbols it paid to have produced. At the same time, Buddhism was effectively and purposefully crafted into a state institution.

In the Nara period, sutra transcription became a widespread Buddhist ritual with extensive state patronage, and was central to ritual activities at Tōdaiji and the provincial temples. The merit accrued from transcribing sutras was directed toward the welfare of the state and the well-being of the monarch. Besides this larger state purpose, sutra transcription was also practiced by individuals and directed toward such personal concerns as curing disease and ensuring a happy rebirth for deceased family members.

The idea of the ritual efficacy of sutra copying dates to at least the time of King Tenmu, who, it is said, sponsored the transcription of the *Issaikyō* – the collection of all Buddhist sutras. Sutra copying on this scale required a dedicated office responsible for this ritual activity. To this end, sutra-copying scriptoria (*shakyōsho*) were established. These scriptoria became especially important to the Shōmu imperial line. During this era, there were two major sutra transcription agencies: one located at court and the other at Tōdaiji. The importance of sutra transcription as a ritual practice is evidenced by the remarkable size of the output that these scriptoria produced during the Nara period. According to Farris (2007: 399), over 100,000 scrolls (*maki*) were transcribed as the result of state sponsorship. These figures strongly suggest that such ritual activity was believed to be both karmically meritorious and effective.

The regulation of monks and nuns

The Taihō Code of 701, promulgated by Monmu *tennō* as a way to centralize power around the newly conceived country of Nihon and its ruling *tennō* family, brought further refinements to the *ritsuryō* bureaucratic state inaugurated in 645. From a Buddhist perspective, this iteration of a *ritsuryō* system of penal (*ritsu*) and administrative (*ryō*) codes was especially significant because it formally established the *sōniryō* – Regulations for Monks and Nuns – which both prescriptively and proscriptively detailed the behavior for monastics and their relationship to the state. These regulations expressed both what the state owed the monastics and what the monastics owed the state. Additionally, the Taihō Code also established a Prelate's Office (*sōgō*) to oversee the monastic community and enforce the monastic regulations.

The *sōniryō*, following a Tang Chinese monastic code known as the Daosengge (Regulations Regarding Daoist and Buddhist Clergies; J. Dōsōkaku), subjected monastics to specific forms of supervision and restrictions on behavior so that Buddhism was firmly controlled by the state. A review of the 27 articles that comprise the *sōniryō* reveals that to a great extent monks and nuns were treated as government bureaucrats – this is apparent in the matching of monastic ranks in relation to the ranks of government officials. The restrictions placed on monks and nuns were largely prohibitions against operating without constraint or permission. Even the extent of ministering to the laity was limited. Restrictions on the movement and behavior of monastics included prohibitions on teaching and practicing Buddhism outside of their assigned monastery. This meant, at least in terms of the formal monastic regulations, that official monks and nuns were to restrict their Buddhist activities to those sanctioned by the state and their rituals for the benefit and protection of the state.

Enforcement of the monastic rules and temple affairs was the direct responsibility of the Prelate's Office (*sōgō*). The earliest known mention of *sōgō* as a formal institution was in the Taihō Code. Senior monks were supposed to be chosen to serve in the Prelate's Office by the monastic community, but, in actuality, rulers selected monks for service in the *sōgō*. Thus, control of the monastic community was very strongly connected to the ruling class. Though the hierarchy changed in subsequent revisions of the *ritsuryō*, there were three main offices comprising the *sōgō*: primary prelate (*sōjō*), secondary prelate (*sōzu*), and chief of the Dharma (*hōzu*). Of these three, the chief of the Dharma – responsible for managing monastic financial matters – was a non-monastic position. Administration of the monastic community at each temple was managed through a tripartite system known as the Three Deans (*sangō*): abbot (*jōza*), rector (*jishu*), and superintendent (*tsuina*).

The monks and nuns regulated by the *sōniryō* and overseen by the *sōgō* were considered "official monastics" (*kansō*) because they had received the permission of the *tennō* to become ordained (*tokudo*; literally, "receive the crossing [to the religious life]"). As a result, such monastics were designated as *kando*, or "officially crossed." Officially ordained monastics were expected – under threat of punishment – to follow the *sōniryō*.

Another significant way in which the state and the Buddhist community were intertwined was through the appointment of 10 annual ordinands (*nenbundosha*), who served at the imperial palace and engaged in rituals, such as sutra chanting, for the protection of the nation. The practice started with Queen Jitō, who, in 696, issued an order permitting 10 ordinands for the year. The 10 were novitiates with, presumably, the promise of important Buddhist careers ahead of them. The prominent early Heian period monk, Saichō, was one such ordinand. Until the early ninth century, the selection of the 10 annual ordinands had no connection with specific Buddhist lineages.

In 803, Japanese Buddhism took a sectarian turn that continues to the present. That year, Kanmu *tennō* declared that the 10 annual ordinands would be assigned to specific lineages – 5 each to Sanron and Hossō – for the purpose of focusing on the texts and doctrines of the particular school. In 806, at Saichō's urging, the number of annual ordinands was increased to 12: three 3 each to Sanron and Hossō, 2 each to Kegon and Ritsu, and 2 ordinands assigned to Saichō's fledgling Tendai lineage, signifying Tendai's recognition as a formal school. (Shingon would be so recognized and assigned 2 ordinands in 835). This significant revision to the yearly ordinand system meant that for the first time doctrinal and other differences between the lineages was acknowledged and codified into separate schools.

Nara monasticism and the state

Tensions existed in the Buddhist monastic community between official monastics (*kansō*) and unofficial (or, self-ordained; *shido sōni*) monastics. The former were recognized by the state while the latter were considered legally outside the monastic regulations because they had not received imperial permission to take the tonsure and were, therefore, subject to punishment. A part of Article 22 of the *sōniryō* section of the *Yōrō ritsuryō* makes this clear:

> Those who falsely claim to be ordained (*shido*) or falsely appropriate the identity of the ordained are to be forced to return to lay life. If the violators, once returned to laity,

dress themselves yet again in priestly robes, they will be chastised in accordance with the penal code (*ritsu*). (translated in Abé 1999: 78; see also Bowring 2005: 54–8)

If we were to take such rules at face value and suppose that the monastic community was successfully regulated according to the monastic rules and regulations of the *ritsuryō*, we would miss much of what was actually occurring in this time period. As Yoshida Kazuhiko points out, we must be careful to distinguish between what the *sōniryō* regulations say and the actual state of Buddhism at the time (Yoshida 2006a: 4). To this end, we briefly review four eighth-century monks whose careers reflect the range of adherence to and divergence from the formal dictates of the *sōniryō*.

Dōji (?–744)

Dōji exemplifies the ideal of the *kansō* – an official monastic actively involved in promoting Buddhism in accord with the interests of the state. Through Dōji's efforts, state-sponsored Buddhism gained a formal narrative (*Nihon shoki*) and witnessed an expansion of its sphere of influence outside the capital (*kokubunji* system). He also received aristocratic support from the increasingly powerful Fujiwara family.

In 701, Dōji accompanied a diplomatic embassy to Tang China, where he studied various forms of Buddhist thought and practice, such as Sanron and esoteric doctrines, for nearly 20 years. After returning to Japan in 718, he became an important Sanron-lineage monk. Importantly, Dōji's time spent in China made him an invaluable resource on Chinese Buddhist and political matters, and he became a strong advocate for utilizing Chinese models in promoting Buddhism and the state.

Dōji's efforts on behalf of the state were many and significant, including involvement in the planning and construction of the *kokubunji* system that was based on a Chinese model that Dōji likely learned about during his years in China. At imperial request, he supervised the rebuilding of the Daianji in 729. That same year he was rewarded for his efforts to promote state Buddhism with his appointment to the high rank of preceptor (*risshi*). His deep understanding of Buddhist texts was acknowledged in 737 when he was invited to the imperial palace to lecture on the *Golden Light Sūtra* (*Konkōmyō Saishō-ō-kyō*), a text he brought back with him from China.

There is also evidence that Dōji may have had much to do with compiling the *Nihon shoki* and with the way the text relates such matters as the transmission of Buddhism to Japan and its early reception. Ōyama Seiichi, among other recent scholars of ancient Japanese Buddhism, argues that Dōji is likely the one who wrote the *Nihon shoki*'s narrative of Buddhism's reception in the Japanese archipelago and crafted the traditional and enduring image of Shōtoku Taishi. Evidence for this view derives from quotations in the *Nihon shoki* that were taken from Buddhist texts, such as Yijing's (635–713) translation of the *Saishōōkyō* (*Sūtra of the Most Honored King*; *Sūvarṇaprabhāsa sūtra*) and Daoxuan's (596–667) *Biographies of Eminent Monks, Continued* (*Zoku kōsōden*). Dōji brought all of these texts to Japan on his return from China, indicating that at least some aspects of Buddhism's reception in the Japanese archipelago were written well after the time it occurred (for a detailed analysis of Dōji's role in the writing of the *Nihon shoki* see Yoshida 2006a: 97–121; see also Ōyama 1999: 140).

Finally, Dōji was critical of the state of monastic practice in his day. His work, *Gushi* (*A Fool's Idea*), outlined principles for proper monastic conduct (Futaba 1984: 180). In 734, a new qualification for ordination was established, likely based on Dōji's ideas, that required aspiring monastics to study the *Suvarṇaprabhāsa sūtra* and the *Lotus Sūtra*.

Gyōki (668–749)

Gyōki's life and Buddhist activities can be gleaned, in part, from texts like the *Shoku Nihongi* and a biography inscribed on an epitaph dated 749 that was unearthed at his gravesite in 1235. According to such sources, Gyōki's family lineage traced to immigrants from the Korean peninsula. At age 15, in 682, Gyōki reportedly began his monastic career, eventually studying for ordination as an official monk under the tutelage of Dōshō, founder of the Japanese Hossō lineage.

At some point after Dōshō's death in 700, Gyōki became a wandering monk unattached to any specific temple, traveling the countryside ministering to the people, preaching the Dharma, and engaging in public works projects such as the construction of bridges, irrigation systems, temples for unofficial monastics, safe houses for travelers, and infirmaries. It is reported that he attracted a large following in both the capital and countryside, and that he provided unofficial ordination to both women and men.

Depending upon the historical source, Gyōki's activities are described as the work of a bodhisattva compassionately caring for the people or the work of a charlatan out to fool the people for his own gain. The *ritsuryō* government held something close to both of these views, though at different times. According to the *Shoku Nihongi*, the government, in keeping with the *sōniryō* prohibition against unofficial monks, attempted to strengthen its control over Gyōki and his followers. In 717, Genshō *tennō* issued an imperial edict saying that monks and nuns must reside in temples, where they should study and uphold the Buddha's teachings. The edict admonishes Gyōki and his followers for disrupting towns and villages and for preaching without permission. Monastic regulations required those who violated the code to return to the laity. There is no record of what Gyōki actually did, but, despite censure from the state, Gyōki's influence was already growing and his preaching continued to attract thousands of people.

Some years later, the state's perception of Gyōki's activities underwent a significant transformation leading ultimately to his acceptance into the Nara monastic mainstream. Gyōki was noted for his ability to raise money among his followers for various causes. Shōmu's Tōdaiji project and its very large bronze image of Dainichi Buddha required an enormous outlay of money and labor. It would have been difficult to complete the project using only the resources of the government. Accordingly, Shōmu sought Gyōki's assistance as a *kanjinsō* – a monk who is adept at raising funds and material – for the construction of the image. For his meritorious service to this project, Gyōki was appointed *daisōjō* in 745, the highest monastic rank and its first recipient.

Ganjin (688–763)

In order to regulate the monastic community, the state sought a specialist in the Buddhist precepts who could also establish an official Buddhist ordination platform. When embassies to Tang China resumed in 732, Japanese monks were dispatched to China to find such a Buddhist specialist. The position was offered to the monk Ganjin (Ch. Jianzhen;), a monk of the Ritsu (Skt. Vinaya) lineage. He accepted in 742, but did not reach Japan until 754 – blind and at the age of 66 – after several failed attempts to make the treacherous sea crossing. Once in Japan, he established an ordination platform (*kaidan*) in Nara at the Tōdaiji temple. In 759, he founded the Tōshōdaiji temple, which became the center of the Ritsu lineage in Japan.

The establishment of an orthodox ordination platform was an attempt to make monastic certification something more than a state ritual, and to ensure proper monastic training and practice. Prior to Ganjin's arrival in Japan, ordination was a rather unsystematic procedure. Ordination was conducted at various temples, such as Asukadera, Daianji, Kōfukuji, and Yakushiji. Traditionally, ordination could only take place when 10 fully ordained monks were present to oversee the proceedings. Ganjin brought with him 24 fully ordained monks, thereby creating a doctrinally correct quorum.

Prior to the establishment of the orthodox ordination platform, if men and women wished to become monastics, they had to be recommended for an initial ordination, which required a vow to uphold the basic 10 precepts. Once ordained, they received a certificate stating that they were now a *shami* (male novice) or *shamini* (female novice). After additional study and practice, they could be recommended to receive the complete precepts. Once fully ordained, they received a certificate stating that they had achieved the status of *biku* (male cleric) or *bikuni* (female cleric). The final stage in this three-rank system was appointment to the status of Dharma Master (*hōshi*) (Sakuma 1994: 10; Matsuo 2007: 21–4).

The Mahayana precepts that Ganjin brought to Japan, though originally based in Theravada practice, became the template for the Vinaya embraced in the Mahayana lineages of East Asian Buddhism. The Vinaya required that monks observe 250 precepts, while nuns had to observe 348 precepts. These monastic regulations, known as the Bodhisattva Precepts (*bosatsukai*), required adherence to vows based on Mahayana doctrine.

Dōkyō (?–772)

The fourth monk, Dōkyō, represents the extent to which some elite Nara-period monastics exerted political power and influence, much to the displeasure and concern of some members of the ruling aristocracy. The possibility of Buddhists wielding political power was perhaps inevitable given the close relationship that the state had itself fostered with Buddhist monasteries and individual monastics. This is underscored by Shōmu's *kokubunji* system. The central temple Tōdaiji in Heijōkyō oversaw provincial temples, thereby extending political power into the provinces with monastics acting as de facto state bureaucrats. In any event, Dōkyō came as close as any Buddhist monastic to disrupting imperial line succession and seizing power for himself.

Dōkyō was a Hossō-lineage monk. He became heavily involved in court politics after gaining the confidence of Kōken *tennō* (719–770; r. 749–758), Shōmu's daughter, who assumed the throne when Shōmu retired in 749. Like her parents, Kōken was a devout Buddhist who was a great patron of temples, images, and sutra transcriptions. She was present at the Tōdaiji dedication ceremonies – it is likely that Dōkyō was also in attendance.

Kōken abdicated in 758, passing rule on to an imperial prince (Junnin *tennō*; r. 758–764), perhaps because she never married and therefore did not produce a male heir. In 761, after having become a nun, she became ill and it was Dōkyō who was called on to perform rituals as a way to effect a cure. When Kōken recovered, she embraced Dōkyō as a religious adviser, but she also began to seek his guidance on matters of state. Kōken appointed Dōkyō to a series of increasingly prestigious and powerful roles that placed a monastic in a central position of power within the government. Kōken, with Dōkyō's direct assistance and guidance, plotted to remove Junnin. After a series of intrigues, banishments, and, ultimately, a failed revolt, Kōken once again ascended the throne in 764, taking the name Shōtoku *tennō*.

Dōkyō's prominence at court was enhanced when, in 764, Shōtoku appointed him to the position of *daijin zenji*, or Buddhist Minister of State. In 765, Dōkyō was promoted with his appointment as Buddhist Prime Minister of State (*daijōdaijin zenji*). Both the *daijin* and *daijōdaijin* positions were court positions, but the innovation here was the addition of the term *zenji*, referring to a monastic serving at court. In effect, with these appointments, Shōtoku was blurring the line between imperial and Buddhist power. Finally, in 766, Dōkyō reached the height of his court career when Shōtoku named him *hōō* (literally, Dharma King) and provided him with an office known as the Imperial Office of the Dharma King (*hōō kyūshiki*).

Dōkyō's downfall occurred as a result of an oracle received at court in 769 from a shrine dedicated to the god Hachiman located on the southern island of Kyūshū. According to the *Shoku Nihongi*, Hachiman is reputed to have communicated through a shrine priestess that a national peace was only possible if Dōkyō was made emperor – theoretically an impossibility given the fact that only members of the ruling family were allowed to assume the throne. Likely horrified at the prospects of Dōkyō becoming emperor, aristocrats in or allied with the imperial lineage sought to prevent this from happening by ascertaining the veracity of the oracle. As a result, a second oracle was issued that overturned the original prophecy with the proclamation that only those of imperial blood could become *tennō*. When Shōtoku died unexpectedly in 770, Dōkyō lost his most powerful patron and was exiled to the provinces, thereby ending his career at court.

The traditional view of Shōtoku is that she was being manipulated by Dōkyō to further his own aspirations, which apparently included ascension to emperor. Recent interpretations view Shōtoku as more likely a savvy politician who found Dōkyō's support useful in frustrating the political challenges to her rule from court rivals.

Expressions of an ancient Japanese Buddhist worldview

Our discussion has thus far focused on the relationship between Buddhism and the state, but what Buddhist beliefs were popularly held in this time period? There are a number of texts and other artifacts of eighth-century material culture – including collections of Buddhist didactic tales (*setsuwa*), temple histories (*engi*), inscriptions found on Buddhist sculpture, and inscribed wooden documents (*mokkan*) from excavated government offices – that reveal details about the kinds of beliefs embraced by Nara-period Japanese Buddhists. One particularly valuable text for understanding the developing Japanese Buddhist worldview is the *Nihon ryōiki*.

The *Nihon ryōiki* (Miraculous Tales from Japan) is the oldest Japanese collection of Buddhist didactic stories (*setsuwa*). Although compiled in the early Heian period (ca. 823) by the monk Kyōkai (or, Keikai) of the Yakushiji temple, this collection of narratives (116 stories in three fascicles) recounts many tales from the Nara period and can be considered at least one monk's view of the state of the Japanese Buddhist worldview at the end of the Nara and beginning of the Heian periods.

The stories told in the *Nihon ryōiki* explore *ryōi*, unusual, supernatural, or anomalous phenomena that reportedly occurred in Japan as a result of the workings of karmic consequence and the power of Buddhist rituals. The central Buddhist idea expressed in these stories is the inexorable workings of the law of cause and effect (*inga*): all actions (Skt. *karma*; J. *gō*) are causes that lead to effects. Good actions yield good results, while bad actions produce negative consequences. This classic Buddhist perspective on karmic consequence is further embellished, in the *Nihon ryōiki*, by the idea that at least certain actions produce immediate consequences. Of the three kinds of recompense (i.e., karmic reward or punishment for one's actions) – recompense in one's present life (*genpō*), one's next life (*shōhō*), and one's life after the next life (*gohō*) – it is the immediacy of recompense in one's present life that is stressed. The collection's full title, *Nihonkoku genpō zen'aku ryōiki* (Miraculous Tales from the Country of Japan Concerning Immediate Recompense for Good and Bad Actions), underscores the significance of this idea by the beginning of the ninth century.

This belief in – and fear of – the immediacy of recompense figures into most of the *Nihon ryōiki* narratives. Readers or hearers of these stories could not have missed the warnings evident in the kinds of karmic consequences these tales relate. For instance, one story describes the riches that are attained by one who prays to the bodhisattva Kannon. Similarly, another story explains how a monk ridiculed another monk who was chanting the *Lotus Sūtra* with an unusual accent. The first monk mimicked the reciter's accent, twisting his mouth up as a way to mock him. Shortly after, the mocking monk's mouth became permanently twisted, immediate retribution for ridiculing the other monk and, by extension, the *Lotus Sūtra*. Whether good action or bad, consequence is inevitable. Although the majority of stories are concerned with karmic consequence in one's present life, there are several stories that also describe recompense in one's next life. At death, one undergoes transmigration (*rinne*) through the samsaric cycle – the cycle of birth–death–rebirth (Skt. *samsara*; J. *rokudō*), resulting in either a better or worse rebirth depending on the sum of the good and bad consequences of one's past actions.

In making the case for the spiritual and material benefits of good actions, additional aspects of the Nara and early Heian Buddhist worldview are revealed. Although karmic consequence is inevitable – it cannot be avoided or cheated – there was a strong belief that adherence to and practice of rituals would bring about good karmic consequence, whether the resolution of some problem in this life or rebirth in a Buddhist paradise, such as the Pure Land. Acting badly, which includes the failure to perform Buddhist rituals, leads to the possibility of rebirth in one of the Buddhist hells, a temporary if especially unpleasant way station through multiple lives.

The idea that one's body and mind transform as the result of good and bad effects of behavioral causes highlights the central tenet that all sentient beings are subject to transmigration though the samsaric cycle. Release from the cycle of birth–death–rebirth occurs only upon attainment of enlightenment or birth in a Buddhist paradise, at which time there are no longer any consequences to one's actions and, hence, no more rebirths. The idea of transmigration was also a significant reason why the idea that impermanence pervades all conditioned reality became such a central theme in Japan and other Buddhist countries.

Finally, the *Nihon ryōiki* tales posit that it is possible for human beings to tap into the salvific power of the universe through belief and ritual praxis directed toward

Buddhas and bodhisattvas. Not only is praying to such a figure spiritually beneficial, but so too is constructing, venerating, or otherwise taking care of statues or paintings of Buddhas and bodhisattvas. It was believed that Buddhist salvific power could be transmitted not only by the Buddhas and bodhisattvas themselves, but also by their images. The transmission of salvific power was not limited to Buddhas, bodhisattvas, and their images. For instance, reciting a sutra or hearing one chanted also enabled one to access salvific power. Ritual practices connected with reading, writing, copying, expounding, or simply holding a sutra could, according to texts like the *Nihon ryōiki*, activate salvific power. The *Lotus Sūtra,* among other sutras, was considered especially powerful in this regard, and there are several *Nihon ryōiki* tales that recount the immediate karmic benefits of even making a vow to copy the sutra (for an extensive discussion of the *Nihon ryōiki*, see Yoshida 2006a: esp. 13–43; this discussion of the *Nihon ryōiki* is based on Yoshida's analysis, and on Nakamura 1973 and LaFleur 1983).

Early Heian Period Buddhism (794–950)

New capital, new lineages

In 784, Kanmu *tennō* (737–806; r. 781–806) ordered construction of a new capital at Nagaoka, to replace the Heijō capital. In 749, with construction still ongoing, Kanmu abandoned the Nagaoka site in favor of a new site – Heiankyō (modern-day Kyōto) – located between mountains and Lake Biwa's south end. The reason for leaving Heijōkyō, the first permanent Yamato capital, has been much debated. Whatever the reasons, this was not a casual undertaking. By some estimates, there were several thousand bureaucrats operating in Heijōkyō and the overall population of the capital at that time is estimated between 70,000 and 100,000 people (Farris 2009: 82–83). In addition to the large bureaucratic infrastructure, Heijōkyō, with its large number of Buddhist temples – many established with the express purpose of providing ritual protection for the well-being of the state and its leaders – was the center of Yamato Buddhism.

One long-held theory attributes the establishment of a new capital to the Dōkyō incident and the ruling family's desire to move away from the machinations of powerful Heijōkyō monks and their meddling in government matters. This theory holds that the rulers had inadvertently invited this state of affairs by imbuing Buddhist institutions with the responsibility for the protection of the state (*chingo kokka*) from natural and human-made disasters. Given the power and economic wealth accrued by monks and their monastic complexes during the Nara period, there was little choice but to abandon Heijōkyō in order to escape this influence. While Dōkyō's actions seem to bear this out, this theory has largely been eclipsed.

Kanmu himself said that he favored the move to the Heian capital for the economic and strategic reasons that it was accessible by both land and water (Toby 1985: 332). Further, as in the former capital at Heijōkyō, Heian Buddhist institutions played significant roles in the life of the city and state. As in the Nara period, Kanmu- and subsequent Heian-period *tennō* were important patrons of Buddhist rituals and material culture. Kanmu himself was a strong supporter of Tendai and sponsored envoys to Tang China that included Buddhist monks seeking new Buddhist texts and practices to bring back to Japan. Thus, it seems an overstatement to argue that the imperial line fled Heijōkyō because of fear of continued Buddhist interventions in the affairs of state. It was in the Heian period, and both in Heiankyō and in the regions beyond, that Buddhism became firmly established and increasingly ubiquitous in the Japanese population, slowly moving beyond the purview of state concerns and control (for a detailed discussion on the move from Heijōkyō to Heiankyō, see Toby 1985).

The move from Heijōkyō to Heiankyō coincided with the development of new Buddhist ideas and practices that were being imported into Japan from the Chinese mainland. This influx was predominantly the result of Japanese pilgrims traveling to China and returning with new texts and ritual practices. By the early Heian period, the Shingon and Tendai lineages, discussed in more detail below, were established and would come to play a significant role in subsequent developments in Japanese Buddhism, at the same time promoting the importance of Buddhist rituals both for the protection of the nation (*gokoku zuhō*) and for the legitimation of the aristocratic ruling elite. These new lineages, however, did not supplant the Nara schools, which remained vibrant monastic communities enjoying continued state and aristocratic support.

From a Buddhist perspective, the early Heian period is especially important for the development of two new Buddhist lineages, Tendai and Shingon. Both Tendai and Shingon – and their respective Japanese founders Saichō and Kūkai – represent a turn toward new Buddhist ideas burnished, in part, by their conversations and debates with the Nara schools and advanced by travel to China for further Buddhist study. Saichō and Kūkai were both heavily involved in court affairs, seeking patronage from powerful courtiers in order to promote their teachings. But both of them also mark a divergence from the notion of the official monk of the Nara period. Despite their strong connections to the state, they also forged independence from the centers of bureaucratic power in the capital at Heiankyō and from the traditional Buddhist monastic centers in Heijōkyō. Still, Saichō and Kūkai continued to support the state ritually through the use of Buddhist rites for the protection of the nation. In short, Saichō and Kūkai maintained traditions, but also set the stage for new Buddhist ideas and practices for centuries to come.

The centrality of Saichō and Kūkai to any narrative of early Heian-period Buddhism is evident from the enormous body of scholarly and sectarian literature that describes and interprets their accomplishments. There is also significant scholarship in English, most notably Groner's (1984) biography of Saichō and Abé's (1999) treatment of Kūkai. Though there is much to be said about both, because of the extensive secondary literature available, we will limit our discussion to brief biographies and overviews of the content and significance of their ideas, practices, and legacies.

We have identified Saichō and Kūkai as founders of new lineages. On the one hand, this is true enough – they were driving forces in getting Tendai and Shingon formally established and recognized as separate lineages by the state. On the other hand, speaking of them this way also generates a problem related to a sectarian, great founder viewpoint: it belies the fact that the religious thought and rituals primarily identified with lineages and their founders were not contained solely within these lineages. As we will see, there was a great deal of sharing and mutual adoption of ideas and practices. For instance, esoteric Buddhist practices associated with Kūkai's Shingon can be found within Tendai. Similarly, Pure Land and Zen schools were established by the early Kamakura period (late twelfth and early thirteenth centuries), but ritual practices and Buddhist doctrine associated with these later lineages were embraced by Tendai from its inception under Saichō's leadership.

The development of sectarian Japanese Buddhism was accelerated by the annual ordination system that went into effect in 806. Saichō, among others, strongly advocated for the change to this system. In the previous allocation system, which was started in 696 during the reign of Queen Jitō, 10 _nenbundosha_ were appointed. Since at this time the notion of distinct schools of Buddhism did not yet exist, only the number of ordinands was specified, but not in relation to a particular school. The revised allocation system assigned ordinands to the Nara schools as before, but added Tendai.

The 806 revision included the term _shūha_ referring to distinctive schools and this was reinforced by the fact that 3 ordinands each were assigned to Hossō and Sanron (Jōjitsu and Kusha were included with Sanron's allocation), 2 each to Ritsu and Kegon, and 2 to the newly emerging Tendai school. The total number of yearly ordinands thus increased by 2, from 10 to 12. This change marked the state's formal acknowledgment of the existence of schools with specific differences. Once Shingon became established, 3 more ordinand appointments were created and assigned to Shingon. As time went on, the 8 schools (_hasshū_) became more and more distinct from each other.

In addition to a new capital and new Buddhist lineages, there were other significant changes occurring in the early Heian period that would greatly affect the future development of Japanese Buddhism. The _ritsuryō_ political system, which had undergirded the Nara Buddhist state, was becoming ineffective and unimportant to Heian aristocrats. The new Buddhist lineages, despite the need for patronage, were developing independently of strong state control. The late ninth-century creation of a regency system (*sekkan seiji*) is of particular note in this changing political climate. This system marked the start of the hegemony of the northern Fujiwara family (*Fujiwara hokke*) over the court and affairs of state that would continue through the eleventh century. The regency system consisted of a regent to an adult *tennō* (*kanpaku*) and a regent to a child *tennō* (*sesshō*), positions occupied by the highest-ranking males of the Fujiwara family. This effectively gave them control of the government even though the *tennō* was the official ruler. Fujiwara control of government was further secured through the practice of marrying Fujiwara daughters into the ruling family, thus giving birth to future *tennō*.

Early Heian Buddhism, with the development of Tendai and Shingon practice and doctrine, introduced the issue of exoteric (*ken*) and esoteric (*mitsu*) Buddhism (*kenmitsu bukkyō*). While the notion of *kenmitsu* Buddhism is especially relevant to medieval Buddhist developments, the notion that there was a significant distinction to be drawn between exoteric and esoteric Buddhist practices is evident by the tenth century and articulated in the Tendai and Shingon lineages. Both Saichō and Kūkai, and their successors, drew distinctions between exoteric and esoteric. The term itself, *kenmitsu* Buddhism, is a twentieth-century construct put forth by the historian Kuroda Toshio (1926–1993). Although the distinction between exoteric and esoteric suggests clear boundaries between these two kinds of Buddhist thought and practice, the reality is that both terms are shorthand for a large array of practices and doctrines that often overlapped and were often complementary. At its most basic, esoteric Buddhism emphasized initiation into rituals that could only be learned and mastered through transmission and training from teacher to disciple. Exoteric Buddhism focused on doctrinal systems that provided an explanation and rationale for the significance of the secretly transmitted esoteric practices. Exoteric Buddhism was also complicated by the fact that different lineages explained esoteric rituals in their own doctrinal terms.

The problem of Heian new Buddhism

Traditional scholarly views of ninth-century Japanese Buddhism have held that the emergence of the Tendai and Shingon lineages in the early decades of the Heian era was the result of a desire to revive a Buddhism that, in the guise of the six Nara lineages, had become a moribund orthodoxy. This perspective views Saichō and Kūkai as rejecting the formal, established, often very abstract, doctrinal formulations of the six Nara lineages. This traditional view is characterized by its focus on schools of Buddhist thought and their founders.

However, recent research, concerned with a cultural history of Japanese Buddhism, yields the possibility of significantly different interpretations. Sone (2003), for instance, questions the extent to which the six Nara lineages were fixed, formalized schools of thought by the early ninth century. The notion that Tendai and Shingon represent "new Buddhism" (*shin bukkyō*) is undermined by evidence that the six Nara lineages were still in the process of formulating their doctrinal positions at the same time that Saichō and Kūkai were developing their doctrinal views. In this sense, says Sone, the notion of "new Buddhism" in the Heian period must take into account active doctrinal development in the six Nara lineages along with Tendai and Shingon (Sone 2003: 32–9; see also Stone 2006: 39–41).

As a result of this revised perspective, traditional methods of studying the great founders of traditions and the history of their schools – starting with Saichō's Tendai and Kūkai's Shingon – have been challenged by viewing Japanese Buddhism in its much broader and nuanced cultural contexts. Stone (2006) has explained that the traditional meta-narrative of Japanese Buddhist history based on sectarian, doctrinal history held that Japanese Buddhism developed in a more or less unitary line from *ujizoku* (extended aristocratic families) Buddhism in the Asuka period to state Buddhism (*kokka bukkyō*) in the Hakuhō, Nara, and early Heian periods to aristocratic Buddhism (*kizoku bukkyō*) in the mid Heian period to popular Buddhism, which starts in the late Heian and reaches fruition in the Kamakura period. As Stone points out, this traditional narrative "was a teleological one, suggesting a gradual shift in Buddhist concerns, from politics and this-worldly benefits to individual liberation … It is now being challenged by the recognition that Buddhism at each juncture of the Heian period (or any period, for that matter) encompassed a range of both social bases and soteriological aims" (Stone 2006: 40–1).

Early Heian Buddhist lineages: Tendai

Saichō (767–822), known posthumously as Dengyō Daishi, was the founder of the Tendai (C: Tiantai) Buddhist lineage in Japan. After studying Buddhist thought and practice in China in the early ninth century he returned to Japan, establishing the Enryakuji temple on Mt. Hiei, northeast of the new capital at Heiankyō. This was the genesis of the great temple complex that played a prominent role in the subsequent development of Japanese Buddhism. Of his many accomplishments, Saichō is especially noted for transforming monastic regulations and discipline, and for his efforts toward creating an independent Tendai ordination system, known as the Bodhisattva Precepts (*bosatsukai*).

Saichō's Buddhist training began in 780 when, at age 13, he entered a provincial temple. Five years later he received full ordination at the Tōdaiji ordination platform (*kaidan*). Thereafter, from 785 to 797, Saichō resided on Mt. Hiei, where he continued his study of Buddhist thought and practice. Although still relatively unknown in Japan at this time, he focused his study on Tendai Buddhism through the writings of the Chinese Tendai founder Zhiyi (J. Chigi), particularly his *Mohezhiguan* (Japanese,

Maka shikan, "Great Calming and Contemplation"), which details the ritual practice of meditation. Zhiyi's Tiantai ideas were based on the *Lotus Sūtra* and its doctrine that the sutra was the "One Vehicle," or teaching, that would lead the faithful to Buddhahood. According to this view, all other Buddhist teachings are only provisionally true – they are, according to the *Lotus Sūtra,* expedient devices (Skt. *upāya;* J. *hōben*) – whereas the *Lotus Sūtra* is understood as the final and ultimate teaching of the Buddha.

Whatever Saichō's intentions were for living a contemplative life on Mt. Hiei, his monastic career took on new directions when the capital was moved to Heiankyō in 794. Mt. Hiei, nearby and northeast of the new capital, took on the geomantic role of protecting the capital from evil spirits that were believed to travel from the northeast. Saichō was brought closer to political affairs when, in 797, he was appointed one of the 10 priests of the imperial court (*nenbundosha*). He earned a reputation as an erudite monk as the result of annual lectures on the *Lotus Sūtra* started in 798. Saichō's lectures stressed the primacy of the *Lotus Sūtra* and Tendai doctrine, and asserted their superiority over the older Nara lineages, especially Hossō.

In 804, Saichō traveled to China to study Tendai doctrine with Chinese Buddhist masters, spending time at Mt. Tiantai, the center of Zhiyi's Tiantai lineage. While there, he studied sutras and Tendai commentaries and received instruction in esoteric texts and rituals and in Zen meditation. Significantly for the subsequent development of Saichō's Tendai lineage, he was instructed in Mahayana monastic regulations – the Bodhisattva Precepts – enumerated in the *Brahmā's Net Sūtra* (Ch. *Fanwang jing;* J. *Bonmōkyō*).

When Saichō returned to Japan in 805 he brought with him a large number of exoteric and esoteric sutras and commentaries that became the focus of study for the Tendai monastic community at Enryakuji. While he may have wished to concentrate on the contemplative life, Saichō was nevertheless drawn more deeply into early ninth-century politics. Saichō's return coincided with the illness of Kanmu *tennō.* He was summoned to the imperial palace in order to recite sutras and perform esoteric rituals in hopes of curing the ailing Kanmu, typical strategies for coping with disease in the Heian period.

In 805, two officially sanctioned ordinands from the official monastic quota system were provided to Saichō and the Tendai lineage for the first time. This system was established as a means of regulating the number of monastics, thereby controlling the monastic community. The allocation of two ordinands to the Tendai confirmed the status of Saichō's Mt. Hiei monastic community as a separate lineage. Of the two initial Tendai ordinands, one studied exoteric thought and practices known as the Meditation Course (*shikango*), Tendai meditation techniques described in Zhiyi's *Mohezhiguan.* The other studied the Esoteric Course (*shanago*), which centered on the study of the *Daibirushanakyō* (Skt. *Mahāvairocana-sūtra*).

Saichō is especially noted for two major accomplishments. First, he was able to defend Tendai against detractors from traditional Nara Buddhist schools, such as the Hossō. The Hossō lineage taught that it was impossible for the most evil people to attain Buddhahood. Saichō's Tendai view held that all sentient beings have the potential to attain Buddhahood because all sentient beings possess the Buddha nature. This and other doctrinal differences were pronounced enough that Saichō engaged in a series of debates with a Hossō monk named Tokuitsu. The Saichō–Tokuitsu doctrinal debates gained a great deal of notoriety. Topics debated included the Buddhahood question and issues concerning how to classify Buddhist teachings.

Second, it was through Saichō's efforts that Tendai was eventually granted permission to use the Bodhisattva Precepts as the basis for Tendai monastic ordination, thus freeing the lineage from attempts at external control. The Bodhisattva Precepts constituted a set of vows intended to induce faithful practice of Mahayana Buddhism. These vows could be taken by both monastics and laypersons, but they were considered secondary to the precepts that were required in the traditional full monastic ordination known as the Four-Part Precepts (C: *sifenlu*; J: *shibunritsu*). In the early Heian period, the Tōdaiji ordination platform was the only legal location for receiving full ordination, a regulation that provided the government a way to control the monastic community. Saichō later tried to replace the traditional ordination performed at Tōdaiji with the Bodhisattva Precepts as a means of ordaining monks directly in the Tendai lineage. Saichō argued that these precepts were better suited to the requirements of Tendai monastic life, especially since the older precepts were based, he said, on conditions no longer relevant to his day.

Not surprisingly, Saichō met with significant resistance from Hossō and other Nara Buddhist lineages, whose prestige and authority were directly threatened by Saichō's attempt to operate outside of their supervision. Saichō's Nara-lineage detractors criticized his proposal as, in essence, ignoring traditional monastic rules for a set of rules that were really intended for lay practitioners and hence secondary, not primary, precepts. Such doctrinal disagreements also had political implications. His attempt to reform the ordination system with new regulations directly threatened the long-held power of Nara Buddhist institutions, which had traditionally been in control of monastic ordination. This quest for an autonomous ordination also required state permission. To this end, Saichō addressed three petitions to the State seeking permission to implement the Bodhisattva Precepts for Tendai ordination. This permission was received on Mt. Hiei seven days after Saichō's death. As a result, monks assigned to Tendai through the annual quota system were now allowed to be ordained at Enryakuji, rather than at Tōdaiji. In the end, not only did Tendai gain independence from the Nara lineages, but this led to increased independence from government control for all lineages.

Although Saichō was primarily focused on study of the *Lotus Sūtra* and related texts, he also studied esoteric Buddhist rituals, practices that were attracting the attention of Heian aristocrats. However, Saichō's grasp of esoteric Buddhism was eclipsed by that of Kūkai (774–835), who established the Shingon esoteric lineage. He traveled to China, on the same occasion as Saichō, in order to study esoteric thought and practice. As we will detail more fully below, Kūkai developed a much deeper understanding of esoteric thought and practice than was possible for Saichō given the latter's brief encounter with Chinese esoteric Buddhism. Saichō recognized Kūkai's esoteric accomplishments: He dispatched Tendai monastics to Kūkai for esoteric training and to borrow esoteric texts. Over time, however, animosity developed between Saichō and Kūkai. Kūkai started refusing to lend Saichō esoteric texts, suggesting that Saichō should study under him. Further, some of the monks Saichō sent to study with Kūkai became Kūkai's disciples instead.

When Saichō died in 822, Tendai was still very much a fledgling school. Paul Groner (2002a: 2) cites evidence that Saichō, around the time of his death, had lost over half of the ordained monks assigned to Tendai yearly through the *nenbundosha* system, some leaving to train in esoteric practices with Kūkai. Prominent challenges confronting the post-Saichō Tendai lineage included disputes over leadership and how to systematize the relationship between exoteric and esoteric practices.

Given Saichō's problematic relationship with Kūkai, it is perhaps ironic that later Tendai monks developed Tendai esoteric practices (known as *taimitsu*), that eclipsed Shingon *mikkyō* (known as *tōmitsu*) as the focus of esoteric practice among the imperial family and aristocracy. Tendai monastics continued to study the *Lotus Sūtra* and related texts, but subsequent monks also focused on esoteric practices, developing Tendai esotericism. The melding of Tendai and esoteric Buddhism was mostly a Japanese innovation. The reason for this was, in part, that after envoys to China were halted about the ninth century, contact with the Chinese mainland became limited, resulting in Japanese Tendai developing independently from Chinese Tiantai. Of particular importance to Tendai's esoteric turn were two of Saichō's successors, the monks Ennin and Enchin. Both Ennin and Enchin traveled to China in order to study esoteric thought and practices. Upon their return, and with many texts in hand, they expanded the esoteric ritual repertoire of Tendai Buddhism, thus competing with Shingon for the patronage of court aristocrats who were frequent sponsors of esoteric rituals.

Ennin (794–864; known posthumously as Jikaku Daishi) was the third abbot (*zasu*) of Enryakuji. When he returned from China to Japan in 847, the esoteric Buddhist texts and ritual manuals that he carried with him became central to the development of Tendai esoteric practices because they filled in many of the lacunae in Tendai's collection of *mikkyō* texts, a result of Saichō's only partial study of Shingon. These texts allowed Tendai to compete with Shingon for imperial and aristocratic patronage. Besides his advocacy of Tendai *mikkyō*, Ennin was responsible for the expansion of the temple complex on Mt. Hiei. He also inaugurated meditation practices that were instrumental in the development of Pure Land practices in subsequent centuries. Of note was the implementation of the *jōgyō zanmai*, or constantly walking meditation, that required one to circumambulate an image of Amida Buddha while contemplating Amida's physical form and reciting his name. This ritual had its origins in a similar ritual advocated by Zhiyi in China.

Enchin (814–891; known posthumously as Chishō Daishi) was the sixth abbot (*zasu*) of the Tendai lineage. Enchin returned to Japan from his China travels in 859, and soon gained the patronage of both the imperial family and the increasingly powerful Fujiwara aristocratic family because of the continued interest in the ritual efficacy of esoteric practices. It was under Enchin's leadership that Tendai fully embraced *mikkyō*. Enchin argued that Tendai and Shingon were co-equal, and that Mahāvairocana and the Buddha in the *Lotus Sūtra* were the same entity.

The Tendai dispute over leadership that challenged the post-Saichō Tendai lineage was the result of factions that developed around the former abbots Ennin and Enchin. At stake, among other things, was control over the future of the Tendai lineage and aristocratic patronage. The Ennin faction (Tendai's *sanmon* lineage) was centered on Mt. Hiei at Enryakuji, while the Enchin faction (Tendai's *jimon* lineage) eventually left Mt. Hiei, taking up residence at the base of the mountain at Enchin's former temple, Onjōji (also known as Miidera). At least some of the rhetoric that animated the dispute included arguments over doctrine and ritual practice.

Early Heian Buddhist lineages: Shingon

Kūkai (774–835), known posthumously as Kōbō Daishi, is traditionally considered the founder of the Japanese esoteric Buddhist lineage known as Shingon (Ch. Zhenyan; "True Word"), and also referred to as *mikkyō* ("esoteric teaching"), or Vajrayana ("Diamond Vehicle"). Kūkai, from a provincial aristocratic family, first studied Confucianism at the state-sponsored university (*daigaku*) in Heijōkyō in preparation for a career as a court official. However, his interests turned to Buddhism – especially texts and rituals associated with esoteric Buddhism, which he initially studied and practiced as a privately ordained monk (*shidosō*). In 804, Kūkai received the official ordination at Tōdaiji, and, soon after, he traveled to China to further his study of Buddhism. He studied esoteric Buddhism under the tutelage of Huiguo (746–805), a Chinese *mikkyō* master. He was introduced to such fundamental esoteric Buddhist texts as the *Mahāvairocana-sūtra* (J: *Dainichikyō*) and the *Vajraśekhara-sūtra* (J: *Kongōchōkyō*). Kūkai received the esoteric Buddhist ordination (Skt. *abhiṣeka*; J. *kanjō*) in recognition of his understanding of the complexities of esoteric texts and rituals.

Kūkai returned to Japan in 806, landing on the southern island of Kyūshū. He brought back with him a large number of Buddhist texts as well as esoteric ritual objects. He did not proceed to Heiankyō until 809, when he received governmental permission to became abbot of the temple Takaosanji (later known as Jingoji), administering esoteric ordination (*kanjō*) to those interested in pursuing *mikkyō* practices, among them Heijōkyō monastics and the abdicated *tennō* Heizei (r. 806–809). He also produced a number of texts in this period that systematized his view of Buddhist teachings and became the doctrinal foundation for the Shingon lineage.

Kūkai was able to expand Shingon's influence quickly because of the interest expressed by the court and aristocrats in esoteric rituals, which were believed to be especially efficacious for both state protection and individual needs. As a result, Kūkai was frequently called to court in order to perform rituals such as the Latter Seven-Day Ritual (*go-shichinichi mishiho*; also pronounced *go-shichinichi mishuhō*) – first conducted in 834 – that were meant to secure the health of the *tennō* and the prosperity of the state. Kūkai's success in his ritual activities is evidenced by the fact that esoteric rituals became central to the ritual life of the court and aristocracy.

In 816, Kūkai sought permission from Saga *tennō* – who had become Kūkai's supporter and patron – to make Mt. Kōya the center for esoteric study and practice, and, in 818, construction began on the mountain's main temple, Kongōbuji. Kūkai was called back to the capital in 823, where he was made abbot of Tōji. This temple became the Shingon center in Heiankyō and an important site for esoteric rituals on behalf of the court and aristocrats. In 834, near the end of Kūkai's life, Shingon began receiving two annual state-sponsored ordinands from the *nenbundosha* system in recognition of its growing state influence and its sectarian differences with other schools. Unlike Saichō's Tendai, which antagonized the Nara lineages through creation of an independent ordination platform, Shingon continued to utilize the traditional ordination platform at Tōdaiji, thus maintaining a good relationship with Kegon and other Nara schools. Due to ill health, Kūkai left Tōji for Mt. Kōya in 832, where he continued to write commentaries on esoteric Buddhism. He died on Mt. Kōya in 835.

Kūkai's Shingon school (Shingon-shū) derives its name from the Chinese esoteric school known as Zhenyan, meaning "True Word." The Chinese term is itself a translation of the Sanskrit term *mantra*. Mantras are ritual words that are chanted in order to activate their spiritual power. The Shingon lineage, though, is referred to by a number of more or less synonymous terms such as two Sanskrit terms: Mantrayāna (Mantra Vehicle) and Vajrayāna (Diamond/Thunderbolt Vehicle). The Japanese term *mikkyō* (esoteric teaching) is also used to describe esoteric practices generally, but without specific reference to Shingon because there are also Tendai *mikkyō* ritual practices. The notion of esoteric teachings stresses the fact that its rituals cannot be learned from reading a text, but must be transmitted directly from master to disciple. In the case of Shingon, the master, or *ajari* (Skt. *ācārya*), is someone who has advanced understanding of Shingon thought and practice and who has been so certified by a master. The disciple is one who has successfully mastered the required initiations, thus certifying through this ordination process that the disciple is able to properly practice *mikkyō* rituals and is therefore ready to begin advanced study.

Kūkai's interpretation of Shingon thought and practice centered on the *Mahāvairocana sūtra* (Chinese translation by Śubhākarasiṃha [637–735] and his disciple Yixing [683–727]) and the *Vajraśekhara sūtra* (Chinese translation by Amoghavajra [705–774]). On the basis of his interpretations of these two texts, Kūkai developed two key ideas that became central to Shingon ritual practice: the importance of the Dharma Body of the Buddha (Skt. *dharmakāya*; J. *hosshin*) and the ritual practice of the three mysteries (*sanmitsu*).

The *dharmakāya* is one of the three bodies of the Buddha (*trikāya*), each body expressing a different but interrelated reality. According to Kūkai's interpretation of the *trikāya* theory, the Dharma body of the Buddha is equivalent to the Buddha Mahāvairocana (J. Dainichi Nyorai). Mahāvairocana's body is itself made up of the six elements (*rokudai*), namely earth, water, fire, wind, space, and consciousness. The universe is nothing but the manifestation of different configurations of the six elements. One's experience of the world is in fact the experience of Mahāvairocana, though this is obscured unless one is enlightened (Abé 1999: 281–282). The other two bodies are the manifestation body (*nirmāṇakāya*) and the celestial body (*saṃbhogakāya*). The manifestation body represents the historical Buddha who is a manifestation of Dainichi in a form through which the Dharma could be preached to human beings. The celestial body refers to the form in which Buddhas such as Amida (Skt. Amitābha) appear in their Buddha-fields, that is, Buddhist paradises. Of note here is the fact that Shingon does not replace the historical Buddha in this system, but rather treats him as a necessary manifestation of Dainichi required in order to approach humans at a level they can understand.

While the *dharmakāya* might be understood as doctrine, for Kūkai it had to be experienced through esoteric rituals involving the three mysteries (*sanmitsu*), that is, practices into which one must be initiated under the guidance of an *ajari*. The practice of the three mysteries (*sanmitsugyō*) is a ritual protocol that through its practice actualizes the Shingon idea that the universe manifests the body, speech, and mind of Mahāvairocana. The mystery of the body (*shinmitsu*) is symbolized through appropriate hand gestures (Skt. *mudrā*; J. *ingei*), the mystery of speech (*kumitsu*) is symbolized through sacred verbal formulae (Skt. *mantra*; J. *shingon*), and the mystery of mind (*imitsu*) is symbolized through mental images of artistic representations of enlightened worlds (Skt. *maṇḍala*; J. *mandara*), the abode of Buddhas and bodhisattvas. Utilizing what Abé (1999) refers to as the "technology" of the three mysteries, the practitioner experiences the spiritual goal of the realization of Buddhahood in this very body (*sokushin jōbutsu*), a notion central to Kūkai's ideas about *mikkyō*.

According to Shingon thought, the universal truth comprises two aspects that are merged in the body, speech, and mind of Mahāvairocana: the phenomenal world and the noumenal world. The phenomenal world is symbolized as the Womb World (*taizōkai*). The Womb World represents the impermanence of samsara (birth–death–rebirth cycle) and contains the elements of earth, wind, fire, water, and space. The noumenal world is symbolized as the Diamond Realm (kongōkai) and is associated with mind (or consciousness) – considered the sixth element. This mind is the absolute, perfect wisdom of Mahāvairocana. Both of these worlds are richly illustrated in esoteric mandalas, or representations of these worlds.

After Kūkai's death, Shingon continued its expansion, in large part because of court and aristocratic patrons, who maintained a strong interest in and sponsorship of esoteric rituals. A further source of support came from the older Nara lineages. Unlike Tendai, which had antagonized the Nara Buddhist schools by circumventing the traditional Tōdaiji ordination platform, Shingon forged ties with these lineages. One source of connection between Shingon and Nara lineages was located in the idea of the fundamental interdependence between esoteric rituals and their exoteric explanation in Nara lineage doctrine. One example of this quest for reciprocity occurred in 875, when Shōbō (832–909), a Shingon monk, founded the subtemple Tōnan'in at Tōdaiji as a site for the study of both Shingon ritual and Sanron doctrine (Abé 1999: 369–370).

It is sometimes argued that Kūkai's philosophical brilliance in theorizing and interpreting Shingon thought and practice (see, for instance, Tamura 2000: 70; Ōkubo 2010: 179) rendered further doctrinal development unnecessary. It is the case that after Kūkai's death Shingon focused mostly on furthering its ritual practices and building new temples as ritual centers. Some of these new temples were built as a result of imperial patronage. Uda tennō (867–931; r. 887–897) established the Ninnaji temple in 888 and his son, Daigo tennō (885–930; r. 897–930), became a patron of the Daigoji temple, which was established by Shōbō in 874. It became Daigo's prayer-offering temple (goganji) in 907. Renewed development of Shingon doctrine did not occur until the late Heian period with Kakuban's (1095–1144) revival movement.

Women in Ancient Japanese Buddhism

In this section on women in ancient Japanese Buddhism, and in related sections in this volume, we discuss the conflicted status of women in Japanese Buddhist history. In examining this history, we are mindful of the work of scholars such as Lori Meeks, who, in her study of premodern female monastic orders, argues that "ideological disjunctures" in Japanese Buddhism, such as the possibility of salvation for women, were not always expressed in simple distinctions between male and female perceptions. Meeks suggests that we also need to take into account other "markers of difference," including social class, education, and monastic status, in order to better understand rhetorical stances regarding women and their roles in Buddhist culture. It is sometimes the case, emphasizes Meeks, that there is a clearer correlation between views on female salvation among men and women of the aristocracy than between male clergy and laymen (Meeks 2010: 7). This methodological and histori-cal viewpoint, which is informed by other scholarly discussions (see, for instance, Faure 2003: 8–15), serves as a backdrop for our discussions of women in Japanese Buddhism throughout this volume.

Until the Heian period, the attitude toward and role of women Buddhists – officially ordained, self-ordained, and lay – was for the most part positive. Although it is impossible to estimate exact numbers of women Buddhists in ancient Japan, there is evidence that they played a significant role in the early development of Buddhist institutions and practices. We have already discussed the sixth-century nun Zenshin-ni – along with two of her female attendants – as the first to take the tonsure and become monastics in Yamato. Several other women also became ordained under Zenshin'ni's direction. By the seventh century, nunneries, such as the Toyouradera (the origin of the Gangōji temple) were becoming a part of the Buddhist landscape.

It may, in retrospect, seem surprising that women were the first Japanese Buddhist monastics, especially given the less generous treatment of women in other Asian Buddhist contexts. Ōsumi Kazuo (2002) argues, however, that the context in which Buddhism was introduced into Japan was significantly different from other locales, such as India. He invokes indigenous ritual practices in which women played an essential role serving as mediums of communication for deities (*kami*). Thus, he observes, "it was only natural that those who would serve the Buddha and become the first acolytes would be women" (Ōsumi 2002: xxxi). Whether this is a sufficient explanation or not, historical sources indicate that women were the first Japanese Buddhist monastics. They were also the first to travel outside of the Japanese archi-pelago – in this case, to Paekche – in order to learn more about Buddhism

We previously examined the strong support for Buddhism by women of the rul-ing elite, such as Kōmyō and Kōken/Shōtoku *tennō*. Kōmyō, Shōmu *tennō*'s consort, was arguably the most powerful female patron of Buddhism in Japanese history. As we saw, she supported nuns in a number of ways, including inviting them to perform rituals at court and advocating for the construction of Kokubunniji. She was also a major sponsor of sutra copying. One scholar has argued that a consideration of Kōmyō's role in promoting "state Buddhism" helps us not merely to gain an under-standing of court women's support of Buddhism but also to question conventional assumptions about the categories of state Buddhism, on the one hand, and "court Buddhism," on the other (Hongō 2002: 46–47). There was, in other words, a "blur-ring" of distinctions between private and official support of Buddhism. In addition to women of the ruling elite, lay women from aristocratic families were also strong patrons. They were involved in various projects that promoted Buddhism, such as sutra copying and the creation of images of Buddhas and bodhisattvas.

Texts, like the *Nihon ryōiki* and other Buddhist tale literature (*setsuwa*), provide some perspective on the situation for women Buddhists beyond the court and officially sanctioned nunneries. The *Nihon ryōiki* includes several stories that underscore the devotion of women to Buddhist practices. In addition, the *Nihon ryōiki* makes an argument for the equality of women and men in matters Buddhist. One such tale (Nakamura 1973: 246–248) recounts the story of a provincial girl born with physical deformities but who was "endowed with wisdom." We are told that she could recite sutras from an early age, and that she eventually decided to become a Buddhist renunciant, compassionately aiding the people she encountered. On the occasion of a series of lectures on the Kegonkyō by a very senior monk from the Nara temple, Daianji, the young nun was always in attendance.

> Seeing her, the lecturer said accusingly, "Who is that nun unscrupulously seated among the monks?" In reply she said, "Buddha promulgated the right teaching out of his great compassion for all sentient beings. Why do you restrain me in particular?" Then she asked a question by quoting a verse from the scripture, and the lecturer could not interpret it. (Nakamura 1973: 248)

After much questioning, it was determined that the nun was in fact an incarnation of the Buddha. We need to be careful, of course, in assuming that this story is somehow indicative of the entire period in which it is located, but it does clearly indicate that gender was a part of the conversation in ancient Japanese Buddhism.

In the early eighth century, the monastic regulations (*sōniryō*) that were instituted as part of the *ritsuryō* government reforms codified the treatment of officially ordained monks and nuns as equals, and specified that both had responsibilities for conducting nation-protecting rituals, among other duties. However, these legal provisions borrowed from Tang Chinese models and, as such, were imbued with Confucian values that articulated a social hierarchy that placed women in an inferior position to men. The temples and nunneries that were constructed in every province as part of the state-supported *kokubunji* monastic system established by Shōmu *tennō* evidences the beginnings of an unequal valuation of monks and nuns. While these temples were built in pairs, the monasteries (*kokubunsōji*) were staffed with 20 monks, while the nunneries (*kokubunniji*) were staffed with only 10 nuns, and were smaller in physical size compared to the monasteries. (Ōsumi 2002: xxxii)

This notion of a separation between men and women came to inform Japanese monastic attitudes. Ushiyama Yoshiyuki (2002: 132) asserts that this led to restrictions on the activity of nuns as officiants on the many Buddhist ritual occasions that marked late Nara and early Heian religious life. As a result, official nuns rapidly declined in authority and number. By the Heian period, women were more and more written out of monastic positions of authority and ritual responsibility. A significant reason for this was the *nenbundosha* yearly ordinand system. When ordinands started getting assigned to specific lineages in the early Heian period, the system favored men, appointing them to the task of studying doctrine and monastic precepts.

By the late Nara period, the extensive role that women played in the development and dissemination of Buddhist practices up to that time began to erode. A number of events marked government withdrawal of support for nunneries as well as the role of nuns in court rituals (Ushiyama 1998: 31; Matsuo 2007: 135–37; Katsuura 2000, 122). In 772, the male *tennō* Kōnin, perhaps in response to the Dōkyō incident that preceded his ascension to power with the death of female *tennō* Shōtoku, instituted a new monastic regulation, *naigubu jūzenji* (Ten Court Meditation Masters). This regulation required 10 monks (and, conspicuously, no nuns) to conduct Buddhist rituals in the Buddha Hall at the imperial palace. Ushiyama Yoshiyuki (1990) asserts that with the revision of the *jūzenji* into the *nenbundosha* system in the early ninth century, women were further excluded from positions of lineage leadership because it was monks, not nuns, who were assigned to specific lineages. Nunneries, too, came to be managed by monks, further diminishing leadership roles for nuns. These various changes conspired to reduce the number of nuns and nunneries and by sometime in the ninth century, women were apparently no longer formally ordained, though women continued to be involved in Buddhist activities in unofficial capacities. The ninth century also witnessed the development of social attitudes – at least among those associated with the court – promoting the chastity of widows following the death of their husbands, which might suggest a more restrictive view of women in general, at least at court (Groner 2002b: 74).

Our discussion might seem to suggest that Buddhism was primarily limited to the court in the Nara and early Heian periods, but this is not the case. Archaeological evidence has established that Buddhism was spread throughout the realm – and that women were active as nuns and supporters. Although additional research is needed, given the fact that more than 700 sites of temples (some nunneries) from the late seventh to eight centuries have been excavated, the traditional interpretation that the dissemination of Buddhism would await the "new Kamakura" lineages is, simply put, incorrect (Yoshida 2006a: 171–173).

References

Abé, Ryūichi. 1999. *The Weaving of Mantra: Kūkai and the Construction of Esoteric Buddhist Discourse*. New York: Columbia University Press.

Aston, W. G., trans. 1972. *Nihongi: Chronicles of Japan From the Earliest Times to A.D. 697*. Rutland, VT and Tokyo: Charles E. Tuttle Company, Inc.

Bowring, Richard. 2005. *The Religious Traditions of Japan, 500–1600*. Cambridge: Cambridge University Press.

Deal, William E. 1995. "Buddhism and the State in Early Japan." In Donald S. Lopez, Jr. (ed.), *Buddhism in Practice*, 216–227. Princeton, NJ: Princeton University Press.

Farris, William Wayne. 2007. "Pieces in a Puzzle: Changing Approaches to the Shōsōin Documents." *Monumenta Nipponica* 62 (4): 397–435.

Farris, William Wayne. 2009. *Daily Life and Demographics in Ancient Japan* (Michigan Monograph Series in Japanese Studies No. 63). Ann Arbor, MI: Center for Japanese Studies, The University of Michigan.

Faure, Bernard. 2003. *The Power of Denial: Buddhism, Purity, and Gender.* Princeton, NJ: Princeton University Press.

Futaba Kenkō. 1984. *Nihon kodai bukkyōshi no kenkyū.* Kyoto: Nagata bunshodō.

Groner, Paul. 1984. *Saichō: The Establishment of the Japanese Tendai School.* Berkeley, CA: Berkeley Institute of Buddhist Studies.

Groner, Paul. 2002a. *Ryōgen and Mount Hiei: Japanese Tendai in the Tenth Century.* Honolulu: University of Hawai'i Press.

Groner, Paul. 2002b. "Vicissitudes in the Ordination of Japanese 'Nuns' during the Eighth through the Tenth Centuries." In Barbara Ruch (ed.), *Engendering Faith: Women and Buddhism in Premodern Japan* (Michigan Monograph Series in Japanese Studies 43), 65–108. Ann Arbor, MI: Center for Japanese Studies, The University of Michigan.

Hayami Tasuku. 1986. *Nihon bukkyōshi: Kōdai.* Tokyo: Yoshikawa Kōbunkan.

Hongō Masatsugu. 2002. "State Buddhism and Court Buddhism: The Role of Court Women in the Development of Buddhism from the Seventh to the Ninth Centuries." In Barbara Ruch (ed.), *Engendering Faith: Women and Buddhism in Premodern Japan* (Michigan Monograph Series in Japanese Studies 43), 41–61. Ann Arbor, MI: Center for Japanese Studies, The University of Michigan.

Inoue Mitsusada. 1971. *Nihon kodai no kokka to bukkyō.* Tokyo: Iwanami Shoten.

Inoue Mitsusada, with Delmer M. Brown. 1993. "The Century of Reform." In Delmer M. Brown (eds), *The Cambridge History of Japan*, vol. 1: *Ancient Japan*, 163–220. Cambridge: Cambridge University Press.

Kasahara, Kazuo, ed. 2001. *A History of Japanese Religion.* Trans. Paul McCarthy and Gaynor Sekimori. Tokyo: Kōsei Publishing Co.

Katata Osamu. 1967. "Shoki no bukkyō." In Ienaga Saburō (ed.) *Nihon bukkyōshi. 1: Kodai-hen*, 46–105. Kyoto: Hōzōkan.

Katsuura Noriko. 2000. *Nihon kodai no sōni to shakai.* Tokyo: Yoshikawa Kōbunkan.

LaFleur, William R. 1983. *The Karma of Words: Buddhism and the Literary Arts in Medieval Japan.* Berkeley, CA: University of California Press.

Matsuo, Kenji. 2007. *A History of Japanese Buddhism.* Folkestone, UK: Global Oriental.

McCallum, Donald F. 2009. *The Four Great Temples: Buddhist Archaeology, Architecture, and Icons of Seventh-Century Japan.* Honolulu: University of Hawai'i Press.

Meeks, Lori. 2010. *Hokkeji and the Reemergence of Female Monastic Orders in Medieval Japan.* Honolulu: University of Hawai'i Press.

Nakamura, Kyoko Motomochi, trans. 1973. *Miraculous Stories from the Japanese Buddhist Tradition: The Nihon ryōiki of the Monk Kyōkai.* Cambridge, MA: Harvard University Press.

Ōkubo Ryōshun. 2010. "Saichō, Kūkai no kaikaku." In Sueki Fumihiko *et al.* (eds.), *Nihon bukkyō no ishizue* (Shin Ajia Bukkyōshi 11, Nihon 1), 138–201. Tokyo: Kōsei Shuppansha.

Ōsumi Kazuo. 2002. "Historical Notes on Women and the Japanization of Buddhism." In Barbara Ruch (ed.), *Engendering Faith: Women and Buddhism in Premodern Japan* (Michigan Monograph Series in Japanese Studies 43), xxvii–xlii. Ann Arbor, MI: Center for Japanese Studies, The University of Michigan.

Ōyama Seiichi. 1999. *"Shōtoku taishi" no tanjō.* Tokyo: Yoshikawa Kōbunkan.

Piggott, Joan R. 1997. *The Emergence of Japanese Kingship.* Stanford, CA: Stanford University Press.

Sakamoto Tarō, Ienaga Saburō, Inoue Mitsusada, and Ōno Susumu, eds. 1965. *Nihon shoki*, vol. 2. *Nihon koten bungaku taikei* 68. Tokyo: Iwanami Shoten.

Sakuma Ryū. 1994. "Gyōgi." In Yūsen Kashiwahara and Kōyū Sonoda (eds.), *Shapers of Japanese Buddhism*, 3–13. Tokyo: Kōsei Publishing Co.

Sone Masato. 2003. *Saichō, Kūkai to Nanto*. In Ōkubo Ryōshun *et al.* (eds.), *Nihon Bukkyō sanjū-yon no kagi*, 32–39. Tokyo: Shunjūsha.

Sonoda Kōyū, with Delmer M. Brown. 1993. "Early Buddha Worship." In Delmer M. Brown (eds), *The Cambridge History of Japan*, vol. 1: *Ancient Japan*, 359–414. Cambridge: Cambridge University Press.

Stone, Jacqueline I. 2006. "Buddhism." In Paul L. Swanson, and Clark Chilson (eds.), *Nanzan Guide to Japanese Religions*, 38–64. Honolulu: University of Hawai'i Press.

Sugimoto Kazuki. 2010. "Tenpyō shakyō." In Sueki Fumihiko *et al.* (eds.), *Nihon Bukkyō no kiso* (Shin Ajia Bukkyōshi, Volume 11, Nihon 1), 132–135. Tokyo: Kōsei Shuppansha.

Tamamuro Taijō. 1940. *Nihon bukkyōshi gaisetsu*. Tokyo: Risōsha.

Tamura Enchō. 1982. "Kokka bukkyō no seiritsu katei." In *Nihon bukkyōshi, Asuka jidai*, 208–26. Kyoto: Hōzōkan.

Tamura, Yoshiro. 2000. *Japanese Buddhism: A Cultural History*. Tokyo: Kōsei Shuppansha.

Toby, Ronald P. 1985. "Why Leave Nara?: Kammu and the Transfer of the Capital." *Monumenta Nipponica* 40 (3): 331–347.

Totman, Conrad. 2008. *Japan Before Perry: A Short History*. Berkeley, CA: University of California Press.

Ushiyama Yoshiyuki. 1990. *Kodai chūsei jiin soshiki no kenkyū*. Tokyo: Yoshikawa Kōbunkan.

Ushiyama, Yoshiyuki. 2002. "Buddhist Convents in Medieval Japan." In Barbara Ruch (ed.), *Engendering Faith: Women and Buddhism in Premodern Japan* (Michigan Monograph Series in Japanese Studies 43), 131–164. Ann Arbor, MI: Center for Japanese Studies, The University of Michigan.

Visser, M. W. de. 1935. *Ancient Buddhism in Japan*. 2 vols. Leiden: E. J. Brill.

Yoshida Kazuhiko. 1995. *Nihon kodai shakai to bukkyō*. Tokyo: Yoshikawa Kōbunkan.

Yoshida, Kazuhiko. 2003. "Revisioning Religion in Ancient Japan." *Japanese Journal of Religious Studies* 30 (1–2): 1–26.

Yoshida Kazuhiko. 2006a. *Minshū no kodaishi: "Nihon Ryōiki" ni miru mō hitotsu no kodai*. Nagoya: Fūbaisha.

Yoshida Kazuhiko. 2006b. "Religion in the Classical Period." In Paul L. Swanson, and Clark Chilson (eds.), Nanzan Guide to Japanese Religions, 144–162. Honolulu: University of Hawai'i Press.

Further Reading

Bender, Ross. 1979. "The Hachiman Cult and the Dōkyō Incident." *Monumenta Nipponica* 34 (2): 125–153.

Bogel, Cynthea J. 2009. *With a Single Glance: Buddhist Icon and Early Mikkyō Vision*. Seattle: University of Washington Press.

Brown, Delmer M., ed. 1993. *The Cambridge History of Japan*, vol. 1: *Ancient Japan*. Cambridge: Cambridge University Press.

Gardiner, David L., trans. "Japan's First Shingon Ceremony." In George J. Tanabe, Jr. (ed.), *Religions of Japan in Practice*, 153–158. Princeton, NJ: Princeton University Press.

Grapard, Allan G. 1993. *The Protocol of the Gods: A Study of the Kasuga Cult in Japanese History*. Berkeley, CA: University of California Press.

Grapard, Allan G. 1999. "Religious Practices." In Donald H. Shively and William H. McCullough (eds.), *The Cambridge History of Japan*, vol. 2: *Heian Japan*, 517–575. Cambridge: Cambridge University Press.

Hakeda, Yoshito S., trans. 1972. *Kukai and His Major Works*. New York: Columbia University Press. 1972.

Hayami Tasuku. 1975. *Heian kizoku shakai to bukkyō*. Tokyo: Yoshikawa Kōbunkan.

Hayami Tasuku. 1996. *Zusetsu Nihon bukkyō no rekishi: Heian jidai*. Tokyo: Kōsei Shuppansha.

Holcombe, Charles, trans. 1999. "The Confucian Monarchy of Nara Japan." In George J. Tanabe, Jr. (ed.), *Religions of Japan in Practice*, 293–298. Princeton, NJ: Princeton University Press.

Holcombe, Charles. 2001. *The Genesis of East Asia, 221 B.C.–A.D. 907*. Honolulu: Association for Asian Studies and University of Hawai'i Press.

Kashiwahara, Yusen, and Koyu Sonoda, eds. 1994. *Shapers of Japanese Buddhism*. Trans. Gaynor Sekimori. Tokyo: Kōsei Publishing Co.

Katsuura Noriko. 1995. *Onna no shinjin: Tsuma ga shukke shita jidai*. Tokyo: Heibonsha.

Katsuura Noriko 2003. *Kodai, chūsei no josei to bukkyō*. Tokyo: Yamakawa Shuppansha.

Kawahashi, Noriko. 2006. "Gender Issues in Japanese Religions." In Paul L. Swanson, and Clark Chilson (eds.), *Nanzan Guide to Japanese Religions*, 323–335. Honolulu: University of Hawai'i Press.

Kiyota, Minoru. 1978. *Shingon Buddhism: Theory and Practice*. Los Angeles and Tokyo: Buddhist Books International.

Ko, Dorothy, JaHyun Kim Haboush, and Joan R. Piggott, eds. 2003. *Women and Confucian Cultures in Premodern China, Korea, and Japan*. Berkeley, CA: University of California Press.

Kornicki, Peter F. 1998. *The Book in Japan: A Cultural History From the Beginnings to the Nineteenth Century*. Leiden: Brill.

Miller, Alan L. 1971. "Ritsuryō Japan: The State as Liturgical Community." *History of Religions* 11 (1): 98–124.

Mitsuhashi Tadashi. 2000. *Heian jidai no shinkō to shūkyō girei*. Tokyo: Zoku Gunsho Ruijū Kansei Kai.

Naoki, Kojiro. 1993. "The Nara State." In Delmer M. Brown (ed.) *The Cambridge History of Japan*, vol. 1: *Ancient Japan*, 221–260. Cambridge: Cambridge University Press.

Nishiguchi Junko. 1987. *Onna no chikara: Kodai no josei to bukkyō*. Tokyo: Heibonsha.

Piggott, Joan R., ed. 2005. *Capital and Countryside in Japan, 300-1180: Japanese Historians Interpreted in English*. Ithaca, NY: East Asia Program, Cornell University.

Reischauer, Edwin O. trans. 1955a. *Ennin's Diary: The Record of a Pilgrimage to China in Search of the Law*. New York: Ronald Press.

Reischauer, Edwin O. 1955b. *Ennin's Travels in T'ang China*. New York: Ronald Press.

Saitō, Enshin, trans. 1992. *Jikaku Daishi Den: The Biography of Jikaku Daishi Ennin*. Tokyo: Sankibō Busshorin Inc.

Sakaehara Towao. 2000. *Nara jidai no shakyō to dairi*. Tokyo: Hanawa Shobō.

Shively, Donald H., and William H. McCullough, eds. 1999. *The Cambridge History of Japan*, vol. 2: *Heian Japan*. Cambridge: Cambridge University Press.

Sueki Fumihiko. 1995. *Heian shoki Bukkyō shisō no kenkyū: Annen no shisō keisei o chūshin to shite*. Tokyo: Shunjūsha.

Sueki Fumihiko *et al.*, eds. 2010. *Nihon Bukkyō no kiso* (Shin Ajia bukkyōshi 11, Nihon 1). Tokyo: Kōsei Shuppansha.

Swanson, Paul L., and Clark Chilson, eds. 2006. *Nanzan Guide to Japanese Religions*. Honolulu: University of Hawai'i Press.

Takagi Yutaka. 1988. *Bukkyōshi no naka no nyonin*. Tokyo: Heibonsha.

Tamura Enchō. 1996. *Zusetsu Nihon bukkyō no rekishi: Asuka, Nara jidai*. Tokyo: Kōsei Shuppansha.

Tanabe, George J., Jr., and Willa Jane Tanabe, eds. 1989. *The Lotus Sūtra in Japanese Culture*. Honolulu: University of Hawai'i Press.

Tsutsui, William M., ed. 2007. *A Companion to Japanese History*. Oxford: Blackwell.

Weinstein, Stanley. 1974. "The Beginnings of Esoteric Buddhism in Japan: The Neglected Tendai Tradition." *Journal of Asian Studies* 34 (1): 177–191.

Weinstein, Stanley. 1999. "Aristocratic Buddhism." In Donald H. Shively and William H. McCullough (eds.), *The Cambridge History of Japan*, vol. 2: *Heian Japan*, 449–516. Cambridge: Cambridge University Press.

Yamasaki Taiko. 1988. *Shingon: Japanese Esoteric Buddhism*. Trans. Richard and Cynthia Peterson. Boston: Shambhala.

Yamashita Yumi. 1999. *Shōsōin monjo to shakyōsho no kenkyū*. Tokyo: Yoshikawa Kōbunkan.

Yiengpruksawan, Mimi Hall. 1998. "The Legacy of Buddhist Art in Nara." In Michael R. Cunningham (ed.), *Buddhist Treasures from Nara*, 1–34. Cleveland, OH: The Cleveland Museum of Art.

Yoshida Kazuhiko, Katsuura Noriko, and Nishiguchi Junko, eds. 1999. *Nihonshi no naka no josei to bukkyō*. Kyoto: Hōzōkan.

3

Early Medieval Buddhism (950–1300): The Dawn of Medieval Society and Related Changes in Japanese Buddhist Culture

Middle Heian- and Late Heian-Period Buddhism (950–1185)

The mid Heian period can be identified with the ritual and political consolidation of the Heian royal court around 950, with the onset of Northern Fujiwara House dominance of governmental and cultural life in the capital of Heiankyō (Kyoto). All of the major cultural features common to the royal court had developed by that time. So well ensconced were these features that most, with the exception of politics based on the regent-chancellor system (*sekkan seiji*), continued in some form until at least the end of the Kamakura period (1192–1333).[1]

This chapter addresses the first part of the medieval era by examining a series of topics that illustrate the relationship between these larger cultural changes and central concerns of Buddhists. Finally, we examine the appearance of what are referred to as "new Kamakura" lineages of Buddhism. Commonly interpreted, until recently, as focused uniquely on the proselytization to the populace and a related simplification of Buddhist teachings and practice, we consider the new consensus among scholars that establishment Buddhism – sometimes called exo-esoteric Buddhism (*kenmitsu bukkyō*) – included many of the presumably novel features of the new Kamakura schools.

A Cultural History of Japanese Buddhism, First Edition. William E. Deal and Brian Ruppert.
© 2015 William E. Deal and Brian Ruppert. Published 2015 by John Wiley & Sons, Ltd.

Annual court ceremonies and envisioning
a Buddhist ritual calendar

Pivotal organizational and philosophical changes begin to arise in the royal court with the consolidation of the annual court ceremonies (*nenjū gyōji*), particularly those corresponding to the 859 advent of the regent-chancellor system.[2] Beginning that year (859), Buddhist ordinands were assigned to pray for the salvation of the *kami*, even at great shrines like Kamo and Kasuga. It is of particular note that the Mt. Hiei monk Eryō, in his petition for those ordinands, was the first to employ the explanation that the *kami* were "traces" (*suijaku*) of the Buddha (*Nihon sandai jitsuroku*, Jōgan 1/8/28, 37), a discourse that would be incorporated into so-called essence-trace (*honji-suijaku*) discussions, which became increasingly prominent over the course of the medieval era.

The effort by noble families to acquire diverse ritual and ceremonial knowledge became particularly clear over the course of the tenth century. Sovereigns (*tennō*) and Fujiwara nobles alike began to write journals (*nikki*) and their families began to compile ritual protocols (*gishiki sho, nenjūgyōji sho*; Matsuzono 2006). As one scholar noted:

> It goes without saying that the personal journals which suddenly became extremely common among the court nobility from the mid Heian period onwards were written for the purposes of aiding, as memos or references, their participation in court rites and official duties. (Hashimoto 1976: 351)[3]

For example, the effort to acquire and transmit Buddhist ritual knowledge within the court is reflected by the extensive representations of Buddhist belief and practice in Minamoto no Tamenori's (d. 1011) didactic tale collection on Buddhism called *Sanbō'e* (The Illustrated Three Jewels), which he completed for tonsured Princess Sonshi in 986. Tamenori's discussions of the Japanese Buddhist monastic community are specifically focused on annual and seasonal Buddhist rites in Japan (*Sanbō'e*, 132–224).[4] His writings, which are roughly contemporary with court families' earliest manuals of annual ceremonial court protocol, make it clear that nobles' knowledge of Buddhism and interest in its ceremonies developed at the same time they accumulated bodies of ritual protocol, both Buddhist and non-Buddhist, for use at the royal court. The rites with specified sites of practice are as shown in Table 3.1. The list indicates that Tamenori had knowledge of a whole range of rites performed in the temples of Heiankyō, Nara, and surrounding areas. It also suggests that Tamenori had particular interest in rites conducted at Enryakuji (Mt. Hiei), headquarters of the Tendai lineages.

Tellingly, only *one* rite is esoteric Buddhist in character – and it is specifically devoted to a discussion of the consecration directed at lay practitioners (*kechien kanjō*). In this way, Tamenori depicts a whole series of Buddhist ceremonies that might be described as "popular" in the sense of broad, trans-institutional rites. While veneration, together with related repentance, expiation of transgression, and avoidance of calamity, seem to have been the most prominent goals, many of the rituals presumably bring together aristocrats of the court and temple practitioners.

Table 3.1 Annual and seasonal Buddhist rites in Japan (from Minamoto no Tamenori's *Sanbō'e*)

Rite	Month	Site
Repentance Rites (*senbō*)	1st	Mt. Hiei (*Hokke senbō*, seasonal)
Repentance Rites (*keka*)	2nd	Sai'in [Junna'in], *Anan keka*
Nirvana Assembly		Yamashinadera (Kōfukuji)
Lecture Assembly (Denbō'e)	3rd	Sūfukuji (Shiga, twice annually)
		(~ "Bodhisattva Maitreya Assembly")
Sūtra of Superlative Kings		Yakushiji
Lecture Assembly		
Lotus Sūtra Assembly		Takaosanji (Jingoji)
Flower Garland Sūtra Assembly		Hokkeji
Myriad Lamps Assembly		Yakushiji
Buddha Relics Assembly	4th	Mt. Hiei
Great Perfection of Wisdom Sūtra Assembly		Daianji
Bodhisattva Precepts		Mt. Hiei
Bodhisattva Precepts	5th	Hatsusedera (Hasedera)
Thousand Flowers Assembly	6th	Tōdaiji
Bodhisattva Mañjuśrī Assembly	7th	(Tōji, Saiji, and realm; food for poor)
Uninterrupted *Nenbutsu* Recitation	8th	Mt. Hiei
Liberation of Beings (Fish, Fowl)		Iwashimizu Hachimangū (Shrine)
Bond-Establishing Consecration	9th	Mt. Hiei (+ Tōji/Hosshōji)
Vimalakīrti Sūtra Lecture Assembly	10th	Yamashinadera (Kōfukuji)
Eight *Lotus Sūtra* Lectures Assembly	11th	Kumano (Shrines)
Commemorative Ten *Lotus Sūtra* Lectures Assembly		Mt. Hiei

Although Tamenori's focus is primarily on aristocrats, he attempts to incorporate other parts of the populace within his narrative, especially as objects of giving. Indeed, his discussion of the Mañjuśrī Assembly (J. Monju'e) invokes the intimate karmic relationship between beings as well as the layered and mysterious character of the Buddhist cosmos in order to legitimize his call to charity.

These folks [the poor, elderly, and ill persons present] may be the manifestations of holy ones or Buddhas of the ten directions, so do not look lightly upon them. All are the [reborn] forms of fathers and mothers of previous eras, and so you should have compassion [for them]. Thus the Venerable Śākyamuni [Buddha] taught that they are a "field of merit" [as an object of giving, establishing thereby good roots (merit)] and Vimalakīrti [Jōmyō] divided his jewels [as a gift] for them. (*Sanbō'e* no. 3.23, 200)[5]

For Tamenori and, presumably, most of those around him, belief in karma and rebirth was a given. Assumptions about the fluidity of the universe, illustrated through teachings of emptiness and expedient devices in works like the *Vimalakīrti sūtra* (J. *Yuimagyō*), also made for an implicit understanding that fellow beings are not necessarily what they seem. Regardless of the criticisms of the lower class made by some court figures (e.g., Sei Shōnagon, b. ca. 966), even class differences were ultimately as empty of substantiality as the persons who embodied them.

Here we begin to see limitations of the "rhetoric of decadence" some scholars attribute to "old" Buddhism. This critical apparatus assumes that practitioners of "old" Buddhism were completely unconcerned with those outside their walls, and that "religious heroes" emerged in reaction to such elitism, acting on behalf of the salvation of the general populace (Payne 1998: 2–11; Stone 1999: 100).

The rising prominence of Tendai lineages and related shifts in Heian Buddhism

In the mid Heian period, the major Tendai temples at Mt. Hiei and Onjōji (Miidera) profited from the combination of their locale in the mountains, comparative geographical proximity to the capital, and close relationships with leading nobles such as those in the Northern Fujiwara House, the family that dominated court politics from the mid ninth to mid eleventh centuries.

Ryōgen (912–985) was in many ways a paradigmatic example of a monk who negotiated the difficult path to clerical success, parlaying personal skills and alliances with powerful figures of his era to his benefit. Following his impressive performance at a debate on the occasion of the Yuima'e assembly at the major Hossō-lineage monastery of Kōfukuji in Nara (clan temple of the Fujiwaras), Ryōgen became known to members of the court. Soon thereafter, Fujiwara no Tadahira (880–949) and Fujiwara no Morosuke (908–960) became his patrons in exchange for a variety of ritual services. Two of the sons of Morosuke were ordained under Ryōgen. One, Jinzen (943–990), eventually became head of the complex at Hiei, where he not only engaged in regular rituals on behalf of his family, but also received large private donations of estates directed to monastic halls he controlled. In this way, Jinzen amassed many estates and effectively directed their earnings to halls where members of his family would, ideally, continue to reside as monks in perpetuity (Groner 2002: 192–198; Stone 1999: 111).

From the late Kamakura period onward, the monastic halls that Jinzen and other sons of noble or royal background controlled in the major temples would become referred to as *monzeki*, which might be translated as "aristocratic cloisters" (Nagamura 1989: 191). The monks as a whole, when seen in terms of the larger temple administration, were typically referred to as the "temple lineage" (*jike*). However, their varying modes of independence were guaranteed by their concurrent residence within a particular hall (*inge*) or aristocratic cloister. Nagamura Makoto has recently clarified that prior to any particular association with class, *monzeki* signified other important monastic features. From the eleventh century onward, its meaning could have included a Dharma lineage (*hōryū*) and the social body of believers who constituted such a lineage (*montei*) and, from at least the Kamakura period, their particular hall of residence (Nagamura 2000: 58–62). Identification of the term *monzeki* with the abbot of the cloister only developed in later eras.

Meanwhile, undoubtedly in part in connection with the patronage of the Tendai lineages by the Northern Fujiwara House, the *Lotus Sūtra* was the central object of veneration and more general ritual concern at court. The *Lotus Sūtra* was already prominently featured in the *Sanbō'e*, which included a discussion of the Eight *Lotus Sūtra* Lectures Assembly at Kumano. It is important here to emphasize that it mentioned the presence not only of lay aristocrats at the assembly but also of "monks" in "deer skin," which suggests the presence of mountain ascetics (*shugenja*), who might be connected to the category of ambiguous religious practitioners called "holy ones" (*hijiri*), discussed in the next section. Indeed, faith in the *Lotus Sūtra* was clearly now not limited to the aristocracy since it had been disseminated to other groups in the populace. For example, the tales in the collection *Honchō hokke genki* (hereafter *Hokke genki*; *Accounts of Lotus Sūtra Anomalies in Japan*) (ca. 1041–1044) depict such anomalies from the standpoint of the so-called "*Lotus* [*Sūtra*] holy ones" (*Hokke hijiri* or *jikyōja*), which makes it clear that such faith spread across classes over the course of the mid Heian period onwards.[6] Indeed, these figures deployed rhetoric of the *Lotus Sūtra* to legitimate their position within the evolving Buddhist communities of their day (Deal 1993: 267–268).

Over the course of the middle to late Heian period, just as groups of holy ones gradually occupied areas of the landscape – albeit often also associated with the monastic complexes – Tendai lineages, like those of Shingon and, increasingly, lineages in Nara temples as well, splintered along lines of distinct ritual and textual transmission; the development occurred contemporaneously with the increase of lineage halls and aristocratic cloisters, and was surely related to it. The writing of Dharma-lineage charts (*kechimyaku*) and other transcriptions of oral transmissions, along with other commentarial works of both Tendai and Shingon monasteries, seem to have arisen, at least in part, in connection with this historical context.

For example, although divisions between the so-called Eshin and Danna lineages may not date to as early a period as suggested by Tendai traditions – from Genshin and his fellow student of Ryōgen, Kaku'un (953–1007) – the next generation, particularly led by Kaku'un's disciple Kōkei (977–1049), seems to have actively formulated a fully developed esoteric Tendai (Taimitsu) ritual system, identified with his "Valley Lineage" (Tani no ryū). Kōkei, in particular, has been described as "a pioneer in the development of secret oral transmission" (Stone 1999: 109–110).

Monks of Tendai lineages in this connection introduced more and more commentarial discourses related to "original enlightenment" (*hongaku*), which were originally rooted in Chinese commentarial works that concerned the dichotomy between gradual or ascending approaches to the Buddhist path and those based on initial acknowledgment of the practitioner's inherently awakened status as "buddha" (Stone 1999). Shingon lineages, for their part, increasingly produced ritual texts and commentaries that went beyond the ritual procedures (J. *giki*) of continental esoteric Buddhism; the new ritual works especially took the form of so-called *shidai* (*shidai sho*) ritual protocols. From the late eleventh century onward, rites such as those focused on the veneration of wish-fulfilling jewels (e.g., Nyohō sonshō hō) were introduced – and, as in Tendai, newly written ritual handbooks and commentaries, which were typically referred to as "notes" (*shōmotsu*) (Kamikawa 2008: 269–316; Nagamura 2000: 191–198).

The advent of Pure Land Buddhist discourses and practices

Throughout the early medieval era, monks in temples of the capital of Heiankyō were interested in activities beyond the study of the *Lotus Sūtra* and esoteric Buddhist practices. One of these interests was the practice of the *nenbutsu*, that is, contemplating on and, particularly, chanting the name of the Buddha Amida (Skt. Amitābha) in hopes of birth in his Pure Land (J. Gokuraku Jōdo; Skt. Sukhāvatī) at the time of death – or of enabling unsettled spirits to find peace. This was first prominent in temples with Tendai lineages. Although there were clearly esoteric Buddhist elements in the Mt. Hiei monk Genshin's *Ōjōyōshū* (Essentials for Birth in the Pure Land; 985), the work featured as its main theme the reasons for and means by which one can be born in the Pure Land. The text had significant influence on the aristocracy.

Meanwhile, semi-independent clerics increasingly inhabited areas adjacent to and sometimes distant from the major Buddhist monasteries. They were referred to by a variety of loose titles – sometimes as *shōnin* (true ones, holy ones), sometimes as *hijiri* (holy ones). Another version of these was the so-called "*[Lotus] sūtra* upholder" (*jikyōja*) that appeared in sundry Buddhist literary and other records of the era. Perhaps influenced in part by the precedent of the ancient figure Gyōki (668–749), such figures typically had much more interaction with those in the general populace than other monks. They were commonly associated with one or the other of the major temple complexes so they seem often to have not been completely independent figures (Kikuchi 2007: 54–55).

The most prominent of these in the mid Heian period seems to have been the "holy one of the marketplace" (*ichi no hijiri*), Kūya (alt. Kōya; 903–972), who was also sometimes called "Amida hijiri." After having wandered through several nearby provinces and presumably engaged in good works (*sazen*) there, Kūya entered Heiankyō in the late 930s and went on to receive the official precepts at the main Tendai lineage center, Enryakuji (Mt. Hiei); he continued to be known by the name Kūya, which was actually an earlier non-official name. He seems to have remained in the capital most of the time, promoting the practice of calling upon Amida Buddha, while also leading so-called Buddhist cooperatives (*zenchishiki*) in the construction of and services to images like that of the Bodhisattva Kannon, especially in connection with pestilence that plagued the city (Takei 1994: 846a–846c). Kūya made a vow to produce a 600-fascicle copy of the *Greater Perfection of Wisdom Sūtra* (J. *Daihannyakyō*), and spent more than 10 years working on it until its fruition, a relatively early example of an individual making a vow to undertake such a substantial scriptural-copying enterprise (Hori 1971: 52–65).

Since even the early ninth century, veneration of prominent bodhisattvas such as Kannon, Miroku (Skt. Maitreya) and Jizō, and sometimes of resident holy ones or mountain ascetics, seems to have become common among aristocrats and the populace in the area in or near the capital and, presumably, in some outlying regions. Apparently, for many in the aristocracy and in the larger populace, Buddhist practice had little to do with scholastic study or participation in a particular school of Buddhism but more with the perceived powers of divinities in specific sites – such as at Kumano, where multiple deities, identified as local manifestations of Buddhist figures like the Pure Land Buddha and Kannon, were prominent objects of pilgrimage and veneration throughout premodern times (Moerman 2006). *Sanbō'e*, which we considered earlier, devoted a section to the performance of the Eight *Lotus Sūtra* Lectures Assembly (Hokke "hakkō'e") and took note that it was conducted before the deities of Kumano – perhaps a reference to their position as "traces" (*suijaku*) of Buddhist figures (*Sanbō'e* no. 3.29, 216–218; Kamens 1988: 357–359).

Moreover, it seems that an initial work of didactic tales outlining the spiritual anomalies of the bodhisattva Jizō, *Jizō bosatsu reigen ki* (Account of Spiritual Anomalies of the Bodhisattva Jizō), was completed in a very early period by an Onjōji (Tendai) monk named Jitsu'e (fl. 1033).[7] Thus tale collections draw our attention to the rapidly increasing interest in Pure Land or related practice, especially among aristocrats of the late tenth century onwards. Although the tale collection *Hokke genki* made clear the broad interest in the *Lotus Sūtra* amongst both clerics and the wider population, it was the novel genre of "hagiographies of birth in the Pure Land" (*ōjōden*) that both illustrated and promoted Amidist practice among lay and monastic aristocrats. The appearance of this genre marked a new moment in the history of Japanese Buddhism. Moreover, lay aristocrats of Heiankyō spearheaded its development (Obara 2007: 222).[8]

Figure 3.1 Jizō Bodhisattva image, circa Edo period, Sanzen'in temple, Ōhara. Photograph by Brian Ruppert.

While Amida's Pure Land was by far the most common object of such birth in the early collections, later collections often depicted an individual's veneration of multiple Buddhas and bodhisattvas – commonly in connection with deathbed practices (typically along with Amida, e.g., *Shūi ōjōden* no. 1.23, 598b; no. 3.9, 616b). As Jacqueline I. Stone has noted, these last hours of life took on new importance for Pure Land believers of the early medieval era. Although among many there was clearly hope for Amida's descent to greet (*raigō*) the dying, many others feared that even a single deluded or distracted thought – away from the Buddha – by a virtuous person in her or his final moment might lead to bad rebirth. Given this anxiety, which became clearly manifest in aristocratic society from the tenth century onward, Tendai clerics and, soon after, monks of other lineages produced writings promoting deathbed rites (*rinjū gyōgi*) they saw as effective in avoiding the problem and ensuring good rebirth. As early as the mid Kamakura period, members of some "single-practice" schools (e.g., the Chinzei line of the Jōdo lineage) also began to adopt such practices, as concerns with the death transition transcended lineage distinction or distinctions such as "exoteric" and "esoteric" (Stone 2008: 66–88).[9]

The prominent literatus Ōe no Masafusa (1041–1111) compiled *Zoku honchō ōjōden* (Continued Hagiographies of Pure Land Births in the Realm; ca. 1101 ~ 1104) and other aristocrats continued the practice of compiling hagiographical accounts of

Pure Land birth. One of the related works Masafusa compiled was the *Honchō shinsen den* (Hagiographies of Hermits with Spiritual Powers in the Realm; ca. 1102 ~ 1109), which depicted figures who had engaged successfully in all manner of practices; although we might associate use of the term *shinsen* (Ch. *shen-xian*) with the continental immortals tradition, almost all of the accounts of the work are of figures directly affiliated with Buddhist institutions or practices. Thus even notions of long life had an intimate connection with Buddhism in Masafusa's day, a discursive and practical link often associated with the practices of mountain ascetics (*shugenja*) or so-called "mountain beliefs" (*sangaku shinkō*; Inoue 1974: 740).

Meanwhile, by the early medieval era, Kūkai clearly stood as a unique figure apotheosized, like Prince Shōtoku, in Japanese aristocratic society. How did Kūkai come to be seen as being in meditation (*nyūjō shinkō*) on Mt. Kōya – his residence in his later years – and how was this related to evolving associations between death, mountains, and Buddhist sacred realms like Amida's Pure Land or the future Buddha Maitreya's Tuṣita Heaven? Undoubtedly, works like the so-called *Twenty-Five Article Last Testament* of Kūkai (*Nijūgokajō go-yuigō*, ca. mid 10th century; T. 77, no. 2431)[10] and Fujiwara no Michinaga's (966–1027) pilgrimage to Kōya (*Nihon kiryaku*, Jian 3.10.17, 260) reflected important symbolic associations of Kūkai with Mt. Kōya, particularly given its character as his resting place.

It was, however, particularly the hagiographies of Kūkai – the so-called *Kōbō Daishi den* – that seem to have represented the master in new ways. For example, Saisen's (1025–1115) *Daishi go-nyūjō kanketsu ki* (Account of Kōbō Daishi's Ongoing Meditation; ca. late eleventh century) is an early depiction of Kūkai in continuing meditation at Kōya. In particular, it is the first work to offer an argument for the *nyūjō* status of Kōbō Daishi by explaining why he took that form. Using a *mondō* dialogue format, Saisen teaches that, first, Daishi takes the *nyūjō* form to benefit sentient beings, explaining that it is like the discussion in the *Golden Light Sūtra* where Śākyamuni Buddha tells Ānanda that sentient beings should do obeisance to his relics to requite their debt to his body – so beings should have the opportunity to venerate Daishi's body on Kōya in order to repay their deep debt for Daishi's practice and transmission. The second reason that Daishi takes the *nyūjō* form is to enable monastics, laymen, and laywomen to plant good roots (*zenkon*) through engaging in esoteric Buddhist practices at Kōya (117a–120b). Later, Kakuban (1095–1144), who seems to have been influenced by Saisen, would go on to not only establish a new line within Shingon and to promote Pure Land practice; he would also, like Saisen, promote lore about and study of Kūkai and his works (Van der Veere 2000).

Kami, Buddhas, and sacred space

Even a cursory glance at the extant works from early medieval Japan suggests that while people inside and outside the capital as well as in other regions saw *kami* and Buddhas as somehow distinct, they also understood them as intimately related to each other. As we saw in Chapter 1, the Buddhas seem to have first been seen as a form of *kami* by some members of the ancient court – foreign or continental (Mori 2003: 28). And yet the tensions over a perceived "threat" from the newly arrived Buddhas that arose in the ancient court are well known, and ritual distinctions such as those manifested explicitly in the seven-day series of banquets of each New Year followed by seven days of Buddhist rites (Mi-sai'e, Go-Shichinichi mishiho, Taigen hō) in the Heian period attest to the fact that Buddhist ceremonies were recognized as distinct from non-Buddhist ones.[11]

In Japan, *kami* and Buddhas – especially bodhisattvas – were also typically associated with specific places and, sometimes, the very same sites.[12] Indeed, although there has been a tendency among some scholars to suggest that the essence of Japanese religion can be found in the mountains, others have more recently drawn attention to the "fluid character" (*ryūdōsei*) of life surrounded by mountainous topography with intermittent influences from the continent as a prime component contributing to the development of religious beliefs and ascetic practices (Kikuchi 2011: 11–16). The most prominent site of a *kami* who was somehow also a Buddhist divinity was originally Usa on the southern island of Kyūshū, where Usa Hachimangū enshrined a *kami* described as the "great Bodhisattva Hachiman" (Hachiman daibosatsu) in a Council of State decree of 798 (Itō 2003: 73, 103ff.) and which seems to have been viewed by the early ninth century as a mausoleum housing the spirit of the sovereign Ōjin: "This great [Usa Hachiman] Bodhisattva is thus the august spirit of the retired sovereign" (Council of State order, dated 816, *Tōdaiji yōroku*, 117–118).

The construction of Buddhist temples within certain major shrines (*jingūji*) and related offering of sutra-recitation by monks to *kami* there were undertaken from the eighth century onward, particularly given the notion that *kami* were seen as karmic beings subject to rebirth and suffering.[13] Moreover, novel private organs of the royal family, such as royal chamberlains (*kurōdo*), dominance of the court by the Northern Fujiwara House, and its "royal court" (*ōchō*) system of governance developed hand-in-hand with a streamlining of court shrine patronage. Sets of decreasing numbers of shrines associated with the royal house became the direct objects of its largess (Breen and Teeuwen 2010: 41). Although the accessional rites included offerings to as many as 57 shrines throughout the land (Ruppert 2000), a 22-shrine set of the capital region rose to clear prominence over the course of the eleventh century (Grapard 1988).[14]

Historically, it is clear that by the late tenth century, mountain ascetics of some sort resided in Kumano and, indeed, the *kami* of Kumano were increasingly represented as local manifestations of specific Buddhas and Bodhisattvas. The essence of the *kami* of the main shrine seems now to have been seen by many as the Pure Land Buddha Amida, and those of the *kami* of the other two shrines were seen as the Healing Buddha (Yakushi) and the Thousand-Armed (Senju) Kannon; the three were together often called Kumano Sansho Gongen, a term indicating their condition as manifestations of Buddhist divinities. Among these three, the site of the *kami* of

Nachi Falls was seen by many in the Heian period aristocracy as the Pure Land of Kannon (Fudaraku Jōdo) and, by the twelfth century, that of the main shrine as Amida's Pure Land. Given notions that pilgrimage gains one access to religious merit or purification, aristocrats and sovereigns increasingly visited Kumano and other areas such as Yoshino (Kinpusen), another major site of belief and ascetic practice along the Ōmine mountain range. Pilgrimages by nobility and, subsequently, warriors and other landholders, were so common to Kumano by the early thirteenth century that the mountain ascetics increasingly served as guides (*sendatsu*) to its sacred sanctuaries (Miyake 2005: 65).

Moreover, the Eight *Lotus Sūtra* Lectures rite, as practiced at Kumano, seems to have been undertaken for reasons distinct from those for the rite when it was practiced in the capital: the Kumano rite was undertaken to expiate transgressions of locals for whom killing was a profession, rather than being focused primarily on transfer of karmic merit to deceased loved ones (Moerman 2006: 57). Indeed, *Sanbō'e*'s depiction of the practice, mentioned earlier, noted that no distinction was made between elite or lowly, young or old, in the audience at the Kumano shrines, suggesting, as Abe Yasurō has emphasized, that the divinities were not only perceived as helping expiate wrongdoing but were also accessible to people at all levels of society (Abe 2001: 208–224).

Figure 3.2　Nachi Falls, with Torii gate in foreground, Kumano. Photograph by Brian Ruppert.

Belief that Kumano was a site for religious practice, particularly in preparation for the afterlife, was so powerful that multiple groups of practitioners developed early on – with varying orientations. We know, for example, that from the late eleventh century on the retired sovereign appointed Buddhist monks to administer three organizations in the area of the Kumano shrines: shrine priests, Buddhist monks, and mountain ascetics. At first, the monk selected was typically the abbot of the Tendai temple Onjōji (Miidera) and much later that of Shōgo'in in Kyoto. By this time, the last of these groups, known especially for their ascetic practices (*tosō*, to cast aside attachment to clothing, food, and lodging) especially developed an orientation that was informed by Buddhism, *kami* worship, and related mountain beliefs – including Daoist hermit beliefs. Regularly entering into the mountains (*nyūbu*), they drew upon examples of ancient mountain ascetics' worship of the powers of *kami* while at the same time incorporating the powerful practices of esoteric Buddhism (*mikkyō*) and of traditional Mahayana ("exoteric") Buddhism, especially that associated with the *Lotus Sūtra* (Miyake 2005: 62–65).

A related goal of pilgrimage in the era was also to meet the *shōjin* – the living body – of Buddhas or Bodhisattvas, even *kami*. Indeed, these *shōjin-no-hotoke* (living Buddhas) were sometimes identified with *kami*. In such a case, the Buddha was seen to be a celestial figure who took presence as a living body in the form of a *kami*, thereby evoking so-called *honji-suijaku* correspondences – between the original ground (one or other Buddha or Bodhisattva) and his local trace (Satō 1997: 67). Sarah J. Horton, in her study of these "living Buddhist statues," takes note of claims that *kami* worship may have influenced notions, for example, of secret Buddhas (*hibutsu*), but makes it clear that Buddhism and "Shintō" are "inextricably inter-twined" – indeed, emphasizing that "the idea of representing *kami* in the form of statues occurred under Buddhist influence in the first place" (Horton 2007: 169).

In all of these cases, pilgrims increasingly approached the *kami* and Buddhist divinities. *Kami* and Buddhas were associated with each other at most of the major pilgrimage sites, often in connection with some layered discourse moving between local appearance and its underlying, often hidden, meaning. Indeed, symbolic discourses such as of *honji-suijaku*, royal glory, religious faith, and memorialization informed pilgrimage to the sites of *kami* and Buddhas – witnessed even in literary diaries such as that of court lady Go-Fukakusa'in Nijō (Abe 1999: 64–65; Abe 2001: 187–188).

Moreover, scholars have drawn attention to the complex interaction between the *kami* (*shin, jin*) and Buddhas in major complexes such as Tōdaiji, the halls of which often enshrined not only Buddhas but also protective deities. Tōdaiji's Hokkedō Hall, for example, enshrined in its rear entryway (*ushirodo*) the deity Shukongōjin (= *kami*) as its secret Buddha (*hibutsu*) (Abe 1998b: 261).[15] A thirteenth-century docu-ment from Tōfukuji, now exclusively Rinzai Zen but originally conceived by the powerful noble Kujō Michi'ie (1193–1252) as a monastery featuring multiple

Buddhist lineages, describes the wood of an image of the cosmic Buddha Dainichi (Mahāvairocana) enshrined in Tōfukuji as having been taken from a pillar at Ise Shrine (Ogawa 2003: 186) – reinforcing the association between the *kami* at the royal family shrine there and the greatest of esoteric Buddhas.

Buddhist performance and the flowering of aesthetic traditions

The arts had long occupied an important part of Buddhist practice in the Japanese isles. In particular, arts seem to have thrived since they commonly represented, in one way or another, narratives or images from Buddhist works. The seminal beginning of "preaching with pictures" (*e-toki*) seems to have been in 931, when the abbot of Jōganji explained the eight phases of the historical Buddha's life to the prince-diarist and his brother (*Rihōō ki*, Jōhei 1.9.30, 57; Kaminishi 2006: 20). By 946, the former noble Tachibana no Aritsura (fl. 944–953) – now a monk – had completed the "praise portraits" (*gasan*) on the wall of the *Lotus Sūtra* Repentance Hall (Hokke zanmaidō) on Mt. Hiei. The site featured images of 31 ancestral masters of India, China, and Japan combined with strands of 4-character lines of praise. The images included not only a series of Tendai (Ch. Tiantai) monks but also esoteric Buddhist masters and Japanese figures like Prince Shōtoku (574 – ca. 622), the precepts master Ganjin (Ch. Jianzhen; 687–763), and the holy one-cum-great-archbishop Gyōki (668–749). A work said to be by the eminent Shingon lineage monk Ningai (951–1046) similarly includes written praises for 13 of its 36 figures of the 3 realms, 7 of which are taken directly from Tachibana's work, illustrating the latter's influence across lineage (Gotō 2002: 90–96, 200). There is no clear evidence that these were used in preaching, but the veneration of these images – perhaps including the reading of these praises – was clearly appropriated as part of Dharma assemblies (*hō'e*).

The complex interweaving of visual representation and the copying of scripture was perhaps most magnificently represented in the so-called "Enshrined Sutra of the Taira Family" (*Heike nōkyō*), an example of an elaborately decorated *Lotus Sūtra* installed at Itsukushima Shrine, placed there by the great warrior Taira no Kiyomori in 1164. This so-called "decorative sutra" (*sōshokukyō*) is remarkable not merely for the brilliance of its representation of *Lotus Sūtra* scenes from all of the major chapters of the work but also in its creative interweaving of scriptural text and visual image (Eubanks 2009: 224–226; Nara Kokuritsu Hakubutsukan 2005: 156).

Depictions of Pure Lands and similar realms in Amidist and other scriptures such as the *Flower Garland Sūtra* (J. *Kegonkyō*, *Avataṃsaka sūtra*) and esoteric Buddhist works and mandalas (Skt. *maṇḍala*; J. *mandara*) clearly formed important objects of visualization and imagination throughout East Asia. Three important early examples of Japanese temples established as simulacra of Amida's Pure Land were

Michinaga's Muryōju'in (hall of immeasurable life) at his Hōjōji, with nine images of Amida representing each level of birth within the Pure Land; the Amida Hall (now called Phoenix Hall) of the Byōdō'in (Uji, near Heiankyō), which was established by Michinaga's son, Yorimichi (992–1074), in 1052 near the graveyard of the clan; and the Konjikidō (Hall of gold) at Hiraizumi, where the "Fujiwara" warrior-kings of northern Honshū enshrined their mummified remains (Yiengpruksawan 1998: 122–142).

The elaboration of performative liturgy at Dharma assemblies from the late tenth century onward was a prominent feature of medieval Japanese Buddhist practice. Rites such as the Repentance Assembly (*keka'e*) at Michinaga's temple Hōjōji featured not only a different schedule of rites from what had previously been the case at temples like Tōdaiji but also increasingly elaborate music, dance, and other performance; by the Retired sovereigns Era, additional temples like the royal Hosshōji included major late-night banquets that included features such as Sarugaku entertainment, the origin of Nō (Noh) Drama. In other words, from the late tenth century onward, entertainment became a feature of the practice of the annual Repentance Assembly (Uejima 2010b: 236).

By the twelfth century, at Ninnaji and other major monasteries such as Kōfukuji, monks of the general assembly (*shuto*) – sometimes together with male youth attached to the temple – began to perform dances and music collectively referred to as celebratory *ennen* ("longevity-enhancing") arts. The monastic cloisters and other residential halls – sometimes used as temporary palaces for a sovereign's visit – often served as the sites of such performances, although major worship halls were also common. The ritual space used was, when recorded, commonly the rear entryway, which we saw in the context of Tōdaiji's Shukongōjin image above. From the thirteenth century, a distinct group of monks specializing in such arts, *yūsō* ("artistic monks"), developed in some Nara monasteries, under the control of the residential halls there. The *ennen* performances, such as that of the Flower Garland assembly (Kegon'e) at the Tōdaiji cloister Sonshō'in in 1212, sometimes included prominent arts of the day like *sarugaku* and *shirabyōshi* dances; they seem to have commonly celebrated the entrance of the presiding abbots at major Dharma assemblies, the latters' assumption of higher clerical status, or the attendance of a royal emissary at an assembly (Matsuo 1997: 42–59).

A number of the scriptures and ritual texts introduced to Japanese Buddhists either depicted the non-dual character of bodhisattva realization or instructed believers as to how such realization would occur in ritual performance. Earlier, we took note of this layered and "empty" character of the Mahayana universe as experienced by Japanese people particularly from the dawn of the early medieval period onward. The continental works that influenced this experience included, of course, the *Lotus Sūtra* – which tells us that the appearance of the historical Buddha was an expedient device (*hōben*) used by the Eternal Buddha to help aid ignorant sentient beings – but they also included a wide range of other works. The pilgrimage of the bodhisattva Sudhana (J. Zenzai dōji) in the *Flower Garland Sūtra* sets him out to study under multiple "friends" in the dharma (J. *zenchishiki*) – including women – who as more advanced bodhisattvas use all manner of devices to teach him. The text compares these devices used by the greater bodhisattva-teachers to magical creations that display the wondrous quality of states of bodhisattva realization while at the same time offering a representation of our world when properly understood – that is, as being marked by the absolute interpenetration of all psycho-physical phenomena (Skt. *dharmas*; J. *hō*).

In Heiankyō, in scenes of the major Buddha relics procession of the mid Heian period described in works like the historical tale *Eiga monogatari* (eleventh century), we see the assemblage of the Sudhana figure, the fabulous jewels associated with both Amida and the *Flower Garland Sūtra*, and performative ritual practice – all projected before the great Fujiwara no Michinaga (966–1027) and the nobles surrounding him:

> The august gallery stands were a magnificent sight! And on that day [of the procession of relics for the assembly] the sounds of the staffs and Sanskrit of more than 300 monks and so on, the various [aristocrats] who arranged their ceremonial dress magnificently, the initial arrival of the two palanquins [housing relics], the two fabulous *Sudhana* figures continuing to walk [together with others accompanying the palanquins] ... [– all were splendid...]

> At Gidarinji, where the regular boy attendants dressed the child dancers in magnificent ceremonial costumes, they danced in the front garden, which was polished like the Pure Land *Sukhāvatī* [of Amida], appearing covered with jewels ... One could only think that this was the Pure Land! (*Eiga monogatari* 2, 150–151)[16]

A spectacular sight, clearly: twin Sudhanas parading with Buddha relics on a route lined with trees covered in jewels for the occasion – and even the destination garden at Gidarinji covered in jewels as if it were the Pure Land.[17] With such performative examples, it is no wonder that, as we saw at Tōdaiji, major rites such as the Flower Garland assembly would eventually feature elaborate artistic performances.

At the beginning of the medieval era, it was not only such written stories and visual media that presented Buddhist narratives and depictions to people in the Japanese isles, since poets were increasingly incorporating Buddhist discourses into their own Japanese-sinic poetry ("Chinese poetry," *kanshi*) and Japanese poetry, *waka*. The writing of *waka* with Buddhist themes became particularly prominent from the late tenth century onward, when figures like Princess Senshi (964–1035) produced her work *Hosshin waka shū* (Collection of *Waka* of the Awakening Mind, 1012; Kamens 1990: 3–4). We might even compare the context within which such an early "Buddhist" *waka* work was written with that in which Tamenori wrote his *Sanbō'e* – for a young princess, thus in keeping with the tendency in the early medieval era to produce these works for particular individuals or one's immediate court milieu.[18]

Completed in the same period as Senshi's collection, the literatus Fujiwara no Kintō's (966–1041) compilation of Chinese and Japanese-sinic poetry as well as *waka*, *Wakan rōei shū* (Collection of Chinese and Japanese Court Performance poetry; ca. 1011–1012), constituted a great innovation in terms of poetry and poetry collections created in Japan. In particular, it not only brought together Chinese and Japanese versions of Chinese poetry into the same collection but also added *waka*, and so it synthesized what would have otherwise been primarily a continentally flavored work into a remarkable product of the early eleventh-century Japanese court that would influence a series of later works, including many Buddhist rites and themes. This work would become a textbook for calligraphy practice, and the practice of *rōei* performance poetry – combining *kanshi* poetry with court instrument music – would develop into lineages in the Fujiwara and Minamoto families; although the Minamoto lineage of *rōei* would survive longer, the Fujiwara form was central early on, and its influence can be seen in the Tendai and Shingon lineages of *rōei* practice, which amalgamated the court practice with Buddhist verses (Skt. *gātha*) and *shōmyō* temple music (*Wakan rōei shū*, "kaidai" 1965: 32–33).

At the same time, we must bear in mind that one of the undoubted motivations for such efforts to incorporate Buddhist concerns into poetry was the perceived tension between the Buddhist imperative to cast off all attachments and avoid falsity, on the one hand, and the seeming intoxication of those who made use of or found beauty in the linguistic arts, on the other. In continental East Asia, the concern dated at least to 839, when the great Tang poet Bojuyi (J. Haku Kyoi; 772–846) made an offering of his poems to a Buddhist treasury, asking that the act "transform the errors of 'wild words and adorning phrases' [Ch. *kuang-yan qi-yu*; J. *kyōgen kigo*] into cause for praising the vehicle of the Buddha and condition for turning the Dharma Wheel."[19] Although the poem would appear in *Wakan rōei shū* (*butsuji*, no. 588, 200), the most prominent early evidence of the impact of Bojuyi's poem in Japan is in the records concerning the Kangaku'e Assembly – the "Assembly of Learning" in which a group of university scholars and Tendai monks, with the intention of expiating the transgression of using "wild words and adorning phrases," met in Sakamoto at the edge of Mt. Hiei to listen to lectures on the *Lotus Sūtra*, contemplate the Pure Land Buddha Amida, and then write poems based on lines in the *Lotus*. *Sanbō'e* describes how the members of the assembly began the twice-yearly rite in 964 and, in addition to the practices we have just noted, chanted together the Bojuyi poem quoted above (*Sanbō'e* 3.14, 172–4; Kamens 1988: 295–298). The scholar-aristocrat Yoshishige no Yasutane (d. 1002), author of the earliest Pure Land birth tale collection, was a leader of the group and made allusions to the presumed problematic relationship between literary writing and the Buddhist path (e.g., *Honchō monzui* 13, 321).

"Women's literature" (*joryū bungaku*) and the related development of literary salons of the early medieval era constituted the other extremely prominent arena that reflected or resolved perceived tensions between Buddhist and literary acts. The earliest of the literary diaries written by a woman, *Kagerō nikki* (Gossamer Journal; ca. 974), was filled with the protagonist's concern about her attachments, belief in the sorrows associated with impermanence, and Buddhist belief. It was, however, with the appearance of *Genji monogatari* (Tale of Genji; ca. 1008) that women's literature brought not only the belief in Buddhism but also perceived tensions between Buddhism and fiction to the fore. Here, however, the problematic concerned not poetry, which was associated with both sexes, but the writing of prose vernacular literature, which was associated with women (*Genji monogatari*, 2: 432–3; *Tale of Genji* 2001: 461). Meanwhile, "Sugawara no Takasue's daughter" (b. 1008) described in her literary diary, *Sarashina nikki* (Sarashina Journal; ca. 1059+), her own acute attachment to tales and their tension with expectations to study Buddhist scriptures like the *Lotus Sūtra* (*Sarashina nikki*, 492–3; Morris 1989, 46–47). The concern with the presumed transgression of enjoying reading and writing tales became great enough within the court that, in the case of *Genji*'s Murasaki Shikibu (ca. 973 – ca. 1014), rites (Genji kuyō) were conducted on a semi-regular basis for her salvation from the twelfth century onward (Komine Kazuaki 2009: 475–490).

The literary salons established in women's circles undoubtedly had some influence on the broad range of those that developed over the twelfth and thirteenth centuries. We can take particular note of those which were held within monasteries, a striking innovation in the use of monks' quarters (*sōbō*) as sites of cultural interaction. Presumably, the *monzeki* cloisters and their immediate precursors on Mt. Hiei (e.g., Jinzen's "hall," or *inge*) and at Ninnaji (the royal "O'muro") constituted a natural source for interaction between lay and monastic believers, since families – noble or royal – controlled these and included both monastic and lay believers; thus with time such quarters more generally came to become independent from the larger monastery economically, a shift that occurred alongside the development of monastic lineages (*monryū*) and included inheritance of the quarter and its contents (Takahashi 2007: 20–21; Kuroda 1992: 118–130).[20]

We now understand that three main types of monks' quarters existed, including traditional monastic compound quarters (*garan* or *sanmen sōbō*), highly functional *inge* residential halls and similar separate halls (*shi'in*), and quarters within worship/practice halls (*sōbō*; Yamagishi 2004: 96). The monks' quarter was a realm in which monks both engaged in study of sacred works (*shōgyō*) and also interacted with other monks and lay outsiders. The Dharma Prince Shukaku's (1150–1202) Kita'in (an *inge*) was the site of the Ninnaji poetry circle (*kadan*), the members of which featured both monks and a wholes series of aristocrats, who came each month for *waka* meetings and musical gatherings (Minobe 2000: 273) and, clearly, Dharma assemblies

Figure 3.3   Entrance to traditional monastic cloister called Sonshō'in (Seigantoji temple) at Nachi, Kumano, currently also used for visitor lodging. Photograph by Brian Ruppert.

(*hō'e*) as well. When we consider these factors together with the extensive record of increasingly mobile performances by Shukaku and other monks of the era at assemblies in royal-vow temples (*goganji*; Yamagishi 2004: 36–93) and of their rites in aristocrats' palaces (Kamikawa 1998: 152–155), we realize all the more the evolving and intimate connection between monastic Buddhists and their lay supporters.

Clearly, cultural salons or enclaves such as that at Shukaku's cloister, or those of certain other mountain temples in the area near the capital, brought together monks and aristocrats (sometimes disillusioned with capital politics) to engage in conversations (*kōdan, zōtan*) over the course of the Kamakura period, and thus helped give rise over time to a variety of aesthetic lineages. Shukaku's *"kōdan"* salon apparently included not only eight of the most prominent Shingon monks of the day but also a series of Confucian scholars and a poet (Yamazaki 1981: 15–16; *Shinzoku kōdan ki*); even if we grant, as a prominent historian claims, that the record of their meeting is a mid Kamakura-period accretion (Gomi 2003: 207), it is clear that Shukaku was the leader of a major salon at Ninnaji O'muro. Shukaku, for example, was not only also the leader of the poetry circle at Ninnaji, but he was also the figure who commissioned the monk Shun'e (1113 – ca. 1180s) to compile his major personal poetry collection. Shun'e was the Tōdaiji monk whose personal quarters in Shirakawa

(Eastern Heiankyō), Karin'en, was the locus of a major poetry salon known for not only its attendance by luminaries like Fujiwara no Toshinari but also general participation by poets of lower status (Smits 2003: 213–216). Indeed, Shingon, Tendai and Nara cloisters had a great impact on the development of literary treatises and poetry houses (Minobe 2000: 273–274).

Shukaku's legacy is ultimately attributable to the broad range of works he wrote and collected. In particular, the breadth and character of the genres which he employed display the intersections between the religious and aesthetic worlds of the court in his day.[21] In terms of Buddhist music, Shukaku wrote manuals and was associated with the figure Fujiwara (Myōon'in) no Moronaga (1138–1192); Moronaga's eminent disciple Fujiwara no Takamichi (1166–1239), father of the original Biwa lineage, would spend his later years in Ninnaji. Shukaku also wrote protocols (*kojitsusho*) concerning not only esoteric Buddhist and monastic practice but also Chinese poetry, *waka*, string music, calligraphy, and ritual records (Abe 1998a).[22] During the same era, the powerful Tendai cleric Jien (1155–1225), son of a Fujiwara regent and younger brother of the noble Kujō Kanezane (1149–1207), was not only abbot of Enryakuji several times and rewarded some 30 times for his ritual services to the court: he was a famous poet, rhetorician, and author of the first treatise on Japanese history, *Gukan shō* (Personal Notes), who was also known for repeated practice of rites like the esoteric celestial ritual Shijōkōhō on behalf of the retired sovereign Go-Toba (Arichi 2006: 200–203; Sueki 2008: 274–284; Yamada 1989: 109–113). Jien indeed was such a great proponent of the Shijōkōhō, and commissioned the construction of a hall (1205) where it would be repeatedly performed for the retired sovereign; the hall had a close association with the *kami* of the Hie shrine at the foot of Hiei, based on the identification of celestial deities with the *kami* as well as with the Buddhas of Hiei.

Of course, performative practice, including Buddhist music, was not limited to the confines of traditional lineages and their temple complexes. As we saw earlier, there were figures like Kūya who, while often nominally affiliated with established temples, engaged in practices such as the *nenbutsu* publicly which over time included some kind of musical accompaniment. Evoking an image that developed of Kūya as having engaged in the "dancing *nenbutsu*" (*odori nenbutsu*) – dancing and chanting the *nenbutsu* with some version of gong or drum, typically – and perhaps also indebted to the Tendai monk Ryōnen's circulating *nenbutsu* (*yūzū nenbutsu*) practice, Ippen (1239–1290), to whom we will turn later, spread his ecstatic joy at assurance of Pure Land birth (and perhaps also promoted repose for the dead) by distributing amulets and circumambulating while dancing the *nenbutsu* with others (Hirota 1997: xxxix–xli). Likewise, mountain ascetics' use of prayer beads and conch shells might be interpreted not only as symbolic of the path to Buddhahood but also as performative and musical notation of their realization onto the ritualized landscape.

Ritual knowledge, transmission, and the increasing prominence of esoteric Buddhist lineages

From the tenth to twelfth centuries, prominent aristocratic families tried to acquire ritual knowledge that would be useful at the royal court. Of course, the leading Fujiwara attempted to acquire such knowledge, and in the era just after the unrivaled leadership of Fujiwara no Michinaga established the first of many great treasuries of the era: Uji-no-hōzō (the treasury of Uji), which was located at the Byōdō'in and included great quantities of documents, objects, and Buddhist scriptures. Later, retired sovereigns would develop their own elaborate treasuries at Shōkōmyō'in (within Toba rikyū, south of Heiankyō) and Rengeō'in (a.k.a. Sanjūsangendō; Hōjūjidono, Higashiyama), illustrative of their own efforts to fortify such knowledge within the royal house (Tajima 2006).[23]

Indeed, the introduction of esoteric Buddhist lineages (*ryū*, *hōryū*), which emphasized the importance of initiation into – and thus access to – secret rituals and the related possession of ritual knowledge was, undoubtedly, also related to this trend in the court. The esoteric Buddhist lineages, while partially influenced by earlier examples of temples' amassing of large collections of Buddhist scriptures, especially attempted to increase their collections of not merely Buddhist scriptures but also ritual treatises as well as oral transmissions (*kuden*, *kuketsu*) concerning ritual practice. These included Tendai esotericism (Taimitsu), noted above, and Shingon esotericism (Tōmitsu).

Shingon traditions focused as a whole on esoteric study and practice. For that reason, and because of their incomparably large extant manuscript collections from the period, we turn to them here. Monks at Shingon temple complexes drew upon and disseminated the charisma associated uniquely with Kūkai's image to legitimize their esoteric lineages. They produced many hagiographies of Kūkai over time, though it is apparent that they wrote little early on concerning the treatises that Kūkai had himself produced as only two treatises seem to have been written about Kūkai's works in the first two centuries after his death.[24]

Shingon lineages also increasingly began to splinter into lines of ritual and textual interpretation, in varied oral transmissions that usually claimed special access to knowledge of the original teachings of Kūkai – interpreted as ortho-practical Shingon instruction based on the esoteric lineage of continental Buddhism. It was partially in an effort to explain the oral transmissions concerning esoteric ritual practice that Shingon monks began to compile copious iconographic commentaries and other works, eventually producing extremely large treasuries of sacred works (*shōgyō*, "sacred teachings"). At the same time, such ritual protocols (*shidai sho*) and related works came to be transmitted as part of the esoteric tradition of any given line within Shingon temples, just as works like Ōe no Masafusa's protocol collection *Gōke shidai* were the products of particular ritual lineages at court. These attempts to explain the transmissions thus intersected with the imperative to construct lineages with distinctive knowledge as well as collections that attested to its authenticity, a concatenation of beliefs and interests which has been described by one scholar as *shōgyō-shugi*, "sacred-works-ism" (Kamikawa 2008: 28).

Sanbō'in in Daigoji monastery illustrates the complexity and evolving character of the relationship between residential "halls" (*inge*) and their larger monastic complexes. This hall was established by the abbot Shōkaku (1057–1129) in the early twelfth century and became thereafter the regular residence of each abbot (*zasu*) of the larger Daigoji monastery, who was likewise usually of Minamoto (Murakami Genji) heritage; in other words, the head monk of Sanbō'in was also the abbot of Daigoji as a whole. The retired sovereign Toba's establishment of an esoteric initiation hall (Kanjō'in, 1131) as a royal-vow temple within Sanbō'in Hall seems to have provided the particular impetus for this transformation (Fujii 2008: 19). Sanbō'in's position as a singular hall within the complex thus intersected with its larger role as governor of the greater temple grounds. What, then, was specifically bequeathed to Daigoji abbots? On the one hand, each Daigoji abbot received the scriptural treasury and sacred implements of Sanbō'in; on the other, he served as head (*bettō*) of other halls of the monastery, such as Enkō'in and Muryōkō'in, and the three official administrators (*sangō*) of the monastery operated within Sanbō'in as well (Tsuchiya 2001: 29–30).

In modern scholarship, we have long described the major lineages or "schools" (*shū*) as the center of Japanese Buddhism, and often assumed that these were somehow sectarian in character; but the manuscript collections remind us that the operative levels of religious, social, and intellectual activity were halls – and related "cloisters" (*monzeki*) – and, in the case of large institutions, their environs of temple complexes. The Daigoji halls, like those in other major monasteries, primarily housed scions of Fujiwara and Minamoto heritage. Careful study of their operative levels must reflect some consideration of familial networks – sometimes transcending barriers of monastic complex and Dharma lineage – in addition to other factors.

What works were particularly important to the Sanbō'in line? Indeed, it is clear that the most treasured of works within the lineage were neither particular sutras – discourses said to record the words of the Buddha Śākyamuni – nor continental esoteric ritual procedures, although these would also be considered sacred. In medieval Japan, although works like the *Lotus Sūtra* and the *Amida Sūtras* were celebrated scriptures, most Buddhist lineages privileged either specific recitations – like the name of Amida or, connected to sutras, the title (*daimoku*) of the *Lotus Sūtra* – or they gave unique attention to particular works, often written in Japan, that were written or uttered by ancestral masters of their lineage. These latter works were seen as the most valuable of *shōgyō* (Skt. *śāsana*, "instructions"), sacred works of a particular tradition, though sometimes the term *shōgyō* also referred to sutras important to it.

The most treasured *shōgyō* in Sanbō'in was the oral transmission of Shōkaku's main disciple Jōkai (1074–1149) evoked in the *Atsuzōshi* (Thick Notebook, *Daigoji monjo* Box no. 144.7; T. 78, no. 2483), *Bekki* (Separate Record) and voluminous added materials known as the *Dai-no-kawago* collection of sacred works which the Daigoji abbot Shōken (1138–1196), son of the prominent scholar-aristocrat Fujiwara no Michinori (Shinzei, 1106–1159), took with him to Mt. Kōya following his temporary ouster from Daigoji (Tanaka 2006: 7, 38–40). Later, Seigen (alt. Jōken, 1162–1231), Shōken's nephew at Daigoji and also a scion of the Fujiwaras, compiled the *Usuzōshi* (Thin Notebook, T. 78, no. 2495), which seems to have been prized most and con-ferred only upon the disciples who received the highest initiations within the line-age. These works transmitted what was seen as the highest ritual knowledge at Daigoji and variously recorded or suggestively pointed to oral transmissions of mas-ters to disciples.

On the one hand, Daigoji history was marked by tension between the Fujiwaras' Shinzei lineage and the main Minamoto lines at Daigoji. For example, the opposi-tion to Shōken at Daigoji, which led to Shōken's multi-year departure for Mt. Kōya in the Kii peninsula further down the Ōmine mountain range, was undoubtedly related to Jōkai's position as nephew of Shōkaku and, thus, member of the Minamoto. On the other hand, there seems to be no suggestion, ritually or other-wise, that the position of the *Thick Notebook* and *Thin Notebook* as sacred works (*shōgyō*) of the Sanbō'in was directly the result of tensions or social contention between these family lineages.

The Shingon lineages, from a very early point, also had a special connection with the royal line, a connection that was undoubtedly reflected in the fact that Tōji, their original administrative center, was uniquely located within the capital of Heiankyō. Kūkai had also managed to acquire permission for the establishment of a "Shingon Hall" (Shingon'in) within the greater palace for the performance of the Latter Seven-Day rite every January, which was likewise a unique development. No other major compound associated with a particular lineage was located in either the capital or the palace. Moreover, the retired sovereign Uda's (r. 887–897) initiation into Shingon at the turn of the tenth century and transformation of Ninnaji O'muro into a royal institution constituted an important precursor (Bauer 2012) to the historical develop-ment of the so-called royal or aristocratic cloisters. The retired sovereign Shirakawa's establishment of the Dharma Prince system began at Ninnaji in 1099 partially in connection with the intimate association between Tendai's Enryakuji (Hiei) and the leading Fujiwaras – the timing of which, we should note, perfectly matched a rare period (1099–1105) in which there was neither a regent nor a chancellor; the difficult relationship between the Fujiwaras and the retired sovereigns would ebb and flow for the next centuries, with Dharma Princes being established, beginning with Sanzen'in (at Hiei, then Ōhara, north of Kyoto) and Shōren'in (Hiei, then Higashiyama, Kyoto) in the twelfth century, at a number of Tendai cloisters as well.

In addition, however, it is essential to emphasize, in this connection, that the Shingon lineages held a position close to the Nara temples, given that both Shingon monks' precept vows were necessarily undertaken at Tōdaiji and Kūkai had founded an esoteric initiation hall there (Abé 1999: 41–46). Indeed, these Shingon-lineage monks, commonly of noble background, not only came to acquire the abbacy of Tōdaiji regularly from the late tenth century onward, but they typically were *not* in residence there, instead administering the monastery from their home quarters in other temple complexes (Nagamura 1989: 342; Horiike *et al.* 2001: 40–41).

Japanese Buddhists within the East Asian cultural sphere

Scholars have typically conceived of Japanese Buddhists of the tenth to twelfth centuries as being largely cut off from the continent, following a trend established when the emissaries – including official-emissary monks (so-called *kentō-sō*) – to the Tang were stopped at the end of the ninth century. Yet was this indeed the case?

In the period of the Fujiwaras' consolidation of their power from the mid tenth century onward, contacts with the continent seem to have become prominent once again. This period coincided with the beginning of the Northern Song Dynasty (960–1127), following the collapse of the Tang in 907, a feature the Japanese court undoubtedly noticed (Uejima 2010a: 19–22).

The interaction with continental Buddhism became all the more visible when the monk Chōnen (938–1016), a Tōdaiji monk trained in Kegon (Ch. Huayan) and Shingon lineages, made a pilgrimage to China in 983. Whether orchestrated with the help of the Fujiwaras or not, Chōnen's reception of a copy of the printed Chinese Buddhist canon from the Song emperor a year after its publication marked a pivotal moment in the history of the relationship between the courts – and, of course, between the Japanese Buddhist community and that on the continent. The diplomatic background evoked by the reception is suggested also by the fact that just four years later, the Chinese emperor would grant another copy to Koryŏ as well. Moreover, the Fujiwaras seem to have been particularly fascinated with the canon, and proceeded thereafter to undertake venerative rites toward the Buddhist canon on numerous occasions. Fujiwara no Michinaga even investigated the possibility of acquiring his own canon from China, and his son Yorimichi would later inaugurate a regular rite to the canon in the scriptural treasury of the Fujiwara chapel Byōdō'in. Meanwhile, Genshin sent a series of Japanese Buddhist works to China, as he was conscious of the position of Japanese Buddhists within the East Asian Buddhist cultural and political sphere (Kamikawa 2008: 140–143, 223–228).

The Tendai monk Jōjin (1011–1081) is well known for his pilgrimage to the Song in the late eleventh century (Borgen 2007). During his stay there, he sent back 422 fascicles of newly translated sutras to be included in the Buddhist canon. A century later, the monk Yōsai (alt. Eisai; 1141–1215), who would go on to be seen as father of the Rinzai Zen lineages, made an agreement to acquire the Song Buddhist canon after returning from his first pilgrimage to China (Kamikawa 2008: 191, 206–207). Meanwhile, a number of the copies of the canon made during the twelfth century included some printed scriptures from the Song canon. Particularly from the late twelfth century onward, rites were commonly held to copies of the Chinese canon, several of which the monk Chōgen (1121–1206) acquired during his pilgrimages to China (Kamikawa 2008: 162–207).

Finally, as we saw, *kanshi* poetry was among a whole series of Chinese genres of writing that was at the very center of cultivation practice within the royal court. Indeed, a bit of reflection concerning the way in which Japanese aristocrats emulated and made Chinese writings their own through creating their own editions and new handbooks based on the influence makes it clear that we must not overemphasize distinctions between "Buddhist" and other continental influences since, as we saw, the handbooks for youth written by a figure like Minamoto no Tamenori included not just *Sanbō'e* but also one on general informational background and another on quotable sayings. That is, didactic handbooks designed for the cultivation of particular youth of the court drew both on Buddhist works and "the classics" since both were the "norm" for scholastics of the day (Obara 2007: 212–216).[25] As with *Wakan rōei shū*, Buddhist sections and even random accounts were, together with those from the Chinese classics, part and parcel of the body of Japanese knowledge in the royal court.

Scripture-copying, fund-raising campaigns, and the explosion of merit in the twelfth century

There was, especially within the royal court and its environs, a perceived urgency to engage in elaborate acts of merit-making. Sponsoring large rites to the Buddhist canon as well as of copying of the canon thus came to be common over the course of the twelfth century, and meanwhile scriptural copying in general took on new and more elaborate features. We can draw attention to just a few of these, but we must also bear in mind that there were multiple variations in scripture-copying in the era.

One feature that was increasingly prominent was the copying of scriptures in the form of "sacred works" (*shōgyō*), which were typically commentarial works written by masters within the Japanese isles in the lineages of the great monasteries identified primarily with Tendai, Shingon, and the so-called Nara lineages. This marked increase in copying and writing occurred initially in the kenmitsu lineages and developed in tandem with the appearance of new lines, including cloisters, within these temples – and, eventually, newly developing lineages often referred to as examples of "new Kamakura Buddhism."

Of course, there are many continental Buddhist precedents. For one, Mahayana Buddhist scriptures like the *Lotus Sūtra* and related commentaries routinely emphasized the efficacy of good acts, especially those undertaken in great numbers. In any event, although the seeds of such elaboration of practice were undoubtedly sown in part in the first half of the eleventh century (Mitsuhashi 2000: 380–395), it is clear that court society of the era was undergoing rapid changes from the second half of the century onward, and was approaching a series of crises. The retired sovereign (*in*) was now typically the most powerful figure in the court, displacing the Fujiwara chancellors and regents. At the same time, the Northern Fujiwara House retained on the whole a large measure of its former power and, certainly, most of its accumulated wealth.[26]

The positions at court were all the more rigidly controlled by those at the top, so that a large number of nobles and lesser-ranked aristocrats found it extremely difficult to establish successful careers. Satō Michio has tied the impulse of the poets of the late Heian period to go into reclusion with such failures, especially that experienced by the prince Sukehito (1073–1119), a son of the sovereign Go-Sanjō (r. 1068–1072) who failed to become crown prince and decided to seclude himself at Ninnaji, writing Chinese poetry and playing music with his aesthete acquaintances. Similarly, nobles sometimes chose to give up their regular life for more rustic and secluded lives, providing models for figures like the great poet-monk Saigyō (1118–1190), a northerner of warrior background who would take up a peripatetic and rustic life (Satō 2003: 28–29).

One scholar has argued that the elaborate sponsorship of various Buddhist works accompanied a "crisis of alienation" in which the aristocrats and royal family witnessed an increasing privatization of lands – in the form of manors (*shōen*) – and experienced great anxiety about their position. Figures like the retired sovereign Shirakawa undertook merit-making as modes of "self-promotion" and, in the latter's case, as part of an effort to gain "control over the physical and symbolic landscape of an increasingly splintered realm" (Yiengpruksawan 1998: 56–58). Indeed, it may be that both the embellished, expensive beautification of scripture and the sponsorship of major aesthetic projects flowed out of concern over a realm that seemed simultaneously splintered in economic terms and stratified in social ones. Others have emphasized that the perceived "extravagance" (*kasa*) of clothing of some nobles and of their ritual giving was intimately related to the competitive symbolism within the court in the late Heian period (Endō 1998: 99–118). Clearly, members of prominent families such as that of Fujiwara no Michinori (Shinzei) and his descendants commonly promoted the production of extravagant patronage of aesthetic productions (Jamentz 2008).

Meanwhile, given financial and other problems at court, temple complexes increasingly found that it behooved them to increase efforts to raise funds toward various modes of image and architectural construction, and in the process groups of "fund-raising" holy ones (*kanjin hijiri*) developed that spurred on efforts to garner material support from the population. This development, although patterned on the earlier example of Gyōki in the Nara period, became prominent beginning in the mid eleventh century and would become extremely common over the course of the medieval era (Hosokawa 1997: 171). The fund-raising monk Chōgen, noted above, proved a pivotal figure in the history of such figures, since he came to be employed by the retired sovereign Go-Shirakawa and others of the court in the effort to repair the Great Buddha at Tōdaiji in the 1180s; moreover, Gyōki was evoked in his efforts and related documents, and Chōgen himself clearly attempted to resonate with the image (Rosenfield 2011: 109–110; 32–34; Itō 2009: 62). Chōgen's official position as "great fundraiser" (*daikanjin-shiki*) would become a regular post sponsored by Tōdaiji, with the interesting development that the vast majority of such figures would operate out of the Zen temple of Kenninji over the course of the thirteenth century, including prominent monks like Yōsai and Enni Ben'en (1202–1280). The fact that such prominent monks served reflects the fact that the position was formulated within the established temple system and provided the "great fundraiser" with even the revenue from sites like Suō and Hizen Provinces (Yoshikawa *et al.* 2008: 135, 143–144). Moreover, such practices also propelled a series of performative arts into great prominence among the populace as such fundraisers would either patronize performances on-site or travel through surrounding regions, where such performances or picture-preaching might be offered for local supporters (Goodwin 1994: 116, 151–152).

Many in the early medieval era were concerned with what they thought was the onset of the Latter Age of the Dharma (*mappō*) – an East Asian concept – which was believed in Japan to have begun in the year 1052. The notion was, of course, very important in the novel Pure Land Buddhist lineages of the Kamakura period, but many scholars have thought that *mappō* was also a central concept from much earlier, given references alluding to it even in early tale collections like the early ninth-century *Nihon ryōiki*. Moreover, the Byōdō'in in Uji was established in 1052, which was clearly related on some level to belief among the Fujiwaras in the onset of *mappō*.

Recently, scholars have increasingly raised new questions regarding the meaning and extent of concern with *mappō* over the course of the Heian period. D. Max Moerman, for example, has examined Heian sutra burials and argued that while there was a connection with concerns regarding *mappō*, the latter was not seen in many cases as a soteriological goal. That is, most typically, rather than constituting efforts to attain "salvation" in the Pure Land, most often the burial was conducted with a view to either birth in Amida's realm to wait for the arrival of Maitreya Buddha to descend again to earth or to go to Maitreya's heaven, Tuṣita (J. Tosotsu), to abide with him and eventually descend together (Moerman 2007).

Presumably, a seminal work like the well-known essay *Hōjō ki* ("Account of my Hut," 1212) had some influence in later centuries on the powerful image of *mappō* along with its connection to Pure Land faith. The author, Kamo no Chōmei (1155–1216), saw his immediate family fall out of favor with the court, and he eventually took the tonsure. He went on to write a major Buddhist tale collection along with the *Hōjō ki*, which was on the catastrophes of Heiankyō of his day. The essay interpreted these events as further reflections of the inexorability of impermanence and instability as well as the need to rely on Amida, while it implicitly alluded to the problematic condition of the royal court in his day (Marra 1991).

Early and Middle Kamakura-Period Buddhism (1185–1300)

Late Heian Buddhist knowledge, proselytization, and "Kamakura Buddhisms"

One part of the increase of religious texts created by the kenmitsu lineages before and during the period of the advent of the so-called new Kamakura "schools" was the vast corpus of their preaching (*shōdō*) works, which represented ritual performances conducted often on behalf of lay believers. For example, although prayers ("vows," *ganmon*) for rites sponsored by the aristocracy are well known (Kudō 2008), a related occasion for preaching practice was that of a Dharma assembly or esoteric ritual (*shuhō*, alt. *suhō*), in which a ritual pronouncement (*hyōbyaku*) would be made, and the texts of such pronouncements came to be commonly assembled in collections by the mid twelfth century (e.g., Yamazaki 1996; Abe *et al.* 2005). Soon after, liturgical prayers (*kōshiki*) also became increasingly common, as they were also read on the occasion of some assemblies (Ford 2006a; Guelberg 2004).

A series of prominent examples of such traditions included the Agui preaching lines, which began with another son of Fujiwara no Michinori, the Tendai monk Chōken (ca. 1126–1203). As has been noted with regard to Agui preaching texts, these pronouncements were viewed as not merely petitioning the figure venerated but also as being potentially efficacious in their own right. On one occasion of the *Saishōkō* liturgy, Chōken felt so compelled by an ongoing drought that he performed a *hyōbyaku* – whereupon, proven successful by rainfall the next day, he went on to receive a reward from the retired sovereign (*Kōsei hyōbyaku*, "Saishōkō daiyonza," Tōji Hōbodai'in-zō, in *Agui shōdō shū* 1979: 480–481).[27] Further publication of a series of additional Agui works has occurred in a variety of venues, which will undoubtedly prove fruitful objects of future study to ascertain the character of preaching and its audiences.[28]

Moreover, as we saw briefly in the context of the Pure Land literatures and collections such as *Sanbō'e*, lay aristocrats were also intimately involved in the "popularization" and intellectual activities of Buddhism in the mid-to-late Heian period. From the late eleventh century onward, such activity was often connected with aristocratic or royal cloisters (*monzeki*) following the same general pattern as represented by the halls Jinzen established at Hiei. Lay involvement was registered not merely in the writing by figures like Ōe no Masafusa of pronouncements, but also in figures such as the powerful scholar-noble Fujiwara no Yorinaga (1120–1156), who studied Buddhist logic under the tutelage of monks of the Nara temples Tōdaiji and, especially, Kōfukuji (Yokouchi 2008: 179–214).

The writings of Kūkai, as suggested above, also became a serious new focus of interest among both aristocrats and monks. For example, the scholar-noble Fujiwara no Atsumitsu (1063–1144) wrote commentaries on Kūkai's esoteric treatises. Atsumitsu was also interested in Kūkai's studies in Chinese poetry (*kanshi*) and in his more general scholarly enterprise (Satō 2003: 13–15). There was, apparently, a kind of nostalgia in the court for what was considered first-rate scholarship of the early Heian period. At the same time, what may have been behind Atsumitsu's fascination with Kūkai's esoteric writings? We should note that just a few decades earlier the monk Saisen organized Kūkai's prayers and related documents anew in the form of the *Seirei shū* (alt. *Shōryō shū*) adding new materials to the original, which had been completed in the ninth century. Saisen, who seems to have been a favorite of the retired sovereign Shirakawa, became the first monk to write large numbers of commentaries on Kūkai's works.

During the same period, a group of warriors governed an autonomous domain in Hiraizumi to the northeast. These so-called "Hiraizumi Fujiwaras" pursued religious patronage policies of the same pattern as the Northern Fujiwara House and retired sovereigns, establishing temple complexes where they entombed their leaders for purposes of Pure Land mortuary practice. In this way, lay believers far from the Heiankyō and Nara appropriated Buddhist practices that promoted their authority while also improving their own afterlife (Yiengpruksawan 1998).

Meanwhile, over the course of the medieval era Buddhist preachers and entertainers came to employ newly developing literatures on major female authors such as Murasaki Shikibu and Izumi Shikibu (ca. 976 – ca. 1030), connected with tensions between Buddhism, fiction, and vernacular literature associated with women noted earlier. These works flourished and clearly depicted them in varied and sometimes extremely negative ways, as has been exhaustively demonstrated (Kawashima 2001). At the same time, scholars have also pointed out that these "staple figures" in preaching and entertaining were often very appealing to audiences. In the case, for example, of Izumi Shikibu, she is depicted as having gained birth (*ōjō*) in the Pure Land and met the wandering founder of Jishū, Ippen; her visual image seems to have replaced that of Amida in one picture scroll, and another temple legend depicted her as a supporter of the Jishū lineages. All of these elements serve to indicate that her image was used, by the late medieval period, in both preaching and fundraising activities (Kimbrough 2008: 241, 180–190).

"Kamakura Buddhisms"

Although the term *shoshū kengaku* ("simultaneous study of [Buddhist] schools") is sometimes associated with study of multiple lines among the traditional eight lineages (six of Nara, along with Tendai and Shingon), almost all of the so-called founders of the new lineages were themselves trained on Mt. Hiei at the great Enryakuji temple complex – all were trained in Tendai lineages – and, in varying ways, continued to incorporate features of the *kenmitsu* or eso-esoteric system in which they studied and practiced. The kenmitsu system here refers to the doctrinal and practitional set of regimes taught at the major temple complexes of the medieval era, which included both traditional Mahayana Buddhist teachings ("exoteric teachings," *kengyō*) and Tantric Buddhist teachings ("esoteric teachings," *mikkyō*), the latter of which as we saw were generally divided into Tendai esoteric and Shingon esoteric categories. There has been extensive study of the political context within which kenmitsu Buddhism developed, as Kuroda Toshio connected it in larger terms with the appearance of power blocs (*kenmon*), which collaboratively and, sometimes, competitively placed their sons or related allies in the cloisters, halls, and adjacent shrines within the major complexes (Kuroda 1975: 413–547; Kuroda 1996).[29]

The phrase "Kamakura Buddhism" or new Kamakura Buddhism has commonly been used to refer to the new lineages that began to develop over the course of the Kamakura period. Indeed, at least until the 1980s, there was a tendency among scholars to assume that new lineages were more prominent politically and culturally than so-called "old Buddhism," and to focus on their ancestral founders (*kaiso, soshi*); in doing so, they celebrated such presumed founders as originators of distinct "sects" viewed variously as accomplishing a kind of Lutheran-style "Reformation," as cultural heroes, and as nascent democratic if not pre-Marxist movements championing the populace (*minshū*; Stone 2006: 41–42). However, Kuroda Toshio and, later, scholars like Taira Masayuki have demonstrated that the established lineages remained most prominent in society throughout the Kamakura period, with the partial exception of movements like Rinzai Zen, which was tied to an influx of Chinese masters from the continent (Kuroda 1996: 265–266; Taira 1996: 431–435), and to which we will turn in the next chapter. Other scholars, building on their work and partially on essays by figures who earlier suggested limitations in the Reformation model (Foard 1980), have conducted sustained analyses of ongoing reconceptualization of Kamakura Buddhism in public and academic discourse of the early modern and modern period. They have pointed to more recent efforts to formulate new theories distinct from the Kuroda model, which has a tendency to apply a normative discourse of corruption / anti-corruption in its claim that the new lineages were not only marginal but also heterodox vis-à-vis established Buddhism (Stone 1999: 58–62; Dobbins 1998).

It is thus with the caveat that the vast majority of so-called "new" lineages did not, in fact, gain great prominence in the Kamakura period, that we begin to turn briefly to their founders and earliest generations of leadership; given their rising prominence

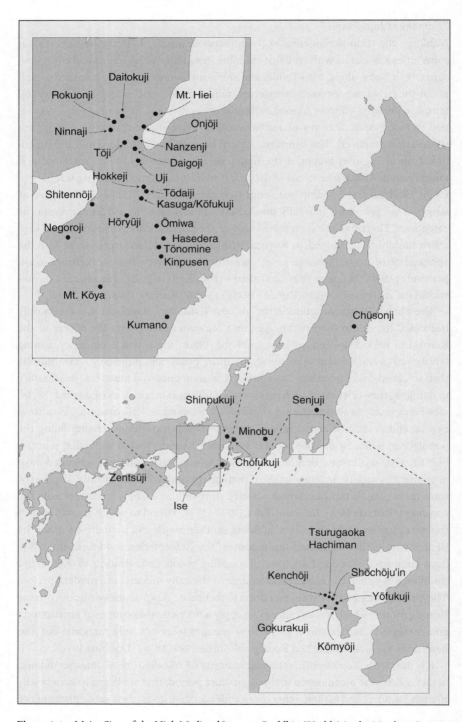

Figure 3.4 Major Sites of the High Medieval Japanese Buddhist World. Map by Matthew Stavros.

over time, we will turn to their development in greater depth in Chapters 4–5. The first figure seen by believers as having been the ancestral founder of a new lineage was Hōnen (1133–1212), viewed as inaugurator of Japan's Pure Land lineages (Jōdo shū), who was of rural warrior background, and had been sent to Hiei after the death of his father, who had been killed in a dispute on the estate where he was employed in Mimasaka Province (Okayama). By Hōnen's day, life at Enryakuji was becoming increasingly difficult if not unstable, given the gradual development of militarized bands that represented the complex and were sometimes in conflict with the court and others; holing himself up in the Kurodani area of Hiei, Hōnen did his best to assimilate the Buddhist canonical traditions, and in the meanwhile encountered Genshin's *Ōjōyōshū*. He would later study Pure Land works by figures such as Tōdaiji's Yōkan (alt. Eikan, 1033–1111) and Chinkai (1092–1152), as well as the oeuvre of the Chinese Pure Land thinker Shandao (J. Zendō, 613–681; Ōhashi 1985: 43–45).

Based on his reading of these works, Hōnen came to have the view by the mid-1170s that in his own age – what he and many other Japanese now interpreted to be *mappō* – the only available means to salvation was the invocation of the Pure Land Buddha's name, "hail to Amitābha Buddha" (*namu amida butsu*), the *nenbutsu* (thinking on or reciting [Amida] Buddha['s name]). In other words, a catholic approach pursued by monks on Mt. Hiei or any other kenmitsu Buddhist institution was ineffective in the Latter Age of the Dharma, as only the repeated and faithful chanting of the invocation to Amida promised transcendence of karma and rebirth. Hōnen left Hiei at that time, and went to study in Nishiyama (Kyoto) under a holy one specializing in exclusive practice (*senju*) of the *nenbutsu*, Enshō (1139–1177) – yet another son of Fujiwara no Michinori (Ōhashi 1985: 55–57).

Hōnen would rise to further prominence and reach a new level of reception with his invitation in 1186 by the Tendai monk Kenshin (1131–1192) to engage him in dialogue at Shōrin'in in Ōhara concerning his teaching of exclusive *nenbutsu* practice. Others who participated were major scholastic monks like Myōhen (1142–1224), a Shingon and Sanron figure who was also son of Michinori and had studied under Hōnen previously, Myōhen's brother, the prominent Hossō monk Jōkei (1155–1213), the monk and fund-raising holy one Chōgen, noted earlier, and the prolific Tendai figure Shōshin (fl. 1186–1204). Hōnen became quite prominent from that point on, and the powerful noble Kujō Kanezane became his patron by 1189. Jōkei would later offer a memorial to the court (1205) denouncing Hōnen's single-practice *nenbutsu* for perceived infractions such as undermining the traditional monastic structure of state protection and establishing a new school without the sovereign's permission; and Hōnen would eventually be exiled for several months in 1207, alongside a group of his disciples, some of whom were accused of licentious practices (Maekawa 2010: 77–80).

It is, initially, almost impossible to overstress the truly novel character of Shinran's view of the *nenbutsu* and Pure Land faith in general. Shinran, unlike Hōnen, was from an aristocratic background, and was presumably of one of the lower aristocratic lines of the Hino house. His undergoing the tonsure at 9 under the great Hiei abbot Jien meant that he received tutelage in Buddhist teachings at a very young age and his experience as a monk attached to Hiei's "Hall of Continuous Practice" (Jōgyōdō), where all manner of *nenbutsu* practices were conducted, meant that he witnessed the Tendai *nenbutsu* on a virtually constant basis (Dobbins 2002: 22–23).

Shinran's turn to the exclusive practice of the *nenbutsu* occurred in 1201, and between that time and 1207 a series of pivotal events occurred that helped shape his spiritual development. Shinran, like the monks Jien and Myō'e (1173–1232) and other prominent people of his day, saw dreams as vehicles of the Buddha's teachings and directives. In the early thirteenth century, Shinran had a dream at Rokkakudō temple in Kyoto that led him to change his course; the records of the dream suggest variously that he saw Kannon in the form of either prince Shōtoku or as a monk, the latter announcing that he would solve a believer's sexual desires by taking form as his female mate and lead him to the Pure Land at death. Shinran became a follower of Hōnen, took a wife between 1204 and 1207, began to describe himself as "neither priest nor layman" (*sō ni arazu zoku ni arazu*), and was exiled to Echigo (Niigata) in 1207 – never to see the Tosa(Shikoku)-bound Hōnen again (Dobbins 2002: 23–26).

Shinran focused on the eighteenth vow among those Amida made when he undertook an oath to create a Pure Land through the merit of his Bodhisattva practice. Thus Shinran emphasized that birth in the Pure Land was based not on good deeds or even on practice of chanting the *nenbutsu* but rather on complete faith in the "other power" (*tariki*) of Amida Buddha. Such faith, which lacks any doubt whatsoever concerning the Buddha's vow to save beings and his unlimited wisdom, retains no suggestion of calculated efforts to achieve or acquire salvation. What, then, is the status of the *nenbutsu* here? The enunciated *nenbutsu* is Amida's rather than the believer's action, and it is the faith instead of the *nenbutsu* that results in birth in the real Pure Land (*shinjitsu hōdo*) as opposed to an expedient Pure Land (*hōben kedo*). Moreover, as Shinran's monumental treatise *Kyōgyōshinshō* argues, Amida and his Pure Land here are infinite – indeed, when beings are born in the real Pure Land they realize that it is none other than "the unconditioned realm of Nirvāna" (*gokuraku wa mui nehan no kai nari*). As for non-Buddhist traditions related to the *kami*, other spirits, divination, star-worship, calendrical taboos, curses and so on, Shinran interpreted these as irrelevant and an impediment to birth in the Pure Land. At the same time, Shinran made it clear that he saw the ultimate object of the Buddha's vow as evil persons (*akunin shōki*) rather than those disposed toward the good, insofar as evil persons recognize their inability to overcome afflicted dispositions (*bonnō gusoku*) through good acts in the era of the Final Age of the Dharma (*mappō*): evil ones who rely on Amida's power constitute, more than any others, the true cause of birth in the Pure Land. Some of Shinran's own followers would interpret this as antinomian license to commit evil acts, but the evil ones he depicted also, by extension, were presumed to possess a sense of weariness toward the world (*ensei*) that precluded intentional evil use of body, speech, and mind (Dobbins 2002: 28–54). Nonetheless, Sueki Fumihiko has stressed that Hōnen had also expressed the belief that evil persons were the objects of Amida's vow (Sueki 1993: 431–438), and so the novelty of Shinran's view on evil may be recognized as an elaboration of Hōnen's views, albeit more forcefully stated and hence potentially subject to all manner of interpretations (Ford 2006b: 97; Taira 2001: 132–134).

Shinran spent a significant portion of his life in the Kantō region. After being exiled to Echigo, he moved to Kantō, settling primarily in the area of Inada in Hitachi Province, where he remained for at least two decades; Shinran enjoyed the patronage of the Utsunomiya clan which had intimate connections with the Hōjō shogunal clan (Imai 1999: 21–23). Thus, as Imai Masaharu has emphasized, within the True Pure Land lineages (Jōdo Shinshū), from the death of Shinran until the rise of Rennyo (1415–1499) and Honganji to eminence, Kantō lines were at the center of the organization – and Kyoto remained "provincial" by comparison (Imai 1999: 2).

One particular aspect of the Pure Land movement more generally was the development of the so-called *dōjō*, "place of practice," which in this case was typically a dwelling converted for worship purposes, where the congregation, known as *nenbutsu* members (*nenbutsu shū*) or lineage disciples (*monto*), gathered. These seem to have been dominated by lay believers of all classes even from the late Kamakura period, perhaps in connection with the approaches of figures like Hōnen and Shinran. Shinran seems to have encouraged believers of varied backgrounds with his innovation of using a Name venerable (*myōgō honzon*) – an inscription of Amida's name – rather than a traditional image venerable (*honzon*); moreover, the Dharma talks (*hōwa*) of these figures, along with the *nenbutsu* and the singing of Japanese-language lauds (*wasan*), seems to have encouraged people from all walks of life to join the movement. Within True Pure Land lineages, these groups initially worshiped together on the 25th of each month, date of Hōnen's death, and would later change to Shinran's on the 28th after his passing (Dobbins 2002: 66–68).

A prominent new Pure Land Buddhist group that was not directly related to Hōnen's and Shinran's movement was that of the monk Ippen, who would have simply become a largely forgotten holy one (*hijiri*) had he not established a movement with multiple followers and they not recorded his sayings and depicted him visually. Ippen was born to the Kōno family in Shikoku, which lost its standing with the Jōkyū War (1221). His father was a True Pure Land monk who had taken the tonsure after the defeat, studied under Hōnen's disciple Shōkū (1177–1247) in Kyoto, and gone back to Shikoku to continue in the priesthood while running the warrior clan. In fact, Ippen was perhaps the first major figure in Japanese Buddhism to experience a religious transformation based on his encounter with an image – in this case, a painting of a wanderer's "white path" to the Pure Land that he saw at the famous temple Zenkōji in Shinano (Nagano) household (Hirota 1997: xxii–xxv).

The visual scrolls of Ippen's life (*Ippen hijiri-e*) that his close relative Shōkai (1261–1323) and other disciples completed in 1299 depict Ippen, upon his return to Shikoku, as having constructed a small retreat, practiced the *nenbutsu* only, and attained a realization. They quote the following Sino-Japanese poem that Ippen wrote to express his realization:

> Perfect enlightenment ten kalpas past – pervading the realm of sentient beings;
> Birth is one thought-moment – in Amida's Land.
> When ten and one are nondual, we realize no-birth;
> Where Land and realm are the same, we sit in Amida's great assembly. (Hirota 1997: xxvii)

Ippen's understanding of the non-duality of Amida's Buddhahood and beings' confirmation of birth in the Pure Land (*ketsujō ōjō*) constituted the fundamental doctrinal vision of his life and teaching. In other words, Ippen believed that Amida's vow spanned all time and was realized in the single utterance of the *nenbutsu* at any one moment; for Ippen, the believer and Amida were ultimately identical (*sokuichi*), a position clearly distinct from that of Hōnen or Shinran and which also entailed his affirmation of the non-duality of *kami* and Buddhas (Nagashima 2004: 56–60). He decided to distribute, together with his disciples, a talisman (*fuda*) saying "Hail to Amida Buddha: Confirmation of Birth [for] Sixty Myriads of People" (*Namu amida butsu: ketsujō ōjō, rokujūmannin*) throughout the realm; according to *Ippen hijiri-e*, he was told, and followed, the following advice from an anonymous mountain ascetic (*yamabushi*) at Kumano – in fact, the deity Kumano Gongen:

> In Amida Buddha's perfect enlightenment ten kalpas ago the birth of all sentient beings was decisively settled as Namu-amida-butsu. Distribute your *fuda* regardless of whether people have faith or not, and without discriminating between the pure and the impure. (Hirota 1997: xxxv)

Ippen was also influenced by the practice of Tendai lineage monk Ryōnin (1073–1132), who had promoted the interpenetrating *nenbutsu* (*yūzū nenbutsu*) and traveled widely to collect the names of those who pledged to practice the *nenbutsu* – and who by the early fourteenth century was depicted in illustrated scrolls (*e-maki*) as collecting names even from the protective deity Bishamonten, who had gathered names of *kami* pledgers in the heavens (*Yūzū nenbutsu e-maki* [Shōwa-era edn] 1.3, image 2.1; Abe 2013: 71–74). Ippen's use of this name – "one instant" (*ippen*) – is thought to be based on the the same notion of interpenetration of time and space, and the extent of his distribution of the *fuda* arguably extended to a large proportion of the populace in the Japanese isles (Hayashi 2000: 127–137).

Ippen was disliked by the shogunate, which was concerned about his near-constant movement (*yugyō*), but it turns out that he and his followers were supported by some

Figure 3.5 Scene from *Yūzū nenbutsu e-maki*, artist unknown, early fourteenth century. Handscroll (ink, colors, and gold on paper), 130.5 × 1,176.9 cm. Kate S. Buckingham Endowment 11956.1256, The Art Institute of Chicago.

sectors of the Hōjō shogunal house (Imai 1993), and the patron who sponsored the writing of *Ippen hijiri-e* may have been a leading Kujō family noble in Kyoto (Kaufman 1992: 70–71). Ippen's activities had a remarkably performative feature, including not only his movement around the realm and distribution of talismans but also his inception of the dancing *nenbutsu* (*odori nenbutsu*) from 1279 onward, although it is important to keep in mind that the latter practice seems to have been common to a series of groups, not just Ippen's, at the time (Hayashi 2004: 96).

Another response to what was clearly a period of perceived religious and societal instability was the movement to return to proper practice of the Buddhist precepts, which cut across both established and novel lineages. There were figures like the Shingon and precepts practitioner Jichihan (d. 1144) and related others originally from Kōfukuji, who became interested in attempting to revive the precepts traditions, such as the then extinct lineage of Ganjin (Ch. Jianzhen; 688–763). At the same time, at Tōdaiji, the so-called Precepts Assembly (Risshū) were monks of the larger clerical assembly (*dōshu*) there who continued to confer the precepts at the Kaidan'in precepts-platform hall in the complex on a semi-regular basis, following the practice of figures like Kakuju (1081–1139). We can take particular note of the prominent Kōfukuji monk Jōkei, who while famous for his denunciation of Hōnen's exclusive *nenbutsu* orientation was extremely influential as a promoter of the return to the precepts – and who also had great interest in Zen meditation (Ford 2006b: 122–124, 131–138). In the meantime, the monk Shunjō (1166–1227), originally of Tendai training, traveled to China to study the precepts, and returned to Kyoto to teach. Shunjō taught not just the precepts but a combination of their strict study and observation with Zen practice as well as doctrinal study and esoteric practice. Thus, on the one hand, Shunjō was a kenmitsu monk and, on the other, he attempted to respond anew to what he perceived as a decline in Buddhist practice in his day by studying Zen meditation and the precepts as two of the traditional foundations of the Buddhist path (Minowa 1999: 74–132; Minowa 2010: 32–34).

Meanwhile, social practices intimately related to conceptions of impurity and associated with marginalization became increasingly prominent in Japanese society. Although the prominent Kegon- and Shingon-lineage master Myō'e was known early on for opening his temple gate to lepers, a variety of beggars, and other marginals (Abé 2006: 156), it was especially precepts masters such as Eison (1201–1290) and Ninshō (1217–1303) who were active in ministering to the needs they perceived. Certain groups or individuals who were often peripatetic came to be called "nonpersons" (*hinin*), a term which has been variously interpreted as being a product of, or at least an adjunct to, the developing status system of the period. Kuroda Toshio, Amino Yoshihiko, and others came to offer interpretations of the relationship between these spheres of society and the larger social framework; one distinction sometimes drawn is between the more general term, associated at points with traveling holy ones, and the figures employed at the bottom end of the structure within temple-shrine complexes (*shukuhinin*) of the time. The latter groups were seen particularly in the Kansai region, especially in the Nara (Nara-zaka) and Kyoto (Kiyomizu-zaka) areas, and it was these to whom figures like Eison ministered, in connection with veneration of the bodhisattva Mañjuśrī (Hosokawa 1996: 137–139; Matsuo 2010: 164–166).

Eison and his group are well known for their development of a ritual regime that combined precepts practice with Shingon-lineage rites as part of their efforts to aid *hinin* and a series of other figures marginalized by the court and others. In particular, Eison and the larger series of what came to be called Shingon Ritsu lineages offered help to those suffering from a series of illnesses, managed funerary practices and areas for locals, and built or maintained various material and medical infrastructure on behalf of the populace (Matsuo 2010; Quinter 2007: 437–438). At the same time, Eison is known for having employed these groups to engage in activities at sites such as cremation grounds, leading some scholars to emphasize what they see as a gap between the ritual view of the poor as manifestations of Mañjuśrī and such social practices (Hosokawa 1996: 143–144); others have argued that there is no such incongruity, ultimately, as the ritual presumably projected a mode of respect that ideally would be remembered and introduced into everyday life (Quinter 2007: 443–444). In any event, Eison and then, especially, his disciple Ninshō were extremely active in ministering to those poor, ill, and otherwise socially marginalized. In particular, under Ninshō's abbacy at Gokurakuji in Kamakura a medical facility was established on the grounds in 1287, perhaps the greatest such facility in Japanese history to that point (more than 88,000 people were apparently treated over a 34-year-period). Buddhist monks there and elsewhere were very active in their additional efforts to acquire new medical knowledge from China, reflective of an ethos very supportive of continental contact, networking efforts, and transfer of multiple kinds of knowledge; indeed, the catalog recording in 1280 the works passed from Tōfukuji's Enni Ben'en to his followers at his death included almost 30 medical manuscripts, further indicating that monks at the forefront of continental Zen and esoteric Buddhist knowledge networks were seriously interested in medicine (Goble 2011: 7–20). Moreover, we should not underestimate the importance of the conferral by the Ritsu leaders of the bodhisattva precepts on what were clearly larger numbers of both lay and monastic adherents (e.g., the account of Eison's 90,710 recipients), and their establishment of large numbers of Saidaiji-lineage affiliate temples (Groner 2005: 220).

We can take note of two other seminal Buddhist figures that were active in the thirteenth century: one, who attempted to revive the ideal path of meditation and precept practice; and another, who tried to enact the teachings of what he saw as the true Tendai doctrine of the *Lotus Sūtra*. In either case, the lineages traced to their teachings will be examined in Chapter 4, since the flourishing of their religious programs only came into effect during or after the fourteenth century. Dōgen (1200–1253) introduced teachings and practices of the Chan lineage of Caodong, which would become known as the Sōtō lineages of Zen in Japan, with a special emphasis on "just sitting meditation" (*shikan taza*) that he justified through referring to its practice by every generation of enlightened teachers (Bielefeldt 1988: 167–169). Originally on Hiei, Dōgen, a scion of the Koga (Tsuchimikado) family, is described by later hagiography in the Sōtō lineages as having been struck by a fundamental question concerning enlightenment: If all beings already have Buddha-nature, why do they need to practice toward realization? Perhaps it would be more accurate to simply note that Dōgen, in his own time, was clearly troubled by another problem – the seeming contradiction between his notion of an ideal teacher and the less-than-ascetic lives of many monks of his day. In any event, Dōgen's thought was clearly closely related to original enlightenment discourse, particularly since he argued that practice and enlightenment realization are identical, that the round of rebirth and nirvāna are nondual, and that particular phenomena express the nondual reality at any specific moment (Stone 1999: 73, 88–89). Following his Zen master Myōzen, a disciple of Yōsai, to China, Dōgen gained access to a blood lineage chart of Chan at Mt. Tiantong and came to be under the Chinese master Nyojō (Ch. Rujing; 1163–1226), who taught of "dropping of the body-mind" (J. *shinjin datsuraku*).

Upon his return to Japan, Dōgen returned to Kenninji, and became a prominent Zen meditation teacher for a range of monks, including Pure Land lineage figures (Maekawa 2010: 110). Dōgen, although criticized by those on Mt. Hiei, did not see Zen as a particular sect within the Japanese Buddhist landscape but rather simply part of a much larger, unified Buddhist tradition (Bodiford 2008: 262–263). Thus it is not surprising that those from other lineages would study underneath him or, for that matter, that as a Tendai-trained monk he would make ample use of the teachings of the *Lotus Sūtra* in his writings (Leighton 2005). Dōgen's advocacy of "just-sitting" meditation did not, in fact, mean that he rejected the study of *mondō* or *kōan* interactions between masters and disciples. At the same time, he did criticize certain teachings common in the early medieval era, such as those promoting the *nenbutsu*, belief in the final age of the Dharma (*mappō*), and many of the apotropaic prayers made to *kami*, bodhisattvas, and Buddhas (Imaeda 2001: 245–246).

The Tendai monk Nichiren (1222–1282), child of a local fishing family in the Eastern Honshū Province of Awa (Chiba), would be remembered as the founder of the Nichiren lineages (Nichiren shū) of Japanese Buddhism, one of the schools often identified by scholars with "new" Kamakura Buddhism. During his life, however, Nichiren did not claim to be attempting, in his devotion to the *Lotus Sūtra*, to do anything other than to resurrect what he saw as the true teaching of earlier Tiantai and Tendai figures like Chigi (Ch. Zhiyi, 538–597) and Saichō (766–822; Maekawa 2010: 124). Nonetheless, his views on issues such as original enlightenment, for example, were very different from those of other Tendai monks historically, since his concern was very different: Nichiren was motivated to discuss original enlightenment to demonstrate that the *Lotus Sūtra* is the exclusively valid object of faith in the age of *mappō*, whereas medieval Tendai esoteric texts typically promoted original enlightenment to counter notions that cultivation of merit would contribution to eventual enlightened realization (Stone 1999: 240).

Nichiren's teaching thus concerned his understanding of his era, not only because he believed in *mappō* but because he saw Japan in his day as crystallizing the narratives outlined in the *Lotus Sūtra* itself. In other words, Nichiren believed that the bodhisattvas and events outlined in connection with *mappō* were being fulfilled in what Japanese Buddhists had until now generally seen as only a set of isles at the edge of the human and Buddhist world – and that he himself had a unique role to play in that Buddho-historical drama. Moreover, he believed that the disasters and violent conflicts of the day were specifically due to the ignorant beliefs of many Buddhists; during the first half of his teaching career, he concentrated his criticisms on Pure Land believers, and in the second half, on esoteric Buddhists. Nichiren argued, moreover, that not only was the *Lotus Sūtra* the only scripture capable of offering the possibility of Buddhahood to all sentient beings but also, given the impediments of the Last Age, that the only effective object of Buddhist faith in his day was its essence, enacted by means of the enunciation of its title, the *daimoku* (i.e., *namu-myōhō-renge-kyō*; Maekawa 2010: 127–132).

Nichiren approached the Kamakura military government with his *Risshō ankokuron* (Treatise for Pacification of the Realm and the Establishment of Truth) in 1260, following studies in Kamakura and at Mt. Hiei and his witness of a series of natural catastrophes, which together convinced him that the source of the realm's ill-fortune was the decline of the Buddha Dharma. In sending his treatise to the *bakufu*, Nichiren differed sharply from earlier kenmitsu figures (e.g., Jōkei), who invariably denounced figures like Hōnen by appealing to the court, an action apparently reflecting his knowledge that actual power lay in the hands of the shogunal regent rather than the retired sovereign (Satō 2008: 25–26). Nichiren, like kenmitsu monks before him, reacted particularly vociferously to Pure Land Buddhists' failure to venerate the "traces" of Buddhas/bodhisattvas – the *kami* – because such rejection was tantamount to denunciation of the very beings who offered mediation to salvation as well as protection and peace to the Japanese isles, themselves the "realm of *kami*" (*shinkoku*); however, Nichiren even argued that the Śākyamuni Buddha of the *Lotus Sūtra*, as the original Buddha of the cosmos (i.e., the Dharma body), acted directly through his traces – the *kami* of Japan as well as the sovereign of the realm – and that if Japanese rejected their roles, Śākyamuni would reprove them (Satō 2002: 146–153). In this way, we can see that Nichiren was originally a kenmitsu monk but he wove the narrative of the *Lotus Sūtra* into his own age, reinterpreting the absolute Buddha as an historical actor capable of engagement with the very conduct and substance of the realm.

Notes

1   See the Introduction for a fuller discussion of these factors.
2   In fact, the fuller outlines of these customary court rites became apparent by the 840 s.
3   Translation by Ruppert.
4   For the English translation, see Kamens 1988: 241–370.
5   Translation by Ruppert.
6   Although not commonly known, a distinct work by the same title was written at roughly the beginning of the tenth century. Compiled by the Hiei monk Yakkō (n.d.), described as a "recluse" of the south valley there, it is described briefly in *Fusō ryakki* (twelfth century) but no longer extant (Chimoto 1999).
7   Tales derived from this early collection also reveal that faith in Jizō sometimes included chanting the bodhisattva's name and was tied to practices such as the Amida *nenbutsu* (e.g., *Jizō bosatsu reigen ki*: 34b–35b, 46b–47a; *Konjaku monogatari shū* 17.2: 505–506, 17.16: 523). It is also known that a variety of lineage figures, like the "Zen" master Yōsai, were Jizō devotees (Glassman 2012: 72).
8   Obara notes that although these were originally patterned upon the genre of such narratives in Tang-period China, the latter were written by monks.
9   See also Uejima 2010a: 497–527.
10 T. = Taishō shinshū daizōkyō 1924–1932.
11 In the case of the Ise shrine complex, taboo words (*imi-kotoba*) were developed by the early ninth century to be used in the stead of Buddhist terminology when anyone entered the premises (Itō 2010: 195).
12 Sueki Fumihiko has succinctly discussed the tendency in Japan to associate Buddhist divinities and, especially *kami*, with particular sites, focusing especially on the period during or after the rise to eminence of retired sovereigns (Sueki 2010: 39–40).

13 *Kami* were only mysteriously and partially assimilated to Buddhas or Bodhisattvas and, moreover, they were seen as inferior beings within the Buddhist cosmos insofar as they were subject as deities to karma within the six courses of rebirth (Yoshie 1996).

14 In fact, Okada Shōji has noted that the basic system, which transformed crisis-driven ritual patronage into customary ceremonies, continued unabated until the late Muromachi period (sixteenth century; Okada 1994: 325–361). Uejima Susumu has recently noted, based on analysis of the governmental provisions (*yōdo*) at the time, that this system promoted shrines and that Buddhist provisions continued for only court rites like the Mi-sai'e since the early Heian period, and offers what he sees as the Buddhist response to the shrines' new precedence – the creation, on the one hand, of new exoteric assemblies (*hō'e*) and, on the other, esoteric royal-guardian monks (*gojisō*; Uejima 2010a: 74–75).

15 A documentary recently produced by Matsuo Kōichi has clarified that the *kami* of Kasuga has offered the topics for discussion at the Kōfukuji clerical debates (*rongi*) since the medieval era, and emphasized that the presiding abbot is understood to be transformed into the *kami* during the ceremony (Matsuo 2009).

16 The italics have been added for stress and reader comprehension. We have adapted the translation from Ruppert (2000: 196–197).

17 Illustrated scrolls depicting the Sudhana narrative became prominent by the thirteenth century (see, for example, *Kegon gojūgosho e-maki*, in Morimoto 1998).

18 The so-called *waka* category of '"Teachings of Śākyamuni" (*shakkyō*) would only be introduced almost a century later, because its inauguration was monarchical in character – as a category within the official collections – beginning with *Goshūi shū* (1086), which coincided with the onset of the Retired Sovereigns Era.

19 The quote is in the sources section of *Wakan rōeishū* 1965: 303b.

20 Yamagishi Tsuneto (2004: 117–123) has noted that such quarters came not only to be inherited but, at least from the second half of the twelfth century onward, to sometimes be sold.

21 We draw here on a vast accumulation of research, most of which has been conducted under the direction of Abe Yasurō; Abe discusses these genres in succinct terms in Abe 1998a: 122–126.

22 Significantly, Shukaku's body of writings and collections – known more generally as the "sacred writings of the Go-ryū" (*Go-ryū shōgyō*) – was transmitted rapidly to the Kantō region (Fukushima 1998).

23 As Tajima notes, Ninnaji housed a royal treasury from much earlier (2006: 45). However, the scale of these later treasuries may indicate a debt to Uji as has been suggested by Uejima Susumu (2001).

24 For a bibliographical essay on the hagiographies, see "Juyō denki shiryō kaidai/nenpu," in Kōbō Daishi Kūkai Zenshū Henshū Iinkai 1985. Concerning the lack of early treatises, this has rarely been noted in scholarship. We should note, however, that the earliest mention of a treatise (*chūshakusho*) on a work by Kūkai in the extensive bibliographical list "Senjutsusho no shohon to chūshakusho ichiran" (Kōbō Daishi Kūkai Zenshū Henshū Iinkai 1985) was Shinzei's (800–860) on *Shōrai mokuroku*, followed only by a single treatise by Shinkaku (955–1043) on *Jūjūshinron*.

25 Members of the court made distinctions between the classics and Buddhist works – they understood the common Buddhist distinction between "inner works" (*naiten*) and "outer

works" (geten) – and it was also common for handbooks to include sections on both, such as can be see in Tamenori's other handbooks (Zoku gunsho ruijū 30, vol. 2: 55a-6a; Zoku gunsho ruijū 32, vol. 1: 67b–71a).

26 Moreover, although the female retired sovereigns (nyo'in) were increasingly powerful figures, they were typically of Fujiwara heritage, so that the family remained at the center of court activity.

27 Michael Jamentz is currently writing a PhD dissertation at Harvard University on the major figures of the Shinzei lineage, which had tremendous influence over the cultural and political landscape of medieval Japan. Chōken is one of the objects of the study, which will shed extensive new light on this topic.

28 Especially notable is a series of Chōsa kenkyū hōkoku publications of original Agui and related liturgical literary sources. Komine Kazuaki and Yamazaki Makoto spearheaded these publications, which were published under the title Agui shōdō shiryō sanshū in eight successive installments (Komine and Yamazaki 1991–1998)

29 With regard to the latter, Hie (alt. Hiyoshi) shrine, for example, is at the foot of Hiei and, together with the temple Enryakuji, historically part of the larger shrine-temple complex commonly referred to as Mt. Hiei (Breen and Teeuwen 2010: 66–128).

References

Abe Mika. 2013. "Chūsei media to shite no Yūzū nenbutsu engi e-maki." In Setsuwa Bungakkai (eds.), Setsuwa kara sekai o dō tokiakasu no ka, 68–88. Tokyo: Kasama Shoin.

Abé, Ryūichi. 2006. "Swords, Words, and Deformity: On Myōe's eccentricity." In Richard K. Payne and Taigen Dan Leighton (eds.), Discourse and Ideology in Medieval Japanese Buddhism, 148–159. London and New York: Routledge.

Abe Yasurō. 1998a. "Shukaku hosshinnō to inseiki no bukkyō bunka." In Hayami Tasuku (ed.), Inseiki no bukkyō, 118–142. Tokyo: Yoshikawa Kōbunkan.

Abe Yasurō. 1998b. Yuya no kōgō. Nagoya: Nagoya Daigaku Shuppankai.

Abe Yasurō. 1999. "The Confessions of Lady Nijō as a 'Woman's Tale' and Its Layering of the Many Spheres of Medieval Literature." In Wakita Haruko, Anne Bouchy, and Ueno Chizuko (eds.), Gender and Japanese History, vol. 2: The Self and Expression/Work and Life, 47–98. Osaka: Osaka University Press.

Abe Yasurō. 2001. Seija no suisan. Nagoya: Nagoya Daigaku Shuppankai.

Abe Yasurō, Yamazaki Makoto, and Kokubungaku Kenkyū Shiryōkan, eds. 2005. Hōgi hyōbyaku shū (Shinpukuji zenpon sōkan series 2, no. 11). Kyoto: Rinsen Shoten.

Agui shōdō shū. 1979. Comp. Nagai Yoshinori and Shimizu Kōsei (Kichō kotenseki sōkan 6). Tokyo: Kadokawa Shoten.

Arichi, Meri. 2006. "The Seven Stars of Heaven and Seven Shrines on Earth: The Big Dipper and the Hie Shrine in the Medieval Period." Culture and Cosmos 10 (1–2): 195–216.

Bauer, Mikael. 2012. "Conflating Monastic and Imperial Lineage: The Retired Emperors' Period Reformulated." Monumenta Nipponica 67 (2): 239–262.

Bielefeldt, Carl. 1988. Dōgen's Manuals of Zen Meditation. Berkeley, CA: University of California Press.

Bodiford, William. 2008. "Dharma Transmission in Theory and Practice." In Steven Heine and Dale S. Wright (eds.), *Zen Ritual: Studies of Zen Buddhist Theory in Practice*, 261–282. Oxford and New York: Oxford University Press.

Borgen, Robert. 2007. "Jōjin's Travels from Center to Center (with Some Periphery in between)." In Mikael Adolphson, Edward Kamens, and Stacie Matsumoto, (eds.), *Heian Japan: Centers and Peripheries*, 384–413. Honolulu: University of Hawai'i Press.

Breen, John, and Teeuwen, Mark. 2010. *A New History of Shinto*. Oxford: Wiley-Blackwell.

Chimoto Hideshi. 1999. "Yakkōbon." In Chimoto Hideshi, *Genki bungaku no kenkyū*, 150–167. Tokyo: Bensei Shuppan.

Daishi go-nyūjō kanketsu ki. By Saisen (1025–1115). In Hase Hōshū (ed.), *Kōbō Daishi denzenshū daii-ikkan*. Tokyo: Pitaka, 1977.

Deal, William E. 1993. "The Lotus Sutra and the Rhetoric of Legitimization in Eleventh-Century Japanese Buddhism." *Japanese Journal of Religious Studies* 20 (4): 262–296.

Dobbins, James C. 1998. "Envisioning Kamakura Buddhism." In Richard K. Payne (ed.), *Re-Visioning "Kamakura" Buddhism*, 24–42. Honolulu: University of Hawai'i Press.

Dobbins, James C. 2002. *Jōdo Shinshū: Shin Buddhism in Medieval Japan*. Honolulu: University of Hawai'i Press.

Endō Motoo. 1998. "Kasa no kenryokuron: kizoku shakaiteki bunka yōshiki to tokuji shugi ideorogi no hazama." In Fukutō Sanae (ed.), *Ōchō no kenryoku to hyōshō: gakugei no bunkashi*, 87–123. Tokyo: Shinwasha.

Eubanks, Charlotte. 2009. "Illustrating the Mind: 'Faulty Memory' Setsuwa and the Decorative Sutras of Late Classical and Early Medieval Japan." *Japanese Journal of Religious Studies* 36 (2): 209–230.

Foard, James. 1980. "In Search of a Lost Reformation: A Reconsideration of Kamakura Buddhism." *Japanese Journal of Religious Studies* 7 (4): 261–291.

Ford, James L. 2006a. "Buddhist ceremonials (*kōshiki*) and the ideological discourse of established Buddhism in early medieval Japan. In Richard K. Payne and Taigen Dan Leighton (eds.), *Discourse and Ideology in Medieval Japanese Buddhism*, 97–125. New York: Routledge.

Ford, James L. 2006b. *Jōkei and Buddhist Devotion in Early Medieval Japan*. New York: Oxford University Press.

Fujii Masako. 2008. *Chūsei Daigoji to Shingon mikkyō*. Tokyo: Bensei Shuppan.

Fukushima Kaneharu. 1998. "Ninnaji go-ryū no Kamakura denpa: Kamakura Sasame Yuishin'in to sono yakuwari." In Abe Yasurō and Yamazaki Makoto (eds.), *Shukaku hosshinnō to Ninnaji goryū no bunkenteki kenkyū, ronbunhen*, 455–502. Tokyo: Benseisha.

Genji monogatari, By Murasaki Shikibu. Modern edn 1977, vol. 2. Edited by Yamagishi Tokuhei. Tokyo: Iwanami Shoten.

Glassman, Hank. 2012. *The Face of Jizô: Image and Cult in Medieval Japanese Buddhism*. Honolulu: University of Hawai'i Press.

Goble, Andrew Edmund. 2011. *Confluences of Medicine in Medieval Japan: Buddhist Healing, Chinese Knowledge, Islamic Formulas, and Wounds of War*. Honolulu: University of Hawai'i Press.

Gomi Fumihiko. 2003. *Shomotsu no chūsei shi*. Tokyo: Misuzu Shobō.

Goodwin, Janet R. 1994. *Alms and Vagabonds: Buddhist Temples and Popular Pilgrimage in Medieval Japan*. Honolulu: University of Hawai'i Press.

Gotō Akio. 2002. *Tendai bukkyō to heianchō bunjin*. Tokyo: Yoshikawa Kōbunkan.

Grapard, Allan G. 1988. "Institution, Ritual, and Ideology: The Twenty-Two Shrine-Temple Multiplexes of Heian Japan." *History of Religions* 2, (3): 246–269.

Groner, Paul. 2002. *Ryōgen and Mount Hiei: Japanese Tendai in the 10th Century*. Honolulu: University of Hawai'i Press.

Groner, Paul. 2005. "Tradition and Innovation: Eison's Self-Ordinations and the Establishment of New Orders of Buddhist Practitioners." In William M. Bodiford (ed.), *Going Forth: Visions of Buddhist Vinaya: Essays in Honor of Professor Stanley Weinstein* (Studies in East Asian Buddhism 18), 210–235. Honolulu: University of Hawai'i Press.

Guelberg, Niels. 2004. *Kōshiki* database (www.f.waseda.jp/guelberg/koshiki/datenb-j.htm).

Hashimoto Yoshihiko. 1976. *Heian kizoku shakai no kenkyū*. Tokyo: Yoshikawa Kōbunkan.

Hayashi Yuzuru. 2000. "Ippen no shūkyō oboegaki: toku ni sono namae wo megutte." In Ōsumi Kazuo (ed.), *Chūsei no bukkyō to shakai*, 108–145. Tokyo: Yoshikawa Kōbunkan.

Hayashi Yuzuru. 2004. "Odori *nenbutsu* no kaishi to tenkai: Ippen to Jishū ni okeru sono igi." In Imai Masaharu (ed.), *Ippen: yugyō no sute-hijiri*, 95–116. Tokyo: Yoshikawa Kōbunkan.

Hirota, Dennis. 1997. *No Abode: The Record of Ippen*. Rev. edn. Honolulu: University of Hawai'i Press.

Honchō monzui/Honchō zoku monzui. 1965. Comp. Kuroita Katsumi *et al.* (Shintei zōho Kokushi taikei 29, part 2). Tokyo: Yoshikawa Kōbunkan.

Hori Ichirō. 1971. *Kūya*. Tokyo: Yoshikawa Kōbunkan.

Horiike Shunpō *et al.*, eds. 2001. *Tōdaiji monjo o yomu*. Kyoto: Shibunkaku.

Horton, Sarah J. 2007. *Living Buddhist Statues in Early Medieval and Modern Japan*. New York: Palgrave Macmillan.

Hosokawa Ryōichi. 1996. "Eison/Ninshō no jizen kyūsai: hinin kyūsai of shujiku ni." In Hosokawa Ryōichi, *Chūsei no mibunsei to hinin*, 131–164. Tokyo: Nihon editāsukūru.

Hosokawa Ryōichi. 1997. *Chūsei jiin no fūkei: chūsei minshū no seikatsu to shinsei*. Tokyo: Shinyōsha.

Imaeda, Aishin. 2002. "The Sōtō Sect." In Kasahara Kazuo (ed.), *A History of Japanese Religion*, 244–254. Trans. Paul McCarthy and Gaynor Sekimori. Tokyo: Kōsei Shuppansha.

Imai Masaharu. 1993. "Tokifusa-ryū Hōjōshi to Jishū." In Ōsumi Kazuo (ed.), *Kamakura jidai bunka denpa no kenkyū*, 167–192. Tokyo: Yoshikawa Kōbunkan.

Imai Masaharu. 1999. *Shinran to tōkoku monto*. Tokyo: Yoshikawa Kōbunkan.

Inoue Mitsusada. 1974. "Bunken kaidai." In Inoue Mitsusada and Ōsone Shōsuke, comp., *Ōjōden/Hokke genki* (Nihon shisō taikei 7), 711–760. Tokyo: Iwanami Shoten.

Itō, Satoshi. 2003. "The Medieval Period: The Kami merge with Buddhism." In Nobutaka Inoue (ed.), *Shinto: A Short History*, 63–107. London and New York: RoutledgeCurzon.

Itō Satoshi. 2009. "The Medieval Cult of Gyōki and Ise Shrines Concerning the Narratives of Gyōki's Pilgrimage to Ise." In Bernard Faure, Michael Como, and Iyanaga Nobumi (eds.), *Rethinking Medieval Shintō, special issue of Cahiers d'Extrême-Asie* 16, 49–69. Kyoto: École francais d'Extrême-Orient.

Itō Satoshi. 2010. "Girei to shinwa." In Sueki Fumihiko (ed.), *Yakudō suru chūsei bukkyō*, 193–233. Tokyo: Kōsei Publishing.

Jamentz, Michael. 2008. "Shinzei ichimon no shinzoku nettowaaku to inseiki kaiga seisaku." *Rokuon zasshū* 10: 1–35.

Jizō bosatsu reigen ki. Attributed to Jitsu'e (fl. 1033). Two fascicles. *Zoku gunsho ruijū* 25, vol. 2.

Kamens, Edward. 1988. *The Three Jewels: A Study and Translation of Minamoto Tamenori's Sanbōe.* Ann Arbor, MI: Center for Japanese Studies, the University of Michigan.

Kamens, Edward. 1990. *The Buddhist Poetry of the Great Kamo Priestess: Daisaiin Senshi and Hosshin Wakashū.* Ann Arbor, MI: Center for Japanese Studies, University of Michigan.

Kamikawa Michio. 1998. "Insei to Shingon mikkyō: Shukaku Hosshinnō no shiteki ichi." In Abe Yasurō and Yamazaki Makoto (eds.), *Shukaku Hosshinnō to Ninnaji goryū no bunkenteki kenkyū, ronbunhen,* 147–194. Tokyo: Benseisha.

Kamikawa Michio. 2008. *Nihon chūsei bukkyō shiryōron.* Tokyo: Yoshikawa Kōbunkan.

Kaminishi, Ikumi. 2006. *Explaining Pictures: Buddhist Propaganda and Etoki Storytelling in Japan.* Honolulu: University of Hawai'i Press.

Kaufman, Laura S. 1992. "Nature, Courtly Imagery, and Sacred Meaning in the Ippen Hijiri-e." In James H. Sanford, William R. LaFleur, and Masatoshi Nagatomi (eds.), *Flowing Traces: Buddhism in the Literary and Visual Arts of Japan,* 47–75. Princeton, NJ: Princeton University Press.

Kawashima, Terry. 2001. *Writing Margins: The Textual Construction of Gender in Heian and Kamakura Japan.* Cambridge, MA: Harvard University Asia Center, Harvard University Press.

Kikuchi Hiroki. 2007. *Chūsei bukkyō no genkei to tenkai.* Tokyo: Yoshikawa Kōbunkan.

Kikuchi Hiroki. 2011. *Kamakura bukkyō e no michi: jissen to shūgaku/shinjin no keifu.* Tokyo: Kōdansha.

Kimbrough, R. Keller. 2008. *Preachers, Poets, Women, and the Way.* Ann Arbor, MI: Center for Japanese Studies, University of Michigan.

Kōbō Daishi Kūkai Zenshū Henshū Iinkai, eds. 1985. *Kōbō daishi Kūkai zenshū Dai 8 kan.*

Komine Kazuaki. 2009. *Chūsei hōe bungei ron.* Tokyo: Kasama Shoin.

Komine Kazuaki and Yamazaki Makoto et al. 1991–1998. *Agui shōdō shiryō sanshū 1~8 (Chōsa kenkyū hōkoku* nos. 12~19).

Konjaku monogatari shū. Anon. 1961. Modern edn., annotated by Yamada Yoshio, Yamada Tadao, Yamada Hideo, and Yamada Toshio (*Koten bungaku taikei 24*). Tokyo: Iwanami Shoten.

Kudō Miwako. 2008. *Heianki no ganmon to bukkyōteki sekaikan.* Kyoto: Shibunkaku.

Kuroda Toshio. 1975. *Nihon chūsei no kokka to shūkyō.* Tokyo: Iwanami Shoten.

Kuroda Toshio. 1992. *Jisha seiryoku: mō hitotsu no chūsei shakai* (Iwanami Shinsho 117). Tokyo: Iwanami Shoten.

Kuroda Toshio. 1996. "The Development of the *Ken-mitsu* System as Japan's Medieval Orthodoxy." Trans. James C. Dobbins. *Japanese Journal of Religious Studies* 23 (3–4): 233–269.

Leighton, Taigen Dan. 2005. "Dōgen's Appropriation of *Lotus Sutra* Ground and Space." *Japanese Journal of Religious Studies* 32 (1): 85–105.

Maekawa Ken'ichi. 2010. "Shinbukkyō no keisei. In Sueki Fumihiko (ed.), *Yakudō suru chūsei bukkyō (Shin ajia bukkyōshi 12, nihon 2),* 65–135. Tokyo: Kōsei Publishing.

Marra, Michele. 1991. "The Aesthetics of Reclusion: Kamo no Chōmei and the Last Age." In Michele Marra, *The Aesthetics of Discontent: Politics and Reclusion in Medieval Japanese Literature,* 70–100. Honolulu: University of Hawai'i Press.

Matsuo Kenji. 2010. "Bukkyōsha no shakai katsudō." In Sueki Fumihiko (ed.), *Yakudō suru chūsei bukkyō (Shin ajia bukkyōshi 12, nihon 2),* 141–186. Tokyo: Kōsei Publishing.

Matsuo Kōichi. 1997. *Ennen no geinōshiteki kenkyū.* Tokyo: Iwata Shoin.

Matsuo, Kōichi. 2009. *Kōfukuji and Kasuga Taisha: Rites of kami-Buddha Amalgamation and the People Who Support Them DVD.* Sakura: National Museum of Japanese History.

Matsuzono Hitoshi. 2006. Ōchō nikki ron. Tokyo: Hōsei Daigaku Shuppankyoku.

Minobe Shigekatsu. 2000. "Bunkaken to shite no sōbō." In Henkakuki no bungaku 1 (Iwanami kōza Nihon bungakushi daiyonkan), 259–278. Tokyo: Iwanami Shoten.

Minowa Kenryō. 1999. Chūsei shoki nanto kairitsu fukkō no kenkyū. Kyoto: Hōzōkan.

Minowa Kenryō. 2010. "Kenmitsu bukkyō no tenkai." In Sueki Fumihiko (ed.), Yakudō suru chūsei bukkyō (Shin ajia bukkyōshi 12, nihon 2), 13–57. Tokyo: Kōsei Publishing.

Mitsuhashi Tadashi. 2000. Heian jidai no shinkō to shūkyō girei. Tokyo: Zoku Gunsho Ruijū Kankōkai.

Miyake Hitoshi. 2005. The Mandala of the Mountain: Shugendo and Folk Religion. Trans., ed., and introduction, Gaynor Sekimori. Tokyo: Keio University Press.

Moerman, D. Max. 2006. Localizing Paradise: Kumano Pilgrimage and the Religious Landscape of Premodern Japan. Cambridge, MA: Harvard University Asia Center, Harvard University Press.

Moerman, D. Max. 2007. "The Archeology of Anxiety: An Underground History of Heian Religion." In Mikael Adolphson, Edward Kamens, and Stacie Matsumoto, (eds.), Heian Japan: Centers and Peripheries, 245–271. Honolulu: University of Hawai'i Press.

Mori Mizue. 2003. "The Dawn of Shinto." In Inoue Nobutaka (ed.), Shinto: A Short History, 12–62. London and New York: RoutledgeCurzon.

Morimoto Kōsei, ed. 1998. Zenzai dōji: gudō no tabi (Kegonkyō nyūhokkaibon Kegon gojūgosho e-maki yori). Nara: Tōdaiji.

Morris, Ivan, trans. 1989. As I Crossed a Bridge of Dreams: Recollections of a Woman in 11th-Century Japan. New York: Penguin.

Nagamura Makoto. 1989. Chūsei Tōdaiji no soshiki to keiei. Tokyo: Hanawa Shobō.

Nagamura Makoto. 2000. "'Monzeki' to monzeki." In Ōsumi Kazuo (ed.), Chūsei no bukkyō to shakai, 56–82. Tokyo: Yoshikawa Kōbunkan.

Nagashima Shōdō. 2004. "Nenbutsu wa nenbutsu wo mōsu shinkō: Amida-butsu to myōgō." In Imai Masaharu (ed.), Ippen: yugyō no sute-hijiri, 43–69. Tokyo: Yoshikawa Kōbunkan.

Nara Kokuritsu Hakubutsukan, ed. 2005. Itsukushima jinja kokuhōten. Osaka: Yomiuri Shinbun.

Nihon kiryaku. Anonymous. (late Heian period compilation of earlier chronicles), modern edn., 1929 (Shintei zōho kokushi taikei 10–11). Tokyo: Yoshikawa Kōbunkan.

Obara Hitoshi. 2007. Chūsei kizoku shakai to bukkyō. Tokyo: Yoshikawa Kōbunkan.

Ogawa Toyoo. 2003. "Chūsei shingaku no mechie." In Nishiki Hitoshi, Ogawa Toyoo, and Itō Satoshi (eds.), "Gisho" no seisei: chūseitekishikō to hyōgen, 155–195. Tokyo: Shinwasha.

Ōhashi Toshio. 1985. Hōnen to jōdoshū kyōdan. Tokyo: Kyōikusha.

Okada Shōji. 1994. Heian jidai no kokka to saishi. Tokyo: Zoku Gunsho Ruijū Kanseikai.

Ōshima Tatehiko et al. 2003. "Jūyonkanbon Jizō bosatsu reigenki kaisetsu." In Ōshima Tatehiko (supervising ed.), Jūyonkanbon Jizō bosatsu reigen ki, ge, 345–395. Tokyo: Miyai Shoten.

Quinter, David. 2007. "Creating Bodhisattvas: Eison, Hinin, and the 'Living Mañjuśrī." Monument Nipponica 62 (4): 437-458.

Payne, Richard K. 1998. "Introduction." In Richard K. Payne (ed.), Re-visioning "Kamakura" Buddhism, 1–23. Honolulu: University of Hawai'i Press.

Rihōō ki, by Shigeakira Shinnō. Shiryō sanshū ed. 1974. Tokyo: Gunsho Ruijū Kanseikai.

Rosenfield, John M. 2011. Portraits of Chōgen: The Transformation of Buddhist Art in Early Medieval Japan. Leiden, Netherlands, and Boston: Brill.

Ruppert, Brian. 2000. Jewel in the Ashes: Buddha Relics and Power in Early Medieval Japan. Cambridge, MA: Harvard University Asia Center, Harvard University Press.

Sanbō'e/Chūkōsen. 1997. Ed. Mabuchi Kazuo, Koizumi Hiroshi and Konna Tooru (Shin koten bungaku taikei 31). Tokyo: Iwanami Shoten.

Sarashina nikki, by Sugawara no Takasue no Musume (b. 1008). 1957. In Suzuki Tomotarō et al. (eds.), *Tosa nikki/Kagerō nikki/Izumi Shikibu nikki/Sarashina nikki* (Nihon koten bungaku taikei 20). Tokyo: Iwanami Shoten.

Satō Hiroo. 1997. "'Nihon no hotoke' no tanjō." In Tamakake Hiroyuki (ed.), *Nihon shisōshi: Sono fuhen to tokushu*, 56–76. Tokyo: Perikansha.

Satō Hiroo. 2002. "Nichiren no jingikan." In Nakao Takashi (ed.), *Kamakura bukkyō no shisō to bunka*, 137–156. Tokyo: Yoshikawa Kōbunkan.

Satō Hiroo. 2008. *Nichiren: Risshō ankokuron*. Tokyo: Kōdansha.

Satō Michio. 2003. "Heian kōki no kanbungaku: honsho no sōron to shite." In Satō Michio, *Heian kōki nihon kanbungaku no kenkyū*, 5–33. Tokyo: Kasama Shoin.

Shinzoku kōdan ki. Kamakura Era, attributed to Shukaku Hosshinnō (1150–1202). GR 28.

Shūi ōjōden. 1974, by Miyoshi no Tameyasu (1049–1139). Mod. edn in Inoue Mitsusada and Ōsone Shōsuke eds., *Ōjōden/Hokke genki* (Nihon shisō taikei 7). Tokyo: Iwanami Shoten.

Smits, Ivo. 2003. "Places of Mediation: Poets and Salons in Medieval Japan." In Michael Hockx and Ivo Smits (eds.), *Reading East Asian Writing: The Limits of Literary Theory*, 204-219. London and New York: RoutledgeCurzon.

Stone, Jacqueline I. 1999. *Original Enlightenment and the Transformation of Japanese Buddhism*. Kuroda Institute. Honolulu: University of Hawai'i Press.

Stone, Jacqueline I. 2006. "Buddhism." In Paul L. Swanson and Clark Chilson (eds.), *Nanzan Guide to Japanese Religions*, 38–64. Honolulu: University of Hawai'i Press.

Stone, Jacqueline I. 2008. "With the Help of 'Good Friends': Deathbed Ritual Practices in Early Medieval Japan. In Jacqueline I. Stone and Mariko Namba Walter (eds.), *Death and the Afterlife in Japanese Buddhism*, 60–101. Honolulu: University of Hawai'i Press.

Sueki Fumihiko. 1993. *Nihon Bukkyō shisōshi ronkō*. Tokyo: Daizō Shuppan.

Sueki Fumihiko. 2008. *Kamakura bukkyō tenkai ron*. Tokyo: Transview.

Sueki Fumihiko. 2010a. *Chūsei no kami to hotoke*. Tokyo: Yamakawa Shuppansha.

Taira Masayuki. 1996. "Kuroda Toshio and the *Ken-mitsu Taisei* Theory." *Japanese Journal of Religious Studies* 23.3-4: 427-448.

Taira Masayuki. 2001. *Shinran to sono jidai*. Kyoto: Hōzōkan.

Taishō shinshū daizōkyō. 1924–1932. 85 vols. Ed. Takakusu Junjirō and Watanabe Kaigyoku. Tokyo: Taishō Shinshū Daizōkyō Kankōkai.

Tajima Isao. 2006. "Chūsei tennōke no bunko/hōzō no hensen: zōsho mokuroku to shūzōhin no yukue." In Tajima Isao (ed.), *Kinri/kuge bunko kenkyū dai-ni shū*, 43–94. Kyoto: Shibunkaku.

Takei Akio. 1994. "Kōya." In Tsunoda Bun'ei and Kodaigaku Kyōkai (eds.), *Heian jidaishi jiten*, vol. 1: 846a–c. Tokyo: Kadokawa Shoten.

Takahashi Shinichirō. 2007. "Chūsei jiin ni okeru sōbō no tenkai." In Ono Masatoshi, Gomi Fumihiko, and Hagiwara Mitsuo (eds.), *Chūsei jiin: bōryoku to keikan*, 17–40. Tokyo: Takashi Shoin.

Tale of Genji. 2001. 2 vols. Trans. Royall Tyler. New York: Viking.

Tanaka Yūbun. 2006. "Chūnagon risshi misono no Jōson denkō. *Mikkyō bunka kenkyūsho kiyō* 19: 1-41.

Tōdaiji yōroku. 1944. Anonymous (early 12th c.), modern edn Tsutsui Eishun. Tokyo: Zenkoku Shobō.

Tsuchiya Megumi. 2001. *Chūsei jiin no shakai to geinō.* Tokyo: Yoshikawa Kōbunkan.

Uejima Susumu. 2001. "Fujiwara no Michinaga to insei: shūkyō to seiji." In Uwayokote Masataka (ed.), *Chūsei kōbu kenryoku no kōzō to tenkai,* 27–67. Tokyo: Yoshikawa Kōbunkan.

Uejima Susumu. 2010a. *Nihon chūsei shakai no keisei to ōken.* Nagoya: Nagoya Daigaku Shuppankai.

Uejima Susumu. 2010b. "Bukkyō no nihonka." In Sueki Fumihiko (ed.), *Nihon bukkyō no ishizue (Shin ajia bukkyōshi 11, nihon 1),* 203–245. Tokyo: Kōsei Publishing.

Van der Veere, Henny. 2000. "Doctrinal Position of Kakuban." In Henny Van der Veere, *Kōgyō Daishi Kakuban,* 57–105. Leiden, Netherlands: Hotei Publishing.

Wakan rōeishū/Ryōjin hishō. 1965. Modern edn, comp. Kawaguchi Hisao and Shida Nobuyoshi (NKBT 73). Tokyo: Iwanami Shoten.

Yamada, Shōzen. 1989. "Poetry and Meaning: Medieval Poets and the *Lotus Sutra.*" In George J. Tanabe, Jr., and Willa Jane Tanabe (eds.), *The Lotus Sutra in Japanese Culture,* 95–118. Honolulu: University of Hawai'i Press.

Yamagishi Tsuneto. 2004. *Chūsei jiin no sōdan/hōe/monjo.* Tokyo: Tokyo Daigaku Shuppankai.

Yamazaki Makoto. 1981. "Shinzoku kōdan ki kō: Ninnaji bun'en no ichikōsatsu." *Kokugo to kokubungaku* 58 (1): 13–27.

Yamazaki Makoto. 1996. "Kokubungaku kenkyū shiryōkan zō Hyōbyaku gosō." *Kokubungaku kenkyūshiryōkan kiyō* 22: 67–105.

Yiengpruksawan, Mimi Hall. 1998. *Hirazumi: Buddhist Art and Regional Politics in Twelfth-Century Japan.* Cambridge, MA: Harvard University Asia Center, Harvard University Press.

Yokouchi Hiroto. 2008. *Nihon chūsei no bukkyō to higashi ajia.* Tokyo: Hanawa Shobō.

Yoshie Akio. 1996. *Shinbutsu shūgō.* Tokyo: Iwanami Shoten.

Yoshikawa Satoshi, Endō Motoo, and Kohara Yoshiki. 2008. "Tōdaiji daikanjin monjo shū no kenkyū." *Nanto bukkyō* 91: 123–220.

Zoku gunsho ruijū. 1929–1933. Ed. Hanawa Hoki'ichi (1746–1821) *et al.* 34 vols. Tokyo: Zoku Gunsho ruijū Kanseikai.

Further Reading

Abe Yasurō, ed. 2010. *Chūsei bungaku to jiin shiryō/shōgyō.* Tokyo: Chikurinsha.

Hayami Tasuku, ed. 1998. *Inseiki no Bukkyō.* Tokyo: Yoshikawa Kōbunkan.

Nagamura Makoto. 2000. *Chūsei jiin shiryō ron.* Tokyo: Yoshikawa Kōbunkan.

Sueki, Fumihiko. 1996. "A Reexamination of the *Ken-mitsu Taisei* Theory. *Japanese Journal of Religious Studies* 23 (3–4): 449–466.

Sueki Fumihiko, ed. 2010. *Nihon Bukkyō no ishizue (Shin Ajia Bukkyōshi 11, Nihon 1).* Tokyo: Kōsei Shuppansha.

Tanabe, George J., Jr., and Willa Jane Tanabe, eds. 1989. *The Lotus Sūtra in Japanese Culture.* Honolulu: University of Hawai'i Press.

4

Late Medieval Buddhism (1300–1467): New Buddhisms, Buddhist Learning, Dissemination and the Fall into Chaos

Late Kamakura-Period and Early Muromachi-Period Buddhism

Given the important historical developments of the late thirteenth and fourteenth centuries outlined in the Introduction, in this chapter we turn first to the broader rise, both geographically and temporally, of the so-called "Kamakura Buddhisms," which developed further during this period and began to consolidate their respective traditions *as* traditions. Most of them remained at the periphery of Buddhist institutional power and, in some ways, discourse during this era, but they likewise clearly represent increasingly centrifugal elements in the evolving history of Buddhist culture, with close ties in many cases to further reaches of the Japanese populace. Moreover, their focus on veneration of their respective lineage founders (*soshi*; *kaiso*) developed in the wake of early medieval trends toward such faith (*soshi shinkō*) within kenmitsu lineages with regard to figures like Kūkai, Ryōgen, Saichō, Shōbō (Shingon and Shugendō, Daigoji), Kakuban, and others, including figures associated with older lineages at Nara temples. That is, the focus on the remains, memory, and veneration of the founders of what became major traditions fit in quite nicely with broader trends toward veneration of earlier Buddhist figures, including trans-lineage figures like Prince Shōtoku, who was venerated increasingly by a series of figures, including Shinran himself, whose Shōtoku worship helped legitimize his movement (Lee 2007: 133).

From there, we turn to what can be called the medieval "culture of learning," which refers to the broader development of centers and networks of study and

A Cultural History of Japanese Buddhism, First Edition. William E. Deal and Brian Ruppert.
© 2015 William E. Deal and Brian Ruppert. Published 2015 by John Wiley & Sons, Ltd.

practice. Such study and practice were, in fact, interwoven, so that monastic and lay modes of study were conceived of as related or identical to Buddhist practice – and Buddhist practice was seen as directly related to cultivation. We then examine women and gender in medieval Japanese Buddhism. Although we have drawn attention to such issues in Chapter 2, here we follow the dynamic developments in their medieval history as well as academic study.

The further development of "Kamakura Buddhisms": Independence from the Kenmitsu monasteries and the consolidation of tradition

Contrary to the images of New Kamakura Buddhism expounded over the course of the twentieth century in Japanese and Western scholarship, which tended to emphasize the institutional and doctrinal centrality of the so-called founders of these movements, recent studies have largely come to the conclusion that the founders and the movements associated with them were not, in fact, at the center of Buddhist political, cultural, and doctrinal practice during most of the Kamakura period. It was, rather, from the late fifteenth century onward that these lineages came to increasingly occupy the center of Japanese Buddhist belief and practice (Yoshida 2006a: 174), although Rinzai Zen lineages had attained prominence from the late thirteenth century onward.

What scholars sometimes call the "height" of the medieval era, when political power was increasingly multi-centered and thus largely decentralized, was a period in which shrine-temple complexes vied with one another for pre-eminence. These complexes, which controlled multiple manors and sometimes possessed their own military might (Adolphson 2000), often encompassed more than one lineage; in fact, as we will see, it is too simple to assume that only temples associated with "old" Buddhism featured multiple lineages (*ryūha* and, often, major *shūha* lines), since those of the New Kamakura Buddhism, such as True Pure Land, Pure Land, and Zen, often included study of the teachings of the "old" lineages as well as interest in creating doctrines and practices concerning *kami*. Most of the "old" lineages continued to exist alongside the "new" lineages – in some cases flourished – during that era. While the newer lineages tended to be more prominent in Kantō (Kamakura and its surrounding region), with local cultures distinct from those in Kansai (capital region), monks of the older lineages were also very active in the Kamakura area from the Kamakura period onward, invited by the shogunate to perform esoteric and exoteric rites in temples sponsored by the *bakufu* and the shōgun's family such as Yōfukuji, Shōchōju'in, and Tsurugaoka Hachimangū ("Kamakura mikkyō" 2012).

Moreover, a related feature of Japanese Buddhism was the common strife between complexes but also within the complexes themselves. As the system of governance became clearer in the major complexes – typically divided between groups of scholar-monks (*gakuryo*, *gakushō*) and lower-level temple assistants (*dōshu*) and, sometimes, itinerants (*hijiri* etc.) – rivalry for the control of these major landholders became prominent, sometimes leading to devastating consequences. Threats by groups within the complexes to set the area on fire were sometimes used as effective techniques to achieve goals, since members of the court, the shogunate, and all classes seem to have believed in the power of Buddhist rituals and that of the Buddhas and *kami* at these sites (Adolphson 2000: 270; Rambelli 2012: 54–61). Over the same period, monks of warrior background became increasingly prominent as did warrior-cum-aristocrats, and a general increase in martial culture within many of the major monasteries (Adolphson 2007: 136), where even decisions of the larger assemblies (*sengi*) took on an increasingly martial- performative character (Matsuo 1997: 80–107).

We turn now to newer lineages and their permutations over the course of the late medieval era, although we will consider Zen lineages in our discussion of the culture of learning. The latter move is not intended to suggest a uniquely scholastic interpretation of Zen Buddhism in the era but rather to place Zen traditions within the context of society at the time and for reasons of explanatory convenience. We will also consider aspects of Kenmitsu lineages in our discussion of the culture of learning.

The "Pure Land lineages" (Jōdo shū), which traced their roots to Hōnen as we have seen, gradually thrived despite the vociferous criticisms and general persecution by authorities under the influence of the Kenmitsu temples. Moreover, their development may challenge some of our assumptions about "new Kamakura Buddhism." Initially, for example, one of the most important issues that Hōnen's lineage had to address was what to do after his death. In fact, it was through the distribution of his ashes to mausolea that multiple lines (sub-lineages) developed in Kyoto itself. One scholar has emphasized that some other lines based on Hōnen's group came to an end "because they lacked tombs containing relics of Hōnen" (Ōhashi 1985: 93–95; Ōhashi 2001b: 177). Thus even a "new Kamakura Buddhist" lineage such as Hōnen's drew upon traditional Buddhist relic beliefs and, moreover, incorporated them in such a way – venerating remains – that they implicitly suggested that a figure like Hōnen possessed the religious authority and status of a Buddha or bodhisattva.

Likewise, we cannot assume that monks of groups such as the Pure Land lineages necessarily only studied works by Hōnen or directly concerning Pure Land teachings. For example, Shōgei (1341–1420) was primarily responsible for providing a doctrinal foundation for these lineages, especially for the Chinzei line (Ōhashi 2001b: 181–182), and not only studied Shingon but wrote an esoteric Buddhist Shintō work on the *Reiki kanjō* initiation (Ogawa 1997: 154; Rambelli 2002: 283–286).

In addition, the assumption that new Kamakura Buddhist lineages developed as institutions completely independent of the kenmitsu Buddhist temple complexes must be re-evaluated. For example, as Ōhashi Toshio has stressed, the leaders of the

Figure 4.1   Grave of Hōnen, Chion'in Temple, Higashiyama, Kyoto. Photograph by Brian Ruppert.

Pure Land lineages and their temples actually "could not claim to be independent of Shingon and Tendai" for much of their early history:

> Chion-in, as the possessor of Hōnen's principal tomb, was dominant within the Jōdo sect but remained under the control of the nearby Tendai temple Shōren-in. Chion-in could not act independently of Shōren-in, nor could any other Jōdo temple. The Jōdo sect was regarded as an offshoot of the Tendai sect and was often referred to as a "temporary sect" or a "subsidiary sect." (Ōhashi 2001b: 181)

As was noted earlier, the new Kamakura Buddhist movements constituted, at most, a heterodoxical – and heteropractical – element for a long period in medieval history, while the Kenmitsu Buddhist institutions continued to dominate the Buddhist social world (Kuroda 1975: 477–503). Moreover, the Kenmitsu Buddhists and the new Buddhists mutually raised arguments that the other taught doctrine marked by prejudicial belief in the "inequality" (*fubyōdō*) of beings; that single-practice was either preparatory to other practice or absolute in its efficacy; and that each was easier to practice than the other (Taira 1992: 190–199).

However, it would also be inaccurate to assume that all of the monks in the major Kenmitsu monasteries took a clearly antagonistic stance toward Hōnen and his followers. Although, of course, figures like Myō'e and Jōkei openly attacked the views of Hōnen and those around him, prominent Tōdaiji monks of a slightly later period like Sōshō (1202–1278) and especially Gyōnen (1240–1321) were extremely interested in the Pure Land lineages. Thus while Gyōnen, in his *Genrushō* (1311), does not comment on particular doctrines of Hōnen's such as that concerning the equality of access of both genders to the Pure Land or of problems related to political persecution of the Pure Land movement, he was greatly concerned with the history of Pure Land belief and practice, and – despite his knowledge of earlier Pure Land figures of the older lineages such as Genshin, Yōkan, and Jichihan (alt. Jippan, Jitsuhan) – he saw Hōnen as "the place where the study of Japanese Pure Land Buddhist thought must begin" (Blum 2002: 25–28, 33–34). We see, then, that some monks of the Kenmitsu institutions studied "new" figures like Hōnen (Nakai 2005: 45–56, 147–151; *Hōnen shōnin denki*, in *Daigoji monjo*, Box 180, no. 5).

Moreover, at least some Pure Land Buddhist figures during the Kamakura period seem to have been well read in Chan/Zen, suggesting especially close relations between Dōgen and his circle with practitioners as varied as Hōnen's disciples at sites like Mt. Hiei, the area within Kyoto proper, and even on Mt. Kōya (Girard 2007: 6–8, 34–37). Meanwhile, we should also bear in mind that the practice of the *nen-butsu* seems to have been influenced by not only Tendai practice of constant-walking *samādhi* (J. *zanmai*) on Mt. Hiei but also esoteric Buddhist practices, reminding us that the influences on Buddhist practices in the era were multifarious.[1]

The Pure Land lineages increasingly thrived in Kyoto, and it was Shōkū (1177–1247), founder of the Seizan line, who proved most influential for their initial dissemination. Shōkū was the adopted son of the prominent noble Tsuchimikado Michichika (alt. Koga or Minamoto Michichika, 1149–1202; father of Sōtō Zen master Dōgen), and he seems to have been the figure who succeeded in winning adherents in the Kyoto aristocracy (Ōhashi 2001b: 177–178).

Shōkū's lineage, along with a series of other Pure Land lineages such as that founded by Chōsai (1184 – ca. 1266), reached the eastern region of Kantō, home to Kamakura, over the course of the Kamakura period. Scholars have also called attention to warrior connections specific to the Pure Land lineages, such as Kumagai Naozane's conversion under Hōnen, Hōnen's own warrior-family background, and the multiple connections between Shōkū, his disciples, and the shogunate (Takahashi 1996: 123–142).

An even more prominent move to Kantō was made ultimately by the Chinzei line. Originally, the monk Ryōchū (1199–1287), disciple of Shōkō (1162–1238) who had proselytized in northern Kyūshū, made headway with the families of prominent samurai families of the Kantō region, especially of the Shimōsa (Chiba) area where he traveled and preached. He later moved to Kamakura, where he established himself at Kōmyōji; Ryōchū was prominent enough in Kamakura for Nichiren to see him and write of him as an opponent (Ōhashi 2001b: 178–186). Meanwhile, another of the Chinzei monks of the same era, Chōen (1290–1371), traveled even further – to

China. There, he made a pilgrimage to Mt. Lu, original site of Huiyuan's (334–416) White Lotus Society, and studied there; he then returned to Japan where he settled in Sakai (present-day Osaka Prefecture) and taught *nenbutsu* (Ōhashi 2001b: 186–187).

The True Pure Land lineages developed significantly through efforts to proselytize, and it was especially mobile figures like Shinbutsu (1209–1258) and Kenchi (1226–1310) who influenced the history of Shinshū near the time of Jōdo Shinran's death and for decades afterward. Their Takada *monto* (also called "Senjuji" lineage) which was at Takada in the Kantō, claimed that Shinran had himself constructed their Nyoraidō Hall, with an Amida triad that was thought to have come from the famed Zenkōji in Shinano. Although their numbers would ultimately be fewer than some other groups in Jōdo Shinshū, the major lineages of the Bukkōji and Sanmonto both "traced their lineages back to Shinbutsu, Kenchi, and the Takada congregation rather than to Kakunyo and the Honganji" (Dobbins 2002: 120). The significance of Takada, in the early period, was its draw as a site of pilgrimage, especially the construction of a memorial chapel (*sōdō*) to Shinbutsu in 1311. Figures like Kenchi used their itinerant practice as *hijiri* to travel throughout the region and gain large numbers of converts, during this early period (Dobbins 202: 121).

Bukkōji, contrary to the tendency of Shinshū to increasingly win adherents in Kantō in the late Kamakura period, developed in Kyoto, although its founder, Ryōgen (1295–1336), was from the Kantō and formerly a disciple of Takada's Shinbutsu. Bukkōji made remarkable strides in proselytization but also in terms of its teachings. For the Bukkōji lineage, the monks and other teachers of the faith were local manifestations of Amida, entering into the world to save it, and their adherents were thus guaranteed birth in the Pure Land (Kasahara 2001b: 201–202).

As James Dobbins has noted, the next development of monumental importance to True Pure Land lineages in the century following Shinran's death was the effort to "imbue the Shinshū with an identity of its own, separate from the broader Pure Land movement." Dobbins emphasizes that Shinran did not make any sharp differences between his path and that of the Pure Land movement more generally, so many of those at the *dōjō* saw the Shinshū as simply an extension of Hōnen's work, which is why some of them continued to observe the death day of Hōnen rather than shift to Shinran's even after the latter's death. Thus the figure Dōshin, of the Kashima line in Kantō, went so far in 1301 as to ask Kakunyo (1270–1351) – the same great-grandson of Shinran who would strive to forge Shinshū's identity through the establishment of Honganji in Kyoto – to write a biography of Hōnen (Dobbins 2002: 80). Several copies were almost immediately made in the form of an illustrative work (*Shūi kotokuden'e*) and thus were used in preaching to the developing communities (Imai *et al.* 1994: 70–71). Meanwhile, institutionally, the True Pure Land lineages would retain important ties with the Kenmitsu complexes in the region in and near the capital, as Honganji had a very close relationship with the Tendai cloister Shōren'in; and Honganji's monks routinely studied doctrine at Nara cloisters like Daijō'in and Ichijō'in, both part of the Kōfukuji complex (Dobbins 1998: 31; Dobbins 2002: 100).

As with Hōnen's remains, those of Shinran became objects of contestation. Shinran's daughter, the nun Kakushin-ni (1224–1283), received Shinran's tomb at Ōtani (Kyoto) at its establishment in 1272 – along with the image of her father that he was thought to have personally carved. As Kasahara Kazuo noted, possession of the tomb and the image meant that Kakushin-ni, by implication, controlled the True Pure Land lineages. However, there was great tension with the leaders at the time, who argued that Shinran's resting place was the common property of everyone in Shinshū; eventually, following a series of episodes revolving around varying claims to the site, Kakunyo, who had created the Hōonkō memorial services in 1294, finally convinced the leaders to appoint him tomb guardian (Kasahara 2001b: 200–201; Dobbins 2002: 80–82; Imai 1999: 92).

Nichiren Buddhist lineages were centered in the Kantō region from the very beginning, as Nichiren was himself of Kantō background. We can point to two pivotal early events in the broader development of these lineages, which are more accurately called Lotus lineages (Hokke shū) in this early period.[2] First, being leader of the movement, Nichiren's death in 1282 had, as with other religious communities of the period, provided for both a crisis and an opportunity – both of which were solved through granting the leading disciples control over the tomb of the master, which was in this case at Mt. Minobu; alternate guarding by the six main disciples seems not to have been effective, as one of them, Nikkō (1246–1333) took over the tomb (Kuonji) two years later. Second, Nisshō (1221–1323) and his fellow disciples in Kamakura resubmitted Nichiren's *Risshō ankokuron* in 1284 to the shogunate, which had seen Hōjō Sadatoki become the new regent that year. The latter event ended up with threats to Nisshō and his compatriots based on the anger of Tendai, Pure Land, and Shingon lineages, and it seems that the group allayed the situation by stating that they were actually Tendai monks who approved of Tendai practices, including its esoteric aspects. Making such a statement undoubtedly averted the confrontation, but monks like Nikkō came to criticize it, helping contribute to a broader rift between the developing Nichiren lineages.[3]

Although Ippen actually had no thought of creating any organization that would outlast him, his followers, led by Ta'amida-butsu Shinkyō (1237–1319), established the beginnings of a lineage after his death, which came to be called the Yugyō-ha (later, Jishū). Shinkyō spent the first many years of his itinerant practice following Ippen's death primarily in the Hokuriku and Kantō regions, and he seems to have consciously approached warrior families and visited the same sites repeatedly. Like Ippen before him, Shinkyō seems to have seen himself as the singular holy one (*hijiri*) within the group. However, Shinkyō was clearly focused on a novel effort to make his group an established presence in the areas he visited. He created more than one hundred sites for the group within less than three decades. By the mid fourteenth century, the figure Takuga (1285–1354) would develop a doctrine of the Yugyō-ha, with emphasis on belief that, in fact, this world should be properly understood as none other than the Pure Land of Amida and that the current leader of the lineages, referred to as their *chishiki* (friend, guide), is invariably a Buddha, reinforcing the latter's authority (Thornton 1999; 17–18, 44–45, 79–85). The Yugyō-ha would not only serve as the deathbed chaplains for warriors in battle (Thornton 1995) but would also have influence over the development of a series of arts, including Nō theater, linked poetry (*renga*), and flower-arranging (Ōhashi 2001a: 221–222; Mitsuta 1996: 146–147).[4]

The Buddhist culture of learning: Zen, Shintō, networking monks, and seminaries

The Buddhist culture of learning, as we refer to it here, does *not* refer merely to doctrinal study. Rather, the culture of learning in medieval Japan was closely related to the "culture of secret transmission" (Stone 1999: 97–152), as it has sometimes been called, as well as the larger culture of "sacred works" (*shōgyō*) of the period: teachings associated with ideals (*ri*) and practice (*ji*) passed from master to disciple by means of all manner of *shōgyō*, including not just paper strips containing esoteric lore (*kirigami*) but also notes (*shō*) related to various rites (*kuyō, shuhō*) or assemblies (*e, hō'e*). One might argue that it is very difficult to clearly divorce doctrinal beliefs from practice throughout the Buddhist world; the combination of wisdom, ethical practice, and meditative practice signified by the term *sangaku*, "the three learnings," is often described in continental Buddhist works as culminating in a subtle interaction of wisdom with meditative practice. Thus the history of Japanese Buddhism may simply provide the best-documented example of the intersection of, if not often the identity between, Buddhist study and Buddhist ritual.

Scholars have recently noted that sacred works of a whole series of esoteric traditions were treated like talismans or jewels more than as objects of intellectual concern (Rambelli 2006: 53–55, 67). Fabio Rambelli focuses on important differences between reading practices of premodern Japan and those we employ today:

> Even when actually read, medieval texts were read in a different way. Reading was usually not silent, but voiced; most medieval texts are actually notes for lectures, transcriptions of actual lectures and oral transmissions, or models for master–disciple interaction. In other words, orality was an important component of medieval textuality. Reading was often not a public and free (also economically) activity. Even the very people who could actually read did not have an easy access to religious texts. It was important to establish connections with some religious and private institution endowed with a library, to create a network of people from whom to borrow (and to whom to lend) books. More often than not, access to texts was controlled by long and complicated initiatory training and procedures known as oral transmission (Jpn. *kuden*). Such ritual procedures actually culminated not just in oral, secret teachings, but also in the transmission of written texts and documents (Rambelli 2006: 55).

Analysis of medieval Dharma-lineage transmission at Daigoji and other temples affiliated with Shingon lineages has offered further support to the notion that reception of a work, via transmission from one's master, came to be construed as a kind of certification that the prescribed practice had been completed. One scholar has taken particular note, in this context, of the drastic changes that occurred between the mid twelfth and early fourteenth centuries, and analyzed examples demonstrating that initiation rites came to be radically abbreviated (Nagamura 1991: 242–243). That initiation came to be radically abbreviated does not, however, mean that learning was no longer involved. Rather, study continued to be related to orality as it at the same time took on increasingly varied forms. The study quoted above notes that scholarship occurred within monastic environs (Rambelli 2006: 55), and it is clear that such practice constituted part of the world of study in Buddhist lineages and their temples, albeit one in which ritual transmission was increasingly abbreviated. Indeed, if we look again at the quotation above, we realize that "most" of the texts were notes related to lectures (*kikigaki* etc.). Lectures were, undoubtedly, partially liturgical in character, but the notes were used in connection with modes of study, albeit ones that are vastly different from those we have experienced in our late modern world.[5]

In fact, although the Retired sovereigns Era featured an unprecedented increase in writing, study, and the inception of movements within and outside the major temple-shrine complexes, it was the fourteenth century – and perhaps the first half of the fifteenth – that may have marked the period of the greatest development of the Buddhist culture of learning prior to the Edo period. When we consider a series of factors, we come to understand that the period was marked by a remarkably active Buddhist culture of learning. Barbara Ruch has offered insights concerning academic presuppositions concerning Muromachi-period literature that we can appropriate for our consideration of Buddhism during roughly the same period; she refers to these assumptions as problems that have prevented us from understanding correctly the literary productions of the era:

> First, an elitism with regard to what is worthy of literary study; second, the inordinate dependence of literary scholars on concepts borrowed from political history; and third, a traditional scholarly vocabulary consisting of terminology that only inadequately applies to the literary phenomena observable during the Muromachi period. (Ruch 1977: 279)

Research at temples and archives throughout Japan, together with a willingness to reconsider our own presuppositions about the character of Japanese Buddhism, has helped contribute to a reconsideration of our field along the lines of what Ruch proposed for the study of literature. In particular, although the social contexts of the scholars engaged in the study of religion and literature are distinct, they have important similarities. The field of religion was dominated in Japan by scholars of the traditional Buddhist universities (*shūmon daigaku*), which are operated by sectarian traditions promoted since the Tokugawa era. Just as literary scholars have had a tendency to focus on the "masters" of lineal literary traditions, Buddhist studies scholars have tended to be interested in those figures who are seen as having "founded" major new "sects" in Japanese history; in particular, they have focused especially on the so-called "founders" (*kaiso*) of the eight schools newly structured by the Tokugawa government as part of its temple reorganization and, later, strengthened in the nineteenth and twentieth centuries with the broad introduction of Christian missionary influence, which undoubtedly helped contribute to sectarian tendencies (Stone 2006: 41–42; Williams 2006: 188–189).[6] Scholarship outside Japan on Japanese Buddhism has followed similar patterns.

Given what we increasingly understand about the collections of the manifold Buddhist lineages of the period and new interpretive lenses through which we take seriously the fluidity, vibrancy, and conflicts in Japanese Buddhist history, one can forcefully argue that the culture of Buddhist learning actually thrived in this period of social change and decentralization of power.

Zen learning and the arts

It is well known that the Kamakura shogunate and, later, the Ashikaga shogunate, supported the "Five Mountains culture" of the Rinzai Zen monasteries. The monks of these monasteries, which were located in both Kyoto and Kamakura, often pursued studies in esoteric Buddhism as well as arts that were beginning to develop at the time. Earlier, in addition to the well-known Yōsai, who studied Tendai esoteric Buddhism and then received the patronage of the Kamakura shogunate, Enni Ben'en had a pivotal influence on the history of Rinzai, together with a series of masters who came over the course of the mid thirteenth to mid fourteenth centuries from Song China. Enni was a remarkable figure in part because he received the patronage of the leading aristocrat Kujō Michi'ie, which enabled him to have the temple Tōfukuji established in southeastern Kyoto (Collcutt 1981: 43; Harada 2006: 88–89); he also gave lectures and conferred the Bodhisattva Precepts on the retired sovereigns (*Genkō shakusho* 7, 86a).

Moreover, it seems actually to have been Enni's position as a monk who had traveled to the continent and was a high-ranking Kenmitsu monk with experience in conducting fundraising campaigns, rather than the fact that he was of the Zen lineage, that gathered the retired sovereigns' interest (Kikuchi 2009: 23–24). Further testimony to monks' and aristocrats' interest in Enni's continental connections is the fact that so many monks, even from Mt. Kōya, came to study under him.[7]

It is important to emphasize that Enni was initiated not only into Rinzai Zen but also, originally, into Tendai and, later, into the Sanbō'in lineage of Shingon esoteric Buddhism. In other words, it is actually not easy to distinguish completely the purposes or practices of Zen at the time from Tendai or from other forms of esoteric

Buddhist lineage, particularly when we consider the beliefs and interests of those serving at court. Zen practitioners, like esoteric practitioners, seem to have been known for their ritual prowess, given stories such as that told of Enni's disciple Mukan Fumon (1212–1291), who is said to have succeeded in quieting an unsettled spirit through Zen practice, whereas Eison's esoteric rite is said to have failed (*Bun'ō kōtei geki, Zoku gunsho ruijū* 8, part 1, 43b–44a); the suggestion is that the ritual powers of Zen practice are superior to the apotropaic rites of esoteric lineage monks (Harada 2007: 45).

Was this simply a temporary "eclectic phase" in the history of Japanese Zen, as some scholars have suggested, or were the texts and practices of other lineages – especially those associated with the major shrine-temple complexes – related closely to the character of the Zen lineages themselves?[8] That is, can we or should we attempt to find a "pure" mode of Zen, that is, some form of Zen that somehow transmitted "true" Zen from the continent? Prominent scholars have argued that the notion of a "pure" monastic form of Zen (Ch. Chan) of Tang/early Song China free of sundry rites, for example, seems to have been a distinct feature of modern Japanese scholarship – and one at variance with Chan sources; monastic codes feature procedures for "worship of the Buddha, funerals, memorial rites for ancestral spirits, the feeding of hungry ghosts, feasts sponsored by donors, and tea services that served to highlight the bureaucratic and social hierarchy" (Foulk 2008: 27; also, Bodiford 1993 and Faure 1991).

Moreover, even the Sōtō Zen master Dōgen, often interpreted as the purist of Zen thinkers and disciplinarians, seems to have owed a debt to Tendai notions of original enlightenment, including with regard to notions such as of the oneness of practice and enlightenment, the radical nonduality of nirvana and *samsāra*, and the dwelling of all phenomena in a "Dharma-position" (*hōi*) (Stone 1999: 88–90).[9] Some scholars have also called attention to the close connection between the emphasis in Yōsai's Zen on absolute nonduality and original enlightenment discourse (Tamura 2000: 96); it is well known that Yōsai was interested in esoteric Buddhist belief and practice throughout his career, and archival research at Shinpukuji (Nagoya) is currently exploring the implications of the discovery of works written in his hand, some prior to his studies in China (Sueki 2013). Bernard Faure has also demonstrated the debt of the later Sōtō master Keizan's (1268–1325) beliefs and practices to esoteric Buddhism, among other influences (Faure 1996: 47–70).

Meanwhile, we should also briefly consider the influence of the newly arriving Chinese Zen masters (Rinzai Zen; Ch. Linji Chan) of the mid thirteenth century onward, who had an impact on the history of Zen in both Kamakura and Kyoto. It is important to initially remind ourselves that this was the largest contingent of continental Buddhist masters to enter the Japanese isles since the period of the origins of Japanese Buddhism. Among these, Issan Ichinei (Ch. Yishan Yining, 1247–1317) proved a particularly influential figure, becoming abbot of Kenchōji and Engakuji in

Kamakura and the great mentor of shogunal regent Hōjō Sadatoki (1271–1311). Issan was the figure who most influenced the developing Zen interest in Chinese literary culture, including also calligraphy and painting. Issan became so prominent in Japanese monastic circles that he decided to introduce an examination system requiring the use of Chinese verse to express Zen teachings; among those who passed the test was Musō Soseki, later to become one of the most influential Zen monks in the history of the Gozan system (Collcutt 1981: 65–66, 74). Issan, however, was only the beginning of the new Zen culture of learning, as Sadatoki and his successors went on to invite more prominent Chinese monks to Kamakura. Some of their disciples would later go to study in Yuan China and return to contribute to the literary environment of the Gozan. For many if not most of these Chinese masters, to study Zen meant to read the Chinese classics, including Confucian and Taoist works, and to have knowledge of Chinese painting, poetry, and calligraphic practice (Parker 1999: 30).

For the first time since the ninth century, when monks went to China to acquire Buddhist teachings, scriptures, and implements, large numbers of Japanese monks and, by extension, the shogunate, had access to modes of contemporary continental Buddhist practice and learning. It was not simply the shogunate and monks who had access, since the royal court had expressed interest in the Chinese monks and women increasingly took the tonsure to become Zen nuns. With the fall of the shogunate in 1333, the sovereign Go-Daigo would displace the Kamakura temples in their position at the apex of the Gozan system, now placing Nanzenji and Daitokuji in Kyoto at the top rank. From figures like Seisetsu Shōchō (Ch. Qingzhuo Zhengcheng 1274–1339), Go-Daigo as well as other sovereigns and the Ashikaga thus became steeped in the culture of learning as taught by the Chinese masters and their disciples, particularly those of the lineage of Musō Soseki. Some scholars have noted that while a large number of the Kenmitsu monks originally close to the Hōjō met their downfall with the end of Hōjō rule, the Zen monks who had arrived from China, along with their disciples, remained in prominent positions (Harada 2007: 47).

The Gozan monks also drew upon the examples of Nara's Kōfukuji (Kasuga-ban), Saidaiji, Tōdaiji, and Daianji, Kyoto's Sennyūji and Pure Land lineage temples and the rural Mt. Kōya (Kōya-ban), on the one hand, and their new interaction with Chinese monks, on the other, to establish their own major printing program (Gozan-ban). Why would lineages that transmitted enlightened mind directly, "without letters," between masters and disciples, make extensive use of not merely manuscripts but also publishing? In fact, while we in the West received a version of Zen, mediated especially by D. T. Suzuki and Western cultural influences like certain leaders of the Beat Generation, that stressed Zen's presumed transcendence of logic (especially via *kōan*), in Japan the *kōan* were historically part of a multifaceted system of learning that combined veneration of Zen/Chan masters, study more generally, and rigorous pursuit of awakening. Few Japanese Zen adherents, except those in the modern period and particularly those with access to the writings of Suzuki translated into Japanese, recognize our version of Zen as matching their own experience. By the mid-to-late fourteenth century, the Gozan were publishing, in addition to masters' records and other specifically Zen/Chan works, a broad cross-section of texts that included writings of Tang poets, Confucian classics, along with Chinese dictionaries, reference works, and medical texts (Kornicki 2001: 121–123).

At the same time, Zen, like several of the other lineages of the era, was increasingly disseminated to areas outside of the capital and Kamakura. For example, even a figure like Seisetsu (Qingzhuo) was supported by powerful rural warriors like Ogasawara Sadamune (1291–1347) of Shinano (Nagano), who invited him there to open the temple Kaizenji *(Kokushi daijiten* 8, 231d–232a; Collcutt 1981: 83–84). Figures associated with Enni Ben'en's line at Tōfukuji seem to have moved into rural areas from a comparatively early point. In particular, Chikotsu Dai'e (Buttsū Zenji, 1229–1312), trained originally at Hiei in Tendai, became a disciple of Enni. Dai'e was especially interested in esoteric Buddhism as well as scholastic study of several lineages. Later, Dai'e would return to his native Ise where he founded the temples Anyōji and Daifukuji. There, he taught a number of students, passing on a number of works containing Enni's lectures, including several on esoteric Buddhism *(Shinpukuji bunko satsuei mokuroku* 1997: 19b–20b, 520a–521a, 664a–666a; Ruppert 2009: 57–58). Dai'e eventually became abbot of Tōfukuji.

Kokan Shiren (1278–1346) likewise would study at Mt. Hiei, but he would go on to study at Nanzenji in Kyoto and Engakuji in Kamakura; in fact, Shiren would also travel to Ise, where he founded the temple Hongakuji, before writing the Buddhist history *Genkō shakusho* and serving as abbot of Tōfukuji and Nanzenji (Kikuchi 2009). Shiren's history, interestingly, included an argument for the uniqueness of the Japanese isles, something which was becoming increasingly common in the fourteenth century, as lineages of Shintō studies developed; however, Shiren claimed Zen had been transmitted to Japan in the Nara era (Bodiford 1993: 9), which was part of his larger argument, by implication, that Zen was central to the history of Japanese Buddhism, that the shogunate leader Hōjō Tokiyori was the greatest supporter of Buddhism in recent history, and that Japan was superior to India or China because of its status as a "Mahayana land" – moreover, bearing a royal line with uninterrupted transmission (Ichikawa 2000: 98–102).

Joseph Parker has called attention to the fact that modern scholars have had a tendency to focus on the influence of Tang poets (fl. late eighth to early ninth century) and Tang Chan on Japanese Zen rather than the more immediate influences of later times. The presupposition behind the tendency is a "devolutionary narrative" that sees later Zen as "advocating study of canonical and *kōan* (Ch. *gong'an*) texts, being syncretic or overly emphasizing poetry, and generally possessing inferior insight" (Parker 1999: 25). Such presuppositions undoubtedly underlay statements of some scholars concerning the presumed "dilution" of Zen following the so-called "bureaucratization" of the Gozan system in the early Muromachi period, after which Zen monks increasingly were concerned with "literary pursuits" (Akamatsu and Yampolsky 1977: 319). These characterizations are convenient fictions that ignore factors that we took note of above (Bodiford 1993: 12–14; Foulk 2008; Faure 1991).[10]

Indeed, it might be suggested that the Gozan monks, while thoroughly entrenched in institutional relations as were Yōsai, Dōgen, and a broad array of other Kenmitsu and Kamakura-lineage monks historically, cultivated new ways to transcend boundaries between the monastic, on the one hand, and the societal, on the other, and appropriated continental discourses anew to their evaluation of the religious significance of the arts. Indeed, following in a long line of figures, both Japanese and continental, these monks employed motifs like the "hermit at court" to re-envision any perceived distinction between (reclusive) nature and (social) culture in their contemplation and depiction of landscape (Parker 1999: 16–20, 51–154). Meanwhile, shogunal families began to establish temples in their residential palaces, where they constructed temples such as the Rinzai Tōjiji, part of the Sanjō bōmon complex of Muromachi, drawing upon the expertise of Zen and other practitioners in a series of regular familial rites (Stavros 2010: 10–17).

Scholars such as Harada Masatoshi have called attention to the appearance of socially liminal Zen figures – so-called *koji*, neither monastic nor lay – who engaged in various forms of (often humorous) performance and Zen dialogue (*mondō*) from the late Kamakura period onward in areas such as ports; they were consciously regarded as a mode of Zen practitioner. Although works like the *Tengu zōshi* ("Booklet of goblins"; 1296) were critical of such practitioners, the representation nonetheless confirms their existence and suggests something of their character. Later works suggest that their appearance actually dates to Enni Ben'en, whom we have seen had connections not only with the continent and powerful figures of his day but also with geographically outlying areas; these figures came to be cast out of the capital area in 1294 due apparently to pressure from Mt. Hiei but would prove to be so prominent as performers that they were portrayed in a series of Nō plays (Harada 1998: 23–28; Marra 1993: 78–82; Wakabayashi 2012: 116–119).

Likewise, we might interpret the seemingly outlandish monk Ikkyū's (1394–1481) behavior and poetic practice as an elaboration of Zen literary practice holding much in common with figures like the earlier Shingon-affiliated Saigyō, who was similarly of moderately upper-class social background, rejected a career near the court, and traveled exhaustively while writing *waka* poetry (LaFleur 2003: 3–29). Ikkyū's poetic practice may have been, indeed, directly related to his pursuit of an enlightened understanding of nonduality as much as it was to his interest in recreation ("trivialities") – particularly since, as William LaFleur has noted, Buddhist practice also can attempt to realize enlightenment through "ludization" (LaFleur 1986: 54–58).

It would, of course, be inaccurate to tie only Zen to the development of the arts, particularly given the influence of original enlightenment discourse and of practices of esoteric transmission on aesthetic lineages in general. Susan Blakeley Klein has analyzed the development of esoteric *waka* commentaries, which were originally innovated by the grandson of Fujiwara no Teika (1162–1241), Tameaki (ca. 1230s – ca. 1295). Tameaki, who became a monk and seems to have been directly influenced by the so-called Tachikawa-ryū line of Shingon Buddhism, wrote esoteric studies of court works like the official collection *Kokin waka shū* (*Kokinshū*, ca. 905) and the tale *Ise monogatari* (mid Heian period) in which he used tantric allegories to explain the ritual character of enlightenment. Tameaki's commentaries would have great influence particularly on the developing traditions concerning the latter work in the Reizei and Nijō poetic houses of the fourteenth and fifteenth centuries, applying sexual interpretation of ritual practice to tales associated with the path of *waka* poetry (Klein 2002).

The inception of Nō theater, unlike the commentaries, had warriors as the initial intended audience, even if its discursive underpinnings were similarly related to Buddhism. Indeed, although Nō authors seem to have expressed at least a filial relationship with the Jishū lineages through using the "-ami" suffix for their names (e.g., Zeami), it is clear that the ideas they expressed were also influenced by esoteric Buddhist ritual, *Lotus Sūtra*-related notions of merit and, of course, Zen tales and concepts (Harada 2010: 277–278).

"Shintō"

There were developments over the course of the late thirteenth to the sixteenth centuries that led to newer use of "Shintō," a term which historically had varying senses, including associations with local beliefs and practices, royal mythological narratives promoted by the court, and general ideas of numinous powers. It is apparent, initially, that the attempted Mongol invasions (1274, 1281) contributed to increased belief in the court and shogunate of a relationship between *kami* and the protection of the Japanese isles. At the same time, monks at the major temple-shrine complexes began to formulate not merely combinatory rites like the *sokui kanjō* royal initiation but also increasingly complex theories concerning the relationship between *kami* and Buddhist divinities; in doing so, they created lineages of "Shintō," the existence of which would form the most immediate context for the development of institutionalized forms of Shintō prominent in later eras. Although there were some scholars of Shintō in the postwar era who took an increasingly complex and historicized view of the development of *kami* worship (e.g., Nishida Nagao), it was the historian Kuroda Toshio who most prominently called attention to the changing contexts in which Shintō lineages developed.[11] His well-known discussion of Shintō, translated in the early 1980s as "Shintō in the History of Japanese Religion," argued that Shintō did not exist as an independent religion throughout the premodern era. Kuroda turned not only to references to "Shintō" in the mytho-history *Nihon shoki* but also to the ceremonies conducted at Ise Shrine, arguing that what we view as early Shintō was "permeated with Buddhist concepts"; the *kami* were "absorbed into Buddhism through a variety of doctrinal innovations and new religious forms" – witnessed particularly in the form of *honji-suijaku* theory and related *hongaku* thought as well as the development of the ritual forms of *jingūji* temples within shrines (Kuroda 1981: 3–8).

Kuroda's interest in Shintō, however, did not end there. Kuroda was especially interested in the activities of the so-called chroniclers (*kike*) on Mt. Hiei and their connection with faith in the *kami* Sannō at Hiesha Shrine, located at its foot and part of the Hiei complex. Kuroda argued that the chroniclers were interested in representing both the *honji*-source level of the Buddhas/bodhisattvas of Hiei and the *suijaku*-trace level of the *kami* and Hiei legend more generally. In other words, they associated *kami* with the local, trace level at which Buddhist divinities appeared (*honji-suijaku*) – but also with the dynamic history (legends) of Mt. Hiei. Indeed, he identified discussions of the *suijaku*, that is Shintō, elements, as the preponderant concern – and highest concern – of their activities:

> The ultimate duty of the chroniclers was the study of the *hon-jaku* combinatory Shinto-Buddhist system of the Hie shrines at the foot of Mt. Hiei. This system was known as Sannō Shinto, and the method of study of the combinatory system was the study of documents. As a result the chroniclers developed and spread the belief that the study of documents enabled one to attain the highest level of Buddhist truth. (Kuroda Toshio 1989: 150).

Kuroda additionally emphasized that the historical concerns of the chroniclers intersected also with the "symbolic" and "mandalized" elements at Hiei such as those represented in legends like *Enryakuji gokoku engi*, chronological accounts (*nendai ki*), and prognostications (*mirai ki*). He suggested that the historical concerns of the chroniclers were connected to both discourses of "history governed by *kami* and Buddhas" and the broad notion of the "adorned realm" (*kokudo shōgon*) based on conceptions of the Japanese isles as a "*kami* realm" (*shinkoku*) (Kuroda 1995: 49–54).

Moreover, over the course of the medieval era, multiple discourses about the relationship between the *kami* and Buddhas/bodhisattvas developed, especially in connection with the major temple-shrine complexes of established Buddhism. As we have seen, the *kami* were generally seen from the Nara period onward as beings just like others in the six realms of rebirth: in need of Buddhist salvation (Yoshie 1996: 11–7; Sueki 2010: 18). Thus they were the object of Buddhist sutra recitation in *jingūji*. The notion that many *kami* were in need of Buddhist salvation continued after the development of the discourses of *honji-suijaku*. By the medieval period, the distinction between the *kami* who were traces and those who needed salvation were formulated, respectively, as "transformed *kami*" (*gonshin*) and "actual *kami*" (*jisshin*). Moreover, there was even blurring of any distinction between these two at points, since it was sometimes claimed that Buddhist divinities occasionally took *kami* form to represent themselves as beings who share in the suffering of this world (*wakō dōjin*; Itō 2003: 75–76).

These multiple discourses growing out of *honji-suijaku* formulations thus took a variety of forms. Given the notion that Buddhas and bodhisattvas dimmed their light to appear directly in front of sentient beings, it is not surprising to realize that their local traces were not necessarily seen as in any sense inferior to their original forms. Itō has emphasized that such notions actually promoted belief in *kami* (Itō 2003: 76); Teeuwen and Rambelli have likewise stressed that such ideas in no fashion suggested that Buddhas were superior to the *kami* (Teeuwen and Rambelli 2003: 21).

We can understand the complex and developing cosmology and relationships between the *kami* and Buddhas by examining the textual genre of medieval "oaths" (*kishōmon*) made to them, which were written by a wide swath of the populace (Satō 2003: 96). Although celestial Buddhas and bodhisattvas were "saving" in their roles represented by the texts, localized beings, including certain Buddhas and bodhisatt-vas, *kami* in general, and a series of other beings like Buddhist holy ones (*shōnin*) and ancestral lineage masters (*soshi*), were commonly represented as potentially threat-ening or "wrathful" in character (Satō 1998: 361; Satō 2003: 105).

The formulations related to *honji-suijaku* also came to be connected to developing claims concerning the doctrine of original enlightenment (*hongaku*), which enabled novel interpretations of the relationship between *kami* and Buddhas. While Ryōbu Shintō is typically identified with Shingon Buddhism, given depictions of corre-spondences between the two main shrines at Ise and the two mandalas of esoteric Buddhism, a seminal text associated with the lineage, *Nakatomi harae kunge* (ca. late twelfth century), came to incorporate elements of Tendai *hongaku* ideas. An account in the work, thought to have been accreted in the mid thirteenth century, describes three types of *kami*, respectively corresponding to original enlightenment, "no enlightenment" (*fukaku*), and acquired enlightenment (*shikaku*), and identified with the following: the *kami* in Ise shrine (*hongaku*), pure and unchanging in their mys-tery; rough *kami* of the kind in Izumo shrine (*fukaku*); and the kind in Iwashimizu Hachimangū and Hirota shrines (*shikaku*), which are capable of pursuing the path (Teeuwen and Rambelli 2003: 33–34; Ōsumi 1977: 273a).

Meanwhile, at Hie shrine, noted above, the incorporation of original enlighten-ment discourse into representation of the main *kami* there, Sannō ("mountain king"), became extrapolated in broader and deeper directions over the course of the thirteenth century. A group of shrine priests (*hafuribe*) compiled the text *Yōten ki* (thirteenth century), which identified Sannō with Śākyamuni and argued that Sannō was equivalent to the Dharma and, indeed, superior to all other *kami* in the cosmos. Within several decades, the chroniclers of Mt. Hiei came to compile major works also arguing for the unique cosmological status of Sannō and, by extension, Mt. Hiei as a whole. *Keiran shūyō shū*, completed by the mid fourteenth century, claimed that

Sannō is the source of existence – including that of Buddhas (Breen and Teeuwen 2010: 87–89; T. 76, no. 2410, 514c–523a). The incorporation of *hongaku* discourse into conceptualization of *kami*–Buddha relations thus enabled the possibility of so-called "reverse" (*han-*) *honji-suijaku* thought, which conceived of the *kami* as original ground and the Buddhas as traces. Indeed, Stone has argued that *hongaku* discourse in itself constituted a kind of reversal of earlier thought – and that it enabled all manner of efforts to "localize" (Stone 1999: 163–164) enlightenment and promote the reversal of traditional original ground-manifest trace discourse, as can be seen in her translation and discussion of a work by the Hiei monk Sonshun (1451–1514):

> "Buddhas achieve the way by acquired enlightenment; thus they are regarded as traces (*suijaku*). *Kami* convert and teach by virtue of original enlightenment; thus they are called "original ground" (*honji*) … *kami* have worldly forms, and Buddhas, the forms of renunciates (*shukke*). "Renunciation" … is the practice of acquired enlightenment. But the lay state (*zaike*) entails behavior stemming from the virtue of one's innate nature and demonstrates the practice of one's present status being precisely the [stage of] wondrous enlightenment (*tōtai soku myōkaku*) … Tenshō Daijin [Amaterasu Ōmikami] is the honest and upright, originally inherent deity; therefore [this *kami*] rejects the twisted mind of acquired enlightenment and takes the straight way of original enlightenment as fundamental."

> It should be noted that Sonshun was a Tendai monk, and that this passage occurs in a commentary on the *Lotus Sūtra*, a Buddhist text. Reverse *honji-suijaku* thought did not originate in an independent Shintō world defining itself over and against Buddhism, though such claims have long been made. It emerged within the Buddhist realm … (Stone 1999: 42).

We can see here not merely the essential influence of *honji-suijaku* and *hongaku* discourse over the development of "Shintō" lineages in late medieval Japan, but also the rising centrality of, on the one hand, the royal *kami* Amaterasu and, on the other, laity – the "lay state" rather than renunciation as the highest religious goal. Meanwhile, there were discourses such as that of the calendrical "thirty protective deities" (*sanjūbanjin*) that existed on Hiei but which were incorporated as early as the fourteenth century into the Hokke lineages; while Nichiren had included the sun goddess Amaterasu and Hachiman in the mandalas he created to be used as objects of veneration (*honzon*), legends were soon produced by Hokke monks that claimed these had been part of Nichiren's own pantheon. With the challenge from the prominent shrine lineage figure Yoshida Kanetomo (1435–1511), the Hokke clerics attempted to systematize their ideas concerning the *kami*, and so it is clear that interaction between these communities contributed to the formation of Hokke Shintō (Dolce 2003: 227–234).

We must also, however, draw careful attention to the intimate connection between Shintō and the struggle for authority between the northern and southern royal courts during the Nanbokuchō Era (1336–1392). For example, there is the religious and social position of Kitabatake Chikafusa (1293–1354), author of the well-known southern royal history *Jinnō shōtō ki* (Account of the Legitimate Reigns of Holy Sovereigns), in which he argued for the unique position of Japan – in comparison to India and China – as home to an unbroken line of royal succession. For Chikafusa, following the Sannō Shintō (Tendai) discourse of reverse *honji-suijaku*, Buddhist teachings and Confucian writings were provisional appearances of the higher *kami* Holy Ones (*shinshō*) that served to disseminate the latter (Shirayama 1998).

Ritually, secrets concerning the powers of the *kami*, in the form of royal regalia and other symbolic objects, wove the significance of the *kami* into esoteric Buddhist practices, including the royal accession rite known as the *sokui kanjō* ([esoteric] accession consecration), which developed in Tendai and Shingon traditions. This rite, which became prominent from the late Kamakura period onward, symbolized the sovereign's initiation into an esoteric rite that enabled him to effectively rule the world, known as the "four seas" (*shikai*). His sovereignty over the world was symbolized bodily by a combination of specific *mudrā* hand-gestures (J. *inzō*) and *mantra* verbal invocations (J. Shingon) performed by the monarch along with the traditional three regalia (mirror, sword, jewel) and an exorcistic scarf known as the *Shinamono no hire*, now defined as a kind of "super-regalia" symbolizing enthronement (Kadoya 2006: 272–277; Matsumoto 2005: 35–151).

Networking monks and seminaries

Many of us who study Japanese Buddhism share the general image of monks as figures who reside in a specific temple or hall throughout most of their monastic careers and are members of a single major lineage of Japanese Buddhism. It turns out, however, that there were monks throughout the medieval era who studied at multiple temples and belonged to more than one lineage. Moreover, some of them achieved a remarkable level of geographical mobility. Given what seems to have been their increasing mobility, common study in multiple lineages, and rising numbers from roughly the second half of the thirteenth century onward, we refer to them here as "networking monks." This category includes figures in more limited categories such as *hijiri* (holy men) and upholders of the *Lotus Sūtra*, but also encompasses a broader range of practitioners.

Although, as we noted earlier, so-called *shoshū kengaku* – practices and study of multiple lineages – was very common, it became all the more prominent as the mobility of many monks increased. Figures like the poet-monk Saigyō (1118–90) appeared earlier, as did monks such as Chōgen (1121–1206), Yōsai (alt. Eisai, 1141–1215), Dōgen (1200–1253), and Enni Ben'en, all of whom are known to have gone to China.[12]

With the establishment of the shogunate in Kamakura in eastern Japan, however, the efforts of monks and their patrons to establish new temples in outlying areas became all the more possible. The interactions of monks like Ippen and Eison with the lower classes is important to take note of, but we should emphasize that they were also representative of the elaboration of the trend toward geographical mobility during the era. The mobility of monks made them potentially close to all manner of classes, including the local gentry and temples or monks previously established in the areas they visited. For example, a Tendai lineage monk named Jūkaku (n.d.) visited one Shida manor in Hitachi Province (Kantō) in 1373, where a series of preaching and worship halls had been constructed since mid-century; Jūkaku taught (*dangi*) at the Bishamondō where he stayed, and a number of local lay believers came to study under him (Ooto 2002: 92).

The prominent Shingon-lineage monk Kōshin (Monkan, 1278–1357) is often noted as promoting hetero-practices (*igyō*) associated with the Tachikawa lineage of esoteric practice, an amorphous set of practitioners who tended toward literal interpretations of sexual symbolism in esoteric Buddhism. However, the ambiguous character of the Tachikawa lineage and of those who came into contact with it can be seen in the example of the prominent work *Juhō yōjin shū* (Collection of Care in Receiving the Dharma [i.e., correct esoteric ritual], 1268), which depicts a "skull rite" usually thought of as transmitted by the Tachikawa; the author of this work was a comparatively obscure Shingon monk named Shinjō (fl. 1215–1268). It turns out that Shinjō describes in his work a sexual skull ritual which was distinct from the Tachikawa lineage and, instead, seems to have been conducted by an unnamed popular esoteric Buddhist movement independent of both Shingon and Tendai (Iyanaga 2006: 207–213).

Shinjō's account of his studies as a monk offers an enlightening window into the careers of networking monks. A monk of a cell called Seiganbō in Echizen Province (Fukui), Shinjō received esoteric initiation from a cleric called Ashō (n.d.) in rural Etchū Province, from whom he also acquired permission to copy the secret works of the Tachikawa lineage. A decade later, he was approached by a monk named Kōamidabutsu of a temple called Shin-zenkōji (Echizen); Shinjō agreed to teach him for several days, and later Shinjō visited the monk's cell at the temple, whereupon he was lent a large new set of *orikami* ritual-sheets of the Tachikawa lineage to copy back at his own quarters. Just a year later, Shinjō went to Kyoto, where he received instruction in Kūkai's *Sokushin jōbutsu gi* (Principle of Attaining Buddhahood in This Very Body) from a monk visiting from Mt. Kōya, Kaiken (n.d.); while there, he was approached by a monk who invited Shinjō to come to his quarters in Higashiyama (Kyoto) to learn about the true significance of Kūkai's work, where he found out about the skull ritual of the unnamed non-Tachikawa lineage and received several hundred fascicles of their sacred works (Iyanaga 2006: 208–210).

We can also note the example of the Shingon monk Nōshin (1291–1353): the founder of Shinpukuji (Owari Province),[13] he was born in the Ise area, studied under a pair of masters at temples there, lived as a recluse, and made a hundred-day pilgrimage to Ise

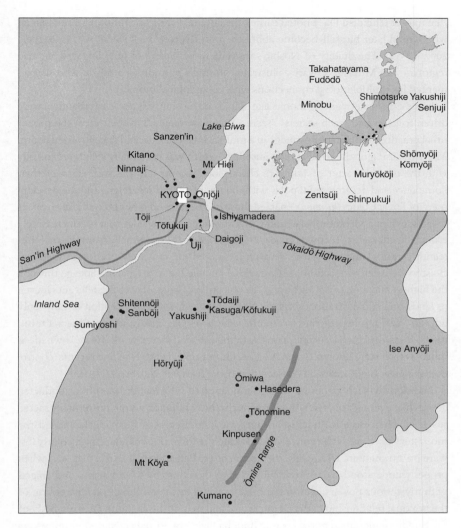

Figure 4.2   Medieval Buddhist Centers and Networking Sites. Map by Matthew Stavros.

Shrine before traveling to study under the monk Gikai (1280 – ca. 1354) at Takahatayama in Musashi (Kantō). Gikai, who seems to have been of higher social standing, had studied and copied the works of the influential Shingon monk Raiyu (1226–1304) throughout Kantō for several years and eventually succeeded in doing so with originals at Raiyu's temple of Negoroji (alt. Negorodera) in the Kansai region. Under Gikai, Nōshin was initiated into Raiyu's lineage and into the Sanbō'in lineage of the monk Bankai of Shimotsuke Yakushiji (present-day Tochigi Prefecture). Nōshin also studied under the monk Jaku'un in Ise, who had been initiated into Shingon esotericism by the

Zen master Chikotsu Dai'e noted earlier, the latter a disciple of Tōfukuji's Enni Ben'en who would later himself become abbot there in Kyoto (Abe 2002: 475–478; Ruppert 2009: 57–59). The fluidity of Nōshin's movement between not only lineages but also regions – Ise, Musashi, Owari – illustrates Nōshin's position as a monk who supplemented his multiple social connections with geographical mobility.[14]

In the case of networking monks like Shinjō and Nōshin, it is also clear that they were driven to learn and teach secrets – secrets that disseminated, in their view, the proper ritual practices and, thus, knowledge in a multilayered universe and decentralized realm. The weakening of the royal court's authority, which was potentially splintered initially with the dual character of Fujiwara chancellors/regents and the sovereigns of their dominance and became multi-polar with the rise of retired sovereigns and the development of lineage blocs (*kenmon*), enabled those in cloisters and other non-official environs to pursue their own non-official modes of knowledge – knowledge that was increasingly esoteric in character (Teeuwen 2006a: 21; Stone 1999: 151), especially from the mid thirteenth century onward. Mark Teeuwen has noted the direct connection in medieval cloisters between acquisition of secret ritual knowledge of a Dharma lineage through the highest initiation (*shabyō sōjō*) and the reception of control over the relevant cloister, its lands, and administration; similarly, he emphasized, with the inception of new "sublineages" the numbers of rites to esoteric venerables (*shosonbō*) and related secret transmissions also increased. Secrets, along with their related sacred works, were "owned" as much as they were known, as can be seen, for example, in the Nijō line regents' control over the *sokui kanjō* accession consecration rites (Teeuwen 2006b: 182–183).[15]

Additionally, such gathering and dissemination of information was often conducted at sites like a monk's quarters, but it might also be conducted within presumably sacred space, which in esoteric Buddhist lineages was identified with the mandala. Indeed, the monastery itself might be conceived as taking the form of a mandala, particularly if it were on a mountain. Ultimately, the notion of participating in a world that was, when properly understood, a cosmos inhabited in all directions by sacred beings and objects with mysterious powers, was undoubtedly related to the esoteric Buddhist notion of the nondual relationship between our world and that of the absolute Dharma-body of the Buddha – identified as the cosmic Buddha Dainichi. Ritual activation or unlocking of that ritual knowledge is necessary, however, so the practitioner must be initiated, using body (correct hand-gestures), speech (correct invocation), and mind (meditative practice) into the secrets ("mysteries") that offer access, like keys, to realization of that nonduality. Kūkai had, of course, introduced such discourse much earlier (Abé 1999: 151–184), and especially from the medieval era onward it was increasingly represented by those within esoteric Buddhist or related circles in the form of ubiquitous, "mandalized" sites, objects, and texts that, with proper ritual activation, manifested the Dharma-body in our conditioned realm (Teeuwen 2006a: 15–16).

Meanwhile, mountain ascetics (*shugenja*) became increasingly prominent in a whole series of mountain ranges, where since at least the thirteenth century they

Figure 4.3   Esoteric Buddhist altar, Daikakuji temple, Kyoto. Photograph by Brian Ruppert.

began to serve as guides (*sendatsu*) for lay believers whom they accompanied to important sacred sites like Yoshino or Kumano and to lodgings (*shukubō*) there, which were run by fellow ascetics (*oshi*). By that period, they were no longer simply seen as affiliated with esoteric Buddhism but had been established, at least in the case of the group overseen by the Tendai temple Onjōji (Ōtsu, just east of Kyoto), as a distinct bloc of practitioners (Sekiguchi 2009: 6–7). The Shingon case of Daigoji Sanbō'in suggests there was a distinction within the complex between esoteric Buddhist ortho-praxis and and *shugenjas'* so-called *tosō* ascetic practices – and the gradual development of some form of distinct headship of the mountain ascetics affiliated with Daigoji (Sekiguchi 2011: 106–111).

Although we saw the seminal presence of mountain ascetics at a setting like Kumano, for example, from the mid Heian period – such ascetics' practices, as early as the Nara period, seem to have included ablutions and esoteric Buddhist invocations (*dhāraṇī*; J. *darani*) – the formulation by the fourteenth century of a basic repentance and purification regime of 10 ascetic practices led, by the Muromachi period, to their identification with progress through the 10 realms of rebirth in the Buddhist cosmos. Such progress culminated ideally in their attainment of Buddhahood: from birth as hell-beings, hungry ghosts, animals, humans, heavenly beings, and so forth to enlightenment in the form of the very body of the ascetic himself, understood as identical with that of Dainichi (Skt. Mahāvairocana), the Cosmic Buddha, the true reality expressed by the Diamond and Womb realm mandalas. That is, mountain ascetics now understood these twin mandalas to be the essence underlying the entire Ōmine mountain range and, ultimately, of their own bodies. The landscape of the Ōmine, which stretched from Yoshino to Kumano, was thus mandalized, as was eventually that as well in the Katsuragi mountains, where the mountainscape was en-texted with the establishment of 28 sacred sites, each housing a sutra mound enshrining a chapter from one of the 28 chapters of the *Lotus Sūtra* (Miyake 2005: 54–65; Miyake 2001: 314–331).[16]

Monks of or associated with Precepts lineages (Risshū), meanwhile, were particularly active in networking with other monks and vis-à-vis both the royal family and the military government of the late thirteenth and fourteenth centuries. That is, these figures actively interacted with a variety of groups of the populace, including not just those in the general population but also the military and court leaders. They were active not only in extensive fund-raising efforts on behalf of certain of the major complexes, such as Tōji (Shingon, Kyoto), Gion Shrine (Kyoto) and those in Nara (Tōdaiji, Kōfukuji, Hōryūji, Saidaiji), but also in using the funds from bridge-construction fundraising and related efforts to engage in shipping-related activities along with establishing new precept-lineage affiliate temples in areas near the sea as distant as Kyūshū as well as nearby eastern/western Honshū; in fact, in eastern Honshū, the Hōjō seem to have had Ritsu monks stationed at bridges to administer them, and precept-affiliate temples such as Senkyōji and Uji Hōjō'in (both south of Kyoto) charged fees for crossing and shipping, although major temples like Kōfukuji often held partial rights to the proceeds (Hosokawa 1997: 172–198; Matsuo 2010: 167–185). Meanwhile, although there is little research on the development of the Precepts lineages over the course of the fifteenth century onward, it is clear that the Precepts groups took multiple forms. At Saidaiji, they existed as an organization of holy ones (*hijiri*) alongside so-called "white-robed" regular monks, and the latter presumably performed official prayer rites (*kitō*) requested variously by the shogunate and court of the Saidaiji abbot at the command of Kōfukuji, the governing complex of a series of seven affiliate temples (Ōishi 2004: 135–141).

By the early fourteenth century, changes came to be recorded concerning how funerals of major court figures and, eventually, shogunal members were conducted, as precept-lineage and *nenbutsu* holy ones (*nenbutsu hijiri*) along with Zen monks were now uniquely employed to handle the bodies of the dead, as opposed to regular monks of Kenmitsu temples, who simply performed the 49 days of memorial rites following death. The roles of these various groups were so intertwined, beginning as early as the end of the fourteenth century, that while Sennyūji, a Ritsu temple complex, served as the site where the bodies of royal dead were placed in coffins, the chanting on the occasion was typically conducted by either Zen monks or Pure Land Buddhist holy men. Thus these groups were incorporated into the larger

Kenmitsu system of ritual practice and patronage, but they also clearly had unique roles as mediators of impurity. They replaced a system in which Yin-yang masters (*onmyōji*) and *kebiishi* policing figures handled the dead, and it is apparent that at Sennyūji and other of the sites of these three kinds of Buddhist monks there were artisans – presumably liminal "non-persons"(*hinin*) – who made coffins and other materials for the dead, contributing to the professionalization of these roles (Ōishi 2004: 214–237). In Saidaiji and related groups, ritual works transmitted from apparently as early as the late thirteenth century suggest the influence of Shingon esoteric lineages on the funerary practice of Ritsu monks (Inagi 2005: 329–331), reminding us of the distinct precept lineages that developed and their often intimate connection with Shingon lines.

The funerals of major patrons such as Hōjō Tokimune (1251–1284) and prince Yoshihito (1351–1416) drew especially upon the ritual abilities of Zen monks, and the contents of the funerals establish that Zen lineages made no distinction between rites for monastic practitioners or lay believers, which marked them as different in that fact from their Chinese Chan counterparts; these differences are attributable to the fact that Japanese Zen groups such as the Rinzai lineages incorporated the Tendai Bodhisattva Precepts into their practice, which dissolved any traditional ritual differences between monk and lay believer. Moreover, Japanese Buddhist lineages innovated with posthumous ordinations, which included a full process of tonsure of the body, placement of the precept-lineage chart (*kechimyaku*) next to the deceased, and the conferral of the precepts. Importantly, funeral sermons were often recorded, revealing through the precept-name of the deceased their gender and status, which – at least in the case of Sōtō lineages – increasingly indicated they were of lower status and, notably, most often women (Bodiford 1993: 193–194).

Kuroda Toshio and later scholars, such as Jacqueline I. Stone, Nagamura Makoto and Taira Masayuki, have drawn attention to the dynamic learning within both the so-called "old" Buddhist monasteries and those of the new lineages of the medieval era. Indeed, a careful examination of the extant sacred works and other documents of the era indicates that the process of consolidating lineages in most of these complexes was also largely completed in this period, with the exception of some of the strains of new lineages. In particular, the inscription of all manner of documents (*kiroku*, *ki*), transmission works (lineage charts, *kirigami* [paper strips recording oral transmissions], and including some *shō* commentaries that were especially valued), hagiographical works (*den*), and scholastic works related to seminary (*dangi*) practice was prominent in many of the halls and cloisters of the major monasteries – and, even, increasingly in semi-rural or rural temples.

What one scholar has called the "interactive model" of the relationship between the teachings of the new Kamakura Buddhisms – including the Hokke lineages (Nichiren) – and medieval Tendai can as readily be applied as well to the Nichiren movements of the later medieval era. They had participated with the Tendai establishment in the "'reimagining' of Buddhist liberation as nonlinear and accessible in the present moment," and now continued to interact with Tendai in the develop-ment of further elaborations on relevant discourses, the most prominent of which were those concerning original enlightenment (Stone 1999: 300–301). However, such discussions were never purely doctrinal in character, because they were was directly related to efforts to establish one's own lineage or the larger Nichiren tradition; achieving legitimacy for a lineage and to question the position of others was always a seminal feature (Stone 1999: 305–307). Particular lineages within Kantō Tendai, such as at the Senba seminary, made claims such as that *shikan* meditation is superior to the text of the *Lotus Sūtra*, which seems to have been at variance not only with the Hokke lineages but also with Tendai on Mt. Hiei (although there is some debate as to whether certain figures originally proposed the idea at Hiei). Some Hokke lineages claimed that Nichiren had received the true transmission of the teachings of the Tendai Eshin Sugiu lineage monk Shunpan (fl. mid thirteenth century), who had been chief instruc-tor (*sōgakutō*) when the latter was originally on Hiei (Stone 1999: 305–318; Shugyō 1960: 82–84).

Meanwhile, on fourteenth-century Hiei, figures like the monk Kōshū (fl. 1311–1348) attempted to elaborate on concepts in Tendai esotericism (Taimitsu). Visually, there are at least three examples of a coupling of the *Lotus Sūtra mandala* (Hokke mandara) with the traditional twin mandalas of the diamond and matrix realms, and Kōshū in his *Keiran shūyō shū* (Collected Leaves of the Valley Mist) argued that the *Lotus Sūtra mandala* integrates the other two into a system of esoteric doctrine and practice alternative to that put forth traditionally in Shingon Buddhism. Such iconography and study suggest that the "esoteric" was broadly defined and fluctuated in diverse ways – represented most perfectly by the esoteric Lotus rite, which was practiced in the lineages of Tendai and Shingon (Dolce 2006: 154–158).

Women and Gender in Medieval Japanese Buddhism

It is well known that, on the one hand, some Buddhist sites (e.g., Hiei and Kōya) excluded women (J. *nyonin kekkai*) from as early as the ninth century, and that, on the other, the Pure Land hagiographies included stories of women's salvation (Kasahara 2001a: 285–291; Groner 2002: 77). But when it came to the recognized Buddhist line-ages, what was their stance? Earlier studies often argued that women were excluded from all salvation by the Buddhist lineages that predated "Kamakura Buddhism," and claimed therefore that the offer of birth in the Pure Land to female believers was an innovation of the Kamakura lineage "founders" (*kaiso*; Kasahara 1975: 392–394). However, earlier lineages also regularly discussed the problem, and sometimes pro-moted the notion that women – as women – can be born in the Pure Land, as seen in writings by figures like the Hiei monk Jōshō (fl. 980–1003) and the Shingon monk Kōzen (1121–1203; Taira 1998: 157; Yoshida 2002: 312).

In any event, while there may have been nunneries in outlying areas, it is clear that official support lapsed and that, at least in certain areas in and around Heiankyō and Nara, the exclusion of women at Buddhist sites became increasingly entrenched over the course of the Heian period. During this gradual official decline, however, women of the capital areas seem to have been as interested in Buddhism as had ever been the case, and it is clear that they found ways to pursue the path of their devotion; we know, for example, that while the government no longer offered official ordination, there were nuns who outside of officialdom privately engaged in preaching and the conducting of rituals (Meeks 2010: 23).

Drawing attention to the relationship between hair length, social status, and Buddhist renunciation, Katsuura Noriko has pointed to multiple modes of tonsure use by the women of the court as expressions variously of their rejection of social status symbols (e.g., hair) to express their faith. While other scholars have previously emphasized that despite female Buddhist practice from a young age the larger society opposed full tonsure (Nishiguchi 1987: 115) – Katsuura stresses that women of the period often took partial tonsure but ultimately hoped to complete the process with full tonsure. Their goals in doing so, in any event, seem to have been varied: to simply follow a path of devotion to a Buddha or bodhisattva, to expiate a perceived sin of being female, to engage in practice in memory of a deceased loved one, and in some cases to improve their destiny in the afterlife (Katsuura 2002: 126).

Meanwhile, mothers continued to be represented as seminal influences in a variety of Japanese Buddhist texts – as in East Asian Buddhism and Japanese society.[17] Mothers together with fathers constituted one of the four fundamental objects of indebtedness in Japanese Buddhism, and Buddhist hagiography in Japan made much of the relationship between monks and their mothers. In larger terms, some scholars have emphasized that categories such as "mother of the realm" (*kokumo*) used in reference to cloistered female sovereigns was intimately connected to familial "matrimonial strategies" in which women were "mere instruments" (Faure 2003: 161–162), but more recent research has demonstrated that some figures referred to with the term *kokumo*, like Jōtōmon'in (Fujiwara no Shōshi, 988–1074), actually led the royal house (Fukutō and Watanabe 2007: 30–32). Clearly, the image of the mother was extremely powerful in cultural terms, and the difficulties monks felt in choosing to travel to the continent – and thus leaving their mothers – reveal how taxonomies like the four debts had meaning in the context of the most intimate of relationships (Ruppert 2001: 41-45).

Over the past few years, the study of female pursuit of Buddhist paths has made tremendous strides. One significant example in the West has been Lori Meeks's study of the role of the nunnery Hokkeji (Nara) in the reappearance of female monastic orders (Meeks 2010). Through the work of a group of women together with the

Precepts-lineage master Eison, this former convent in the official system of provincial nunneries spearheaded by Kōmyō in the eighth century was energetically revived. The work is particularly apt in its treatment of the meaning and significance of the contradiction between, on the one hand, women's new opportunities to undertake ordination and leadership positions in Buddhist groups and, on the other, increasingly androcentric tendencies in Buddhist doctrinal discourse.

We know now that the expansion by Hokkeji nuns and their patrons over the course of the late Heian period laid the grounds for the resurgence of Hokkeji's convent through a combination of expanding the Hokkeji pilgrimages, disseminating legends (*engi*) related to Hokkeji as well as promoting other popular forms of religious literature. Moreover, in the background of the eventual re-establishment of an official ordination platform for Hokkeji's nuns was not merely a romanticization of convents of a court culture perceived as waning in the wake of extreme political changes, but also developing religious environs, in the late Heian and early Kamakura periods, in which nuns taught other women. Meanwhile, male monastic society generally viewed women, particularly from the mid Heian period onward, as essentially potential patrons rather than practitioners; it would be the Zen and Ritsu lineages[18] – especially Eison – that began to treat women as potential disciples who would ideally bow themselves to illustrious masters of lower social status, ironically granting them position within the organization while transgressing the social code (Meeks 2010: 27–116). Indeed, the Zen lineages seem to have been a seminal influence among the Ritsu communities, and the teaching of Chinese Chan masters and, in particular, the relocating of Chan masters to Japan – like Rankei Dōryū (Ch. Lanxi Daolong, 1213–1278) and Mugaku Sogen (Ch. Wuxue Zuyuan, 1226–1286) – expressed admiration for female followers and nuns; one follower of Mugaku was Keiaiji abbess Mugai Nyodai, whom he described as a "great teacher" (Meeks 2010: 107).

Ritsu nuns of Hokkeji and Chūgūji would later interpret the re-emergence of the female monastic movement not in connection with Eison's movement but instead would attribute it to the ancient actions of queen-consorts like Kōmyō, whom they describe as behaving as or like bodhisattvas on behalf of others. Even the males in the Ritsu order of the thirteenth century had comparatively positive interpretations of women generally, as they neither held that women's bodies were particularly impure nor that the blood of childbirth was especially negative (Meeks 2010: 271–300).[19]

The dawn of the True Pure Land lineages ushered in a set of temple institutions that were very different from the situation with Zen and Ritsu nuns. From as early as the life of the founder Shinran himself, temples in these lineages featured shared leadership by the abbot and his wife, who was referred to typically with the term "temple guardian" (*bōmori*). The fact of marriage itself should not surprise us, since there were already examples of monks serving in temples and taking wives at that time (Nishiguchi 1987: 201–209). However, in the True Pure Land lineages, the legend of Shinran's dream of Kannon, in which the bodhisattva promised to take the form of a woman to lead him to birth in the Pure Land at the time of his death, took on particular force because it was conjoined in texts like the hagiographic *Shinran shōnin go'innen* (Karmic Causes [of the Life] of Holy Man Shinran) with the tale that Shinran took a daughter of the powerful noble Kujō Kanezane as his first wife with permission from his master Hōnen – and that, from that point onward, the *bōmori* was the "proprietor" of the *dōjō* where the congregation gathered.[20]

The *Blood-bowl Sūtra* (J. *Ketsubonkyō*) came to be introduced from the continent by roughly the fourteenth or early fifteenth century, and seems to have had extensive implications for gender representations and practice. This apocryphal scripture depicts the presumed physical impurity of women – particularly in connection with childbirth – and a karmic damnation in which the latter must swim in blood pools filled with their own secretions in a hell specific to them. The earliest known text dates to 1429, but the work may have been introduced slightly earlier (Matsuoka 1998: 276 n. 1). The appearance of this sutra also, it turns out, coincided with the period of change within Japanese families and the eventual adoption of the "household" (*ie*) as the family unit; women's inheritance rights – along with those of non-heir sons – thus became temporary from the late Kamakura period, albeit with the important caveat that women in families without male heirs continued to enjoy full inheritance of property (Kurushima 2004: 240–241; Mass 1989: 100–105). The end of prominent aristocratic women's literature likewise, for unknown reasons, came roughly at the end of the early medieval era, with Lady Nijō's completion of her journal *Towazugatari* (An Unrequested Tale) in 1306; it would not be until the Edo period that women's literary works would resurface to any great degree. When considered alongside these other factors, it seems evident that the sutra was introduced in a social climate that was increasingly restrictive for many women.

At the same time, we should not assume that these new restrictive environs necessarily or universally meant that women lost their agency as religious actors. Meeks's study has clarified the extent to which Ritsu nuns engaged in what can fairly be described as "priestly" function activities for lay believers: "like the male members in the Saidaiji order, [they] acted as members of a vocational priesthood who made their living through the performance of ritual" (Meeks 2010: 245). Moreover, we know that there were itinerant "nuns," clearly influenced by so-called female *miko* (oracular mediums), who were involved in proselytizing from the medieval era (Hagiwara 1983; Faure 2003: 250–254). However, it seems to have been from roughly the fifteenth century onward that these figures, to whom were eventually ascribed the title "Kumano nuns" (*kumano bikuni*), brought such proselytization to a new level of prominence. Pictorial recitation (*e-toki*), in particular, was by roughly the sixteenth century the best-known practice in which these figures typically engaged, as they traveled around using visual images drawn from texts like the *Blood-bowl Sūtra* and *Urabonkyō* ("Ghost Festival" *Sūtra*) to preach to other women

(Ruch 2002: 567–573; Hagiwara 1983: 34–38). The basis for the development of the use of the pictorial-recitative work most often used, the *Kanjin jikkai mandara* (Mandala of Mind-Visualization of the Ten Realms of Rebirth), is thought to have been a Song dynasty pictorial work (*Yuandun guanxin shi fajie tu*, J. *Endon kanjin jūhokkai zu*; Kuroda Hideo 1989: 219–222), illustrating once again the continued intimate connection between innovations in Japanese and continental Buddhism.

We do not here take as our focus the problem of sexuality in Japanese Buddhism, but it is important to take note, in conclusion, of a leading contribution to its study. Bernard Faure has innovated with theoretical considerations of both sexuality and gender in Buddhism in general, with special emphasis at many points throughout on the Japanese case (Faure 1998; Faure 2003). He considers in topical terms the relationship between sexuality and Buddhist problems such as transgression by considering ways in which Buddhist discourses are variously reinforced or undercut. For example, the figure Ikkyū was someone who exemplified the paradoxical justification of transgression through "holy madness" – in his case a monk who is thought in the tradition to have transcended even sexual transgression through his affirmation of all manner of sexual activities in his own life. Ikkyū's case expressed in part the hyperbolic and antinomian extravagance in Muromachi-period Japan that was sometimes referred to with the esoteric Buddhist term *basara* (Skt. *vajra*) which was presumably related to the tendency in the late medieval era for the weak to overcome the high (*gekokujō*; Faure 1998: 111–118).

Notes

1   Esoteric Buddhist ritual activation of body, speech, and mind was one seminal influence on the gradual shift among many Japanese Buddhists from practicing introspective meditative techniques to vocalizing enunciations such as the *nenbutsu* and the title of the *Lotus Sūtra* (*daimoku*; Stone 1998: 145).

2   We should note that the Tendai lineages were also sometimes referred to as *Hokke shū*.

3   In fact, although it is important to note that these early monks shared a sense of shared identity in their exclusive devotion to the *Lotus Sūtra*, their reception of the *nichigō* name with the master's "sun" character in their names, use of stern proselytizing (*shakubuku*), and a common identity when faced by opposition from other lineages (Stone 1999: 304), Takagi Yutaka has emphasized that what we might speak of as a "Nichiren sect" was in fact a movement of "numerous separate schools and groups" (Takagi 2001: 268–270).

4   Despite these cultural connections, unlike the Nichiren and other major lineages of this period, however, those that came to be called Jishū did not enjoy large increases in adherents in future eras.

5   The colophons the disciples wrote to record their initiations may have constituted for them and those around them, in part, verification that they completed the practice. However,

they also clearly understood such initiation as part of a broader course of study within the monastery, including sitting in lectures, engaging in debates (*rongi*) and dialogues (*mondō*), and often consulting a variety of ritual texts and other commentarial works.

6   That is, studies of Japanese Buddhism of the late medieval era – otherwise known as the early to mid-Muromachi period – were clouded by assumptions that analysis should focus on presumed "sect-founding" figures from the Heian and Kamakura periods, including Kūkai, Saichō, and the founders of the six most significant lineages of the latter period, especially Hōnen, Shinran, Nichiren and Dōgen.

7   They undoubtedly knew that after his six years in the Song (1235–1241), he had founded a temple in Hakata (Kyūshū), preached to Chinese in the port city, and later maintained his contacts overseas (Enomoto 2010: 151–160).

8   Martin Collcutt, in his groundbreaking study on the Five Mountains monastic system of Rinzai Zen, formulated the argument that Enni's was part of an "eclectic phase" (1981: 43–48).

9   We should note that Stone bases much of her argument, in this segment, on the earlier work of Tamura Yoshirō.

10 The attention we pay to this account is not to discredit two important postwar contributors to the historical and literary study of premodern Japan and of Zen, but to consider carefully presuppositions that have until recently been commonplace in Zen studies – and to clarify the character of the problems inherent therein.

11 Sueki Fumihiko has taken note of Kuroda's analysis but also of the influence of the early figure Tsuda Sōkiichi, who recognized that the term *Shintō* was drawn from Chinese classics (Sueki 2010: 9–10).

12 These figures had varying reasons for travel, as Saigyō rejected his position as a retainer under retired sovereign to devote himself to writing and a monk's life, Chōgen seems to have traveled to China for purposes which significantly included pilgrimage; Yōsai, Dōgen and Enni seem to have been primarily motivated by the goal to obtain the "true" Dharma in order to transmit it on the Japanese isles.

13 Shinpukuji was originally in Ōsu-no-shō in Nakajimagun of Owari, and would only be moved to its current site in Nagoya in 1612 (Inaba 2012: 10).

14 In fact, Nōshin did not apparently have access to all collections of sacred esoteric works in which he had interest, so his own mobility had to be supplemented by the access of his masters to esoteric knowledge held at other sites.

15 Networking monks thus pursued secrets as part of an assemblage of knowledge, ritual protocol, related authority and, sometimes, wealth; moreover, as we have seen, they attempted to acquire initiation into multiple lineages of their concern, and through their teaching to others helped propel new networks of religious interaction.

16 See also Allan G. Grapard's study of the cult on the Kunisaki peninsula (Grapard 1989).

17 For a study of the Chinese case, see Alan Cole (1998).

18 An exception was Myō'e, who was a monk of Shingon and Kegon lineage (Meeks 2010: 93–95, 112).

19 Abe Yasurō, from a literary standpoint, has noted that, in addition to the bodhisattva symbolism associated with Kōmyō, she was also seen as representing the mysterious female who, simultaneously as sovereign (empress), has the religious power to purify and mediate between worlds and levels of society (Abe 1998: 59–64).

20	Figures like Shinran's historical wife Eshin-ni (1182 – ca. 1268), though of lower status than the Kujō figure of the legend, would have great influence within True Pure Land groups, especially beginning with the Araki *monto* in eastern Hōnshū, and the partnership of monk and wife would be a standard feature throughout their history more generally; she also wrote of a dream she had revealing that Shinran was himself the bodhisattva Kannon (Dobbins 2004: 26–27). The image of Shinran and his wife propagating the Dharma together became a leitmotif of visual works like *Shinran shōnin e'den*, which would come to be disseminated over the course of the late medieval era (Endō 2007: 120–52, 502–509).

References

Abé, Ryūichi. 1999. *The Weaving of Mantra: Kūkai and the Construction of Esoteric Buddhist Discourse*. New York: Columbia University Press.

Abe Yasurō. 1998. *Yuya no kōgō: chūsei no sei to seinaru mono*. Nagoya: Nagoya Daigaku Shuppankai.

Abe Yasurō. 2002. "Shinpukuji shōgyō no keisei to Raiyu no chosaku." In Sanha Gōdō Kinen Ronshū Henshū Iinkai (ed.), *Raiyu sōjō nanahyaku go-onki kinen ronshū: Shingi Shingon kyōgaku no kenkyū*, 471–500. Tokyo: Daizō shuppan.

Adolphson, Mikael. 2000. *Gates of Power*. Honolulu: University of Hawai'i Press.

Blum, Mark L. 2002. *The Origins and Development of Pure Land Buddhism: A Study and Translation of Gyōnen's "Jōdo Hōmon Genrushō"*. New York: Oxford University Press.

Bodiford, William M. 1993. *Sōtō Zen in Medieval Japan*. Honolulu: University of Hawai'i Press.

Breen, John, and Teeuwen, Mark, 2010. *A New History of Shinto*. Oxford: Wiley-Blackwell.

Cole, Alan. 1998. *Mothers and Sons in Chinese Buddhism*. Stanford, CA: Stanford University Press.

Daigoji monjo. Sacred works and documents collection in Daigoji temple, Kyoto. Photographic facsimiles of roughly the first 230 boxes out of the 800 boxes in the collection are held in the Historiographical Institute of the University of Tokyo.

Dobbins, James C. 1998. "Envisioning Kamakura Buddhism." In Richard K. Payne (ed.), *Re-Visioning "Kamakura" Buddhism*, 24–42. Honolulu: University of Hawai'i Press.

Dobbins, James C. 2002. *Jōdo Shinshū: Shin Buddhism in Medieval Japan*. Honolulu: University of Hawai'i Press.

Dobbins, James C. 2004. *Letters of the Nun Eshinni: Images of Pure Land Buddhism in Medieval Japan*. Honolulu: University of Hawai'i Press.

Dolce, Lucia. 2006. "Reconsidering the taxonomy of the esoteric: Hermeneutical and ritual practices of the Lotus sutra." In Bernhard Scheid and Mark Teeuwen (eds.), *The Culture of Secrecy in Japanese Religion*, 130–171. London and New York: Routledge.

Endō Hajime. 2007. *Chūsei nihon no bukkyō to jendaa: Shinshū kyōdan/nikujiki futai no bōmori ron*. Tokyo: Akashi Shoten.

Enomoto Wataru. 2010. "Nissō bukkyōkai wo tsunaida jinmyaku: nissō sō Enni." In Enomoto Wataru, *Sōryo to kaishōtachi no higashi shina kai*, 147–165. Tokyo: Kōdansha.

Foulk, T. Griffith. 2008. "Ritual in Japanese Zen Buddhism." In Steven Heine and Dale S. Wright (eds.), *Zen Ritual: Studies of Zen Buddhist Theory in Practice*, 21–82. New York: Oxford University Press.

Girard, Frédéric. 2007. *The Stanza of the Bell in the Wind: Zen and Nenbutsu in the Early Kamakura Period*. Tokyo: International Institute for Buddhist Studies.

Grapard, Allan G. 1989. "The Textualized Mountain – Enmountained Text: The Lotus Sutra in Kunisaki." In George J. Tanabe, Jr. and Willa Jane Tanabe (eds.), *The Lotus Sutra in Japanese Culture*, 159–189. Honolulu: University of Hawai'i Press.

Groner, Paul. 2002. "Vicissitudes in the Ordination of Japanese 'Nuns' during the Eighth through the Tenth Centuries." In Barbara Ruch (ed.), *Engendering Faith: Women and Buddhism in Premodern Japan*, 65–108. Ann Arbor, MI: Center for Japanese Studies, University of Michigan.

Hagiwara Tatsuo. 1983. *Miko to bukkyōshi*. Tokyo: Yoshikawa Kōbunkan.

Harada Masatoshi. 1998. *Nihon chūsei no zenshū to shakai*. Tokyo: Yoshikawa Kōbunkan.

Harada Masatoshi. 2006. "Kujō Michi'ie no Tōfukuji to Enni." *Kikan Nihon shisōshi* 68: 78–97.

Harada Masatoshi. 2007. "Chūsei bukkyō saihenki to shite no jūyon seiki." *Nihonshi kenkyū* 540: 40–65.

Harada Masatoshi. 2010. "Muromachi bunka to bukkyō." In Sueki Fumihiko (ed.), *Yakudō suru chūsei bukkyō*, 237–278 (Shin ajia bukkyōshi 12, nihon 2). Tokyo: Kōsei Publishing.

Hosokawa Ryōichi. 1997. *Chūsei jiin no fūkei: chūsei minshū no seikatsu to shinsei*. Tokyo: Shinyōsha.

Ichikawa Hirofumi. 2000. "'Suterareta' kuni/Nihon." In Ōsumi Kazuo (ed.), *Chūsei no Bukkyō to shakai*, 84–107. Tokyo: Yoshikawa Kōbunkan.

Imai Masaharu. 1999. *Shinran to honganji ichizoku: chichi to ko no kattō*. Tokyo: Yūzankaku.

Imai Masaharu et al., eds. 1994. *Shūikotokuden'e*. Tokyo: Seikōsha.

Inaba Nobumichi. 2012. "Shinpukuji no sōken." In Nagoya-shi Hakubutsukan/Shinpukuji Ōsu Bunko Chōsa Kenkyūkai (eds.), *Ōsu Kannon: Ima hikarareru kiseki no Bunko*, 10–11. Nagoya: Nagoya-shi Hakubutsukan.

Inagi Nobuko. 2005. *Nihon chūsei no kyōten to kanjin*. Tokyo: Hanawa Shobō.

Itō, Satoshi. 2003. "The Medieval Period: The Kami merge with Buddhism." In Nobutaka Inoue (ed.), *Shinto: A Short History*, 63–107. London and New York: RoutledgeCurzon.

Iyanaga, Nobumi. 2006. "Secrecy, Sex and Apocrypha: Remarks on Some Paradoxical Phenomena." In Bernhard Scheid and Mark Teeuwen (eds.), *The Culture of Secrecy in Japanese Religion*, 204–228. London and New York: Routledge.

Kadoya, Atsushi. 2006. "Myths, Rites, and Icons: Three Views of a Secret." In Bernhard Scheid and Mark Teeuwen (eds.), *The Culture of Secrecy in Japanese Religion*, 269–283. London and New York: Routledge.

"Kamakura mikkyō." 2012. In Kanagawa Kenritsu Kanazawa Bunko, *Kamakura mikkyō: shōgun goji no tera to sō*, 5–16. Yokohama: Kanazawa Bunko.

Kasahara, Kazuo, ed. 2001a. *A History of Japanese Religion*. Trans. Paul McCarthy and Gaynor Sekimori. Tokyo: Kosei.

Kasahara, Kazuo. 2001b. "The Jodo Shin Sect." In Kazuo Kasahara (ed.), *A History of Japanese Religion*, 191–210. Tokyo: Kosei Publishing.

Katsuura, Noriko. 2002. "Tonsure Forms for Nuns: Classification of Nuns According to Hairstyle." In Barbara Ruch (ed.), *Engendering Faith: Women and Buddhism in Premodern Japan*, 109–130. Ann Arbor, MI: Center for Japanese Studies, University of Michigan.

Kikuchi Hiroki. 2009. "Kokan Shiren no rekishiteki ichi." *Bukkyō shigaku kenkyū* 51 (2): 21–46.

Klein, Susan Blakeley. 2002. *Allegories of Desire: Esoteric Literary Commentaries of Medieval Japan.* Cambridge, MA: Harvard University Asia Center, Harvard University Press.

Kuroda Hideo. 1989. "Kumano kanjin jikkai mandara no uchū." In Miyata Noboru (ed.), *Sei to mibun*, 207–272. Tokyo: Shunjūsha.

Kuroda, Toshio. 1981. "Shinto in the History of Japanese Religion." *Journal of Japanese Studies* 7: 1–21.

Kuroda, Toshio. 1989. "Historical Consciousness and Hon-jaku Philosophy in the Medieval Period on Mount Hiei." In George and Willa Tanabe, eds., *The Lotus Sutra in Japanese Culture.* Honolulu: University of Hawai'i Press. Pp. 143–158.

Kuroda Toshio. 1995. "*Kenmitsu* bukkyō ni okeru rekishi ishiki: chūsei Hieizan no kike ni tsuite." In Kuroda Toshio, *Kuroda Toshio chosakushū daisankan: kenmitsu bukkyō to jisha seiryoku*, 39–57. Kyoto: Hōzōkan.

Kurushima, Noriko. 2004. "Marriage and Female Inheritance in Medieval Japan. *International Journal of Asian Studies* 1 (2): 223–245.

LaFleur. William R. 1986. *The Karma of Words: Buddhism and the Literary Arts in Medieval Japan.* Berkeley and Los Angeles: University of California Press.

Lee, Kenneth Doo Young. 2007. *The Prince and the Monk: Shōtoku Worship in Shinran's Buddhism.* Albany: State University of New York Press.

Marra, Michele. 1993. *Representations of Power: The Literary Politics of Medieval Japan.* Honolulu: University of Hawai'i Press.

Matsumoto Ikuyo. 2005. *Chūsei ōken to sokui kanjō.* Tokyo: Shinwasha.

Matsuo Kenji. 2010. "Bukkyōsha no shakai katsudō." In Sueki Fumihiko (ed.), *Yakudō suru chūsei bukkyō (Shin ajia bukkyōshi 12, nihon 2)*, 141–186. Tokyo: Kōsei Publishing.

Matsuo Kōichi. 1997. *Ennen no geinōshiteki kenkyū.* Tokyo: Iwata Shoin.

Meeks, Lori. 2010. *Hokkeji and the Reemergence of Female Monastic Orders in Medieval Japan.* Honolulu: University of Hawai'i Press.

Mitsuta Kazunobu. 1996. "Renga no nagare." In *Iwanami kōza Nihon bungakushi dairokkan: 15–16 seiki no bungaku*, 131–155. Tokyo: Iwanami Shoten.

Nagamura Makoto. 1991. "'Inge' to 'Hōryū': omo ni Daigoji Hōon'in o tōshite." In Inagaki Eizō (ed.), *Daigoji no mikkyō to shakai*, 235–271. Tokyo: Sankibō Busshorin.

Nakai Shinkō. 2005. *Hōnen e'den o yomu.* Kyoto: Shibunkaku.

Ogawa Toyoo. 1997. "Chūsei shinwa no mechie: henjō suru Nihongi to *Reiki ki (Amefuda maki).*" In Mitani Kuniaki and Komine Kazuaki (eds.), *Chūsei no chi toGaku: 'chūshaku' o yomu*, 143–178. Tokyo: Shinwasha.

Ōhashi Toshio. 1985. *Hōnen to jōdoshū kyōdan.* Tokyo: Kyōikusha.

Ōhashi, Toshio. 2001a. "The Ji Sect." In In Kazuo Kasahara (ed.), *A History of Japanese Religion*, 211–225. Tokyo: Kosei Publishing.

Ōhashi, Toshio. 2001b. "The Jōdo Sect." In Kazuo Kasahara (ed.), *A History of Japanese Religion*, 169–190. Tokyo: Kosei Publishing.

Ōishi Masaaki. 2004. *Nihon chūsei shakai to jiin.* Osaka: Seibundō.

Ooto Yasuhiro. 2002. "Chūsei shakai ni okeru kyōiku no tamensei." In Tsujimoto Masashi and Okita Yukuji (eds.), *Kyōiku shakai shi (Shin taikei Nihon shi 16)*, 65–119. Tokyo: Yamakawa Shuppan.

Ōsumi Kazuo, ed. 1977. *Chūsei shintō ron*. Tokyo: Iwanami Shoten.

Rambelli, Fabio. 2002. "The Ritual World of Buddhist 'Shinto': The *Reikiki* and Initiations on *kami*-Related Matters *(jingi kanjō)* in Late Medieval and Early-Modern Japan." *Japanese Journal of Religious Studies* 29 (3–4): 265–98.

Rambelli, Fabio. 2006. "Texts, Talismans, and Jewels: The *Reikiki* and the Performativity of Sacred Texts in Medieval Japan." In Richard K. Payne and Taigen Dan Leighton (eds.), *Discourse and Ideology in Medieval Japanese Buddhism*, 52–78. London and New York: Routledge.

Rambelli, Fabio. 2012. "Iconoclasm and Religious Violence in Japan: Practices and Rationalizations." In Fabio Rambelli and Eric Reinders, *Buddhism and Iconoclasm in East Asia*, 47–88. London and New York: Bloomsbury.

Ruch, Barbara. 2002. "Woman to Woman: Kumano bikuni Proselytizers in Medieval and Early Modern Japan." In Barbara Ruch (ed.), *Engendering Faith: Women and Buddhism in Premodern Japan*, 537–580. Ann Arbor, MI: Center for Japanese Studies, University of Michigan.

Ruppert, Brian. 2001. "Sin or Crime? Debts, Social Relations, and Buddhism in Early Medieval Japan." *Japanese Journal of Religious Studies* 28 (1–2): 31–55.

Ruppert, Brian. 2009. "A Tale of Catalogs and Colophons: The Scope of the Lineage, the Touch of the Master and Discourses of Authenticity in Medieval Shingon Buddhism." In James Baskind (ed.), *Scholars of Buddhism in Japan: Buddhist Studies in the 21st Century*, 49–66. Kyoto: International Research Center for Japanese Studies.

Satō Hiroo. 1998. *Kami/hotoke/ōken no chūsei*. Kyoto: Hōzōkan.

Satō, Hiroo. 2003. "Wrathful Deities and Saving Deities." In Mark Teeuwen and Fabio Rambelli (eds.), *Buddhas and kami in Japan: "Honji Suijaku" as a Combinatory Paradigm*, 95–114. New York: Routledge Curzon.

Sekiguchi Makiko. 2009. *Shugendō kyōdan seiritsushi*. Tokyo: Bensei Shuppan.

Sekiguchi, Makiko. 2011. "The Sanbōin Monzeki and Its Inception as Head Temple of the Tōzan Group." In Bernard Faure, D. Max Moerman, and Gaynor Sekimori (eds.), *Shugendō: The History and Culture of a Japanese Religion*, 103–121 *(Cahiers d'Extrême-Asie 18)*. Kyoto: École française d'Extrême-Orient Centre de Kyoto.

Shinpukuji bunko satsuei mokuroku jō, ge. 1997. Edited by Chizan Denpō'in, 2 vols. Tokyo: Chizanha Shūmuchō.

Shirayama Yoshitarō. 1998. "Chusei Shintō to Bukkyō." In Nihon Bukkyō Kenkyūkai (ed.), *Bukkyō to deatta Nihon*, 51–67. Kyoto: Hōzōkan.

Shugyō Kaishū. 1960. *Nichirenshū kyōgaku shi*. Tokyo: Heirakuji Shoten.

Stavros, Matthew. 2010. "The Sanjō bōmon Temple-Palace Complex: The First Locus of Ashikaga Authority in Medieval Kyoto." *Japan Review* 22: 3–29.

Stone, Jacqueline I. 1998. "Chanting the August Title of the Lotus Sutra: Daimoku Practices in Classical and Medieval Japan." In Richard K. Payne (ed.), *Revisioning "Kamakura" Buddhism*, 116–16,. Honolulu: University of Hawai'i Press.

Sueki Fumihiko. 2010. *Chūsei no kami to hotoke*. Tokyo: Yamakawa Shuppansha.

Sueki Fumihiko. 2013. "Yōsai shū sōsetsu," and "Kaihen kyōshu ketsu/Chōshu kyōshu ketsu kaidai." In Chūsei Zenseki Sōkan Henshū Iinkai (ed.), *Chūsei zenseki sōkan daiichi: Yōsai shū*, 503–514, 515–528. Kyoto: Rinsen Shoten.

Taira Masayuki. 1998. "Kyūbukkyō to josei." In Kojima Kyōko and Shiomi Minako (eds.), *Josei to bukkyō (Nihon joseishi ronshū 5)*, 150–179. Tokyo: Yoshikawa Kōbunkan.

Takagi Yutaka. 2001. "The Nichiren Sect." In Kasahara Kazuo (ed.), *A History of Japanese Religion*, trans. Paul McCarthy and Gaynor Sekimori, 255–283. Tokyo: Kosei.

Takahashi Jun'ichirō. 1996. "Toshi Kamakura ni okeru bushi to jiin." In Takahashi Jun'ichirō, *Chūsei no toshi to bushi*, 121–182. Tokyo: Yoshikawa Kōbunkan.

Tamura, Yoshirō. 2000. *Japanese Buddhism: A Cultural History.* Tokyo: Kōsei Publishing.

Teeuwen, Mark. 2006a. "Introduction: Japan's Culture of Secrecy from a Comparative Perspective." In Bernhard Scheid and Mark Teeuwen (eds.), *The Culture of Secrecy in Japanese Religion*, 1–35. London and New York: Routledge.

Teeuwen, Mark. 2006b. "Knowing vs. Owning a Secret: Secrecy in Medieval Japan, as Seen Through the *sokui kanjō* Enthronement Unction." In Bernhard Scheid and Mark Teeuwen (eds.), *The Culture of Secrecy in Japanese Religion*, 172–203. London and New York: Routledge.

Teeuwen, Mark, and Rambelli, Fabio, eds. 2003. *Buddhas and kami in Japan: Honji Suijaku as a Combinatory Paradigm.* New York: RoutledgeCurzon.

Thornton, S. A. 1995. "Buddhist chaplains in the field of battle." In Donald S. Lopez, Jr. (ed.), *Buddhism in Practice*, 586–591. Princeton, NJ: Princeton University Press.

Thornton, S. A. 1999. *Charisma and Community Formation in Medieval Japan: The Case of the Yugyō-ha (1300–1700).* Ithaca, NY: Cornell University Press.

Wakabayashi, Haruko. 2012. *The Seven Tengu Scrolls: Evil and the Rhetoric of Legitimacy in Medieval Japanese Buddhism.* Honolulu: University of Hawai'i Press.

Yoshida, Kazuhiko. 2002. "The Enlightenment of the Dragon King's Daughter in *The Lotus Sutra*." In Barbara Ruch (ed.), *Engendering Faith: Women and Buddhism in Premodern Japan*, 297–324. Ann Arbor, MI: Center for Japanese Studies, University of Michigan.

Yoshida Kazuhiko. 2006a. *Kodai bukkyō wo yominaosu.* Tokyo: Yoshikawa Kōbunkan.

Yoshie Akio. 1996. *Shinbutsu shūgō.* Tokyo: Iwanami Shoten.

Further Reading

Faure, Bernard, Michael Como, and Iyanaga Nobumi. eds. 2009. "Rethinking Medieval Shintō." Special Issue, *Cahier d' Extrême-Asie* 16–17. Kyoto: École Française D'Extrême-Orient.

Hayami Tasuku, ed. 2006. *Nihon shakai ni okeru hotoke to kami*, 2–26. Tokyo: Yoshikawa Kōbunkan.

Nishi Yayoi. 2008. *Chūsei mikkyō jiin to shuhō.* Tokyo: Bensei Shuppan.

Ruch, Barbara, ed. 2002. *Engendering Faith: Women and Buddhism in Premodern Japan.* Ann Arbor, MI: Center for Japanese Studies, University of Michigan.

Scheid, Bernhard, and Mark Teeuwen, eds. 2006. *The Culture of Secrecy in Japanese Religion.* London and New York: Routledge.

Sueki Fumihiko, ed. 2010. *Yakudō suru chūsei Bukkyō (Shin Ajia Bukkyōshi 12, Nihon 2).* Tokyo: Kōsei Publishing.

5

Buddhism and the Transition to the Modern Era (1467–1800)

Late Muromachi-Period Buddhism (1467–1600)

A compelling case can be made for the notion that the period from 1467 onward is of a piece with developments such as centralized administration of Buddhism and of what we think of as Japanese "sectarian" Buddhism, associated with the Edo (Tokugawa) and later periods. One prominent scholar has reformulated the periods of Japanese Buddhism, concluding that the final of the three major periods is that of "New Buddhism" (*shinbukkyō no jidai*), which he sees as beginning in the second half of the fifteenth century – focused particularly on the development of sects (*kyōdan*) and "mortuary Buddhism" (*sōsai bukkyō*), especially of the True Pure Land and Sōtō lineages (Yoshida 2003: 29–34).

At the same time, the centralization achieved by the shogunate in the so-called Edo period must also be recognized as unprecedented. Moreover, it is now well understood that the Muromachi shogunate, based in Kyoto, was largely functional until at least the point of the coup d'état of 1493 and, arguably, thereafter, so to claim that Kyoto's Ōnin War constituted the "opening curtain" (*maku-ake*) of the so-called "Warring Provinces" (*sengoku*) period would be anachronistic (Ishida 2008: 8–9). However, the *destruction* wrought by the Ōnin War surely laid the groundwork for the *possibility* of a broad series of developments associated with the "early modern" (*kinsei*). That is, there are important ways in which, at least in historical terms, after the Ōnin War – and, perhaps, as well the destruction caused by the Tenbun War (Tenbun no ran, 1536) – one might no longer speak of "medieval Buddhism" as we have explored it. The Ōnin War, and the roughly half-century period of its aftermath, seems to have contributed directly to a fundamental shift in the larger Japanese political economy and culture.

Before we dismiss Tsuji Zennosuke's well-known criticisms of Edo-period Buddhism out of hand – and what is clearly in many ways an anachronistic application of modern-era philosophical concepts and prejudices to historical interpretation – let us

A Cultural History of Japanese Buddhism, First Edition. William E. Deal and Brian Ruppert.
© 2015 William E. Deal and Brian Ruppert. Published 2015 by John Wiley & Sons, Ltd.

remember that he seems to faithfully represent a strain of discourse that can be traced, at least in part, to the expressed concerns of the shogunates of the Kamakura and later periods. For example, legal texts of the Kamakura shogunate and later military governments repeatedly attempt to curb "selfish" behavior of monks. *Go-seibai shikimoku* (1232), the major legal code of the Kamakura shogunate, which begins with a discussion of stipulations for temples and shrines, emphasizes that personal use of temple funds is prohibited. Later, it warns monks in Kamakura against exploiting official clerical (*sōgō*) status to selfishly violate traditional lines of monastic seniority and increase the number of monks (*Go-seibai shikimoku*, 8–9, 30).[1]

Tsuji's emphasis seems to reflect, in part, his reliance on the materials he had available to him at the time. Moreover, close examination of this stress reveals that Tsuji's "selectivity" in choosing his sources and emphasis, while problematic, was integrally related to his awareness that many practices he associated with "corruption," even in the case of Edo Buddhism, dated to much earlier periods of Japanese history. Nonetheless, Sueki Fumihiko is correct to emphasize that arguments by some scholars for the notion of early-modern Buddhist corruption (*kinsei bukkyō daraku ron*) presuppose that the presumed problematic character of late Edo and modern Japanese Buddhism has its source in the degeneracy of the Edo period as a whole (Sueki 2010: 4–5).

Where, then, might we draw lines to demark the clearly important shift from the medieval to the early modern period in the history of Japanese Buddhism? If continuity is the rule by which historical periods are imagined and constructed, how might we make distinctions useful for interpreting the fifteenth to early nineteenth centuries? What might we learn by returning to the sources remaining from the period while bearing in mind their limitations?

Returning to the primary sources, we see that a number of major changes came about in the late fifteenth and sixteenth centuries, and continued over the course of the period typically referred to as the early modern (*kinsei*). Bearing in mind historians' cautions against assuming that the Ōnin War marked the very beginning of the Warring Provinces period, let us consider ways in which the war and related societal contexts may have influenced the course of Buddhist history over the next centuries.

Anyone who has visited Kyoto notices that much of the temple architecture seems extremely similar. If these temples were built in different periods over a thousand years, why do their architectural and garden patterns often look so much alike? A careful examination of the historical record reveals that the great monasteries were destroyed in the Ōnin War and over the century thereafter. These monasteries were reconstructed in the main between the late sixteenth and seventeenth centuries, most often through the financial support of figures like the unifier Toyotomi Hideyoshi (1537–1598), the third shōgun Tokugawa Iemitsu (1604–1651), sovereigns and Dharma princes of the period (Miyamoto 2006). Undoubtedly, the lack of reconstruction over the course of a century after the destruction is related in part to a dearth of financial resources though, perhaps more importantly, in the period after the establishment of shogunal legal codes, major rebuilding or repair of any temple required an order from the military government (*Go-seibai shikimoku*, 8). Surprisingly, one ancient temple, Kōryūji, survived the mayhem, as did a few other sites like the mountain-top complex at Daigoji (Kami Daigo) and its vast sacred works collection. Tōfukuji also survived, but a large proportion of the complex was destroyed by fire in the late nineteenth century. So while the Ōnin War and the wars that ensued in the century thereafter did not recreate Buddhism, they created a Kyoto akin to the devastation witnessed at the end of World War II – what Japanese call to this day the reduction of the isles to "scorched fields" (*yake nohara*) in 1945.

To emphasize the inauguration of numerous *kaichō* – rare public viewings of hidden images – in the period of the mid-to-late fifteenth century is to run counter to the general associations many scholars have of *kaichō* with the Tokugawa period.[2] Yet despite associations with the Tokugawa period and its popular culture, *kaichō* were common features of much earlier periods, especially the mid fifteenth to sixteenth centuries. We know of examples of the multiple *kaichō* at Hasedera and Togano'o (north Kyoto) which demonstrate that not only were secret images made available for viewing; they were available for viewing by large numbers of people and were the objects of veneration that inspired generous offerings, which were then used for temple-shrine income (Yasuda 2003).

Although research does not currently tie the *kaichō* to the Ōnin War specifically, the broad increase at both sites of showings from the mid fifteenth century onward bespeaks, on the one hand, the increasingly unstable political and, by extension, financial situation in the period, but also on the other the realization at these temple complexes that *kaichō* could supplement or match other *kanjin* methods as a major form of fundraising. In the case of Hasedera, which had been a subsidiary temple of the cloister of Daijō'in in Kōfukuji for centuries, the *kaichō* were controlled by the cloister and the funds went largely to support the latter. In fact, fundraising monks (*kanjin hijiri*), along with the resident monks (*shuto*) of Hasedera, together performed the rite for which the materials were assembled; prior to the occasion, they had to request the conducting of the *kaichō* together with certain major assemblies, an effort which required first and foremost the permission of the sovereign – Hasedera was originally a royal-vow temple – together with that of the Kōfukuji cloister and, oftentimes, the added stamp of the shogunate and other powerful regional warriors. The proceeds of the events went to temple repairs and to the chief of Daijō'in cloister, who also served as abbot of Hasedera during the period (Ōishi 2003).

Meanwhile, by the 1490s, the purchase by monks of *shōgyō* sacred works sometimes occurred, an activity that seems to have been unheard of previously and which would often occur afterwards. Although major nobles like the great Fujiwara no

Michinaga had attempted to purchase Buddhist scripture as long ago as the early eleventh century (*Midō kanpaku ki, ge,* Chōwa 4.7.15 [1015]: 20; Kamikawa 2008: 189), it was virtually unheard of for monks to attempt to purchase sacred works prior to that time. The colophon at the rear of the manuscript held in the temple Kōzanji of the catalog of works Kūkai brought back from China, *Shōrai mokuroku* (Catalog of Imported [Scriptures and Implements]), signed by a monk named Benjo (n.d.) in 1494, describes the text as having been "purchased" (*baitoku*; Tsukimoto 1983: 63).

Factors clearly beyond the monasteries also came to affect Buddhist practice. There were, for example, some fundamental changes in the ritual life of the royal court and the shogunate which did so. An annual rite as significant as the court's Latter Seven-Day Rite (Go-shichinichi mishiho) was suspended from the period of the Ōnin War until 1623, when it was revived; the cessation of the rite during this period undoubtedly reflected a sharply weakened royal court. Similarly, the court's Eight *Lotus Sūtra* Lectures rite was ended in 1524, only to be revived near the end of the sixteenth century, and its shogunal equivalent, which with its monastic debates (*rongi*) constituted a prominent site for monks' advance in the clerical hierarchy, was dissolved in 1493. These developments reflected the marked decrease in economic power of the governing elites during the period (Sonehara 2010: 100).

The late fifteenth century also witnessed an effort by elite merchants and Buddhist monks to establish a new mode of tea practice that was very different from the Sino-centric, expensive, mode supported by the wealthy warriors of the time. These new figures argued that performance informed by knowledge of utensils native to the Japanese isles, such as those of Shigaraki and Bizen, and thus of proper aesthetic "taste" was more important than mere symbolic expression of wealth and power. The "grass-hut" mode of tea culture carved out a new field of aesthetic knowledge for merchants and the monks in their milieu that used notions of bodily initiation and training in tea practice as a "way" (*michi*), and it would become extremely prominent among the burgeoning merchant class over the course of the sixteenth century (Slusser 2003: 42–48).

The continuing development of Kamakura Buddhisms, the arrival of the West, and the new world of Japanese Buddhism

Given the chaotic religious and social landscape, those traditions that later came to be collectively called "Kamakura Buddhism" (*Kamakura bukkyō*) now rose to a new level of prominence and were reformed along lines that would remain for centuries. A figure like the True Pure Land-lineage monk Rennyo (1415–1499), among leaders of new Kamakura lineages, forged a larger following while imposing order on them through newly interpreting Shinran's teachings on faith and developing extensive rules for the community. This point is not to suggest that, following the war, which undoubtedly offered an opening to increased activity to movements distinct from the powerful Kenmitsu traditions, there was *only* chaos. One scholar has emphasized that Kōfukuji master Jinson's (1430–1508) description of a Japan in which none of the vassals of the regional warrior-lords (*daimyō*) continued to hold allegiance to the shogunate was simply an expression of the experience of his own temple-shrine complex and its holdings; the shogunate continued to function despite its greatly weakened condition (Imatani 2006: 208–211).

Rennyo's most active proselytizing occurred during the Ōnin War: "The ordinary strictures and conventions of society were not as rigidly enforced, so there was greater latitude for innovation and experimentation" (Dobbins 2002, 133). Moreover, Rennyo was able through his efforts in Hokuriku and later in the capital region to raise support, including from figures who undertook *ikki* league uprisings, to a degree sufficient enough to contravene any further threat from Mt. Hiei, enabling him to successfully reconstruct Honganji in 1483. The example of Rennyo making a pledge with his followers as a league in Yoshizaki (Echizen, Hokuriku) and their uprising nearby soon after in Kaga Province, in which they ultimately defeated both the Takada monto (also of Jōdo Shinshū) and their supporter, the warrior-governor of the Togashi family, set the stage for similar uprisings throughout the Hokuriku and Kansai regions.

In considering Rennyo's contribution to the cultural history of True Pure Land lineages, it is important to emphasize that Rennyo accomplished broad reform of devotional practices with a reconstituted emphasis specifically on Shinran and the standardization of *nenbutsu honzon* scrolls (so-called "*myōgō* scrolls") as the main objects of veneration in temple sanctuaries (*dōjō*). Rennyo is also well known for his use of vernacular letters of instruction (*o'fumi*) as well as his ritual incorporation of Shinran's *Shōshinge* (Verses of True Faith) and vernacular hymns (*wasan*) into the daily practice of his community. Just as important for Rennyo's institutional success was his increased promotion of local meetings (variously *kō* or *yoriai*) in True Pure Land Lineages, which were patterned on the largely aristocratic assemblies (*e*) and liturgical lectures (*kō*) that first became prominent over the course of Heian period (Yasutomi 2006: 27–29).

Rennyo thus propagated his religion through the coordinated emphasis on Shinran, vernacular writing, vernacular ritual performance, and broader promotion of local meetings of the faithful. Having first succeeded in Hokuriku, he went on to successfully create a vast network of temples and believers under Honganji – an achievement that ensured Honganji, even after divided into Higashi Honganji and Nishi Honganji monasteries, was a pre-eminent site among Buddhist institutions. Although it is important to note that Rennyo typically opposed efforts by his followers to clash physically with authorities – he even wrote at one point that they should respect the "Royal Law / Buddhist Dharma" (ōbō buppō), a term commonly used by the established Kenmitsu complexes – their leagues were often extremely successful in military efforts even during his lifetime. Rennyo returned to Kyoto in the year after the conclusion of the Ōnin War, 1478, and constructed the new Honganji there in the Yamashina area within a few years.

Like the True Pure Land lineages, the Zen lineages were by this period thoroughly disseminated throughout the Japanese isles. Their activity in funerals and mortuary rituals more generally clearly contributed to such dissemination, as we noted in Chapter 4 (Bodiford 1993), as did Zen's intimate involvement in the culture of learning. Several major complexes in Kyoto, such as that at Myōshinji, were reconstructed from the 1570s to the early 1640s, often in connection with the new temple regulations ordered by the Tokugawa shogunate in the Genna period (1615–1624); many among them were also renamed in connection with the fact that most new halls were now established as mortuary temples (bodaiji) for the patrons of Myōshinji on the sites of extant halls (Takenuki 1993: 303–304).

Mortuary temples, and the patronage relations with which they were connected, had developed over several hundred years, and multiple lineages increasingly offered mortuary services to their believers. In addition to the Zen lineages, large numbers of temples were constructed or renovated as mortuary temples – sometimes including a change of lineage in the process – in the Pure Land lineages over the course of the sixteenth century, though especially in the period between the 1570s and 1640s (Hōzawa 2003: 214).

Sites of veneration such as the tassho (also, jutō), established to requite indebtedness to the lineage master, were also constructed by the mid fifteenth century in Zen complexes such as Daitokuji (Kyoto). Such sites were also intimately related to the efforts of local Zen monto to establish themselves as affiliate temples (matsuji) of the major complexes and to improve their relations with their local patrons (danna; Takenuki 1993: 247–251). The promotion of master veneration follows the pattern we saw in our discussion of the consolidation of other traditions during the late medieval era, and these movements were thus often conducted in tandem with local monto efforts rather than simply a "top-down" creation of the complexes. We also witness in these sites developing mortuary temples and their sponsoring patrons (jidan seido) – including both regional lords and the local populace – as well as "main-temple-affiliate-temple" (hon-matsu) relations, both prior to the production of the well-known systems of the same name by the Tokugawa shogunate (Sueki 2010: 36–37). As one scholar has noted, in the medieval era believers had great freedom to select the temple or particular worship group with which they would affiliate – and such groups might be semi-independent or independent of any particular lineage of Buddhism or even associated with non-Buddhist beliefs or practices – and were thus the object of intense competition for patronage across the Japanese isles. By the early modern period, their increasing affiliation with a specific temple complex or singular lineage would become subject to official regulations developed by the shogunate. The pivotal turn occurred between these eras (Sonehara 2010: 82–83).

These new developments thus began prior to the advent of the Edo period. Furthermore, we can see that other vital changes occurred, especially during the so-called "Warring Provinces period" (Sengokuki). For example, even when the traditional "eight lineages" (Hasshū) discourse was invoked in documents of the sixteenth century, it no longer necessarily referred to those of "old Buddhism" but a combination of Shingon, Tendai, Nichiren, Gozan Zen, Jōdo Shinshū, and other lines of new Buddhism (Ōta 2007: 342). Perhaps most symbolic of the change in the Buddhist order was the court's orchestration of the conferral of the status of *royal cloister* (*monzeki*) on Honganji in 1559, which was propelled undoubtedly by the perceived threat of the Christians (Andō 2007: 379).[3]

Indeed, we might follow Ōkuwa Hitoshi in describing the Warring Provinces period as the era in which the transformation of Japanese religion, including Buddhism, from the "medieval" to the "early modern" (*kinsei*) became "overt" (*henkaku no kenzaika to shite no sengokuki*; Andō 2007: 369). This transformation included not merely organizational aspects as seen in True Pure Land lineages, but also expansion of religious ideas in a newly internationalized context that significantly featured both Neo-Confucianism and Christianity; Fukansai Habian (1565–1620?), for example, came to reject Buddhist lineages and even wrote anti-Buddhist tracts before his *reconversion* to the Buddhist fold, a sign of the instability ideologically and otherwise still present at the end of the Warring Provinces period (Baskind 2012). While the relationship between the shogunate, Gozan Zen and the continent in the context of the fourteenth century has recently been demonstrated (Harada 2007), it may be that the extensive economic interactions of Zen monks and others with the continent in the sixteenth century, like the purchase of sacred works (*shōgyō*) mentioned earlier, offers a glimpse of the dawn of a new and very different religious and social order. As an economic basis for the temple complexes, the system of manors (*shōen*) had now given way to the market economy using currency, a change which suggests that the Sengokuki was the period of not just the rise to prominence of the new Kamakura Buddhisms but also of an entirely new series of financial and transcultural orders that re-inscribed the religious landscape with displaced, reordered, and reconceived interactions.

Scholars of Pure Land traditions have suggested that Rennyo should be interpreted as having established something on the order of the "roots" of cultural and institutional changes assumed to be "emblematic of Japanese Buddhist institutions in the modern period" (Blum 2006: 12). It seems evident that the beginnings of the sectarian character of Japanese Buddhism were in the Warring Provinces period when various lineages that had extended their reach into rural and semi-rural regions were able to become organizationally and doctrinally self-sufficient. Groups such as that of Rennyo, the Hokke lineages (i.e., the Nichiren school), and Sōtō Zen lineages, for example, building on earlier efforts within their schools, developed comprehensive regimes of study that, from their perspective, allayed any need to systematically be taught directly by Tendai teachers – instead of recognizing a need to study multiple lineages in the traditional fashion (*shoshū kengaku*; Sueki 2010: 20–22). In these cases, such regimes were accompanied by decision-making marked by self-governance and equality in the form of the league (*ikki*), which reinforced the trend toward sectarian independence, albeit with the added necessity of material support of the regional lord (Kanda 2010b: 131–136).

Meanwhile, as noted above, even Rennyo could not stop the True Pure Land leagues from undertaking military action, the consequence of which might be described as a novel effort to wholly incorporate the royal law into the Buddhist dharma. During the same period, the leader of the Nakayama line among the Hokke lineages, Nisshin (1407–1488), led his group in the formation of an uncompromising approach to religious practice, symbolized most clearly in the movement's refusal to either give or receive donations (*fuju fuse*) from anyone outside of the Hokke, a practice that was radical in its social implication – an expression of sectarian self-sufficiency. Both of these examples assimilated all governance to the organization and would come to be seen as posing a direct threat to legal authorities. Thus such assimilation of the royal (secular) law to the Buddhist dharma set the stage for its violent opposite – the complete subjugation of Buddhism by the government with the destruction by the powerful warrior Oda Nobunaga of major Buddhist temples a century later (Sueki 2010: 22–26).

Virtually all of the Hokke lineages had established themselves in Kyoto from the fourteenth century onward. By the mid fifteenth century, they had established not only major *monto* groups affiliated with Myōkenji, Honkokuji, and Honnōji, but also a series of temples associated with other Hokke groups throughout the capital; thus they acquired supporters throughout the aristocratic, warrior, and the rising urban merchant class (*machishū*; Stone 1999: 304). The Hokke leagues (*hokke ikki*) there would become extremely powerful by 1532, when they came into conflict with the True Pure Land *ikkō ikki* leagues and destroyed the Honganji in Yamashina (Higashiyama). Until 1536, the Hokke leagues dominated capital life, a situation that would only change when Enryakuji gathered its forces and added supporters in an attempt to force the 21 major Hokke temples into Enryakuji affiliation. The Hokke leagues did battle against a force that seems to have numbered some 60,000 in what has come to be called the Tenbun Period War (Tenbun no ran), which led to the complete burning of all 21 temples and a fire so virulent that its destruction of the city was compared to that of the Ōnin War (Yuasa 2009, 154–156).

Strikingly, as if in tandem with this breakdown of central authority and major developments in Japanese Buddhism, Westerners arrived in Japan in 1543. Scholars have recently drawn attention to the profound impact of the introduction of Christianity in the mid sixteenth century, including the recurrent debates between

Christian and Buddhist monks concerning their faiths. One part of the so-called "Yamaguchi sectarian debates" (*yamaguchi no shūron*) was described in a letter from the missionary Fernandez to Francis Xavier in 1551 in which he described the argument between himself and Zen Buddhist monks in some detail. In it, he outlined the stark distinction between the theistic argument, on the one hand, and the argument according to "nothingness" (*mu*, i.e., emptiness) on the other. However, it has been noted that Buddhist and Shintō lineages had already begun to pursue the possibility of the existence of an ultimate deity, given Rennyo's strongly theistic bent and certain trends in Shintō thought (Sueki 2010: 24–29, 63–64). In this connection, use of the term for the highest divinity, conceived as the "way of Heaven," *tentō* (alt. *tendō*), common among Buddhist and Shintō lineages, Christians, and the powerful warriors of the era, clearly had subtly distinct senses yet the term also evoked a kind of discursive common ground from which to imagine the highest forces of destiny and sacred power. Thus, on the one hand, the term invariably evoked the highest sacrality, but to most people, it undoubtedly evoked the world of *shinbutsu* – Buddhas and *kami* seen as inhabiting visible and invisible realms – on the other. That is, the way of Heaven, like Buddhas and *kami*, acted in the world by variously responding to oaths (*kishōmon*) and related prayers, by punishing transgression, and offering salvation (Kanda 2010b: 51–59).

Kanda Chisato has called attention to the inclusion of the life of Śākyamuni in the preaching at the debate recorded by the Catholic monks, emphasizing the prominence of the oral transmission of stories of the historical Buddha in the fifteenth and sixteenth centuries. Works like the monumental *Hokekyō jikidan shō* depicted tales of Śākyamuni as part of the developing genre of stories concerning the historical founder; although these stories along with a whole range of *jātaka* (J. *honjōtan*) tales had been told throughout Japanese history, the increasing preaching of the tales to the general populace, most of which remained illiterate, offered narratives that in their presumed singularity provided a measure of counterweight to Christian efforts to preach the uniqueness of their gospel (Kanda 2010b: 28–31). Undoubtedly, the increasing dissemination of Zen and Hokke lineages throughout the isles, combined with the continued presence of those of Tendai, all of which focused on Śākyamuni (or some interpretation thereof) as their central Buddha figure, contributed to the proliferation of such tales.

Efforts of True Pure Land (Jōdo Shinshū) and Pure Land lineage (Jōdo shū) preachers to disseminate the story of Amida's vow and his grace were also increasingly prominent during the period, given the successes of Rennyo and his successors as well as the continued spread of the lineages tracing themselves to Hōnen. Even the temporary prohibition of True Pure Land lineages undertaken by some regional lords was undertaken to undermine the perceived political threat of the Honganji partisans rather than the True Pure Land teachings per se. In fact, a whole series of itinerant figures, such as mountain ascetics, female oracles (*miko*), yin-yang masters (*onmyōji*), *biwa hōshi* entertainers and amateur healers, were often prohibited under the category of *ikkō shū* (i.e., True Pure Land lineages), illustrating some lords' association of the True Pure Land lineages with a whole range of *nenbutsu* practitioners and, as noted by some scholars, the belief in *kami*–Buddha combinatory relations in Jōdo Shinshū since Rennyo's time, if not earlier (Kanda 2010b: 80–81, 150).

Thus despite conceptions that, on the one hand, the True Pure Land lineages were active only among the peasants, that they did not feature *kami*–Buddha combinatory beliefs or practices, and that they had little to do with the development of funerary or mortuary practice, and on the other, that Zen lineages were primarily close to regional lords, that they did feature such combinatory beliefs and practices, and that they were involved in the development of funerary Buddhism, the situation seems to have been much more complicated. In fact, True Pure Land lineages were actually not only close in many cases to regional lords and encouraged *kami*–Buddha combinatory beliefs and practices but also, in cases such as the Honganji and affiliated lineages, featured their own funerary and mortuary rites (Kanda 2010a: 294–298).

These manifold social associations remind us of the prominence of not merely Honganji partisans but also of a wide range of itinerant practitioners – and the perceived threat experienced by *daimyō* lords of the era. The powerful warrior-lord Oda Nobunaga (1534–1582) subjugated Mt. Hiei and eventually also Honganji (1580), destroying the Buddhist military threat. Any significant remnants of the Kenmitsu "system" (Kenmitsu Taisei), which had been vibrant for some half a millennium, now came to an end. Besides, it was the broad appeal of the True Pure Land lineages and the power of the Honganji in particular which led Neil McMullin to describe the "Ishiyama Honganji War" (1570–1580) as "the major event of Nobunaga's life and, indeed, of the entire Sengoku period" (McMullin 1984: 101). In any event, as we will see, the Tokugawa shogunate would, over time, develop a series of strategies to ensure that Buddhist institutions and itinerant practitioners never constituted a threat to its authority.

By the fifteenth and the sixteenth century, all manner of itinerant practitioners traveled the landscape. Some groups of practitioners, such as the mountain ascetics (*shugenja*), had already been organized for a significant period under the leadership of major Buddhist institutions. Their status in their affiliation with these temples was on a par with other lower-ranking monastic figures at the level of the *dōshu* (temple assistant, also called *zenshu*, *gyōnin*, *gesu*) class (Sekiguchi 2009a: 7). The group that came to be known as the Honzan-ha only geographically expanded their influence significantly from the late fifteenth century onward; they actually came under the supervision of the major Tendai temple Onjōji (Kyoto) only since the late thirteenth century, when the former gained complete control of the administration of Kumano.[4] Figures like Dōkō (1430-1501) traveled throughout the isles, disseminating stories about the ancient mountain ascetic En no gyōja, and attempted to establish further control over groups of ascetics who were, in many cases, largely independent in their activities (Miyake 2005: 54–56), but who seem to have often welcomed sponsorship by the Onjōji-affiliated Shōgo'in cloister (Kyoto). The other major lineage, the group later called the Tōzan-ha, practiced in the area near Yoshino along the same Ōmine mountain range, and was originally sponsored in their practice by officials at halls of the powerful Nara monastery Kōfukuji. They eventually gained instead Daigoji's Sanbō'in cloister as their major patron by roughly the early seventeenth century. This shift might initially seem somewhat surprising, since some Shingon temples, like Negoroji (alt. Negorodera), featured mountain ascetics who had been associated with the Honzan-ha, but these lower-status temple figures seem to have gained greater unity and autonomy by choosing an affiliation with Sanbō'in, the relationship with which was less hierarchical than that fostered under Shōgo'in (Sekiguchi 2009a: 141–145).

During the same period, the expansion of Buddhist lineages from major centers like Kyoto into the countryside became much more pronounced. There are presumably many examples of heads of cloisters and halls within Kenmitsu temple complexes like Daigoji who commonly traveled into the provinces. Abbots of Hōon'in in Daigoji such as Ryūzai (1409–1470) gave initiation to rural monks who came to them for this purpose and for permission to make copies of sacred works (*shōgyō*) and, in the case of Ryūzai, also sought to have their temples be made branch temples (*matsuji*) of Hōon'in in the 1450s and 1460s (Fujii 2008: 238–239). Hōon'in's Chō'e (1432–1516) was one of the first to actually travel to relatively distant regions, where he bestowed consecrations and seals of transmission (*inka*) on at least 15 monks. Moreover, having been initiated in both the Hōon'in and Muryōju'in lines, Chō'e gave initiations in *both* lineages to some of the rural monks, a new development, going additionally to areas of Ōmi as well as Hitachi, Mutsu, Shimosa, and Shimotsuke Provinces in Kantō in connection with the Muryōju'in conferrals and, apparently, promoting the conversion of Shingon temples there into branch temples (Fujii 2008: 234–245). Daigoji Muryōju'in's abbot Gyōga (1511–1592) would go to areas of north Kantō and gave initiation to almost 600; their temples would later become the branch temples of the Muryōju'in line (pp. 251–254).[5] The influence of Daigoji became pronounced through much of Kansai and Kantō, as clerics of local temples, most typically through initiation, acquired sacred works of Daigoji lineages.

At the same time, trans-lineal beliefs and practices had become all the more prominent in the populace and even, in some cases, in temples. For example, images of and related devotion toward ancient figures like Prince Shōtoku and Gyōki had transcended lineage affiliation since at least the early medieval era. Gyōki, for example, had become a prominent model for the fundraising holy ones (*kanjin hijiri*) from the late twelfth century onward, and Shōtoku's position was as an anomalous, apotheosized, figure sometimes seen as a transformation of the Buddha; some scholars have suggested that worship of Shōtoku and figures like Gyōki (even Kannon)

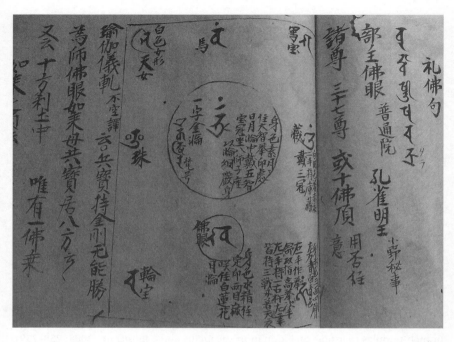

Figure 5.1   Ichiji Kinrin rite divinities (Sanskrit and Japanese), copy of Daigoji sacred work *Genpi shō* made by monk Taijō (n.d.), Hagaji temple (Wakasa, now Fukui Prefecture), signed Meiwa 5 [*tsuchinoene*].8.20 (1768), 16.4 × 19.6 cm. Ruppert personal collection.

offered believers a solution to the threat of the Last Age (*mappō*) – interpreted, as of the fourteenth century, by some as not so much decline as "shorthand for the preeminence of Japan over the rest of Buddhist Asia" (Carr 2012: 92–93).

More generally, the appellation of *daishi*, "great teacher," although originally an official posthumous proclamation of the court, took on special meaning for believers across the vast religious landscape of the late medieval and early modern eras. Veneration related to figures like Kōbō Daishi, Ganzan Daishi (Ryōgen), and Shōtoku thus often transcended any discursive or ritual limitations related to lineage as, for example, a Tendai-affiliated temple like Kokawadera came to house a Kōbō Daishi image (Itō 2008: 162–167).

Figures like Kōbō Daishi and Shōtoku were central also to newly developing Shintō lineages, as described by Urabe Kanekuni in 1486; Kanekuni noted that of the four Shintō lineages existing in his day, one was devoted to Prince Shōtoku and another was to Kōbō Daishi (Itō 2010: 223). Mountain ascetic practitioners of Tōzan groups prior to their affiliation with Daigoji prominently included *dōshu* attendants of Kōfukuji, who like others in these groups possessed deep belief in the *shugen* tradition associated with the early Shingon monk Shōbō, and so veneration of Shōbō transcended lineage affiliation. Daigoji's Sanbo'in, in the early seventeenth century, would thus draw to itself the already extant trans-lineal cult of Shōbō among the *shugenja* (Sekiguchi 2009b: 115–116).

Among those outside monastery walls who greatly influenced Japanese Buddhist cultural history, warrior-lord Toyotomi Hideyoshi is notable for a variety of reasons. Unlike Nobunaga, who we might say triangulated his policies vis-à-vis religious institutions by continuing comparatively tolerant policies toward Christians while crushing Buddhist military powers, Hideyoshi did not continue the policy of tolerance, at least toward the end of the 1580s, when he began to take stricter measures against the Christians. Hideyoshi also attempted to prop up his leadership through renewed support of Buddhist institutions that did not threaten him – the militarized Negoroji being an exception – and thus established a "great Buddha" (*daibutsu*) at Hōkōji in Kyoto (Higashiyama). He also began to attempt to have himself apotheosized as a great *kami* defending/ruling Japan (Hōkoku Daimyōjin), a novel development at that point in the history of Japanese military leaders. Hideyoshi's move followed the trend to incorporate religious belief – the mysterious world of *kami* and Buddhas – into absolute rule, an effort that reversed tendencies in groups such as the True Pure Land and Hokke leagues to attempt establishment of complete self-rule and presaged the apotheosis of the founder of the Tokugawa regime, Tokugawa Ieyasu (1542–1616; Sueki 2010: 22–34). It would, indeed, be the influential Tendai monk Tenkai (1536–1643) who specifically succeeded in transforming Ieyasu into a *kami* (*daigongen*) – in fact, as a "universal god" at Nikkō "whose authority would be acknowledged even beyond Japan's borders" as came to be seen in the performative symbolism of visits by Korean embassies to Ieyasu's memorial at Tōshōgū in future years (Ooms 1989: 181–182).

Early and Middle Edo-Period Buddhism (1600–1800)

The effects of the Tokugawa regime

The sheer quantity of manuscript sources for study of the Edo period continues to grow as scholars explore more and more sites. These enable us to understand "local" or "lived religion" at a depth previously unimaginable. Comparative studies can be conducted of Buddhist lineages within and between regions; analysis can be undertaken of shogunal policies toward religious groups; and investigation can be made of ways in which lay believers and religious specialists engaged in religious life (Williams 2006: 185). The archival work of scholars at the Historiographical Institute of the University of Tokyo and, particularly, figures like Tamamuro Fumio has made it clear that a vast untapped set of sources are held in sites as varied as temples and family collections – and these scholars regularly uncover new materials. Many of the

Edo-period materials are documentary sources, created in connection with require-ments or needs associated with the demands of the Tokugawa shogunate, which attempted to acquire as great as possible a level of control over the populace, and so intensive demographic analysis has become a potential option for scholars of religion.

Moreover, although wood-block printing had existed for centuries, print publish-ing occurred on an unprecedented level in the Edo period, so that a variety of works, including increased numbers of genres of temple literature, became available. In fact, the number of Buddhist works printed was vast, so that even if we exclude temple publishing, we see that the booksellers' catalog of the 1660s includes 117 pages of Buddhist works out of 266 altogether. The Zen monk Suzuki Shōsan (1579–1655) noted that Buddhist books sold especially well and that private publish-ers were even trying to find old preaching materials to publish (Kornicki 2001: 156). Tenkai, with the support of the third Tokugawa shōgun, Iemitsu, began the printing of the Buddhist "canon" (*issaikyō*) near the end of his life – a project which would be completed five years after Tenkai's death (Mizukami 2010: 125). Meanwhile, in cases such as that of the influential *Shōshinge* (full title: *Shōshin nenbutsuge*), a compilation of verses of Shinran that came to be incorporated into proselytizing in True Pure Land lineages, printed commentaries appeared in the seventeenth century, when such dissemination became extremely prominent (Kusaka and Mannami 2005).

These developments suggests that Buddhist interest – at least in the early Tokugawa period – lay in a broad range of masters' writings more than a sectarian focus on the founder, even in lineages with seemingly strong emphasis on ancestral master veneration. Additionally, given the substantial numbers and the broad publi-cation of Buddhist works in Kyoto and, soon after, Osaka and Edo as well, we should question any claim that religion in the Edo period was dominated by Neo-Confucianism.[6] As illustrated by Tenkai's canon and the proliferation of new *hatto* regulations meant in part to encourage monastic learning, it is clear that the shogu-nate's support was an essential component in what was in fact a broad revival of Buddhist learning, to which we will later turn (Nishimura 2010: 188–195).

In institutional terms, the most visible developments occurred over the course of the seventeenth century, when the Edo shogunate increased its supervision over reli-gion and created an administrative system that would remain largely unchanged until the dawn of the Meiji Period. A grandson of Ieyasu, the shōgun Iemitsu quick-ened the process of rooting out Christians, drew upon Tenkai's writings to promote the apotheosis of Ieyasu as "Gongen-sama," and attempted to require affiliation of all residents with temples of one of the officially designated lineages – lineages that were now officially separate and, presumably, increasingly sectarian in character. It is important to emphasize again that groups such as the Nichiren, Pure Land, True Pure Land, and Sōtō (Zen) lineages had consolidated their place in rural society over the course of the sixteenth and seventeenth centuries, so that the institutional ground was already prepared for these developments – especially in connection with the developing "clan" (*ie*) in Japanese society and related ancestor veneration. Indeed, as noted above, recent research suggests that both the head–branch system (*hon-matsu seido*) and the temple affiliation system (*jidan*; alt. *danka seido*) arose primarily as a response of the authorities to developing trends among the temples and populace (Sonehara 2010: 93–96; Takenuki 1993) as was also suggested in connection with Daigoji's Hōon'in above,[7] although one function of the latter system was undoubtedly the "domestication of Buddhism" noted by one scholar (Josephson 2007: 41).

Moreover, it is also important to emphasize that before the consolidation of the shogunate's full version of the head–branch system, distinctions like that between "old order" Shingon (Kogi Shingon) and "new order" Shingon (Shingi Shingon) were essentially doctrinal categories. Monks could be initiated into multiple lineages of varied branches of any one school of Japanese Buddhism. Even in the eighteenth century, the determination of a temple as Kogi or Shingi would often be reclassified according to the training of the resident abbot if he were from the other "order" (Ambros 2011: 1010–1011).[8]

In any event, the early Tokugawa regime clearly took advantage of such developing trends and succeeded in a variety of ways to broaden the impact of Buddhist temples on the larger populace. The temples and lineages promoted, however, were especially those to the shogunate's liking – especially the Tendai and Pure Land lineages (Jōdo shū; Ooms 1989: 173–175) – and these lineages were treated in terms increasingly sectarian in character. Sectarian treatment, for example, can be seen in policies toward temples such as Onjōji and Enryakuji, which had been at loggerheads throughout the medieval era, but were now treated as simply representatives of "the Tendai school" (Tendai shū); and in warrior-sponsored One Thousand Monk assemblies (Sensō'e), which since the late sixteenth century included four of the "new" Kamakura lineages (Zen, Nichiren, Jōdo, Jishū) as part of eight traditional "schools" of Buddhism, but were now conducted alternately on a monthly basis by 100 monks of just one lineage among the eight, who would in combination complete the performance over an extended period (Sonehara 2010: 101–103).

One of the most profound influences the Tokugawa shogunate had was on the variegated religious groups *associated* with Buddhism, such as those of mountain ascetic traditions. The goal of the early shogunate was clearly to weaken the authority of the traditional Kenmitsu institutions over such groups. Thus the shogunate mandated in the early seventeenth century that the so-called Honzan-ha centers at Mt. Haguro, Hiko, Yoshino and others be subsidiary temples (*matsuji*) under the authority of Kan'eiji in Edo – instead of directly under Kyoto's Shōgo'in. Meanwhile, the regime, increasingly supported Tōzan-ha in an effort to weaken the power of the Honzan-ha and create a balance of authority between the two major lineages, which was undertaken in partial response to the efforts of the Yamato region groups of the Tōzan-ha, who were under Daigoji's authority, to gain the shogunate's patronage. At the same time, these groups, to which all individual mountain ascetics were required to be affiliated, were not treated like Buddhist monks because the halls and shrines they operated were not classified as "temples" and so not defined as religious institutions (Hayashi 2010: 250–253).

Other such groups defined as lacking an institutional base included, for example, the itinerant *komusō* Buddhist entertainer groups as well as the lineages of Yin-yang practitioners. *Komusō*, however, were recognized as Buddhist lineages (the Fuke shū) and came to receive special treatment due, ironically, not to their affiliation histori- cally with Zen but to their fictive claim to have a special connection with the warrior class. They acquired unique benefits from this association, as the shogunate came to forbid farmers and merchants from becoming *komusō* and the latter's groups were often able to avoid supervision by the local governor and the shrine-temple magis- trates (*jisha bugyō*; Hayashi 2010: 259–260).[9]

Although we saw that Buddhist groups partly laid the ground for increased con- solidation of governmental authority, it is, in fact, hard to exaggerate the effects of the policies undertaken by the early Tokugawa regime, which intermittently inter- vened from the beginning of the seventeenth century with a series of regulations, became more expansive with the crushing of potential Christian anti-shogunate ele- ments at mid-century, and introduced the temple affiliation system as well as a broad set of newer regulations over the latter half of the seventeenth and into the early eighteenth century. Temple affiliation that was local but also, at least in terms of the policy of the shogunate, increasingly marked by exclusivity of lineage developed throughout the Japanese isles. At the same time, traditional interests in Buddhist learning were strengthened, in part, by the new regulations and clearly by increased patronage at local and national levels. As one scholar has emphasized, Buddhist tem- ples and their organizations, on the one hand, and shrines and their organizations, on the other – which had now been officially separated from mountain ascetics and yin-yang masters – served for the first time as *public* entities throughout the land, distinct legally from a whole variety of itinerant groups that were designated very differently. Specific lineages were designated as official leaders of such groups, but none of these groups was recognized as a public entity by the regime, and in most cases they were seen as potential sites for social mobility and unrest, as farmers and merchants sometimes entered such groups in the developing metropoles of Japan. Their way of life could only be supported through fundraising (*kanjin*), which now became increasingly associated with such groups rather than with the established Buddhist temples or their affiliates (Hayashi 2010: 265–266).

Buddhist learning, dissemination and permutations of Buddhist culture

With the development of Tokugawa rule, Buddhist institutions, now patronized and regulated in ways unheard of over the course of the medieval era, adopted not only new organizational structures but also made renewed efforts to consolidate their cultures of learning while they also explored a broad range of cultural practices. The

Kenmitsu Buddhist complexes had been shorn of their former sovereignty, and even Tendai was compromised with the establishment of Kan'eiji as the "Eastern Hiei" in Edo. The Zen lineages were still very prominent, and yet former Zen monks became independent Confucian thinkers, as Confucianism became an alternative source of authoritative learning with an institutional base in a way that had not been the case throughout Japanese history. There had always been scholars of Chinese learning in Japan, but their lineages were limited to small groups within the court and their achievements were arguably overshadowed by Chinese studies within Buddhist monasteries throughout much of the medieval era, as major monasteries typically included cloisters where the sons of nobles lived and studied and had regular access not only to significant monastic treasuries but also, presumably, the libraries (fumi-kura) of court scholar families. Confucian scholars like Fujiwara Seika (1561–1619) and, especially, Hayashi Razan (1583–1657) – and, undoubtedly, their increasing patronage by the shogunate – contributed to a sea-change of study practice that became particularly prominent from the late eighteenth century onward.

What kinds of changes occurred within Zen lineages themselves? As with the other major Buddhist lineages, the Zen lineages had to deal with the new regulations imposed on them, but that is not to imply that they blindly followed the shogunate. On the one hand, prominent figures like Takuan Sōhō (1573–1645) suggested that the spirit of Ieyasu, enshrined as Tōshō Daigongen at Nikkō, was a kami, and Suzuki Shōsan saw the Tokugawa shōgun as a "holy king" (shōō; Sonehara 2010: 112). Nonetheless, Takuan led a protest against the shogunate's infringement on the sovereign's right to confer purple monastic robes on the abbots of Daitokuji and Myōshinji. Takuan was especially upset that the shogunate dared to mandate that any abbot of these temples who would receive the robe, first complete over 30 years of training and solve 1,700 kōans – this was a position for which he was exiled (Nishimura 2010: 197).

Meanwhile, Zen also enjoyed a revival in direct influence from Chinese Chan masters. Amidst the decline of the Ming Dynasty, Chinese merchants increased their trade with Japan, especially in the port of Nagasaki, where a significant Chinese community developed and constructed a few independent, nominally "Chan" Buddhist temples. Like temples in China, they enshrined various deities, like the sea and merchant-related gods Ma-zu and Guan-di, and invited little-known Chinese monks to serve the temple communities. With the 1650s arrival of prominent Chinese masters Dōja Chōgen (Ch. Daozhe Chaoyuan, 1602–1662) and, especially, Ingen Ryūki (Ch. Yinyuan Longqi, 1592–1673), the situation changed. Ingen would found the first new Zen lineage in Japan in several centuries, the Ōbaku school, which was originally an outgrowth of the Linji (Rinzai) in Ming China. Indeed, Rinzai Zen monks calling for monastic rigor at Myōshinji purchased some volumes by Ingen prior to his arrival in Nagasaki and attempted to have him installed as abbot of Myōshinji, which proved to no avail (Baroni 2000: 31–44). Yet this incident also indicates the extent to which the book business was not merely thriving but also sometimes interwoven with religious developments. Ultimately, the strict monastic monks of Myōshinji changed their plan and convinced the shogunate to permit the construction of a temple for Ingen in Uji near Kyoto, whereupon Manpukuji was built in Ming style during the 1660s by Chinese artisans. The Ōbaku lineages would be remarkably successful, with more than one thousand temples officially placed under its leadership by the mid eighteenth century. The several Chinese masters at the temple in its early phase undoubtedly helped provide an image of monastic rigor, which invoked reactions from Rinzai temples like Myōshinji. The Myōshinji master Mujaku Dōchū (1653–1745) thus wrote the monastic regulations *Shōsōrin ryakushingi* in 1685, a little over a decade after Ingen's *Ōbaku shingi* code was completed (Mohr 2000: 254–255).

Ōbaku Zen introduced to Japan a form of Zen that explicitly promoted the dual use of *zen* meditation and *nenbutsu* recitation. Although earlier Japanese Zen practitioners had been aware of the great Chan master Zhung-feng Ming-ben's (J. Chūhō Myōhon, 1263–1323) promotion of such dual practice, the systematic use of it seems to have been absent in Japanese Zen, with the exception of Suzuki Shōsan and the Myōshinji abbot Ungo Kiyō (1583–1659; Baroni 2000: 112–114). There had been few Zen masters with interest in Pure Land Buddhism historically, perhaps in connection with the rising institutional prominence of True Pure Land Buddhism and its drastic reformulation of monastic practice in the form of clerical marriage in Jōdo Shinshū.[10] Doctrinally, Zen masters typically did not acknowledge the notion of the decline of the Buddhist dharma (*mappō*), and so they did not grant that reliance on "other power" (*tariki*) was of fundamental importance to pursuing the path in their own day.

Thus while Ingen was simply practicing Zen in Japan as it was practiced in China at the time, Japanese monks who followed him were often resistant to Pure Land Buddhist features of his teaching and practice. His morning and evening services included *nenbutsu* recitation and chanting of Pure Land scriptures, which some of his monastic followers did not acknowledge. Meanwhile, like the Chan masters, he commonly assigned the *nenbutsu* as a *kōan* for lay believers, particularly those already of Pure Land orientation. One scholar has stressed that the emphasis on assigning the *nenbutsu* to lay believers is very similar to that of Rinzai's Hakuin Ekaku (1685–1768), who noted the benefit of such practice early on in Buddhist training. Moreover, Ingen, like Hakuin, additionally drew upon a variety of Daoist and Confucian discourses, illustrating his broad incorporation of multiple traditions in his teaching (Baroni 2000: 114–121).

Hakuin, like these other figures, thus seems to have partially represented a renewed incorporation of broad continental influence into Zen practice, a feature that may have influenced the rethinking of *kōan* practice at the time, as has been emphasized by Michael Mohr (Mohr 2000: 256–258). *Kōan* use, which was not originally prominent in Sōtō Zen, had even greatly increased at the main Sōtō monastery Eiheiji, where masters produced both catalogs of *kōan* from the late Muromachi period and established a large body of *kirigami* transmission manuscripts in the seventeenth and eighteenth centuries (Iizuka 2009: 197–204). For Hakuin, however, the *kōan* was somatically interpreted based on general assumptions regarding medicine in Ming China – informed originally by Daoist notions – rather than any connection with Pure Land practice. Hakuin undoubtedly saw the newly arrived Chinese masters as a threat to his own vision of proper Zen practice, which can be seen in his suggestions that the Ōbaku masters were outwardly devoted to Zen but inwardly devoted to the Pure Land path. Hakuin explicitly warned against combining Zen and Pure Land and warned that such combining would destroy the Zen traditions (Baroni 2000: 156–159). Hakuin was thus influenced by continental beliefs and practices, while also being wary of certain continental influences. Indeed, as he lived in an age when the Japanese cultural landscape featured alternative religious visions, he sometimes responded to criticisms of Buddhism, seen, for example, in *Doku jinjakō bengi*, his response to Hayashi Razan's Confucian critique of Buddhism (Maeda 2010: 128).

It is very likely that Hakuin was aware of the increasing prominence of literati monks during his lifetime, especially from the 1750s onwards. Of course, the Haiku master Matsuo Bashō (1644–1694) was an early Edo example of a literati figure strongly influenced by Buddhist, especially Zen, discourses and practices, but the influx of Chinese trade, including the arrival of Chinese monks, and the rapid development of Edo and other metropoles seem to have propelled aesthetic developments among monastic Buddhists as much as among the rest of the population. It was in this regard as well that Ōbaku figures were particularly prominent. For example, the monk Baisaō (Gekkai Genshō, 1675–1763) was well known for the tea-stands he established as a peripatetic peddler in Kyoto and his position within the lineage of *sencha* tea culture that developed in contradistinction to the formal Chanoyu tea ceremony. While formal Chanoyu had the appeal of conferring status on practitioners while transmitting ideas broadly associated with Zen, Baisaō and others promoted drinking *sencha* as part of an alternative tea rite deriving its symbolism from a combination of ideas associated with Wang Yang-Ming Confucian studies, the Daoist thinkers Lao-zi and Zhuang-zi, and Zen lineages – a combination invariably related to the influx of Chinese influence and the renewed fascination with "Chinese things" (*karamono*; Graham 2003: 111–116).

As Hakuin was responding to a series of challenges and undertaking with the Rinzai monks around him with a renewal and full institutionalization of the *kōan* system of training, popular Buddhist preachers were increasingly frequenting public spaces and developing new modes of performance. One early famous example had been the peripatetic Pure Land lineage monk Sakuden (1554–1642) who studied at Zenrinji (Higashiyama) and went on to travel and preach throughout the Kyoto and

Sanyō regions, wrote the ambiguous and often humorous work *Seisui shō* and is seen as an originator of Rakugo humor. Taichū (1552–1639) was also a Pure Land lineage monk who was a prominent preacher, in this case possessing special interest in the record of the Ōhara *mondō* debate between Hōnen and his critics and in the Taimadera Pure Land mandala; he is also known in part for having traveled to and preached in the Ryūkyū islands. The prominent True Pure Land lineage monk Asai Ryōi (d. 1691) was known not only for his preaching and interest in the Pure Land mandala but also for his didactic commentaries on Pure Land sutras, Japanese Pure Land works, as well as a variety of narratives drawn from encyclopedic Buddhist story collections from the continent (Tsutsumi 1996: 233–237; Sekiyama 1973: 200–216, 291–306).

The novel preaching genre called *kange-bon* was particularly prominent in the publishing boom and thus larger audience for Buddhist teaching and performance, with roughly 500 such works published over the course of the Edo period. These works, sometimes referred to as *dangi-bon*,[11] were focused on themes as varied as simple explanations of scripture, homilies, accounts of anomalies and karmic causation (*innen*), legends of temple complexes, monastic hagiography, and birth in the Pure Land, all of which had existed since earlier eras but were now informed anew by continental collections and made accessible to the general population. The Shingon Ritsu monk Rentai (1663–1726) was an early example of a peripatetic preacher who taught about the powers and benefits of the bodhisattvas Kannon and Jizō, karmic retribution, and the importance of the Kōmyō Shingon memorial rite in areas from Shikoku to Kantō, and published a series of *kange-bon* in this connection. A number of the stories he told, as well as those of others in this preaching genre, were related to local oral legends that had been handed down and thus figures like Rentai were also transmitters and transformers of a wide variety of folklore, especially from the eighteenth century onward. Such figures also innovated by making large compilations of, on the one hand, medieval stories, particularly those which featured tours of hell, biographies of famous historical or legendary persons, and anomalous legends, while on the other, embellishing all manner of tales to appeal in the new era, which presumably both edified and entertained the new urbanites (Tsutsumi 1996: 235–254).

A recent study summarized the *kange-bon* sub-genres, especially in connection with the True Pure Land lineages, by highlighting the following components: explication of sutras and sacred works (*shōgyō*), such as of the 48 vows of Amida Buddha and the writings about them, which constitute the largest number in the genre; those which draw on *waka* poetry rather than sutras or sacred works as the source for preaching; presentations on a series of topics such as the six perfections and impermanence; legends of temples, their images, and individual biographies, which were numerous and especially presented on occasions of *kaichō* public image viewings; collections of didactic tales, including ghost stories; and preaching manuals

(Ushiroshōji 2010: 587–588). These varied works proved controversial in True Pure Land, where a large number of new writings claiming to be authored by Shinran and Rennyo also appeared; particularly given the emphasis on karmic merit, thaumaturgy, and *kami* worship of many of these novel writings, the leadership in True Pure Land established new publications like the large collection *Shinshū hōyō* (Essentials of Shinshū, 1765) designed to offer tales for preaching that were in line with official doctrine (Nishimura 2010: 205).

Performance by Buddhist practitioners outside of monastic walls continued to flourish while, within, performance thrived and appealed to pilgrims and other visitors. We saw above the unique position of the *komusō* groups and evolving place of *shugenja*, but it is also important to take note of developing ritual organizations like the so-called *sanmai hijiri*, a self-identified group of "holy men" who, while originally listed officially as *danka* parishioners, conducted funerary rites. Dating from the medieval era, the groups existed throughout the Kansai region and were led by the organization at Ryūshō'in at Tōdaiji since at least the fundraising efforts toward the reconstruction of the Great Buddha there in the late seventeenth century (Takada 2000: 128–132).

There were, of course, various groups of fundraising "holy ones" (*hijiri*) in the Japanese religious landscape. The precursors of the itinerant Hamurogumi, a 33-Kannon fund-raising group in the Kansai region that would develop in the mid-Tokugawa period, were the Hongan (original vow) fundraisers of Nachi at Kumano, who came under the authority of one of the Kazan'in court noble family in the first half of the eighteenth century (Sawa 1999: 118–135). Such fund-raising practitioners were often directly affiliated with major temple complexes since the medieval era (e.g., Mt. Kōya), and the *hijiri* group within Tōji in Kyoto controlled its own nominations for the "great fundraiser" position (*daikanjin-shiki*) from the late fifteenth century onward, an innovation at variance with what had come before. The *hijiri* group at Tōji, intimately related to the first prominent group of such holy ones at Kiyomizudera, invariably selected the great fundraisers from holy ones outside the organization – figures who had demonstrated success in such activity and related networking skills, in this case a group called the "wood-eating holy ones" (*mokujiki shōnin*).

These *mokujiki* holy ones, supported originally also by both the court and shogunate, innovated by leading the *Heart Sūtra* assembly as an annual rite in which numerous copies of the scripture were made and, along with paper amulets of the god Daikokuten, distributed. The activity was conducted in the Sai'in Mi-eidō memorial hall at Tōji, dedicated to Kōbō Daishi Kūkai's memory, and the Daikokuten venerated was believed to have been personally carved by the Great Teacher himself. This rite fit in perfectly with Tōji's traditions, as the original request to the court to reinstate the "great fundraiser" position at Tōji described its goal as the requital of indebtedness to the master and its audience as Tōji lineage members living throughout Japan (Ōta 2008: 242–274).[12]

We can also see here the evolving practice of worshipping deities (*shin*, *kami*) within the Buddhist monasteries. Within monasteries, for example, the Shuni'e (i.e., Tōdaiji's O'mizutori rite) featured elaborate performances of a series of Buddhist and other rites. Among them was the Nakatomi-no-harae exorcism, associated with *kami* worship and yin-yang practice. Although monks performed versions of the rite even in the Heian period and saw the rite as expiating transgression in connection with repentance, their rendition of the rite at the Shuni'e later should also be understood in the context of Yoshida Shintō promotion of its performance, Shugendō practices, and the training of some Tōdaiji monks in Shingon Shintō lineages. At the Shuni'e, the performance of the rite was thought to prevent intrusion into the ritual space by *tengu* or other demons that might interfere with its execution (Daitō 2009: 153–169). Such performances may have accompanied what some scholars have emphasized as the "ritualization" of even large monastic meetings (*sengi*) from the late fifteenth century onward. What had been primarily decision-making gatherings now prominently included performative rituals following the patterns of celebratory banquets (Matsuo 1997: 98–106).

Over the course of the Edo period, monasteries and more regional temples increasingly hosted pilgrims within their grounds, sometimes in connection with the *kanjin* campaigns noted above but also in connection with the development of local confraternities (*kō*), which responded variously to the performances and other appeals of the temples. The scale of such activities reached new heights over the course of the eighteenth century. Mt. Ōyama in Sagami Province (Kantō) had been a center of mountain asceticism, but with the aid of the shogunate converted to a Shingon monastery, assigning more than 20 monks in the first part of the seventeenth century. By 1609, new legally binding regulations had been distributed by both the shogunate and Mt. Kōya, which established rules for the monks and gave control over the premises to the newly established Shingon temples at Ōyama. The main hall, which enshrined the Buddhist protective divinity Fudō, was the greatest object of pilgrimage at the mountain, and in the late seventeenth century, as pilgrimage there began to flourish, the *oshi* innkeeper / guides likewise increased their prominence, acting as intermediaries between pilgrims and the Shingon monks (Ambros 2008: 62–77, 130–133).

There was also a series of major pilgrimage sites that flourished during the period, such as the 88-site pilgrimage route memorializing Kōbō Daishi's legendary practice as well as the increasingly *kami*-centric Mt. Konpira, both of which were on Shikoku island. Undoubtedly, the Kōbō Daishi pilgrimage practice developed at the intersection of the Daishi cult which stemmed from Mt. Kōya, on the one hand, and features of Kumano-pilgrimage-related beliefs and practices, on the other, and both were informed by local religion and were trans-lineal in character as Ian Reader has noted. The development of the Daishi pilgrimage practice was also informed by legendary and, sometimes, historical associations of figures like Gyōki, Saigyō and, especially,

Ippen with the Shikoku sites. It would be seventeenth-century Shingon figures like Chōzen (1613–1680) and Shinnen (d. 1691) who developed accounts featuring the number 88, pilgrimage tale collections and, eventually, guidebooks and so-called pilgrimage stones (*henro ishi*) to provide directions along the route. By the last part of the century, the pilgrimage had become a mass phenomenon attracting believers from around the isles, including varieties of ascetics and monks of multiple lineages (Reader 2006: 111–121). As for the pilgrimage routes to see the 33-Kannon mentioned above and which existed in both Kansai and Kantō, pilgrims enjoyed guidebooks employing multiple written media – print and faux cursive, variation between *kanbun* lists and vernacular descriptions as well as mixed reference to the regional pilgrimage (e.g., Kansai) and more local pilgrimages (e.g., Kyoto).

Legends about the transformations of sacred beings such as Kannon were also prominent and, as mentioned above, were sometimes newly published together with the illustrated guidebooks for the pilgrimage routes. In the case of the guidebook in Figure 5.2, where the guidebook was combined with the legend of 33 transformations based on the twenty-fifth chapter of the *Lotus Sūtra* – the so-called

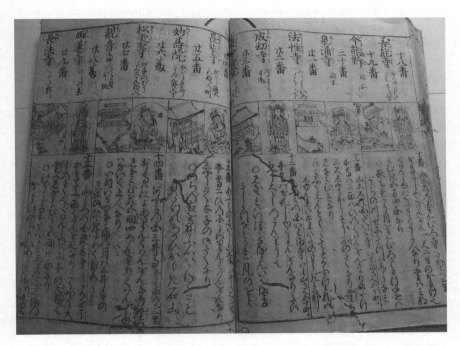

Figure 5.2   Illustrated guidebook mixing (top) non-iconic list of 33-Kannon of Kyoto (*Rakuyō sanjūsan ban fudasho*) with visual depictions and descriptions (bottom) of the 33-Kannon of the Kansai region (*Saigoku sanjūsan sho*), attached to rear of *Kannongyō hayayomi e shō*, Osaka and Kyoto, 1739, 22.4 × 14.8 cm. Ruppert personal collection.

Kannon Sūtra (Kannongyō) – the work was published in both Kansai and Kantō regions and, given the geographical multiplicity and ongoing publishing of the work over the Edo period, seems to have been a relatively prominent publication in pilgrims' circles. Similar to the attached guidebook, the legend *Kannongyō hayayomi e shō* (Illustrated Notes for Quick Reading of the *Kannon Sūtra*) combines written media, in this case of the Chinese passage of the scripture on the particular transformation, the visual illustration of the passage, explanation largely in *kana* and a Sino-Japanese exegesis above (see Figure 5.3). The foci include prominent themes to which most readers in the period could relate, including rescue from fire, as well as ones with more limited connections to most readers, such as rescue from dragons and other threats at sea. The emphasis on "quick reading" presumably would have appealed to lay believers, who could read the book quickly and understand the merits of calling on Kannon without the necessity of more time-consuming study of difficult Sino-Japanese commentaries on the scripture.

Konpira, which had esoteric and Pure Land Buddhist associations since the medieval era, would only become a prominent pilgrimage destination in the late eighteenth century with the vast increase in the market economy, as the mountain came to be associated with financial profit, seafaring safety and curative powers. Although thoroughly combinatory in character, the site would come to be redefined as "Shintō," especially with the rise of nativists such as Hirata Atsutane (1776–1843) who recreated the legends and cosmological underpinnings of Konpira so as to reject any Buddhist element (Thal 2005: 46–118).

Just as preaching practices, publishing, and pilgrimage flourished on a new level, so did the activities of Buddhist institutions as entrepreneurs of rituals and related objects. Sales of posthumous names (*kaimyō* precept-names and *igō* rank names) constituted a major source of revenue for temples throughout the land by the beginning of the seventeenth century, as they served to promote temple connections with wealthy or prominent donors. Moreover, as Duncan Williams has noted, "the ability of money to override matters of faith or social standing was a chief characteristic of the increasingly money-driven Tokugawa society"; thus the stated position of Sōtō Zen was that farmers were prohibited from received high-ranking posthumous titles, but wealthy peasants succeeded at acquiring such conferral for their deceased. Such entrepreneurial interventions were undoubtedly related, as Williams emphasizes, to the dual ritual logics of the Zen monks and their parishioners, which were evident in the effort to provide for some kind of realization of salvation at the time of death and karmic merit in the ongoing perceived necessity of continued ancestral memorial rites for decades afterward. The funerals ordained the dead and conferred lineage charts for entrance into the Buddha's lineage, while memorial rites spoke to parishioners' concerns over the karmic destiny of their loved ones (Williams 2005: 28–29, 58–59).

Geographically, as well, monks at traditional institutions such as cloisters at Mt. Kōya performed regular ancestral rites for believers from distant locales such as

(a)

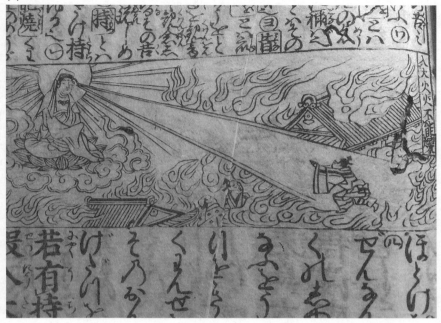

(b)

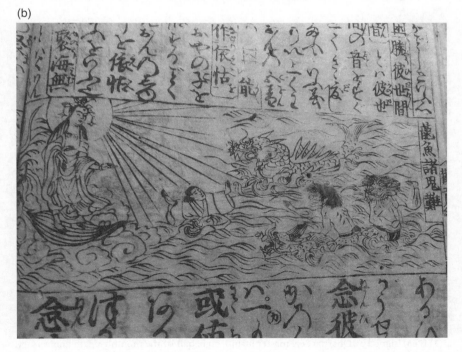

Figure 5.3 *Kannongyō hayayomi e shō* illustrations of Kannon saving a man, respectively, from fire (Figure 5.3a) and from dragons, fish, and demons (Figure 5.3b). Kundoku reading together with scriptural text below, and Japanese exegesis above. Osaka and Kyoto, 1739, 22.4 × 14.8 cm. Ruppert personal collection.

the Shinshū region (Kantō). In some cases they combined colophons and titles written by hand with printed Kōya petitions in their prayers, a practice which undoubtedly yielded substantial income through easing the process of production but at the same time preserved a kind of ritual authenticity through the use of hand-writing (see Figure 5.4).

Sōtō Zen lineages, like many others in the mid Tokugawa period, increasingly sold numerous talismans such as that of the monk-cum-*tengu* (goblin) Dōryō Daigongen at the increasingly powerful temple complex of Daiyūzan in Sagami province (Kantō), typically in connection with the rise of the pilgrimage confrater-nities (*kō*) and the more common use of *kaichō* viewings. Meanwhile, Daiyūzan and other temples increasingly sold a series of medicines that were not simply endorsed in a variety of new visions or dreams, in which figures like the bodhisat-tvas Kannon, Jizō, and the Buddha Yakushi told legends that emphasized their sacred beginnings, but the sales were also connected with changes in shogunate laws that ended the exclusive rights of government and clan physicians to produce and distribute medicines in the late seventeenth century. Within several decades of

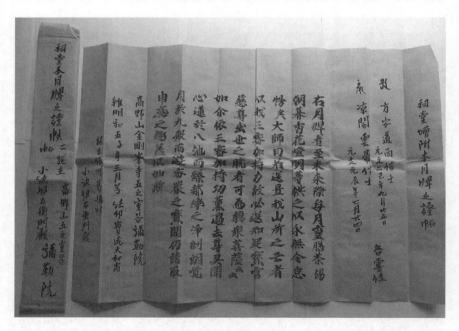

Figure 5.4   Prayer petition of Koike Iemon of Kazurashima village, Shinshū (Kantō), Meiwa 5.3 (1768), signed by Dharma Seal master Jitsujō, on behalf of the monthly-death-anniversary rites of two departed spirits, memorial hall (*shidō*), Miroku'in cloister, Kōyasan Kongōbuji monastery, 35 × 51.1 cm. Note larger characters of printed main prayer in center. Ruppert personal collection.

such changes, groups such as the "holy men of Kōya" (*Kōya hijiri*), prominent since the medieval era, had established networks as far away as the Kantō region to distribute their Daranisuke medicine (Williams 2005: 59–116).

From the late fifteenth century, professional groups increasingly began to construct narratives to depict not just their ancestors but also the sacred character of the tools they used, a part of what one scholar calls the sacralization of "tools and labor." Such groups typically traced their legends to a divinity explained in terms of *honji-suijaku* relations between Buddhist figures and *kami*, and represented their tools as sacred objects traceable to that founding figure or divinity; moreover, they represented everyday work practices as modes of interaction between human beings and divinities. One prime example was that of the Miwa shrine-temple complex and its lineages, the majority of whose works and practices flourished in the eighteenth and nineteenth centuries. Miwa works thus traced the origin of carpenters to *kami* who aided the first emperor, Jinmu. Miwa ritual instructions for carpenters consisted primarily of mantras and related instructions for every step in successful carpentry, as ritual labor effected an atonement and hence reconciliation with cosmic harmony – harmony recovered after the invariable violation of cosmic order by the very act of construction (Rambelli 2007).

Finally, contrary to the impressions given by earlier claims of Tsuji and others, scholars now increasingly emphasize that Buddhist learning in the form of Buddhist scholasticism (*kyōgaku*) reached new heights in a series of Buddhist lineages during much of the Edo period. The strict regulations (*hatto*) conformed to the Tokugawa regime's efforts to maintain a close eye on the Buddhists, but they also fueled an extremely vibrant period of Japanese Buddhist studies. With the financial support of the shogunate, major Buddhist schools (Jōdo shū, Tendai shū, Jōdo Shinshū, Shingon shū, Nichiren shū and, later, Yūzū Nenbutsu shū) developed the so-called *danrin* and related seminaries, requiring extensive training for monastic certification. Famous examples of such seminary systems included the 18 *danrin* in Kantō of the Jōdo school (Jōdo shū), which were especially patronized by the Tokugawa family, with the most prominent one established at Zōjōji in Edo. With a lecture and dialogue format, Jōdo monks studied not only the works of Hōnen, Zendō (Ch. Shandao), and the medieval scholiast Shōgei but also the Nara lineages, Tendai, and non-Buddhist writings. There were also Jōdo figures like Ninchō (1645–1711) who on their own undertook revisions of the Buddhist canon. The Chisan and Buzan groups, which stemmed from the Negoroji tradition of Shingon scholasticism, made important strides in commentarial study (*chūshakugaku*) of the major works of Kūkai and Kakuban and also devoted themselves to interpretation of Nara lineages, including Buzan monks who cultivated critiques of Hossō teachings (Nishimura 2010). Sanskrit studies in Shingon achieved a kind of "renaissance" with the figures Jōgon (1639–1702) and Jiun Sonja (1718–1804; Murphy 2011), and monks like Gien (1558–1626) of Daigoji began to consolidate as well as reorganize scriptural collections (*shōgyō*) and ritual traditions of the major Shingon complexes. The True Pure Land lineages, now split between the Nishi Honganji and Higashi Honganji branches, established elaborate study and publication of Shinran's works from roughly the mid seventeenth century onward; Nishi Honganji's study featured debates about the role of body/speech/mind in ensuring birth in the Pure Land, and its seminary featured over a thousand monks by the eighteenth century, and constituted what would eventually be established as Ryūkoku University. Meanwhile, True Pure Land monks often pursued study of other traditions (*yojō*) such as those of Nara Buddhism, recovering scholastic traditions that dated originally to Zonkaku (1290–1373) in the fourteenth century (Nagamura 2009).

Sōtō Zen scholars undertook annotation of the writings of their ancestral master Dōgen in this period as part of a broader reform movement attempting to base Sōtō life on Dōgen's writings (which had been little studied within Sōtō Zen for centuries). The greatest contribution was that of Menzan Zuihō (1683–1769). The shogunate eventually permitted major print publication of the Dōgen's commentary *Shōbō genzō* and his temple regulations *Eihei shingi* (Nishimura 2010: 188–206; Riggs 2008: 225–227). Such study in these schools tended toward conservative interpretations focused on the teachings of the figure seen as ancestral master of the school and related sacred works and helped enable monks to acquire higher clerical status or their temple to acquire official status.[13]

Nuns in royal convents, most of which were of Rinzai Zen lineage, increasingly enjoyed patronage and the opportunity to engage in privileged ritual practice and more intensive study. Although more investigation is needed to clarify the breadth of study and activity of the nuns of the convents, it is clear that Hōkyōji (in Kyoto), which together with Daishōji stood at the official apex of the royal convent system, featured an extremely active community of nuns. The princess-nun Rihō (1672–1745), in particular, spearheaded the organization and production of large quantities of official convent documents, ritual documents, legends, and other sacred works at Hōkyōji, and had an extremely close association with major Ōbaku monks from Manpukuji (Oka 2000: 47–56). The roughly 30 boxes of manuscripts preserved at Hōkyōji reveal a world revolving around study of Zen records, legends of a wide range of lineages, *waka*, Sino-Japanese poetry, didactic tale collections, the *Tale of Genji*, illustrated guides to famous sites, as well as practical guides on the ways of tea, flowers, medicine, and clothing etiquette – signifying what has been called a kind of "cultural salon" of interaction between the nuns and other members of the imperial house (Komine 2001: 4).

Efforts to recover the precepts

Much Buddhist scholasticism, with its general tendency to try to recover a perceived "authentic" past of lineages or temples, was combined with a vibrant effort to reinstitute the Buddhist precepts. Indeed, the Precepts movement was as broad as and arguably deeper even than earlier reform iterations such as in the early medieval era. It was pronounced across a series of lineages in temples and nunneries throughout the Japanese isles (Dobbins 2005: 248). The Ōbaku masters were part of an effort toward monastic rigor that, in fact, became common throughout a series of lineages of Zen and elsewhere. Sōtō lineages featured figures like Menzan, noted above, who not only attempted to re-present and reinstitute Dōgen's monasticism but also studied at Reiunji in Edo, the main temple of the Shingon Precepts school (Shingon risshū), where he received esoteric initiation (Bodiford 2011: 932) but also, presumably, received some instruction in the precepts. In any event, Menzan was very concerned with the precepts, and took a position different from Dōgen's – arguing that reception of the precepts constituted only one stage of the path rather than being properly understood as the equivalent of attainment of enlightenment; Menzan's argument was just one among a series of interpretations made by Sōtō teachers on the precepts over the course of the Tokugawa period (Riggs 2002).[14] Nichiren lineages also featured new concern over the precepts, with figures like Gensei (1623–1668) establishing hermitages for following the Bodhisattva Precepts in accordance with their respective interpretations of the *Lotus Sūtra* (Nishimura 2010: 214).

Of course, the Shingon Precepts school, mentioned above, was very prominent among the precept movements. The tradition's origins lay in Eison's and Ninshō's efforts many centuries earlier, though its lineages had essentially disappeared by the latter part of the fifteenth century, only to be resurrected by the remarkable figure of Myōnin (1576–1610), who received the precepts at Kōzanji in northern Kyoto and reestablished the temple Saimyōji nearby in his effort to revive the traditional "Four part *vinaya*," the *Dharmaguptakavinaya* precepts (J. *shibunritsu*). Myōnin inspired others to further revive the Shingon Precepts movement, and so temples were also established at hermitages at Mt. Kōya, Izumi, and Kawachi in Kansai (Nishimura 2010: 207–209; Pinte 2011: 849). Jōgon, noted above, would also receive the precepts at Kōzanji, but would be patronized by the shōgun to establish Reiunji as a Precepts center in Edo in 1684. The most prominent Shingon Precepts monk of the mid Edo period would be Jiun Sonja, who preached the "precepts of the True Dharma" (*shōbōritsu*) and in his effort to recapture the precepts of Śākyamuni essentially established a trans-lineal movement that crossed sectarian boundaries. Toward this end, Jiun undertook not only extensive study of Sanskrit but also of the monastic robes of the Buddha's day and wrote a major vernacular work on the precepts for popular consumption (Nishimura 2010: 207–210; Watt 1982).[15]

Pure Land lineages (Jōdo shū) also engaged in prominent efforts to reform precepts practice, including a so-called a "world-abandoning" (*shasei*) movement as well as a specific Jōdo Precepts (Jōdo ritsu) movement. The world-abandoning movement was represented prototypically by Ninchō, who followed a long tendency within Pure Land movements for specific practitioners to attempt to follow a rigorous monastic lifestyle while engaging in exclusive *nenbutsu* practice. The Jōdo

Precepts movement was led by Reitan (1676–1734), who forcefully promoted the precepts as essential to monastic *nenbutsu* practice. Both movements looked favorably on the traditional *Four part vinaya* in addition to the Bodhisattva Precepts (Dobbins 2005: 248–250).

In the meantime, among the world-abandoning monks, there were innovative figures like Kantsū (1696–1770) and Fujaku (1707–1781). Kantsū, a seminarian, is thought to have been the greatest proselytizer of the period and is said to have spread the precepts across a very large swath of the population, converting his temple in Owari Province into a precepts hall while maintaining his strict practice. In the village where he lived, it was said that the children avoided killing insects and even fish venders passed over the area (Nishimura 2008: 55). Fujaku knew Kantsū and was inspired by him to convert from True Pure Land to Jōdo shū. After going on pilgrimage and undertaking ascetic practice in a series of provinces, Fujaku became resident monk at the Precepts temple Chōsen'in in Edo, served as a lecturer on Kegon thought at the head Jōdo shū seminary-temple, Zōjōji, there, and wrote responses to tracts critical of Mahayana Buddhism by figures like Tominaga Nakamoto (1715–1746). Fujaku believed that, in fact, Mahayana was taught specifically for the bodhisattvas, and so people in general should follow the Nikāya precepts during their lives – and, ideally, be born as bodhisattvas in the Pure Land at death. In this way, he bridged the interpretive gap between the new "scientific" criticisms made of Mahayana in his combination of the precept-driven life and practice aimed at Pure Land birth. We can take note that, among the issues debated among Precepts thinkers of the day, there were problems concerning meat-eating, clerical marriage, and silken robes. Although the True Pure Land lineages had long been criticized for the practice of clerical marriage, the eating of meat and use of silken robes became objects of concern on a level never previously seen in Japanese Buddhism (Nishimura 2010: 212–226). For example, prohibitions against meat-eating were common in medieval temple regulations, but there was no extensive monastic literature dealing with the eating of meat until the early seventeenth century. The second monk to become head scholar of the seminary at Nishi Honganji (True Pure Land lineage), Chikū (1634–1718), is one example of a scholiast who argued extensively, drawing on a broad array of continental Buddhist sources, that Buddhist teachings on consumption of meat were subtle and often permissive, and strongly criticized the selective reading of Buddhist proscriptions in Japanese lineages (Jaffe 2005: 256–260).[16]

Nuns in Tokugawa Japan were particularly active in pursuing the precepts. A prime example was Bunchi (1619–1697), daughter of the emperor Go-Mizuno'o (r. 1611–1629). Go-Mizuno'o's court was very supportive of new temple projects, but nunneries such as Bunchi's were especially active in acquiring such patronage and using it toward their own promotion of the precepts. Bunchi, who established Enshōji in the Nara area, was clearly a pioneering figure not only in the vibrant group of nuns who were well connected to both the shogunate and imperial court but also in the nuns' Precepts movement. A Zen nun, Bunchi promoted the Zen Precepts movement but also was initiated into the Shingon Precepts movement under her teacher, the Rinzai Zen master Isshi Bunshu (1608–1646), and had connections with the Shingon Precepts school monks of the area of Makinoo near Kyoto. Moreover, just as Bunshu had been initiated into both the Shingon precepts and the Bodhisattva Precepts as practiced in Zen, Bunchi received both initiations and even received initiation into the *jūhachidō* esoteric practice of Shingon (Cogan 2014). Bunchi's varied initiations thus constitute another example of trans-lineal practice that existed before the Tokugawa period and continued to be pursued by many believers for centuries thereafter.

Notes

1   Moreover, the supplemental section of the code, actually dated to 1231, describes "mountain monks" and shrine-partisans (*jinin*) as having used the pretense of needing supplies for Buddha/*kami* offerings to acquire materials (*Tsuika-hō*, 138).

2   Nam-Lin Hur, for example, in his seminal study of prayer and play at Sensōji temple in Edo (Tokyo), has associated it specifically with the culture of Edo, especially in the latter part of the era; he concludes his work with the note that "'[K]aichō' as a signifier for both prayer and play captures the essence of late Tokugawa Buddhist culture" (Hur 2000: 217). It is clear that Hur deftly analyzed *kaichō* as an extremely important feature of Buddhist practice in the Tokugawa period, but it is also evident that the *kaichō* became prominent as early as the period around the Ōnin War.

3   *Monzeki*, as noted in earlier chapters, were variously aristocratic or royal, so the royal conferral was particularly salient for a monastery not of Kenmitsu tradition.

4   Although Onjōji monks were the most common supervisors (*kengyō*) of Kumano, the control of Kumano had remained in the hands of the administrator lineage (*bettōke*) there. That is, the position of *kengyō* was, fundamentally, not sectarian until the late Kamakura period (Sekiguchi 2009a: 9).

5   Fujii Masako has characterized the main reasons for these travels as, first and foremost, the consolidation of head-branch ties between Muryōju'in and temples throughout the northeast, followed by the abbot's efforts to make copies of sacred works (*shōgyō*) held by the rural temples as well as to raise *kanjin* and other funds, particularly in the wake of the Ōnin War (Fujii 2008: 310–321).

6   Admittedly, however, the number of Buddhist works in book firm catalogs declined from the mid eighteenth century onward, which Kornicki attributes to the later Edo focus on Shintō and "anti-Buddhist sentiment" (2001: 156).

7   This point seems to depart from some recent English-language research, such as that of Nam-Lin Hur, who argues that the "anti-Christian policy" gave rise to the temple affiliation system (Hur 2007: 13–15, 34–36).

8   Thus after the consolidation of the head–branch system, earlier practices and associations often continued and developments were influenced by the immediate temples or lineage

traditions. Even Raiyu, known as the great consolidator of Shingi Shingon, was initiated into multiple lineages and was arguably most influenced by dharma lineages of Daigoji, which were doctrinally classified as Kogi Shingon. (It was, in fact, primarily Raiyu's rather than Kakuban's works that were the objects of study in the "new order" Shingon lineages of the medieval and early modern eras; Sakamoto 2011: 191–192).

9   As Hayashi notes, by the late Tokugawa these groups came sometimes to be unruly and fractured organizationally.

10   The situation was thus very different from the influence of esoteric Buddhism on Zen, which could be seen not just in figures like Rinzai's Yōsai but also Sōtō's Keizan and in deep structural similarities in terms of master–disciple transmission.

11   *Dangi-bon*, we should note, sometimes refers to a specific genre of humorous texts connected with Buddhism.

12   Mt. Kōya, likewise, featured as *kanjin* figures from the late fifteenth century on *mokujiki* holy ones, who variously may have been connected with Jishū lineages but seem to have been more directly related to so-called "traveling monks" (*kyakusō*), who included both monk-students and *mokujiki* practitioners – those who avoided consuming the 10 grains (*jikkoku*). As with the Tōji holy ones, those at Kōya specifically targeted faith in Kōbō Daishi as the central theme of most of their fundraising, and dominated the Oku-no-in mausoleum area (Ōta 2008: 292–315, 326–348).

13   Buddhist scholasticism, together with related publication of a series of works of lineage masters, generally promoted the tendency to clarify distinctions between schools of Japanese Buddhism, even if clearly sectarian distinctions would only be consolidated after the Tokugawa period.

14   Menzan argued for the necessity of novice ordination in addition to the Bodhisattva Precepts, a clear distinction between precept conferral and precept transmission, and the position of the precepts as one of the three features of the Buddhist path (along with meditation and wisdom),

15   While Jiun additionally studied the *Mūlasarvāstivāda-vinaya* (J. *uburitsu*), it would be the Mount Kōya Precepts monk Myōzui (1696-1764) who would argue for the latter's pursuance instead of that of the *Dharmaguptaka-vinaya*, founding a new Precepts movement that would debate with others over the proper course of Precepts practice, and demonstrate, moreover, that discussion of the precepts was a very prominent aspect of Shingon temple life (Clarke 2006: 39-40).

16   After the apex of Precepts interest in the late seventeenth century, when all Precepts lineages are considered, there were apparently some 7,000 Precepts temples altogether (Nishimura 2010: 207–208).

References

Ambros, Barbara. 2008. *Emplacing Pilgrimage: The Ōyama Cult and Regional Religion in Early Modern Japan.* Cambridge, MA: Harvard University Press.

Ambros, Barbara. 2011. "Shingon Buddhism in the Early Modern Period." In Charles D. Orzech, Henrik H. Sorensen, and Richard K. Payne (eds.), *Esoteric Buddhism and the Tantras in East Asia*, 1009–1017. Leiden: Brill.

Andō Wataru. 2007. "Sengokuki shūkyō seiryokuron." In Chūsei kōki kenkyūkai (ed.), *Muromachi/Sengoku-ki wo yominaosu*, 356-386. Kyoto: Shibunkaku.

Baroni, Helen J. 2000. *Obaku Zen: The Emergence of the Third Sect of Zen in Tokugawa Japan.* Honolulu: University of Hawai'i Press.

Baskind, James. 2012. "'The Matter of the Zen School': Fukansai Habian's *Myōtei mondō* and His Christian Polemic on Buddhism." *Japanese Journal of Religious Studies* 39 (2): 307–331.

Blum, Mark L. 2006. "Introduction: The Study of Rennyo." In Mark L. Blum and Shinya Masutomi (eds.), *Rennyo and the Roots of Modern Japanese Buddhism*, 1–13. New York: Oxford University Press.

Blum, Mark L., and Yasutomi, Shin'ya, eds. 2006. *Rennyo and the Roots of Modern Japanese Buddhism.* New York: Oxford University Press.

Bodiford, William M. 1993. *Sōtō Zen in Medieval Japan.* Honolulu: University of Hawai'i Press.

Bodiford, William M. 2011. "Zen and Esoteric Buddhism." In Charles D. Orzech, Henrik H. Sorensen, and Richard K. Payne (eds.), *Esoteric Buddhism and the Tantras in East Asia*, 924–935. Leiden: Brill.

Carr, Kevin Gray. 2012. *Plotting the Prince: Shōtoku Cults and the Mapping of Medieval Japanese Buddhism.* Honolulu: University of Hawai'i Press.

Clarke, Shayne. 2006. "Miscellaneous Musings on Mūlasarvāstivāda Monks: The *Mūlasarvāstivāda Vinaya* Revival in Tokugawa Japan." *Japanese Journal of Religious Studies* 33 (1): 1–49.

Cogan, Gina. 2014. "Precepts and Ordination at Enshōji." In Gina Cogan, *The Princess Nun: Bunchi, Buddhist Reform, and Gender in Early Edo Japan*, 214–229. Cambridge, MA: Harvard University Asia Center, Harvard University Press.

Daitō Takaaki. 2009. "Tōdaiji shuni'e 'Ōnakatomi harae' no kaishaku to tenkyo." In Arai Daisuke, Daitō Takaaki, and Mori Gorō (eds.), *Gensetsu/girei/sanke: 'ba' to 'itonami' no shintō kenkyō*, 153–202. Tokyo: Kōbundō.

Dobbins, James C. 2002. *Jōdo Shinshū: Shin Buddhism in Medieval Japan.* Honolulu: University of Hawai'i Press.

Dobbins, James C. 2005. "Precepts in Japanese Pure Land Buddhism: The Jōdōshū." In William Bodiford (ed.), *Going Forth: Visions of Buddhist Vinaya*, 236–254. Honolulu: University of Hawai'i Press.

Fujii Masako. 2008. *Chūsei Daigoji to Shingon mikkyō.* Tokyo: Bensei Shuppan.

Go-seibai shikimoku. 1981. In Ishii Susumu, Ishimoda Shō, Kasamatsu Hiroshi, Katsumata Shizuo, and Satō Shin'ichi (eds.), *Chūsei seiji shakai jō (Nihon shisō taikei 21)*, 7–41. Tokyo: Iwanami Shoten.

Graham, Patricia J. 2003. "Karamono for Sencha: Transformations in the Taste for Chinese Art." In Morgan Pitelka (ed.), *Japanese Tea Culture: Art, History, and Practice*, 110–136. London and New York: RoutledgeCurzon.

Harada Masatoshi. 2007. "Chūsei bukkyō saihenki to shite no jūyon seiki." *Nihonshi kenkyō* 540: 40–65.

Hayashi Makoto. 2010. "Bakufu jisha bugyō to kanjin no shūkyōsha: yamabushi, komusō, onmyōji." In Sueki Fumihiko (ed.), *Minshū bukkyō no teichaku (Shin ajia bukkyōshi 13, Nihon 3)*, 235–268. Tokyo: Kōsei Shuppansha.

Hayashi Ryōshō and Sakamoto Shōjin. 1993. *Hasedera ryakushi. Kōgyō Daishi Happyakugojūnen go'onki kinen shuppan.* Tokyo: Shingon Buzanha Shūmusho.

Hōzawa Naohide. 2003. "Jidan seido to sōshiki bukkyō." In Ōkubo Ryōshun, Satō Hiroo, Sueki Fumihiko, Hayashi Makoto, and Matsuo Kenji (eds.), *Nihon bukkyō 34 no kagi*, 212–219. Tokyo: Shunjusha.

Hur, Nam-lin. 2000. *Prayer and Play in Late Tokugawa Japan: Asakusa Sensōji and Edo Japan.* Cambridge, MA: Harvard University Asia Center, Harvard University Press.

Hur, Nam-lin. 2007. *Death and Social Order in Tokugawa Japan: Buddhism, Anti-Christianity, and the "Danka" System.* Cambridge, MA: Harvard University Asia Center, Harvard University Press.

Iizuka Hironobu. 2009. "Eiheiji shozō no zenseki shōmotsu ni tsuite: sōden shiryō wo chūshin ni." In Hirose Ryōkō (ed.), *Zen to chiiki shakai*, 196–211. Tokyo: Yoshikawa Kōbunkan.

Imatani Akira. 1993. *Muromachi no ōken: Ashikaga Yoshimitsu no ōken sandatsu keikaku.* Tokyo: Chūō Kōronsha.

Imatani Akira. 2006. *Sengokuki no Muromachi bakufu.* Tokyo: Kōdansha.

Ishida Haruo. 2008 *Ōnin/Bunmei no ran.* Tokyo: Yoshikawa Kōbunkan.

Itō Masatoshi. 2008. *Jisha seiryoku no chūsei: muen/yūen/imin.* Tokyo: Chikuma Shobō.

Itō Satoshi. 2010. "Girei to shinwa." In Sueki Fumihiko (ed.), *Yakudō suru chūsei bukkyō*, 193–233. Tokyo: Kōsei.

Jaffe, Richard M. 2005. "The Debate over Meat Eating in Japanese Buddhism." In William Bodiford (ed.), *Going Forth: Visions of Buddhist Vinaya*, 255–275. Honolulu: University of Hawai'i Press.

Josephson, Jason Ānanda. 2007. *The Invention of Religion in Japan.* Chicago: University of Chicago Press.

Kamikawa Michio. 2008. *Nihon chūsei bukkyō shiryōron.* Tokyo: Yoshikawa Kōbunkan.

Kanda Chisato. 2010a. "Ikki to bukkyō." In Sueki Fumihiko (ed.), *Yakudō suru chūsei bukkyō*, 283–328. Tokyo: Kōsei.

Kanda Chisato. 2010b. *Shūkyō de yomu sengoku jidai.* Tokyo: Kōdansha.

Kanmuri Ken'ichi. 1983. *Kinsei Nichirenshū shuppanshi kenkyū.* Kyoto: Heirakuji Shoten.

Komine Kazuaki. 2001. "Myōhō tenjin gyō kaishaku o meguru jo." In Komine Kazuaki (ed.), *Hōkyōji zō Myōhō tenjin gyō kaishaku: zenchūshaku to kenkyū*, 1–8. Tokyo: Kasama Shoin.

Kornicki, Peter. 2001. *The Book in Japan: A Cultural History from the Beginnings to the Nineteenth Century.* Honolulu: University of Hawai'i Press.

Kusaka Yukio and Mannami Hisako. 2005. "*Shōshinge* chūshakusho no shuppanshi kenkyū (fu '*Shōshinge* chūshakusho kanki shūsei')." In Ōtori Kazuma (ed.), *Chūsei to bungaku to gakumon (Ryūkoku Daigaku bukkyō bunka kenkyō sōsho 15)*, 425–492. Kyoto: Shibunkaku.

Maeda Tsutomu. 2010. "Bukkyō to Edo no shoshisō ." In Sueki Fumihiko (ed.), *Minshū bukkyō no teichaku*, 127–177. Tokyo: Kōsei.

Matsuo Kōichi. 1997. *Ennen no geinōshiteki kenkyū.* Tokyo: Iwata Shoin.

McMullin, Neil. 1984. *Buddhism and the State in Sixteenth-Century Japan.* Princeton, NJ: Princeton University Press.

Midō kanpaku ki, by Fujiwara no Michinaga (966–1027).

Miyake Hitoshi. 2005. *The Mandala of the Mountain: Shugendo and Folk Religion.* Trans., ed., and introduction, Gaynor Sekimori. Tokyo: Keio University Press.

Miyamoto Kenji. 2006. *Kyōto kakubetsu na tera.* Tokyo: Kōbunsha.

Mizukami Fumiyoshi. 2010. "Tenkai no isan: Tenkaihan issaikyō mokukatsuji." In Sueki Fumihiko (ed.), *Minshū bukkyō no teichaku*, 124–126. Tokyo: Kōsei.

Mohr, Michael. 2000. "Emerging from Nonduality: Kōan Practice in the Rinzai Tradition since Hakuin." In Steven Heine and Dale S. Wright (eds.), *The Kōan: Texts and Contexts in Zen Buddhism*, 244–279. New York: Oxford University Press.

"Muromachi bakufu hō." 1981. In Ishii Susumu, Ishimoda Shō, Kasamatsu Hiroshi, Katsumata Shizuo, and Satō Shin'ichi (eds.), *Chūsei seiji shakai, jō* (*Nihon shisō taikei 21*), 145–176. Tokyo: Iwanami Shoten.

Murphy, Regan. 2011. "Sanskrit Studies in Early Modern Japan." In Charles D. Orzech, Henrik H. Sorensen, and Richard K. Payne (eds.), *Esoteric Buddhism and the Tantras in East Asia*, 985–996. Leiden: Brill.

Nagamura Makoto. 2009. "Shinshū to yojō: Zonkaku no chojutsu o tōshite." *Nihon joshi daigaku daigakuin bungaku kenkyūka kiyō* 16: 73–85.

Nishimura Ryō. 2008. *Kinsei bukkyō shisō no dokusō: sōryo Fujaku no shisō to jissen.* Tokyo: Transview.

Nishimura Ryō. 2010. "Kyōgaku no shinten to bukkyō kaikaku undō." In Sueki Fumihiko (ed.), *Minshū bukkyō no teichaku*, 183–228. Tokyo: Kōsei.

Ōishi Masaaki. 2003. "Chūsei kōki no kaichō ni tsuite: yamato Hasedera wo chūshin ni." *Naruto kyōiku daigaku kenkyū kiyō (jinbun/shakaigaku hen)*, vol. 18: 11–18.

Oka Yoshiko. 2000. "Kinsei no bikuni gosho (jō): Hōkyōji o chūshin ni." *Bukkyō shigaku kenkyū* 42 (2): 30–60.

Ooms, Hermann. 1989. *Tokugawa Ideology: Early Constructs, 1570-1680.* Princeton, NJ: Princeton University Press.

Ōta Naoyuki. 2008. "Tōji daikanjin no henshitsu to shūen: jūkoku hijiri to daikanjinshiki." In Ōta Naoyuki, *Chūsei no shaji to shinkō: kanjin to kanjin hijiri no jidai*, 241–288. Tokyo: Kōbundō.

Ōta Sōichirō. 2007. "Muromachi bakufu shūkyō seisakuron." In Chūsei kōki kenkyūkai (ed.), *Muromachi/Sengokuki wo yominaosu*, 327–355. Kyoto: Shibunkaku.

Pinte, Klaus. 2011. "Shingon Risshū: Esoteric Buddhism and Vinaya Orthodoxy in Japan." In Charles D. Orzech, Henrik H. Sorensen, and Richard K. Payne (eds.), *Esoteric Buddhism and the Tantras in East Asia*, 845–853. Leiden: Brill.

Rambelli, Fabio. 2007. "Tools and Labor as Mediators Between the Sacred and the Profane." In Fabio Rambelli, *Buddhist Materiality: A Cultural History of Objects in Japanese Buddhism*, 172–210. Stanford, CA: Stanford University Press.

Reader, Ian. 2006. *Making Pilgrimages: Meaning and Practice in Shikoku.* Honolulu: University of Hawai'i Press.

Riggs, David E. 2002. "Ordination Precepts." In David E. Riggs, "The Rekindling of a Tradition: Menzan Zuihō and the Reform of Japanese Sōtō Zen in the Tokugawa period," 177–190. PhD dissertation, University of California, Los Angeles.

Riggs, David E. 2008. "Meditation in Motion: Textual Exegesis in the Creation of Ritual." In Steven Heine and Dale S. Wright (eds.), *Zen Ritual: Studies of Zen Buddhist Theory of Practice*, 223–259. New York: Oxford University Press.

Sakamoto Masahito. 2001. "Shiryō shōkai Ryō'e sōjō montei meichō." *Buzan Gakuhō* 44: 185–253.

Sakamoto Masahito. 2011. "Shingi Shingonshū ni okeru honmatsu kankei no tokushoku." In Chisan Kangakukai (eds), *Kinsei no Bukkyō: Shingi Shingon o chūshin to shite*, 185–207. Tokyo: Seishi Shuppan.

Sawa Hirokatsu. 1999. "Saikoku sanjūsando junrei gyōja no katsudō to soshiki." In Sawa Hirokatsu, *Kinsei no shūkyō soshiki to chiiki shakai: kyōdan shinkō to minkan shinkō*, 118–167. Tokyo: Yoshikawa Kōbunkan.

Seita Yoshihide. 1995. *Chūsei jiinhō shi no kenkyū.* Tokyo: Keibundō.

Sekiguchi Makiko. 2009a. *Shugendō kyōdan seiritsushi.* Tokyo: Bensei.

Sekiguchi, Makiko. 2009b. "The Sanbōin Monzeki and Its Inception as Head Temple of the Tōzan Group." In Bernard Faure, D. Max Moerman, and Gaynor Sekimori (eds.), *Shugendō: The History and Culture of a Japanese Religion* (Cahiers d'Extreme-Asie 18), 103-121. Kyoto: École francaise D'Extreme-Orient.

Sekiyama Kazuo. 1973. *Sekkyō no rekishiteki kenkyō.* Kyoto: Hōzōkan.

Slusser, Dale. 2003. "The Transformation of Tea Practice in Sixteenth-Century Japan." In Morgan Pitelka (ed.), *Japanese Tea Culture: Art, History, and Practice,* 39–60. London and New York: RoutledgeCurzon.

Sonehara Satoshi. 2010. "Kinsei kokka to bukkyō." In Sueki Fumihiko (ed.), *Minshū bukkyō no teichaku* (*Shin ajia bukkyōshi 13, Nihon 3*), 81–122. Tokyo: Kōsei Shuppansha.

Stone, Jacqueline I. 1999. *Original Enlightenment and the Transformation of Japanese Buddhism.* Kuroda Institute. Honolulu: University of Hawai'i Press.

Sueki Fumihiko. 2010. *Kinsei no Bukkyō.* Tokyo: Yoshikawa Kōbunkan.

Takada Yōsuke. 2000. "Sanmai hijiri: kinai sōbochitai no shudan." In Takano Toshihiko (ed.), *Minkan ni ikiru shūkyōsha,* 127–156. Tokyo: Yoshikawa Kōbunkan.

Takenuki Genshō. 1993. *Nihon Zen shū shi kenkyū.* Tokyo: Yūzankaku.

Tanizaki Junichirō. *Some Prefer Nettles.* Trans. Edward Seidensticker. Tokyo: Charles E. Tuttle, 1985.

Thal, Sarah. 2005. *Rearranging the Landscape of the Gods: The Politics of a Pilgrimage Site in Japan, 1573–1912.* Chicago: University of Chicago Press.

Tsuika-hō. In Ishii Susumu, Ishimoda Shō, Kasamatsu Hiroshi, Katsumata Shizuo, and Satō Shin'ichi (eds.), *Chūsei seiji shakai, jō* (*Nihon shisō taikei 21*), 55–144. Tokyo: Iwanami Shoten, 1981.

Tsuji Zennosuke. 1970a. *Nihon bukkyō shi: daihachikan, kinsei ni.* Tokyo: Iwanami Shoten.

Tsuji Zennosuke. 1970b. *Nihon bukkyō shi: daijikkan, kinseihen no yon.* Tokyo: Iwanami Shoten..

Tsuji Zennosuke. 1970c. *Nihon bukkyō shi: dairokkan, chūsei hen no go.* Tokyo: Iwanami Shoten.

Tsukimoto Masayuki. 1983. "Kōzanjibon Kūkai senjutsusho ichirankō (ho'i)." In Kōzanji Tenseki Monjo Sōgō Chōsadan (ed.), *Kōzanji shozō no tenseki monjo no kenkyū narabi ni Kōzanji shiryō sōsho no hensan,* 59–65. Kyoto: Kōzanji.

Tsutsumi Kunihiko. 1996. "Bukkyō to kinsei bungaku." In Iwanami Kōza Henshū Iinkai (eds.), *Iwanami Kōza Nihon bungakushi dai 8 kan,* 229–258. Tokyo: Iwanami Shoten.

Ushiroshōji Kaoru. 2010. *Kangebon no kenkyū.* Osaka: Izumi Shoin.

Watt, Paul Brooks. 1982. "Jiun Sonja (1718–1804): Life and Thought." PhD dissertation, Columbia University.

Williams, Duncan Ryūken. 2005. *The Other Side of Zen: A Social History of Sōtō Zen Buddhism in Tokugawa Japan.* Princeton, NJ: Princeton University Press.

Williams, Duncan Ryūken. 2006. "Religion in Early Modern Japan." In Paul L. Swanson and Clark Chilson (eds.), *Nanzan Guide to Japanese Religions,* 184–201. Honolulu: University of Hawai'i Press.

Yasuda Jirō. 2003. "Chūsei no kaichō." In Ōsumi Kazuo (ed.), *Buppō no bunkashi,* 267–289. Tokyo: Yoshikawa Kōbunkan.

Yasutomi, Shin'ya. 2006. "The Life of Rennyo." In Mark Blum and Shin'ya Yasutomi (eds.), *Rennyo and the Roots of Modern Japanese Buddhism,* 17–37. New York: Oxford University Press.

Yoshida Kazuhiko. 2003. "Nihon bukkyōshi no jiki kubun." In Ōsumi Kazuo (ed.), *Bunkashi no kōsō*, 20–57. Tokyo: Yoshikawa Kōbunkan.

Yuasa Haruhisa. 2009. *Sengoku bukkyō: chūsei shakai to Nichirenshū*. Tokyo: Chūō Kōron Shinsha.

Further Reading

Haskel, Peter, and Ryūichi Abé. 1996. *Great Fool: Zen Master Ryōkan: Poems, Letters, and Other Writings*. Honolulu: University of Hawai'i Press.

Rambelli, Fabio. 2007. *Buddhist Materiality: A Cultural History of Objects in Japanese Buddhism*. Stanford, CA: Stanford University Press.

Sawa Hirokatsu. 1999. *Kinsei no shūkyō soshiki to chiiki shakai: kyōdan shinkō to minkan shinkō*. Tokyo: Yoshikawa Kōbunkan.

Sueki Fumihiko, ed. 2010. *Minshū Bukkyō no teichaku*. (*Shin Ajia Bukkyōshi 13, Nihon 3*). Tokyo: Kōsei Shuppansha.

Takano Toshihiko, ed. 2000. *Minkan ni ikiru shūkyōsha*. Tokyo: Yoshikawa Kōbunkan.

6

Modern Buddhism (1800–1945)

Buddhism in the Transition to the Modern Period

To chart religious history following periodization schemas that cohere to political and regime change can be problematic, but the transition from the Edo to the Meiji periods is arguably an exception. In 1868, the Tokugawa shogunate was overthrown and the restoration of direct imperial rule (*ōsei fukkō*) was declared, thus inaugurating the Meiji Restoration (*Meiji ishin*). Buddhism's long-held ideological dominance was at an end; indeed, Buddhism was forced into a defensive stand against those calling for the restoration of a true Japanese spirit.

Japanese historians have debated the many causes and pressures that resulted in the overthrow of the shogunate and the establishment of the Meiji Restoration. For our purposes, what is important is that the restoration of imperial rule was accompanied by a deliberate move toward valorizing Shintō as the legitimating religion or, perhaps better, ideology. According to traditional scholarly interpretations, Buddhist lineages were largely irrelevant in the restoration process and ineffective in countering the nativist voices calling for a return to a valorized Shintō past. More recent scholarship, however, redeems Buddhism's place and significance in the period of the Meiji Restoration. James Ketelaar (1990), for instance, has argued persuasively that Meiji-period Buddhists, despite being under siege by Shintō nativists, responded to these difficult circumstances by re-examining and re-inventing the role that Buddhism could play in a modernizing Japan, even a Japan in which the restored imperial system was tethered to a largely invented Shintō nationalism.

One additional problem with researching and describing modern Japanese Buddhism is that Meiji-period – and later – studies have tended to underplay or ignore the role of religion in shaping the social and cultural lives of the period. No doubt influenced by Marxist and other socio-historical critiques, some scholars view religion as an epiphenomenon ill-suited to the processes required to modernize a country. Political, economic, social, and other factors are given explanatory precedence over religious ones. One glaring example of this lacuna is the volume on

A Cultural History of Japanese Buddhism, First Edition. William E. Deal and Brian Ruppert.
© 2015 William E. Deal and Brian Ruppert. Published 2015 by John Wiley & Sons, Ltd.

nineteenth-century Japan in the *Cambridge History of Japan* series (Jansen 1989). This volume lists only three pages on which the term "Buddhism" can be found in the 782-page text. Similarly, the volume on the twentieth century (Duus 1989) contains no references to the term "Buddhism" and only one reference – in a 774-page book – to the term "Buddhist lay organization (Sōkagakkai)." Perhaps more surprising is the listing for "Shinto": there is one reference to "Shinto: discontinued as state religion" and one for "Shinto: emerging system of state." It is unclear how any serious overview of Japan's twentieth century could neglect a discussion of Shintō as a state ideology.

The argument here is not that Buddhism – or Shintō – was somehow the most important factor operating in the processes that brought about the Meiji Restoration, but rather to assert that Buddhism is more important than many historical accounts give it credit for. As we will see, Meiji-period anti-Buddhist sentiment was a catalyst for significant political and social change, but such sentiments also required creative responses on the part of Buddhists to make their teachings and practices relevant in a rapidly changing society.

From the beginning of the nineteenth century to the 1868 overthrow of the Tokugawa *bakufu*, there is arguably more significance to ideas and movements occurring outside of Buddhism – but which impacted post-Meiji Restoration Buddhism – than particular developments within Buddhism itself. In 1798, the Kokugaku (National Learning) scholar Motoori Norinaga (1730–1801) completed work on his *Kojiki-den* (A Commentary on the *Kojiki*). In this text, Norinaga asserts that it is possible to reclaim the origins and essence of the Japanese spirit in the pristine Shintō sensibilities apparent in the *Kojiki* narrative. Significantly, the loss of this pure Japanese spirit was purported to be the direct result of foreign influences, especially Buddhism. The only way to reclaim it, according to Norinaga, was to expunge all Buddhist influences. In keeping with *Kojiki* stories of the origins of Japan, the restoration of direct imperial rule was also required.

The Kokugaku (often referred to as "nativism") movement of Norinaga and others became ideologically important in efforts to transform Japan into a modern nation-state and became coupled with the movement that generated the Meiji Restoration. This movement sought to restore imperial rule and to mitigate the influence of, or outright reject, centuries of foreign influence in Japan. Buddhism was one of the foreign influences that these reformers sought to reject. This nativist perspective was further elaborated by Hirata Atsutane (1776–1843). His Restoration Shintō (*fukko* Shintō) movement extended the nativist critique beyond linguistic study of ancient texts and focused instead on specific critiques of Buddhism and Confucianism. He also advocated reverence for the emperor. These various forms of nativism undergirded Meiji-period nationalist ideas advocating *saisei itchi*, the unity of (Shintō) rites and government (Harootunian 1978; Endō 2003: 145–156).

Meiji Restoration

Feudal domains (*daimyō*), long antagonistic to the shogunate, led the pro-imperial restoration forces against the warrior government. Part of their motivation stemmed from the increasing pressure exerted by Western nations to open trade relations with Japan and a sense that Japan needed to become a nation that could defend itself against possible outside aggression – an ability that they believed the shogunate lacked. Interaction with Western nations also confronted Japan with new political, social, and religious ideas, new technologies, and new military weapons and battle strategies. In short, the reformers who brought about the Meiji Restoration supported a nationalism centered on imperial rule and the symbol of the emperor coupled with a desire to match or exceed Western powers through modernization. On April 6, 1868, soon after the restoration of direct imperial rule, the newly formed Meiji government issued an edict proclaiming the renewal of Shintō-based state rituals. These rituals, previously suppressed by the shogunate, directly supported the legitimacy of imperial rule.

The new government embraced Kokugaku, Restoration Shintō, and related ideologies, and deployed these in support of creating a national polity (*kokutai*) in line with the goals of the restorationists (see, for instance, Hardacre 1989; Havens 2006; and Murakami 1980). To this end, the new ruling order proclaimed the unity of government and (Shintō) ritual (*saisei itchi*) on April 8, 1868. The Meiji Restoration did not so much seek to become a Shintō state as it selected aspects of Shintō that undergirded claims about the legitimacy of imperial rule. In many respects, it was this use of Shintō that created a sense of its historical longevity and consistency, a uniformity that does not actually exist when Shintō is examined historically. Restoration ideology was a mix of both backward-looking and forward-looking perspectives: on the one hand it looked back to what it understood as Shintō ritual and other trappings of imperial rule; and, on the other hand, looked forward to the West for ideas about industrialization, technology, and other trappings of modernity in order to become a modern nation equal to the likes of the United States, Great Britain, and Germany.

The Meiji government's new policies had significant ramifications for the Japanese religious landscape, and especially for Buddhism and Buddhist institutions (for an overview of the impact of these policies on Shintō and Buddhism, see Breen 2000). Although there were great changes to Buddhism, there were also changes to Shintō. There were factions within Shintō that argued over which rituals should be performed at shrines that left shrine priests wondering about the appropriateness of specific rites. The government also closed or merged thousands of shrines as a way to reconstitute them as administrative units of the government with one shrine in each unit area. Similar to the Edo period requirement of household registration at

Buddhist temples, registration (*ujiko shirabe*) was now required of all households at the shrine in their administrative area. However, the situation for Buddhism was arguably far worse. New government policies ended economic and other benefits of state patronage of Buddhism. Buddhism also lost its centrality among the population at large because families were no longer required to register at local temples (Kashiwahara 1990: 18–20).

Meiji-Period Anti-Buddhist Sentiments

The Meiji Restoration marked a significant reversal of fortune for Buddhism. With the rise of a newly conceived monarchy and the nationalism that attended it, there was strong sentiment throughout Japan that a return to native traditions untainted by foreign influences was the only viable way for Japan to survive in an increasingly international world demanding open ports and trade. Anti-foreign sentiment extended especially to Buddhism. The Kokugaku movement was one of the drivers of anti-Buddhist sentiment among restorationists, who viewed Buddhism as a deleterious foreign influence, which, having led the Japanese people away from a pure Shintō, needed to be expunged. Consequently, the newly established government issued a number of decrees and proclamations to curb Buddhist influence and to further attempt to unify the nation by appropriating Shintō ideas for this purpose. Although it would never have been possible to extricate the many centuries of interaction between Buddhism and Shintō, nativist reformers nevertheless attempted to do so.

In March 1868, the Restoration government issued a decree requiring the separation of Buddhism and Shintō (*shinbutsu bunri*, literally, the separation of *kami* and Buddhas). While some Tokugawa-era feudal domains had enacted similar policies, the Meiji version was a government-initiated policy that applied to all of Japan. Intended to disentangle a pure Japanese spirit from the detrimental influences of Buddhist thought and practice, the policy also aimed to promote Shintō as the de facto state ideology (Hardacre 1989: 27–28; Ketelaar 1990: 5–14).

This decree significantly impacted Buddhism, shifting its centuries-long relationship to the state and to Shintō traditions, and severely diminishing its sometimes hegemonic role as overarching ideology. The decrees required the dismantling of the combined temple-shrine complexes that had existed for centuries. This forced separation of Buddhism from Shintō (*shinbutsu hanzen*) meant that shrines and temples were no longer allowed to share the same space. Additionally, Buddhist priests were forbidden to practice at shrines. As a result, Buddhist priests serving at Shintō shrines were forced to choose whether to leave the monastic order, to become shrine priests, or to accept a new post at a Buddhist temple.

Other symbolic steps were implemented to try to extract Buddhism from Shintō. For instance, the use of *honji-suijaku* ("original ground and manifest traces") Buddhist titles used for Shintō *kami* were no longer allowed. Similarly, Buddhist ritual objects, statuary, paintings, and other objects of worship and practice were no longer allowed at Shintō shrines.

Anti-Buddhist language was also sometimes accompanied by anti-Buddhist violence. Under the banner of "expelling Buddhism and destroying Śākyamuni" (*haibutsu kishaku*), temples, images, and other objects of Buddhist material culture were destroyed and Buddhist monastics were sometimes forced to leave the religious life. The intensity of the violence depended on the particular region, but in areas where anti-Buddhist sentiment was especially palpable, the majority of temples were razed and many monks killed. Although intense at times, the worst aspects of *haibutsu kishaku* lasted only a short time, between 1869 and 1871 (Murakami 1980: 22–26; Kashiwahara 1990: 15–20).

There was one additional Meiji government policy that impacted Buddhist institutions and practices: Whereas the government had previously enforced rules of Buddhist monastic discipline, these injunctions were lifted in 1872. Prohibitions regulating meat-eating and monastic marriage (*nikujiki saitai*), as well as tonsure and dress, were lifted so that the government no longer oversaw adherence to prescribed monastic behavior concerning the precepts. This also meant that monastics lost a significant aspect of what set them apart from other, non-monastic, Japanese. Prior to 1872, only Jōdo Shinshū and Shugendō priests were exempt from the celibacy rule (see Jaffe 2001). In 1873, this change in monastic rules was extended to nuns, but since nuns did not run temples and resided in convents once they took the tonsure, the only way for them to observe rule changes was to leave the monastic order altogether. For this reason, nuns still do not marry in Japan. Some Buddhist leaders, like Fukuda Gyōkai (1809–1888) and Shaku Unshō (1827–1909) urged Buddhist monastics to continue to observe the precepts and to maintain traditional Buddhist thought and practice as a way to counter criticism that Buddhist clerics were decadent and Buddhist monastic life was no longer relevant to a modernizing Japan (Jaffe 2001).

Meiji Buddhists had mixed responses to these changes in monastic rules. Some Buddhist traditions such as Tendai, Shingon, and Zen, which were more traditionally monastic, were significantly more impacted than those that had more worldly direction to their activities, such as Pure Land and Nichiren lineages. The result of this legislation over the subsequent three or four decades was that most Buddhist priests married. Many temples became hereditary holdings within a family, the head of the temple passing from father to son. It should be noted that recent scholarship (Jaffe 2001) has questioned the assertion that priestly marriage in, for instance, the Sōtō Zen lineage only started at this time and has argued that the history of monastic marriage is more complicated.

Buddhist Responses to Anti-Buddhist Sentiments

One of the significant results of this anti-Buddhist rhetoric and violence was an emerging sense among Buddhists that they needed to re-imagine Buddhist thought and practice in order to maintain their relevance in a rapidly changing Japanese social and political milieu. Anti-Buddhist rhetoric argued, *inter alia*, that Buddhism was unproductive to the welfare of the nation, that foreign influences – and especially Buddhism – had harmful effects on Japan, and that Buddhists beliefs were ahistorical, unscientific myths. Buddhist reformers, both monastics and laity, responded in diverse ways to these and other criticisms. Responses invoked a number of perspectives to argue for the relevance and legitimacy of Buddhist thought and practice.

During the violence against Buddhism, there were some Buddhists who rioted in protest – the so-called Dharma-protection uprisings (*gohō ikki*) are one example (on Dharma-protection [*gohō*] societies, see Yoshida 1998: 66–74). However, Buddhist leaders made more important and enduring responses to anti-Buddhist sentiment by attempting to locate Buddhist thought and practice within governmental efforts to modernize Japan under the banner of the imperial restoration. Some Buddhists tried to counter the nativist critique that Buddhism had a negative impact on Japanese culture by arguing that Buddhism was an important partner in the efforts to build a strong and modern Japan and that Buddhists were loyal to the emperor.

Buddhism developed a broad range of reform strategies, both at the institutional and individual levels, to position itself as a relevant partner to modernizing Japan. Some Buddhist movements sought clerical reforms in order to address strong concerns that abuses of monastic rules and protocols had contributed to anti-Buddhist sentiments. There were responses by monastics and monastic scholars that attempted to reform Buddhist practices and doctrine outside of official lineage initiatives. These reforms took a variety of forms. Some blended Buddhist thought with Western science and philosophy as a way to remake Buddhism to fit modernizing times.

These reform movements sometimes understood themselves as representing the "new Buddhism" (*shin bukkyō*) – in contrast to the forms of Buddhism, now discredited, of the Tokugawa period. In 1899, the Bukkyō Seito Dōshi Kai (Buddhist Puritan Association) was founded by Sakaino Kōyō (1871–1933), Takashima Beihō (1875–1949), and others. Renamed the Shin Bukkyōto Dōshikai (New Buddhist Friends' Association) in 1903, these lay Buddhist reformers published a monthly journal titled *Shin Bukkyō*, "New Buddhism" and advocated social justice activities. Furukawa Rōsen (1871–1899), among others, founded Keii-kai (Woof and Warp Society) in 1894, marking another attempt at remaking Buddhism into something new. This group was critical of traditional Buddhist institutions for their doctrinal rigidity. Keii-kai championed what they termed "free investigation" (*jiyū tōkyū*) as a way to create a Buddhism responsive to the rapid political and social changes occurring in the late Meiji period. According to Ketelaar (1996: 31), "New Buddhism" coupled Japanese nationalistic virtues such as patriotism and loyalty with Buddhist virtues such as compassion. In this way, reformers maintained a Buddhist worldview but situated it in relation to the demands of modern Japanese citizenship (Ōtani 2014).

Lay Buddhists responded as well, most notably in the founding of organizations and societies. Some of these groups were strongly nationalistic while others pursued more liberal agendas. Regardless of political orientation, these groups played with ideas current in this time period, such as interests in self-cultivation, Western philosophy and science, and ways to promote the nationalism supporting the Meiji state. Kiyozawa Manshi's Seishin-shugi (Spiritualism) movement is one important example of a response which proposed self-cultivation as a means by which to reform Buddhism.

Kiyozawa was a Jōdo Shinshū priest working outside of formal sectarian structures. He was critical of Jōdo Shinshū, judging its clerics to be too worldly and prone to corrupt practices. Kiyozawa had to look no further than his own chief abbot who kept a mistress and assumed an aristocratic rank. Kiyozawa believed that self-cultivation required introspection and, for this reason, he was particularly interested in ascetic practice. His own life was punctuated by his assumption of the role of an ascetic monk, living a simple life separate from his family. His notion of reform involved going back to the original teachings of Shinran, Jōdo Shinshū's founder. He coupled this with ideas about remaking monastic life in such a way that it was responsive to a modernizing Japan. In terms of ascetic practice, Kiyozawa wanted Buddhist practitioners to cultivate awareness that salvation required reliance on an "other power" (*tariki*) in the face of their own moral imperfectability. Kiyozawa wedded this idea with social welfare, arguing that one's own spiritual development and awakening was necessary to fulfilling one's social responsibilities.

Kiyozawa's own ascetic turn was formalized when, in 1900, he began to live communally with friends and disciples. The Tokyo commune, Kōkōdō (Vast Cavern), originally began as a Jōdo Shinshū reform movement, but Kiyozawa's ideas moved beyond the interests of his Buddhist lineage. Kiyozawa's vision for the Spiritualism movement was articulated in a journal called *Seishinkai* (Spiritual World) that was started by Kōkōdō members. His essays in *Seishinkai* demonstrate that Kiyozawa was clearly concerned about the state of Buddhism in a modernizing Japan. He and his followers became disenchanted with the notion of Buddhist lineages reacting to the dictates of a nationalist state. Instead, they advocated Buddhist self-cultivation, a personal spiritualism, that gave individuals control over their own wellbeing without reliance on organized Buddhism or the state (Kashiwahara 1990: 113–120; Sueki *et al.* 2011: 85–89).

Meiji-period anti-Buddhist sentiment became an opportunity for Buddhists to rethink the importance and necessity of adhering to the 10 major precepts, ethical rules for both monastics and laypersons. In the history of Japanese Buddhism, the precepts have sometimes been viewed as important, and sometimes they have been either dismissed or ignored. The Meiji period, however, was a time in which some clerics sought to revive the precepts and make them central to Buddhist life. This reconsideration of the place of the precepts in Japanese Buddhist life was precipitated, in part, by the Meiji government's decriminalization of the requirement that all monastics remain celibate and refrain from meat-eating. This decriminalization also undermined an aspect of Buddhist monastic life that had set apart the Buddhist lifestyle from that of a non-monastic life.

Such reformers as Fukuda Gyōkai, a Pure Land priest, and Shaku Unshō, a Shingon priest, sought reforms to monastic rules and to Buddhist organizations, seeking thereby to re-establish Buddhism's relevance for a modernizing Japan. They focused on making the 10 primary Buddhist precepts relevant again and stressed the importance of their observance. To this end, they advocated the continued, if voluntary, observance of the precepts. They believed that if clerics adhered to strict ethical guidelines like those proscribed in the 10 precepts, then the significance of Buddhism would be maintained even in the face of anti-Buddhist sentiment. They also enjoined the Buddhist laity to observe the precepts as an ethical underpinning necessary to be a good Japanese citizen.

Shaku Unshō created a lay Buddhist organization known as the Jūzen-kai (Association for the Ten Precepts), in which he advocated for strict observance of the 10 precepts by lay Buddhists. Unshō also stressed the importance of repentance in cases where his followers violated a precept. Fukuda Gyōkai was particularly eager to find ways to end sectarian corruption and clerical misdeeds. He looked to Indian Theravada Buddhism, mostly ignored in Japan until the Meiji period, for advice on how to address current abuses. The notion was that over the long centuries of Buddhist transmission, certain Buddhist practices had become corrupt and it was only by returning to a pristine Buddhism reflected in the earlier Theravada teachings that these errors could be understood and corrected. Fukuda was one of many Meiji-period Buddhists who expressed this kind of reform in the expression, *haja kenshō* (rejecting false teachings and manifesting truth). Fukuda's efforts were also driven by the idea, shared with Unshō, that they lived in a decadent Buddhist age known as the Period of the Decay of the Law (*mappō*) (Jaffe 2001).

In 1873, the formal ban on Christianity, still in place from the Tokugawa period, was lifted, in part because it was becoming a hindrance to relations with Western Christian countries. With the ban lifted, Christian proselytization activities increased. Hoping to gain inroads into Japanese culture, Christians adopted the strategy of joining the nativist anti-Buddhist critique in their depiction of Buddhism as corrupt and out of step with changing times. Regardless of this rhetoric, Christianity, a foreign religion associated with powerful Western nations, was looked upon with great suspicion by the Meiji government as a potential threat to the Japanese spirit and indigenous culture the restorationists sought to foster. Thus, the anxiety that Christianity produced for Japanese leaders became a way for Buddhism to assert its loyalty to the nation over and against Christianity. From the late 1880s on, backlash against Christianity increased. This provided Buddhist reformers with the opportunity to align their interests with the nationalist movement that placed the emperor at the center of the nation (Murakami 1980: 33–40).

Buddhist reformers represented themselves as loyal and patriotic nationalists who were more than capable of countering any Christian threat. In so doing, Buddhists aligned themselves with the state – and, by extension, Shintō – and they sought opportunities to demonstrate their nationalist credentials. Buddhists engaged in a scathing criticism of Christianity that was motivated by an incident related to the Imperial Rescript on Education. Promulgated in 1890, the Rescript articulated Japanese virtues such as loyalty to the imperial line and other moral foundations necessary for a strong and unified nation. The Rescript led to the expectation that students and teachers would start each day by bowing to a portrait of the emperor. Famously, Uchimura Kanzō (1861–1930), a Christian teacher at a national high school, hesitated to bow before the emperor's image – effectively denying the emperor's divinity. He was roundly criticized by Buddhists like Inoue Enryō and Inoue Tetsujirō, who argued that Christianity was counter to the Japanese spirit, unlike Buddhism, which is focused on "this-worldly" concerns, as opposed to the transcendent teachings of Christianity. Inoue Enryō also saw Christianity – and, especially, Christian missionaries – as a threat to a Japan attempting to modernize on its own terms. Other Buddhist leaders also expressed strong anti-Christian sentiments.

Inoue Enryō (1858–1919), a Buddhist philosopher and intellectual, interpreted Buddhist thought through the lens of Indian, Chinese, and Western philosophy (on Inoue, see Staggs 1983). He had been a Jōdo Shinshū priest, but later left the priesthood to carry out his work as a layperson. He studied philosophy at Tokyo Imperial University, graduating in 1885. Philosophy informed both his critique of Christianity as inferior to Buddhism – that it was, in part, scientifically and philosophically contradictory and incoherent – and his ideas for reforming Buddhism, especially Buddhist clerical practices, of which he was strongly critical.

Inoue wanted to create a more rational perspective on Buddhism. In 1887, he founded the Tetsugakukan (Institute of Philosophy). This institute, and Inoue's philosophical interests in general, were focused on understanding Buddhism through the perspectives of both Asian and Western philosophical and religious traditions, particularly the teachings of the historical Buddha, Confucian thought, and the thought of Socrates and Immanuel Kant.

Inoue was well traveled – he visited the West on three different occasions – and a prolific writer, authoring over 120 books. Works such as *Shinri kinshin* (The Guiding Principle of Truth, 1886–1887) and *Bukkyō katsu ron* (Enlivening Buddhism, 1887–1890), are deeply critical of Christianity as unscientific and irrational, in distinction to

Buddhism, which is scientific, for instance, in its view of causation. For Inoue, Buddhism was superior to Christianity because of its congruence with scientific fact. Inoue sought a more rational, science-based version of Buddhism, exemplified by his construction, in 1904, of Tetsugaku-dō (Hall of Philosophy), which was dedicated to Shakyamuni, Confucius, Socrates, and Kant.

Inoue was also concerned about how Buddhism was perceived by the government as well as the Japanese people. In particular, he worried that if Buddhists focused on world-renouncing aspects of the Dharma, it would push Buddhism into irrelevance in the face of a modernizing Japan. To counter this possibility, Inoue sought to promote programs that would help the people and, at the same time, underscore the fact that Buddhism could prove supportive of the nation, and not a hindrance. He thus advocated Buddhist social welfare activities as a way to provide concrete assistance to the Japanese people (Staggs 1983).

Shimaji Mokurai (1838–1911), a Jōdo Shinshū priest, and Ōuchi Seiran (1845–1918), a former Sōtō Zen priest, were both involved in reforms that aimed to bring the Buddhism of their day into conversation with the new philosophical and religious ideas that were a part of Japan's modernization process. Shimaji firmly believed that Buddhism was integral to Japan's modernization and wellbeing as a nation. He was concerned that Buddhism had been diminished as a result of government focus on Shintō. In part because of his travels in Europe and India in 1873–1874 with a group of Jōdo Shinshū scholars, he came to the conclusion that separation of religion and state was necessary in Japan to ensure that Buddhism would not be subsumed by Shintō as a state religion. Interestingly, although Shimaji advocated that religion be freed from state control, he was more concerned about advancing the interests of Buddhism, and Jōdo Shinshū in particular. This reflects his anti-Christian sensibilities – he wanted a strong Buddhism to counter what he saw as the threat of Christianity, asserting that Christian doctrine was fundamentally antithetical to the imperial way. He attacked Christianity on the grounds that Western rationalist philosophy revealed it to be unscientific, while Buddhism, with its doctrine of cause and effect, was in accord with a scientific understanding of the world (Kashiwahara and Sonoda 1994: 207–218; Sueki *et al.* 2011: 51–53).

Ōuchi Seiran, a former Sōtō Zen priest, founded a lay Buddhist movement, the Sonnō Hōbutsu Daidōdan (Federation for the Great Way of Venerating the Emperor and Repaying the Buddha) in 1889. This movement is one of several examples of Meiji- era lay Buddhist movements that embraced nationalism and were, at the same time, very critical of Christianity. Ōuchi was particularly concerned with how to make Buddhism relevant to the everyday lives of lay people. He thus advocated that lay people follow the 10 major precepts as a guide for life (Kashiwahara 1990: 98–100).

Tanaka Chigaku (1861–1939) founded the Kokuchūkai (Pillar of the Nation Society) in 1914. This society became one of the chief platforms for Tanaka's views on Buddhism and the nation. He was staunchly nationalistic, concerned with Buddhism's role in Japan's modernization, and volubly anti-Christian. Derived from

Nichiren-lineage doctrine and focused particularly on lay people, this society advocated what was termed Nichiren-*shugi* (Nichirenism). Tanaka coupled Japanese nationalism with Nichiren's desire to create a nation aligned with the teachings of the *Lotus Sūtra*. For Tanaka, Japan's imperial expansion into other parts of Asia was a vehicle for spreading wider Nichiren's doctrine and the *Lotus Sūtra*. This perspective was attractive to both the government and the military.

In his reading of Nichiren's writings, Tanaka saw upholding the national polity (*kokutai*) as fundamental. Tanaka associated the eternal Buddha described in the *Lotus Sūtra* with the Shintō deity Amaterasu, from whom the emperor was claimed to be directly descended. In this way, Tanaka's Buddhism was connected with and in support of national interests, even to the extent of advocacy for outright military intervention under the banner of establishing the truth of the *Lotus Sūtra* in concert with the Japanese imperial agenda. For Tanaka, the *Lotus Sūtra* formed the basis for the wellbeing and prosperity of the nation (Jaffe 2001: 165–188; Kashiwahara 1990: 100–104; Lee 1975; Sueki *et al.* 2011: 176–179).

Other interpretations of Nichiren countered Tanaka's extreme nationalist views. Takayama Chogyū (1871–1902) became familiar with Nichiren's life and teachings through Tanaka's writings. However, Takayama was skeptical of Tanaka's nationalist interpretation of Nichiren's works and instead was drawn to what he perceived to be Nichiren's universal vision that transcended nation. He was particularly struck by Nichiren's view that though a person's actions my be in accord with a ruler's policies, this did not mean that a person had to ascribe universal truth to what a ruler decreed. For Takayama, religious truth – in this case, Nichiren's teachings on the *Lotus Sūtra* – transcended national interests and laws (Tamura 2000: 179–180).

Japanese Buddhists Overseas: Scholars and Missionaries

Particularly after the end of the Russo-Japanese War, and as a result of more and more Japanese living overseas, Buddhist missionary activities increased in such places as China, Korea, Hawai'i, and North and South America. Various Buddhist lineages were active in missionary activities. Jōdo Shinshū engaged in missionary work with Japanese immigrants living in Hawai'i and established a mission there in 1899. In 1904, they established a mission in California. Missionaries from Nichiren and Shingon lineages also engaged in active missionary work in Hawai'i and California starting in the early twentieth century.

Zen lineages established missions, and Zen Buddhism became of religious and intellectual interest to Westerners, particularly Americans. Of the several different Japanese Buddhist lineages, the Western focus on Zen had its inception when, in 1893, Shaku Sōen (1859–1919), a Rinzai Zen priest, attended the World's Parliament of Religions in Chicago as one of Japan's representatives. Sōen, whose formal Buddhist training began when he was 11, came to believe that Meiji-period Japanese Buddhism was too traditional and resistant to change in a time of rapid transformations in Japanese society. Sōen was outward looking: he began studying at Keiō University in 1884 in order to expand his intellectual horizons. After graduation, in 1887, he went abroad for the first time. He spent three years studying Theravada Buddhism and Sanskrit in Sri Lanka (then called Ceylon). He also visited India, Thailand, and China. Sōen became head abbot at Kamakura's Engakuji temple. In 1893, he traveled to Chicago for the World's Parliament of Religions, an event connected to the World's Columbian Exposition that was commemorating the four-hundredth-year anniversary of Columbus's arrival in the New World. At the Parliament, Sōen's presentation, "The Law of Cause and Effect, as Taught by the Buddha," was read to those assembled. Sōen traveled to San Francisco in 1905 as the guest of Mr and Mrs Alexander Russell, who had studied with Sōen at Engakuji. As a result of this trip to the United States, Sōen had the opportunity to teach about Zen Buddhism in San Francisco, Chicago, Washington, DC, and New York City (Snodgrass 2003).

Sōen's disciples also played an important role in cultivating the American engagement with Zen. Of particular note is Suzuki Daisetsu Teitarō (D. T.; 1870–1966), a scholar of Zen Buddhism – and a student of Sōen at Engakuji – who was instrumental in making Japanese Buddhism known internationally. Sōen sent Suzuki to the United States to study with Buddhist advocate and editor Paul Carus (1852–1919), author of *The Gospel of Buddha* (1894), whom Sōen had met in Chicago at the World's Parliament of Religions. It was during his time with Carus that Suzuki wrote his first English-language book on Buddhism, *Outlines of Mahayana Buddhism* (1907). Upon returning to Japan, he taught Buddhist thought at Kyoto's Ōtani University, affiliated with Jōdo Shinshū, and started the journal, *The Eastern Buddhist* (Snodgrass 2003: 259–277).

After the war, in 1950, Suzuki once again traveled to the United States, teaching and lecturing at Columbia University, where he became a visiting professor, among other universities. Suzuki's scholarship ranged over a number of topics, including Zen thought and practice, Zen history, and the impact of Zen on Japanese culture. It is largely because of Suzuki's influence that Zen Buddhism became central to some of the 1950s American Beat Generation poets and authors, like Jack Kerouac, Gary Snyder, and Allen Ginsberg (Kashiwahara and Sonoda 1994: 241–250).

The Study of Buddhism as an Academic Discipline

According to Hayashi (2011), Buddhism, in the Meiji period, became for the first time both a lived experience and an object of academic study. There were earlier precedents for Buddhism as an academic field: In 1804, the Shingon priest Jiun Onkō

(1718–1804) completed an encyclopedic 1,000-volume guide to the study of Sanskrit texts and grammar called *Bongaku shinryō* (Guide to Sanskrit Studies). But it was not until the Meiji period that the study of Buddhism became an academic discipline. Academic interests were fueled, in part, by the overseas travel of Japanese scholars, who studied the research methods and theories of European, American, and other scholars. Of particular interest to these early Japanese academics was Buddhist textual studies and, in particular, the study of Indian Buddhism and its languages, Pali and Sanskrit. Such studies led some Japanese Buddhists to question the orthodoxy of Japanese Buddhist traditions in relation to earlier forms of Buddhism that sometimes seemed quite contrary to Japanese understandings.

Nanjō Bunyū (1849–1927), schooled in the Jōdo Shinshū tradition, was a Japanese Buddhist scholar who traveled to England in 1876 where he studied Buddhist Sanskrit at Oxford University with F. Max Müller and others. Upon returning to Japan in 1884, he took an academic position teaching Sanskrit at Tokyo Imperial University. This marked one of the earliest examples of Japanese academics utilizing Western academic methods to study Buddhism. Similar to Nanjō, Kawaguchi Ekai (1866–1945) traveled to Tibet in 1899 to study Tibetan Buddhism (Sueki *et al.* 2011: 118–120, 126–128, 319–321).

Murakami Senshō (1851–1929), a Jōdo Shinshū priest and Buddhist scholar, was a central figure in efforts to study Buddhism as an academic discipline. He focused on the study of Buddhist texts written in Pali and Sanskrit and was interested in the history of Buddhism. His studies prompted a desire to go beyond sectarian interests that often informed Japanese Buddhist scholarship. He wrote critically of sectarian biases in books such as *Bukkyō tōitsu ron* (The Unity of Buddhism, 1898) and *Daijō bussetsu ron hihan* (A Critique of the Theory that Mahayana Is the Direct Teaching of the Historical Buddha, 1903). In his writings, he called instead for a consideration of a universal or transnational Buddhism on the basis of his research into Buddhist history. He concluded that Mahayana Buddhism was in some ways mistaken and erroneous, especially with regard to the idea that Mahayana sutras were the actual words of the historical Buddha, Śākyamuni. Murakami refuted this idea, arguing instead that Mahayana doctrine was a later elaboration on the original and direct teaching of the historical Buddha. From this line of historical observation, Murakami understood important Buddhas in the Mahayana pantheon, such as Amida, as merely abstractions and analogies pointing toward ideal qualities suggested by the life of Śākyamuni (Ikeda 1996: 80; Kasahara 2001: 554–555).

This pan-sectarian viewpoint sought commonalities in what were, from a sectarian perspective, sometimes disparate teachings that set lineages apart from each other. Not surprisingly, Murakami's work was widely condemned by traditional Buddhist institutions. His own lineage, Jōdo Shinshū, was especially critical and Murakami was forced for a time to remove himself from the monastic order, though he was later re-instated. His example also underscores ways in which the academic study of Buddhism sometimes intersected with and impacted Japanese Buddhist practice.

Buddhist New Religions

Despite anti-Buddhist sentiment and policies detrimental to Buddhism, there were a number of new Buddhist movements popular in the Meiji period through 1945. Three Buddhist new religions that we will consider in this chapter – Sōka Gakkai, Reiyūkai, and Risshō Kōseikai – will also be discussed in the next chapter because they have continued to be an important aspect of contemporary Buddhist religiosity. One significant feature of many of the Buddhist-derived new religions is that they were or are based on Nichiren-lineage and *Lotus Sūtra* thought and practice. They also share other characteristics, such as programs of active teaching and proselytization, and a strong focus on this-worldly, personal benefits (as opposed to more abstract notions of enlightenment or salvation). These groups, despite having similar origins, ran the gamut from staunch nationalism to a universalist perspective in which religious truth trumps national interests.

Sōka Kyōiku Gakkai

Sōka Gakkai (Value-Creating Society) was originally founded under the name Sōka Kyōiku Gakkai (Value Creation Education Society) in 1930 by Makiguchi Tsunesaburō (1871–1944) and Toda Jōsei (1900–1958). The foundation for this lay Buddhist organization was Nichiren-lineage Buddhism blended with Makiguchi's views on education. Makiguchi and Toda had rather pragmatic ambitions for their new organization: applying universal truth to the welfare and benefit of both individual and nation. They found the blueprint for such human and social happiness in the *Lotus Sūtra* and Nichiren's teachings. Their focus was on this-worldly benefits, rather than the notion of an ideal, abstract truth. In 1930, Makiguchi and Toda published *Sōka Kyōikugaku Taikei* (System of Value-Creating Pedagogy) that outlines many of their religious ideas. Sōka Kyōiku Gakkai was mostly a small group that met to discuss Nichiren and other topics related to Buddhist practice. The group might have escaped larger notice except that in 1942 the government, desiring greater control over religious institutions and at its totalitarian pinnacle, called on all Nichiren-related lineages and organizations to combine. When Makiguchi and Toda refused to do so, they were imprisoned. Makiguchi died in prison in 1944. As we will see in the next chapter, Toda re-organized the group as Sōka Gakkai in 1946 and it has played a significant role as a postwar new Buddhist movement.

Sōka Kyōiku Gakkai underwent further state oppression in 1943 when the organization was accused of treason and violating the Public Peace Preservation Law. Sōka Kyōiku Gakkai taught that the emperor, and by extension, the nation, should embrace *Lotus Sūtra* faith in order to create a perfect world. Although Sōka Kyōiku

Gakkai did support the war effort, their larger teaching was clearly at odds with official state policy (Tamura 2000: 210–211).

Reiyūkai Kyūdan

Reiyūkai Kyōdan (Spiritual Friendship Association), a Nichiren-related Buddhist lay organization, was founded in the early 1920s by Kubo Kakutarō (1890–1944) and Kotani Kimi (1901–1971), his sister-in-law. Reiyūkai is an amalgam of *Lotus Sūtra* faith and rituals combined with ancestor veneration. According to Reiyūkai doctrine, one's own salvation depends on the prior salvation of one's ancestors. Reiyūkai teaches that the faithful can effect the salvation of ancestors by reciting passages from the *Lotus Sūtra*.

Kubo emulated Nichiren and believed he would play a role in the contemporary moment that matched the one that Nichiren envisaged for himself in the thirteenth century. Just as Nichiren had warned the Japanese nation that its social and political destruction was imminent if the country did not convert to faith in the *Lotus Sūtra*, so Kubo believed that the Japan of his day faced the same possibility. Kubo judged the Buddhist clerics of his day to be corrupt and incapable of leading people to religious conduct suitable to the times. Dissolute Buddhist clergy, in his view, were to blame for a world in crisis. He interpreted this situation in terms of ancestor veneration: Buddhist clerics traditionally conducted ancestor veneration rituals but their degeneracy caused their inattention to the spiritual needs of the ancestors. This, he asserted, was the cause of current political and social strife. The only resolution was for people to venerate their own ancestors directly and this necessitated that they themselves perform ancestor veneration rites. Doing so would appease the ancestors and natural and human disasters would subside (Hardacre 1984).

Dai Nippon Risshō Kōseikai

Risshō Kōseikai (Society for Establishing Righteousness and Harmony) was founded in 1938 by Niwano Nikkyō (1906–1999) and Naganuma Myōkō (1889–1957), a housewife with shamanic abilities. It prized the *Lotus Sūtra* as the central teaching. In 1938, Niwano and Naganuma, then Reiyūkai members, left Reiyūkai because of disagreements with its founders to start their own *Lotus Sūtra*-based Buddhist movement called Dai Nippon Risshō Kōseikai (after the war, in 1948, they shortened the name to Risshō Kōseikai). Like Reiyūkai, Risshō Kōseikai engaged in ancestor veneration rituals. This movement also stressed the need for penance rituals in order to overcome the bad karmic consequence that immoral behavior engenders.

According to Risshō Kōseikai doctrine, bad karmic consequence is the result of either bad actions done by one's ancestors or by oneself in a previous existence. Adverse karmic consequence can be ameliorated by means of proper ancestor veneration rituals. For Risshō Kōseikai, as with Reiyūkai, these rites centered on *Lotus Sūtra*-chanting. Risshō Kōseikai also urged its members to join a group counseling session known as *hōza* (literally "Dharma seat;" the organization translates this term as "circle of compassion"). The aim of *hōza* sessions was to offer participants both help for themselves and to aid them in providing solace to others (Sueki *et al.* 2011: 280–284).

Japanese Buddhism and the Fifteen-Year War (1931–1945)

As we have seen, Japan's modernization strongly impacted the relationship between religion and state, and was a catalyst for Buddhists to reform their practices and attitudes in order to remain relevant in this rapidly changing atmosphere. It was one thing for at least some Buddhists to assume a nationalist stance and position Buddhist thought and practice as a benefit to the state. However, Japan's modernization and its growing power in East Asia and beyond also involved it in a series of incursions and wars: the Sino-Japanese War (1895), the Russo-Japanese War (1904–1905), the annexation of Korea (1910), participation in World War I (1914–1918), the invasion of Manchuria (1931), and World War II (1941–1945). Japanese Buddhist lineages and new religions were implicated in these events in a variety of ways.

Japan's Fifteen-Year War began in 1931 with the Japanese imperial army's invasion and occupation of Chinese Manchuria and ended with the 1945 atomic bombings of Hiroshima and Nagasaki, and Japan's subsequent surrender to the Allied forces, which ended World War II. It might be supposed that Buddhism, with its pacifist tendencies, would have played no supporting role in Japanese war efforts. However, this is decidedly not the case. Traditional Japanese Buddhist institutions, and some of the Buddhist new religions, generally supported the war effort, though there were also Japanese Buddhists who were opposed to Japan's militant imperialism. This section explores the role that Japanese Buddhism played in supporting Japanese military expansion and aggression between 1930 and 1945.

The notion of Buddhist nationalism, that eventually led to Buddhist support of Japanese military aggression, is evident as early as the late nineteenth century. Part of the reason for this development is that some Buddhists felt it was imperative that they clearly demonstrate Buddhism's relevance to Japan's efforts to modernize and become a world power. Some Buddhists expressed the notion that Japanese Buddhism was the pinnacle of the religion's development and that, therefore, military expansion was necessary for the spread of Japanese Buddhist teachings. Tanaka Chigaku, for instance, held this view. Ishiwara Kanji (1889–1949), one of the architects of the Manchurian invasion, was a follower of Tanaka and saw a war between Japan and the United States as expressing Nichiren's apocalyptic vision of major conflict resolved with a victory inaugurating a Buddhist state (Sueki *et al.* 2011: 184–186).

In 1904, after the start of the Russo-Japanese War, religious leaders representing Shintō, Buddhism, and Christianity issued a statement supporting the war effort. They argued that war with Russia was justified and necessary for national security and future peace. Buddhist institutions assisted in the war effort in a number of ways: They sent priests to attend to the needs of Japanese soldiers, engaged in rituals intended to secure a Japanese victory, and ministered to the families of fallen soldiers.

In similar fashion, during the Fifteen-Year War period, Buddhist priests were associated with Imperial Army regiments in order to minister to the needs of soldiers, both spiritually and, sometimes, medically. Brian Victoria (1997) has studied in detail the role that Zen Buddhists played in the war effort. He cites many examples of Zen Buddhist leaders speaking out in strong support of the war. Myōwakai (Society for Light and Peace), a transsectarian Buddhist organization, was an important source of wartime support to Japanese troops. Victoria reports the following 1937 response Myōwakai made to complaints by Chinese Buddhists about Japanese military aggression on the Chinese mainland:

> In order to establish eternal peace in East Asia, arousing the great benevolence and compassion of Buddhism, we are sometimes accepting and sometimes forceful. We now have no choice but to exercise the benevolent forcefulness of "killing one in order that many may live" ... In general it can be said that Chinese Buddhists believe that war should absolutely be avoided no matter what the reason. Japanese Buddhists, on the other hand, believe that war conducted for a [good] reason is in accord with the great benevolence and compassion of Buddhism. (Victoria 1997: 87)

The role that various Buddhist lineages and new religions played in supporting the Japanese war efforts continues to be debated today, and we will examine some of these issues in the next chapter.

In the midst of war, the government attempted to gain even greater control over religions operating outside the state's official Shintō ideology. In some instances, Buddhist lineages and new religions ran afoul of the government because their writings and doctrines, even though in many instances hundreds of years old, expressed ideas that located religious truth beyond the kind of state interests being expressed in Japan during the early decades of the 1900s. Between 1931 and 1945 – the period of the Fifteen-Year War – the government, on a number of occasions, demanded that

Buddhist lineages and lay organizations expunge from their doctrines and teachings any language or ideas that showed less than full allegiance to the emperor or diminished the significance of Shintō *kami*. For example, in the thirteenth century Shinran, the founder of Jōdo Shinshū, wrote a major work titled *Kyōgyōshinshō* (full title: *Ken jōdo shinjitsu kyōgyōshō monrui*; Textual Passages Expressing the True Teaching, Practice, and Realization of the Pure Land) that includes a line instructing people to be angry when rulers and other officials go against the Dharma and act immorally. In 1939, some 700 years later, this particular sentiment was viewed by government authorities as dangerous to the national polity and an order was issued to change or delete it. Similarly, some of Nichiren's thirteenth-century writings include statements critical of imperial rule – these were marked for deletion by the government in 1941 (Tamura 2000: 208).

Buddhist new religions, like Sōka Kyōiku Gakkai (Sōka Gakkai), Reiyūkai Kyōdan, and Dai Nippon Risshō Kōseikai (Risshō Kōseikai), were particularly distrusted by the government and their leaders often faced persecution and imprisonment because their doctrines were deemed to be detrimental to national interests or because, in the eyes of the government, they failed to show proper respect for emperor and nation. As a way to ascertain allegiance and loyalty to the ultranationalist state, Buddhist and other religions were ordered to venerate talismans from the Ise Shrine – and there were serious consequences for groups that did not do so. We have already encountered the example of Makiguchi Tsunesaburō, one of the founders of Sōka Kyōiku Gakkai, and his imprisonment for refusal to combine his movement with all the other Nichiren-related lineages. In addition, Makiguchi was an outspoken critic of the imposition of Shintō nationalism on the Japanese people during the 1930s and 1940s. He no doubt secured his imprisonment when, along with other Sōka Gakkai officials, he also refused to venerate the Ise Shrine talismans. The Ise Shrine was directly connected to the imperial family, so rejecting the talismans was equivalent to rejecting the authority of the emperor and the legitimacy of the state.

There were some examples of Buddhists voicing outright opposition to the war, such as Itō Shōshin (1876–1963), a former Jōdo Shinshū priest, who founded a movement in 1905 known as Mugaen (Garden of Selflessness). His movement attracted intellectuals like Kawakami Hajime (1879–1946), a Marxist economist who wrote for the *Yomiuri Shinbun*, an important national newspaper, and later served as a professor at Kyōto Imperial University. Itō stressed the idea of selfless love (*muga no ai*) and advocated a life of service to others as the way to avoid the kind of self-attachment that was so detrimental to human interests. He wrote about his philosophy in a journal he founded called *Muga-ai* (Selfless Love). His articles, and those of others published in the journal, often discussed socialist principles – anathema to ultranationalists among the Japanese government and military. Itō also championed a notion of peace that could only come from an absolute, universal, and selfless love, which, for Itō, clearly transcended the untranationalist demands for loyalty to emperor and state. Itō was imprisoned for views that the government deemed treasonous (Tamura 2000: 190–191).

References

Breen, John. 2000. "Ideologues, Bureaucrats, and Priests: On 'Shintō' and 'Buddhism' in early Meiji Japan." In John Breen and Mark Teeuwen (eds.), *Shinto in History: Ways of the Kami*, 230–251. Honolulu: University of Hawai'i Press.

Duus, Peter. 1989. *The Cambridge History of Japan*, vol. 6: *The Twentieth Century*. Cambridge: Cambridge University Press.

Endō Jun. 2003. "The Early Modern Period: In Search of a Shinto Identity." In Nobutaka Inoue (ed.), *Shinto: A Short History*, trans. Mark Teeuwen and John Breen, 108–158. London and New York: RoutledgeCurzon.

Hardacre, Helen. 1984. *Lay Buddhism in Contemporary Japan: Reiyūkai Kyōdan*. Princeton, NJ: Princeton University Press.

Hardacre, Helen. 1989. *Shinto and the State: 1868–1988*. Princeton, NJ: Princeton University Press.

Harootunian, H. D. 1978. "The Consciousness of Archaic Form in the New Realism of Kokugaku." In Tetsuo Najita and Irwin Scheiner (eds.), *Japanese Thought in the Tokugawa Period: Methods and Metaphors*, 63–104. Chicago: University of Chicago Press.

Havens, Norman. 2006. "Shinto." In Paul L. Swanson and Clark Chilson (eds.), *Nanzan Guide to Japanese Religions*, 14–37. Honolulu: University of Hawai'i Press.

Hayashi Makoto. 2011. "Japanese Buddhism and its Modern Reconfiguration." *The Eastern Buddhist* 42 (1): 1–8.

Ikeda Eishun. 1996. *Zusetsu Nihon bukkyō no rekishi: Kindai*. Tokyo: Kōsei Shuppansha.

Jaffe, Richard M. 2001. *Neither Monk nor Layman: Clerical Marriage in Modern Japanese Buddhism*. Princeton, NJ: Princeton University Press.

Jansen, Marius B. 1989. *The Cambridge History of Japan*, vol. 5: *The Nineteenth Century*. Cambridge: Cambridge University Press.

Kasahara, Kazuo, ed. 2001. *A History of Japanese Religion*. Trans. Paul McCarthy and Gaynor Sekimori. Tokyo: Kōsei Publishing Co.

Kashiwahara Yūsen. 1990. *Nihon bukkyōshi: Kindai*. Tokyo: Yoshikawa Kōbunkan.

Kashiwahara, Yūsen, and Koyu Sonoda, eds. 1994. *Shapers of Japanese Buddhism*. Trans. Gaynor Sekimori. Tokyo: Kōsei Publishing Co.

Ketelaar James Edward. 1990. *Of Heretics and Martyrs in Meiji Japan: Buddhism and Its Persecution*. Princeton, NJ: Princeton University Press.

Ketelaar, James E. 1996. "Kaikyōron: Buddhism Confronts Modernity." *Zen Buddhism Today* 12: 25–39.

Lee, Edwin B. 1975. "Nichiren and Nationalism: The Religious Patriotism of Tanaka Chigaku." *Monumenta Nipponica* 20 (1): 19–35.

Murakami, Shigeyoshi. 1980. *Japanese Religion in the Modern Century*. Trans. H. Byron Earhart. Tokyo: University of Tokyo Press.

Ōtani Eiichi. 2014. "The Movement Called 'New Buddhism' in Meiji Japan." In Makoto Hayashi, Eiichi Ōtani, and Paul L. Swanson (eds.), *Modern Buddhism in Japan*, 52–84. Nagoya: Nanzan Institute for Religion and Culture.

Snodgrass, Judith. 2003. *Presenting Japanese Buddhism to the West: Orientalism, Occidentalism, and the Columbian Exposition*. Chapel Hill, NC: University of North Carolina Press.

Staggs, Kathleen M. 1983. "'Defend the Nation and Love the Truth': Inoue Enryō and the Revival of Meiji Buddhism." *Monumenta Nipponica* 38 (3): 251–281.

Sueki Fumihiko *et al.*, eds. 2011. *Kindai kokka to bukkyō* (Shin Ajia bukkyōshi 14, Nihon 4). Tokyo: Kōsei Shuppansha.

Tamura, Yoshiro. 2000. *Japanese Buddhism: A Cultural History*. Tokyo: Kōsei Shuppansha.

Tsutsui, William M., ed. 2007. *A Companion to Japanese History*. Oxford: Blackwell.

Victoria, Brian (Daizen). 1997. *Zen at War*. New York and Tokyo: Weatherhill.

Yoshida Kyūichi. 1998. *Kin-gendai bukkyō to rekishi*. Tokyo: Chikuma Shobō.

Further Reading

Bernstein, Andrew. 2000. "Fire and Earth: The Forging of Modern Cremation in Meiji Japan." *Japanese Journal of Religious Studies* 27 (3–4): 297–334.

Bernstein, Andrew. 2006. *Modern Passings: Death Rites, Politics, and Social Change in Imperial Japan*. Honolulu: University of Hawai'i Press.

Breen, John, and Mark Teeuwen, eds., 2000. *Shinto in History: Ways of the Kami*. Honolulu: University of Hawai'i Press.

Collcutt, Martin. 1986. "Buddhism: The Threat of Eradication." In Marius B. Jansen and Gilbert Rozman (eds.), *Japan in Transition: From Tokugawa to Meiji*, 143–167. Princeton, NJ: Princeton University Press.

Davis, Winston. 1992. *Japanese Religion and Society: Paradigms of Structure and Change*. Albany, NY: State University of New York Press.

Ellwood, Robert. 2008. *Introducing Japanese Religion*. New York and London: Routledge.

Gluck, Carol. 1985. *Japan's Modern Myths: Ideology in the Late Meiji Period*. Princeton, NJ: Princeton University Press.

Grapard, Allan G. 1984. "Japan's Ignored Cultural Revolution: The Separation of Shinto and Buddhist Divinities in Meiji (*shinbutsu bunri*) and a Case Study: Tōnomine" *History of History of Religions* 23: 240–265.

Hardacre, Helen. 1986. "Creating State Shinto: The Great Promulgation Campaign and the New Religions." *Journal of Japanese Studies* 12: 29–63.

Hardacre, Helen. 1988. "The Shintō Priesthood in Early Meiji Japan: Preliminary Inquiries." *History of Religions* 27: 294–320.

Hardacre, Helen. 2002. *Religion and Society in Nineteenth-Century Japan*. Ann Arbor, MI: Center for Japanese Studies, University of Michigan.

Harootunian, H. D. 1988. *Things Seen and Unseen: Discourse and Ideology in Tokugawa Nativism*. Chicago: Chicago University Press.

Havens, Thomas R. H. 1978. *Valley of Darkness: The Japanese People and World War Two*. New York: Norton.

Hayashi Makoto. 2006. "Religion in the Modern Period." In Paul L. Swanson and Clark Chilson (eds.), *Nanzan Guide to Japanese Religions*, 202–219. Honolulu: University of Hawai'i Press.

Hayashi Makoto, Eiichi Ōtani, and Paul L. Swanson, eds. 2014. *Modern Buddhism in Japan*. Nagoya: Nanzan Institute for Religion and Culture.

Inoue Nobutaka, ed. 2003. *Shinto: A Short History*. Trans. Mark Teeuwen and John Breen. London and New York: RoutledgeCurzon.

Ives, Christopher. 2009. *Imperial-Way Zen: Ichikawa Hakugen's Critique and Lingering Questions for Buddhist Ethics*. Honolulu: University of Hawai'i Press.

Jaffe, Richard M. 2004. "Seeing Śākyamuni: Travel and the Reconstruction of Japanese Buddhism. *Journal of Japanese Studies* 30: 65–96.

Jaffe, Richard, and Michel Mohr. 1998. "Editors' Introduction: Meiji Zen." *Japanese Journal of Religious Studies* 25: 1–10.

Jansen, Marius B. 2000. *The Making of Modern Japan*. Cambridge, MA: Harvard University Press.

Matsuo, Kenji. 2007. *A History of Japanese Buddhism*. Folkestone, UK: Global Oriental.

Moriya, Tomoe. 2005. "Social Ethics of 'New Buddhists' At the Turn of the Twentieth Century: A Comparative Study of Suzuki Daisetsu and Inoue Shūten." *Japanese Journal of Religious Studies* 32 (2): 283–304.

Murakami, Shigeyoshi. 1980. *Japanese Religion in the Modern Century*. Trans. H. Byron Earhart. Tokyo: University of Tokyo Press.

Murata Yasuo. 1999. *Shinbutsu bunri no chihōteki tenkai*. Tokyo: Yoshikawa Kōbunkan.

Ōkubo Ryōshun et al., eds. 2003. *Nihon bukkyō sanjū-yon no kagi*. Tokyo: Shunjūsha.

Ōsumi Kazuo and Nishiguchi Junko, eds., 1989. *Shirizu josei to bukkyō*. 4 vols. Tokyo: Heibonsha.

Ōtani Eiichi. 2001. *Kindai Nihon no Nichirenshugi undō*. Kyoto: Hōzōkan.

Rimer, J. Thomas, ed. 1990. *Culture and Identity: Japanese Intellectuals during the Interwar Years*. Princeton, NJ: Princeton University Press.

Sawada, Janine Tasca. 2004. *Practical Pursuits: Religion, Politics, and Personal Cultivation in Nineteenth-Century Japan*. Honolulu: University of Hawai'i Press.

Seager, Richard Hughes. 1999. *Buddhism in America*. New York: Columbia University Press.

Selden, Mark, and Alvin Y. So, eds. 2004. *War and State Terrorism: The United States, Japan, and the Asia-Pacific in the Long Twentieth Century*. Lanham, MD: Rowman & Littlefield.

Sharf, Robert H. 1993. "The Zen of Japanese Nationalism." *History of Religions* 33 (1): 1–43.

Sueki Fumihiko. 2004a. *Kindai Nihon to Bukkyō*, (Kindai Nihon no shisō, saikō 2). Tokyo: Transview.

Sueki Fumihiko. 2004b. *Meiji shisōka ron* (Kindai Nihon no shisō, saikō 1). Tokyo: Transview.

Swanson, Paul L., and Clark Chilson, eds. 2006. *Nanzan Guide to Japanese Religions*. Honolulu: University of Hawai'i Press.

Tamamuro Fumio. 1977. *Shinbutsu bunri*. Tokyo: Kyōikusha.

Tamamuro Fumio. 1999. *Sōshiki to danka*. Tokyo: Yoshikawa Kōbunkan.

Uan Dōnin. 1999. "A Refutation of Clerical Marriage," trans. Richard M. Jaffe. In George J. Tanabe, Jr. (ed.), *Religions of Japan in Practice*, 78–86. Princeton, NJ: Princeton University Press.

Victoria, Brian Daizen. 2010. "A Buddhological Critique of 'Soldier-Zen' in Wartime Japan." In Michael K. Jerryson and Mark Juergensmeyer (eds.), *Buddhist Warfare*, 105–130. Oxford and New York: Oxford University Press.

7

Buddhism Since 1945

Buddhism in the Allied Occupation

World War II ended when Japan surrendered on August 15, 1945, following the devastation wrought by the atomic-bombing of Hiroshima (August 6) and Nagasaki (August 9). By war's end, Japan's major cities were in ruins, many people homeless, and food scarce. The Allied Occupation of Japan, with General Douglas MacArthur serving as Supreme Commander of the Allied Powers (SCAP) and de facto ruler of the country, lasted seven years: from 1945 to 1952.

In addition to the momentous changes occurring in Japan in this traumatic period, religion and its relation to the state were of great importance to Occupation officials and to those responsible for crafting new policies and a postwar constitution. Although many Buddhists had supported the war effort, it was Shintō that most centrally concerned the Occupation. The interim government issued the Shintō Directive in December 1945. It abolished State Shintō, the name for the Shintō ultra-nationalism that fueled the war effort. Most significantly, the directive prohibited any kind of state support of Shintō practice and Shintō shrines – shrines were now considered to be independent institutions located in particular communities. In short, the Shintō Directive sketched out a new religious landscape for postwar Japan. It made clear that no Japanese citizen was required to believe in any doctrines or participate in any rituals that were state sponsored. Besides separating matters of religion and state, the directive was also an attempt to foreclose any possibility of renewed Japanese nationalism wrapped in Shintō trappings.

Underscoring the anti-nationalist agenda was the emperor's so-called "Declaration of Humanity," a radio address to the nation on January 1, 1946. Emperor Hirohito declared that he was not a living god but a human being. Though there had been discussions among Occupation leaders about whether the emperor should be charged with war crimes, in the end it was decided that the Occupation, and Japan's recovery, was better served by allowing the emperor to remain as figurehead of the nation, but with no legislative power. Further, the emperor could continue to engage in Shintō rituals at shrines already associated with the imperial family, but

A Cultural History of Japanese Buddhism, First Edition. William E. Deal and Brian Ruppert.
© 2015 William E. Deal and Brian Ruppert. Published 2015 by John Wiley & Sons, Ltd.

these were to be treated as acts of personal worship, not state rites (Hardacre 1989; Murakami 1980; Shimazono 2006: 220–222; Woodard 1972).

The postwar Japanese constitution, promulgated in November 1946, went into effect on May 3, 1947. It contains two articles, 20 and 89, that are of particular importance to the legal status of religion in postwar Japan.

Article 20 states:
Freedom of religion is guaranteed to all. No religious organization shall receive any privileges from the State, nor exercise any political authority. No person shall be compelled to take part in any religious acts, celebration, rite, or practice. The State and its organs shall refrain from religious education or any other religious activity.

Article 89 states:
No public money or other property shall be expended or appropriated for the use, benefit or maintenance of any religious institution or association, or for any charitable, educational or benevolent enterprises not under the control of public authority.

These two articles are cited as the basic guarantees of religious freedom for postwar Japanese, and are meant to ensure the separation of religion and state, and to prohibit state support of any religion. Further, the state no longer controlled the practices of religions and religions were no longer required to get state approval to function. Legislation also made it possible to establish new religious organizations with relative ease.

One of the implications of this new legislation for Buddhism was that temple affiliations could be freely changed. Some temples chose to become independent from traditional sectarian connections, sometimes for doctrinal reasons and sometimes due to economic exigencies. One famous example is the Hōryūji temple's assertion of its independence from the Hossō lineage and the creation of its own Shōtoku denomination. Disputes over doctrine, practices, and temple administration that would have been internal lineage matters prior to religious freedom became open disagreements resolved by dissidents splitting off from traditional institutional arrangements. Similarly, disagreements between main and branch temples sometimes resulted in disaffiliation.

One other piece of legislation had a lasting impact on the postwar Japanese religious landscape. The Religious Corporations Ordinance (*shūkyō hōjin rei*) made it possible for a religious organization to become recognized as a formal religion simply through a process of government registration. Established in December 1945, it was revised in April 1951 as the Religious Corporations Law (*shūkyō hōjin hō*).

Regardless of the fact that Buddhism was not punished by the Occupation for its wartime cooperation, the Japanese populace was certainly aware of Buddhist involvement in aiding and promoting the war effort. In order to avert the possibility of diminishing public support, Buddhist lineages engaged in acts of repentance for their wartime activities. At least some Buddhists, such as Nichiren lineages, became active in peace movements.

Temples, the center of Buddhist life for most Japanese, entered the postwar period in difficult circumstances. Besides the damage and destruction of many temples, there was little or no financial support available, making temple maintenance, performance of rituals, and other temple activities next to impossible. By the early 1950s, although the situation had generally improved, those temples that were tourist attractions or that were well-known for providing this-worldly comfort and benefits were quickest to achieve financial recovery. Buddhists were also outward looking, and there were efforts to harness Buddhist compassion for social welfare programs for the homeless and starving. In Tokyo, for instance, various Buddhist groups took to the streets to collect money for social welfare programs.

Occupation-period social and economic policies were sometimes detrimental to traditional Buddhist lineages. Postwar land reforms, for instance, deprived temples of land they had long possessed. Further, the increasingly mobile population of the 1950s and 1960s undermined the notion of the family temple – those who moved to cities did not necessarily maintain their ties with the rural family temple. These same city immigrants were also among the population that was attracted to new religious movements, Buddhist or otherwise. These new movements gained followers in urban settings in part because they were more attuned to the problems of postwar life than were traditional lineages, which maintained a rather conservative perspective.

Buddhist new religions, with the exception of Sōka Gakkai, permitted their followers to keep their connection with and participate in rituals with family temples. It was at these temples that memorial rituals would be performed for one's ancestors and it is to these temples that people would likely return for funeral rituals when family members died. Over time, however, the strength of the ties between city immigrants and rural Buddhist communities diminished, becoming increasingly routinized and formal. In 1963, the Buddhist scholar Tamamuro Taijō coined the phrase *sōshiki bukkyō* (funerary Buddhism), in a book of the same title, to describe what he perceived as the moribund state of traditional Buddhism in postwar Japan. Temples, he claimed, were reduced to ritual formality revolving around life changes such as death.

The immediate postwar period was also a time of reflection for the traditional Buddhist lineages. Various denominations engaged in reforming their monastic structures and their relationship to temple parishioners. There were also calls to move beyond sectarian interests to create a renewed, more universal, Buddhism freed from the constraints of the interests of the traditional lineages. The possibility of real transsectarian change was conceivable, in part, because Buddhist institutions and Buddhist individuals were free to express their religiosity in ways not permitted before the end of the Fifteen-Year War. Impetus for a truly universal Buddhism was largely a result of the World Buddhist Conference. The first conference was held in Sri Lanka in 1950. Buddhists and other representatives from 25 countries attended, including a Japanese delegation. A second conference was held in Japan in 1952.

Buddhist New Religions in Postwar Japan

Postwar laws protecting religious freedom had a particularly significant impact on the Buddhist new religions. Nichiren-based new religions, for instance, grew very rapidly in the postwar era because they were now free to teach, practice, and proselytize more or less as they wished. Much of this growth occurred among the increasingly urban postwar Japanese population. Among Buddhist new religions Sōka Gakkai and Risshō Kōseikai were especially popular to Japan's growing middle class and are, today, the two largest lay Buddhist organizations in Japan. Though they promote different doctrines and practices, these two movements share some commonalities. They are both grounded in *Lotus Sūtra* faith. They have attracted followers, in part, by offering this-worldly benefits, such as financial security, happiness, and health. They engage in spiritual and physical healing practices. They are both United Nations NGO (non-governmental organization) members, active in social justice and peace issues.

We encountered Sōka Gakkai in the last chapter. Although persecuted by the wartime government, its fortunes revived significantly after the war under the leadership of Toda Jōsei (1900–1958), one of its original founders, and subsequently by Ikeda Daisaku (b. 1928; president 1960–1979). From a few thousand members in the 1950s, the movement had grown to more than seven million members by the early 1970s. Today, Sōka Gakkai is a global organization with adherents around the world.

Sōka Gakkai practice focuses on group meetings that engage members in core rituals. Central rites include chanting of the title of the *Lotus Sūtra* (*daimoku*): "*namu-myōhō-renge-kyō*," or "praise to the *Lotus Sūtra* of the fine Dharma." This recitation occurs while facing the *gohonzon*, or object of worship. Considered a sacred object, the *gohonzon* is a copy of the *daimoku* phrase composed in Nichiren's calligraphy. Sōka Gakkai doctrine teaches that engaging in this rite leads the believer to a happy life and to the attainment of this-worldly benefits. Salvation is directed at this world instead of enlightenment transcending this life.

In the postwar period, Sōka Gakkai has been noted for two aspects of their practice that have been at times controversial. The first involves the practice of active proselytization incumbent upon the faithful. Known as *shakubuku* – literally, "break and subdue" – Sōka Gakkai active proselytization has been criticized by some as an attempt to gain adherents through forced conversion. Similarly, the movement has sometimes been viewed as intolerant of other religious lineages and movements.

The second aspect of practice concerns Sōka Gakkai's active involvement in Japanese politics. On the one hand, the movement's political activities focus on salvation and world peace. On the other hand, there have been direct attempts to shape the Japanese political landscape in such a way that Sōka Gakkai's agenda is directly addressed by the government. Political activity was especially promoted under Ikeda's leadership. In 1964, he formed a Sōka Gakkai political party called Kōmeitō (Clean Government Party). Although Kōmeitō was always a minority party, it nevertheless had enough political power to sway elections in ways beneficial to Sōka Gakkai's interests, such as electing candidates against increased defense spending and for increased spending on social welfare and related programs. In 1970, Sōka Gakkai officially split from Kōmeitō in order to forestall criticism that the movement was violating laws concerning the separation of religion and state. Nevertheless, Sōka Gakkai members remain strong Kōmeitō supporters.

The other large postwar Buddhist new religion is Risshō Kōseikai (Society for Establishing Righteousness and Harmony). Like Sōka Gakkai, Risshō Kōseikai was founded before World War II, but its real impact is as a postwar movement. It is especially known for its worldwide peace activities promoted by its two founders, Niwano Nikkyō (1906–1999) and Naganuma Myōkō (1889–1957). While Niwano was the architect of Risshō Kōseikai doctrinal ideas, Naganuma was charismatic, and many followers believed her to be a living buddha (*ikibotoke*) with shamanic abilities.

Risshō Kōseikai's brand of lay Buddhism has its origins in a prewar new religion, Reiyūkai, discussed in the previous chapter. While both Reiyūkai and Risshō Kōseikai have religious roots in Nichiren, under Niwano's guidance the focus shifted to ideas derived from his own interpretation of the central Nichiren-lineage text, the *Lotus Sūtra*. In Niwano's reading, the object of veneration is the eternal Buddha revealed in the sutra. Chanting passages from the *Lotus Sūtra* is a part of the ritual life of Risshō Kōseikai adherents.

Traditionally, Risshō Kōseikai doctrine and practice was concerned in part with reincarnation and how to ensure a good rebirth. The problem was that bad karmic consequence is the result of either one's own negative behaviors in a past life or the bad behaviors of an ancestor. It is through attention to cultivating good deeds and mitigating bad deeds of ancestors through rites of ancestor veneration that bad effects are overturned.

Contemporary Risshō Kōseikai doctrine stresses perfection of the self in order to create a harmonious society and achieve world peace. Members engage in small group therapy and counseling meetings called *hōza* ("Dharma seat"; also referred to as "circle of compassion/harmony"). Though *hōza* includes both women and men, these sessions have been especially popular among urban housewives. The purpose of *hōza* is to get help for one's personal problems – whether spiritual, social, or material – from other members. The idea is that this kind of personal self-cultivation, involving the development of altruistic, moral behavior, leads to perfection of self.

In the 1970s, Risshō Kōseikai promoted an initiative they termed the Brighter Society Movement (Akarui Shakai Zukuri Undō), which was intended to bring people together to work for the betterment of Japanese society. More globally, the Niwano Peace Foundation was created in 1978 to promote initiatives aimed at fostering international understanding and world peace (Shimazono 2003; Tamura 2000).

Buddhist New New Religions

The 1970s witnessed the rise in popularity of religious movements that have come to be known as "new new religions" (*shin shin shūkyō*), a term first used by Nishiyama Shigeru in a 1979 article discussing new religious movements. Though some of these new movements were founded before the 1970s, it was in this decade that they began to attract followers on a much wider scale. New new religions tended to appeal to a different demographic than the older new religions and articulated doctrines that were also departures from previous traditions. Buddhist new new religions have figured prominently in this group of religious movements. The new new religions appeared at a time when Japan's economy was growing at an extremely fast pace. This accumulation of wealth was accompanied by changing lifestyles and shifts in traditional Japanese values, and marked needs and interests that went beyond Japan's immediate postwar period.

For some younger Japanese, neither the traditional Buddhist lineages nor Buddhist new religions conveyed a spiritual message that resonated with the dynamism of the contemporary moment. Buddhist and other new new religions appeared to provide thought and practice for the changing social and economic conditions. Whereas new religions are usually discussed in terms of their emphasis on this-worldly benefits (*genze riyaku*), the new new religions have tended toward a more pessimistic view of the world.

We have noted that Buddhist new religions have had a particular connection with Nichiren-lineage thought and practice, albeit in modified form. Buddhist new new religions have evolved from a richer palette of Buddhist ideas. For instance, there are several examples of new new religions with, among other religious interests, strong connections to Shingon-lineage doctrines, such as Agon shū (Āgama School; *Āgamas* are a collection of Theravada texts), Gedatsukai (Enlightenment Society), and Shinnyoen (Garden of True Thusness, i.e., true reality).

Of particular importance among these Shingon-related movements is Agon shū, founded by Kiriyama Seiyū (b. 1921) in 1978. A charismatic figure, Kiriyama studied Shingon esoteric Buddhism but was never fully ordained as a priest. Although Shingon ideas are evident in Agon shū practice, the movement represents itself as acting in accord with the Dharma as taught by the historical Buddha – Śākyamuni – and recorded in the early texts known as the Āgamas (or, in Japanese, *agon*). Kiriyama claims to have been visited by the bodhisattva Kannon in a dream, and was directed by Kannon to become a religious leader and to practice the Shingon fire ritual (*goma*). For Kiriyama, the purification derived from engaging in the fire ritual can free one of bad karmic consequence. To this end, Agon shū is noted for its large-scale, outdoor *goma* rituals. Followers also believe that Kiriyama is capable of acting as an intermediary between this world and the next (Reader 1988).

The most famous of the new new religions is also the most notorious: Aum Shinrikyō (Aum Truth Religion). Aum Shinrikyō was founded by Asahara Shōkō (b. 1955) in 1986. Unlike other Buddhist new and new new religions, Aum Shinrikyō does not derive from a particular Japanese Buddhist lineage. Rather, this movement's teaching is based on Asahara's interpretation of Tibetan Buddhist thought and practice blended with Christian and Jewish religious and millenarian ideas. Aum Shinrikyō's notoriety is the result of the group's 1995 sarin gas attack in the Tokyo subway system in which 12 people died and many thousands were hospitalized. This shocking act – Armageddon from the perspective of Aum Shinrikyō – was meant to inaugurate the millennium prophesied by Asahara. Investigations revealed that Aum Shinrikyō had engaged in numerous crimes, including the murder of members deemed apostates. Asahara was sentenced to death in 2004, but, as of 2014, he remains in prison.

Asahara was, at one point in the early 1980s, an Agon shū member, but he also studied an eclectic assortment of religious ideas and practices, including Tibetan Buddhism, yoga, and forms of meditation. He claimed to have become enlightened and began to attract followers by around the mid to late 1980s. His message of meditation leading to what the movement called "final liberation" was particularly attractive to young Japanese, especially to disaffected youth in their twenties and thirties. Asahara justified acts of violence in the movement by claiming that Armageddon, the ultimate battle of good against evil, was imminent. Sarin gas was one of the weapons in this cosmic war. Not surprisingly, one of the results of Aum Shinrikyō's actions was the government's decision to revise the 1951 Religious Corporations Law, which, when it was originally enacted, was meant to make it easier for movements to become recognized religions with certain rights. The reform that was a response to the Aum Shinrikyō sarin gas attack made it simpler for the government to make a case for removing religious status from a movement (Kisala and Mullins 2001; Reader 2000; Shimazono 1992; Shimazono 1995; Shimazono 1997).

The Kyoto School

Some modern and contemporary Japanese Buddhists have been interested in understanding Buddhist thought from a broader intellectual perspective. A group of twentieth-century Kyoto University professors were particularly important in this endeavor: Nishida Kitarō (1870–1945), Tanabe Hajime (1885–1962), and Nishitani Keiji (1900–1991). These Buddhist philosophers attempted to express a perspective on reality that incorporates both Western philosophical views and Buddhist notions of enlightenment. Their Buddhist insights were drawn from Zen and Pure Land thought. Their engagement with Western philosophy focused especially on the works of German philosophers such as Kant, Hegel, and Nietzsche.

A key concept for Kyoto School thinkers is Nishida's notion of "absolute nothingness" (*zettai mu*) that includes the Mahayana stress on the concept of emptiness (Skt. *śūnyatā*). Emptiness articulates the idea that things in the world owe their existence to "interdependent origination" (Skt. *pratītya-samutpāda*; J. *engi*), the notion that all is a matter of cause and effect. As such, all things are "empty" of any independent or independently arising self or self-nature (Skt. *svabhāva* or "own-being"). Such a perspective stands in sharp contrast to Western notions of "being" as having an essence or self that is permanent and endures. Nishida's concept of absolute nothingness transcends distinctions between subject and object. For Nishida, one seeks "self-awareness" (*jikaku*), which is the mindset that one has attained when the mistaken perception of subject/object duality is transcended. Nishida's self-awareness is related to William James's concept of "pure experience" – an intuitive understanding of the world in which the absolute is revealed.

Subsequent Kyoto School philosophers engaged in dialogue with and were critical of Nishida's ideas. Tanabe Hajime overlaid a Pure Land reading of these ideas, replacing Nishida's Zen sensibility of intuited insight with an emphasis on faith in an "other power" (*tariki*). Nishitani Keiji approached Nishida's notion of absolute nothingness from the vantage point of phenomenological and existential philosophy, and stressed the need to engage with the nihilist elements of Nishida's ideas.

The Kyoto School is also important for another reason: They are connected with a postwar idea referred to as Nihonjin-ron (literally, "theory of the Japanese people"). Nihonjin-ron asserts that Japanese people and culture are unique in the world and, by extension, superior to others. Some scholars trace this idea back to Kyoto School philosophy, which, they assert, was used for the ultranationalist purpose of justifying Japanese militarism in Asia during the Fifteen-Year War. The Kyoto School, too, made the implicit assertion that the Japanese are inherently superior people. Since the 1990s, Kyoto School philosophy has been the subject of much debate over its role, intended or not, in promoting Japanese ultranationalism in the 1930s and early 1940s.

Critical Buddhism

Another Buddhist area of inquiry that has attracted much interest is known as Critical Buddhism (*hihan bukkyō*), and is associated with two Japanese Buddhist scholars (both Sōtō Zen priests), Hakamaya Noriaki (b. 1943) and Matsumoto

Shirō (b. 1950). The notion of "critical" in Critical Buddhism refers to the use of contemporary academic methods and theories drawn from linguistics and history to gain insight into what critical Buddhists refer to as "authentic" Buddhism. On the basis of this kind of research, scholars like Hakamaya and Matsumoto assert that certain bedrock doctrines in East Asian Mahayana Buddhism, and especially their own Sōtō Zen lineage, are in fact mistaken and debased versions of true inter-pretations of what the Buddha taught. For critical Buddhists, certain ideas such as "inherent Buddha-nature" (busshō) and "original enlightenment" (hongaku, also referred to as "original awakening") often lead to the erroneous view that human beings have an enduring self. This, they claim, clearly violates one of the historical Buddha's fundamental teachings of "no self" (Skt. anātman), that there is no per-manent self or soul.

Critical Buddhists are concerned that such a worldview justifies most any behavior – such as actions taken out of extreme loyalty to the emperor – if one understands those actions as in accord with an inherent Buddha-nature or original enlightenment. Critical Buddhists argue that to avoid this dangerous view, strict adherence to fundamental Buddhist moral rules, such as the original five precepts (abstaining from killing, stealing, sexual misconduct, lying, and intoxication) and the exercise of compassion, is necessary. These moral rules pre-date the introduction of Buddhism to Japan and therefore should be used to guide one's life over later notions such as original enlightenment.

There are many Buddhist scholars who have disagreed with the view that an authentic, true, or pristine Buddhism is discoverable through academic investiga-tion. Instead, they argue, it is not possible to recover an authentic Buddhism, but only local versions of Buddhism as pondered and practiced in particular historical contexts. Further, even if there have been historical moments when a Mahayana Buddhist idea has been unethically applied to a particular situation, it does not mean that Mahayana is itself to blame or that it should be abandoned. There are examples, these critics of Critical Buddhism say, of ideas like original enlightenment being employed ethically and with compassion.

Critical Buddhist scholarship has directed attention to problems that might other-wise have been ignored. One, in particular, was widely discussed: the historical use of posthumous precept names that were discriminatory. Precept names (kaimyō) are religious titles given to the deceased. These discriminatory precept names made it clear that the deceased person given the posthumous name was a member of the outcast social group known in Japanese as burakumin. Thus, in death, as in life, such people were being singled out in a discriminatory manner. Critical Buddhists revealed that their own Sōtō Zen lineage engaged in the use of discriminatory pre-cept names (sabetsu kaimyō) and demanded that this practice be abolished (Hubbard and Swanson 1997; Stone 1999).

Women in Contemporary Japanese Buddhism

Research by scholars like Kawahashi Noriko (1995) demonstrates that traditional Buddhist lineages, for the most part, continue to treat women unequally, especially with regard to their institutional roles and doctrine. Kawahashi's work discusses the particular gender problem posed by temple wives (*jizoku*; literally, "temple family") in the traditional Buddhist monastic lineages (sometimes referred to as Temple Buddhism). Temple wives are the conjugal partners of male priests, but their treatment suggests significant issues in how Buddhist lineages differentiate between men and women. The role of the temple wife is traditionally clear: She hopefully bears and raises a son who will become the next head of temple. She is engaged in the administration of the temple's activities. Yet, as Kawahashi points out, the priest can teach about Buddhist doctrine but the wife can only be a passive receiver of this knowledge and does not herself teach. But this marital/religious structure and the attitudes which accompany it are deceptive because they are based on the notion that the priest is a religious renunciant (as in centuries past and certainly before the 1872 decriminalization of clerical marriage) and the woman is not. Even so, the fact of marriage underscores this fiction – a married priest is no more or less a renunciant than is his temple wife. For Kawahashi and other feminist interpreters of contemporary Japanese Buddhism, this fiction means that a temple wife's work and dedication to the temple comes with little or no recognition for its importance to the life of that particular temple community (Kawahashi 2012: 200–202).

If the lives of temple wives are complicated by outmoded ways of thinking, what about the lives of renunciant nuns residing in nunneries? We discussed in the previous chapter that in the 1870s the Meiji government legislated the decriminalization of clerical marriage for both priests and nuns. We observed, however, that given the fact that temples were handed down from father to son, if a nun married she was effectively leaving the religious life for a secular one. This situation has changed in postwar Japan, though not radically. Zen nuns, for instance, now live according to a clerical ranking system that is the same for their male counterparts. This apparent equality, however, is mostly cosmetic because common attitudes toward nuns place them below priests in the monastic hierarchy. There are examples of well-known Japanese Buddhist nuns, but they are the exception rather than the norm. Buddhist nuns face an image problem: Constructions of feminine beauty in contemporary Japanese culture do not include the simple robes and shaved heads that set nuns apart from secular women. As Jørn Borup (2012: 125) remarks, this non-feminine appearance works, however, to a nun's benefit because the common layperson's attitude is that anyone who would abide by such rigorous standards of appearance must be an ardent Buddhist (see also Arai 1999).

The role of women in Buddhist new religions has been varied, but conservative gender expectations remain the norm. According to Watanabe Masako (2002), contemporary Buddhist lay movements, including Buddhist new and new new religions, have tended to view women in terms of more traditional gender roles. For some of these groups, she says, the ideal woman strives for self-cultivation that then allows her to better serve her husband and children. In so doing, a woman's model behavior will have a spiritually transformative effect on her family. Importantly, says Watanabe, traditional gender roles are preserved at the same time as a woman is able to cultivate herself and attain happiness.

Scholarly studies of contemporary Japanese Buddhism have typically focused on Buddhist males, whether monks or laymen, rather than on nuns or Buddhist laywomen. Happily, that is beginning to change. The academic study of women in contemporary Japanese Buddhism, though still nascent, has seem some significant strides thanks to the work of such scholars as Watanabe Masako and Usui Atsuko (new religions), and Kawahashi Noriko (Buddhism), among others. Stone (2006) has noted a number of areas needing research on the relationship of women to Buddhist practices in contemporary Japan. These include additional work on temple wives, feminist perspectives on Japanese Buddhism in general, women Buddhist reformers, and the relationships and networks that exist between nuns, temple wives, laywomen, and feminist scholars of Japanese Buddhism.

Traditional Buddhist Lineages in Contemporary Japan

Traditional Buddhist lineages (or Temple Buddhism) still play an important role in contemporary Japanese religious and cultural life. As we will see, this is a view contrary to some observers of contemporary Japanese Buddhism who claim that Japanese Buddhism is nothing but a shell of its former vibrancy, that it is spiritually stagnant, and that its chief functions are to officiate at funerals and to sponsor tourist opportunities for the general public. Many challenges confront traditional Buddhist lineages such as attracting new priests and nuns, maintaining and creating new and younger followers in an aging population, welcoming women into important organizational roles, engaging religious practices meaningful to contemporary Japan, addressing technological changes especially with regard to medicine and medical ethics, and otherwise flexibly addressing institutional problems when they arise.

Some of these challenges are already being addressed, even if eventual outcomes are not always clear. One important way in which the traditional lineages deal with the need for trained clerics is through the maintenance of colleges and universities that both offer a broad curriculum but also provide specific training in the history, doctrine, and practices of the denomination. Tendai, for instance, maintains such institutions for training clerics: Eizan Gakuin at Mt. Hiei and Taishō University in Tokyo. Another example is Jōdo shū, which also maintains two Buddhist universities and several educational institutions such as high schools and women's colleges.

Initiatives to attract lay followers have also been implemented. For instance, Tendai's Light Up Your Corner Movement (Ichigū Wo Terasu Undō), which started in 1969 and continues today, is actively engaged in trying to retain temple members and to find ways of attracting new followers. The Light Up Your Corner Movement, according to Covell (2005), was originally focused especially on two areas of concern. The first deals with what Tendai sees as the negative changes in Japanese values that have led to the breakdown of traditional Japanese family values. The denomination urges believers to follow Tendai doctrine, and its associated lifestyle, in order to restore the family and family values. The second issue involves creating stronger ties between followers and Tendai temples. Hoping to work against the conception of temples as simply places to go for funeral and memorial rites, Tendai has tried to reframe temples as relevant to Tendai family values and as institutions that can aid followers in understanding the role of families in Japanese society. Both of these areas of concern are animated by the drive to make a Tendai way of life relevant to contemporary life.

Activism and social welfare activities are the focus of several Buddhist lineages. Nichiren shū is active in issues related to peace movements, including a strong anti-nuclear weapon stance. Nipponzan Myōhōji, a Nichiren monastic order, is pacifist, following the example of Gandhi. The order works toward absolute nonviolence and sometimes engages in civil disobedience. Other lineages place an emphasis on missionary activity, such as Jōdo Shinshū. They have engaged in postwar foreign missionary activity in various countries, especially North and South America, and wherever significant populations of Japanese reside.

We have already discussed Tamamuro Taijō's assertion that in the postwar period, especially, Buddhist lineages have become nothing more that funerary Buddhism (*sōshiki bukkyō*), reduced to activities concerned with funerals and ancestor memorial rituals. It is true that Temple Buddhism has had a primary role in providing funeral rituals and other rites that commemorate deceased family members and ancestors, although the lineages would argue they do much more than this to care for their temple families. It has been noted, for example, that land reforms in the early postwar period devastated temple incomes. This created a situation in which priests and their families became dependent on money generated from funeral and memorial rites as their main source of income, a development that matched the rapid increase in the number of nuclear families for whom such services were welcome (Rowe 2011: 26–31). Regardless of the cogency of Tamamuro's argument, the role of Temple Buddhism in funerary matters is changing in contemporary Japan. For one thing, traditional Buddhist lineages have the unfortunate image, among some of the Japanese public, of greedily charging people for their mortuary services.

Some Japanese now prefer alternatives to temple funerals, such as freely scattering the cremated ashes of the deceased or utilizing common graves over expensive temple cemeteries. Recently, too, traditional lineages have been confronted with the outsourcing of roles once played by Buddhist temples, Buddhist priests, and Buddhist rituals. Increasingly, there is a move toward the secularization of funerals performed by a newly emerging industry of professional funeral directors (*sōgiya* or *sōgisha*) (Kawano 2012; Walter 2008; Itō and Fujii 1997).

Moreover, there has also been a quiet revolution in memorial practices for some, spawned in part by innovative temple priests like Ogawa Eiji, but also by female and male believers who have drawn on the new practices to make Buddhist memorializing something starkly personal. Ogawa, a Nichiren-school abbot of Myōkōji in Niigata Prefecture, began in the early 1990s to offer eternal memorial graves (*eitai kuyōbo*) as a challenge to patrilineal and extended-family approaches to burial and memory, which had, for example, often left unmarried or divorced women quite literally out of the (p)lot – unless allowed or hoping to enter the family grave of the former husband – and consigned to communal graves (Rowe 2011).

The long history of Buddhist funeral and memorial rituals has shifted in another direction in contemporary Japan. Since the 1990s, pet ownership has increased dramatically. For those who treat their pets as family members, pet memorial rituals (*petto kuyō*) have become important events. Barbara Ambros (2012a), in her study of the relationship between animals and religion in Japan, notes that over 900 pet cemeteries exist in Japan and that Buddhist temples manage some 120 of these. She also points out that even pet cemeteries that operate outside of the control of Buddhist temples have affiliations with Buddhist monastics who conduct rituals. Interestingly, the traditional Buddhist calendar of memorial days, such as *obon* (festival of the dead), is also a time when pet memorial rituals are performed. For at least some contemporary Japanese, there is little distinction between the spiritual needs of human beings and pets.

There have been attempts by scholars of Japanese religion to characterize in broad strokes the nature of contemporary Japanese religious life, including the many forms of Buddhist thought and practice, both monastic and lay. One important concept used to describe the nature of contemporary Japanese religion is "vitalism." According to Tsushima *et al.* (1979) and Shimazono (2004), vitalism or vitalistic thought is concerned with the notion of salvation in this life. This idea, though derived from the study of new religions, is also discernible in contemporary Buddhist thought and practice. Shimazono describes characteristics that are typically found in vitalistic conceptions of salvation in this life. In brief, these characteristics point to belief in a life-nurturing universe in which human beings and other sentient beings actively participate. Religiously, there is an ultimate reality or a transcendent being that is the source of life. Human beings spring from this source. Salvation involves connecting to the source of life here and now. From a Buddhist point of view, human suffering is the result of separation from this source of life. Depending on the Buddhist tradition, the source of life is Amida Buddha, or the eternal Buddha, or Dainichi Nyorai, or one's own self-cultivation that brings one to a transcendent understanding of this vitalistic notion. Buddhist salvation, or enlightenment, entails complete happiness or bliss in this life.

Contemporary Buddhist Rituals: Monastic and Lay

Traditional practices are important to Temple Buddhism. They provide opportunities for rigorous ascetic practice for those so inclined, but also attract attention when their clerics successfully accomplish a difficult religious practice. Tendai's extreme ascetic practice known as *kaihōgyō* (literally, "ascetic practice of circling the mountains") is a particularly good example of this combination of difficult spiritual practice coupled with deep public interest in the outcome. In addition to monastic practices, there are important examples of contemporary rituals that are especially popular among the Buddhist laity, such as pilgrimage circuits that attract thousands every year. Finally, there are rituals, sometimes controversial, that are focused on particular social or personal problems, such as *mizuko kuyō* rites dealing with spiritual issues related to abortion.

In the Tendai lineage *kaihōgyō* ritual – the ascetic practice of circling the mountains – the ritual practitioner traverses paths through the sacred mountainside of Mt. Hiei, the location of Tendai's main temple and spiritual center. Ascetic monks (*gyōja*; sometimes referred to as "marathon monks") who engage in this practice daily stop at over 250 sacred sites along the pilgrimage path. These sites include everything from temples, Shintō shrines, graves, trees, stones, waterfalls – any place along the mountainside associated with sacred events and occurrences.

The *kaihōgyō* practice that is most famous is also the most difficult. It is a seven-year, thousand-day circumambulation (*sennichi kaihōgyō*) of Mt. Hiei and environs, in some years including the city of Kyoto. *Sennichi kaihōgyō* includes the equivalent of running a marathon a day for 100 or 200 days in a row (depending on the year) over a seven-year period. In the fifth year, there is an additional component of this ritual that includes nine days without food, water, or sleep.

There are a number of rites that are performed within the larger context of the seven-year practice. Some of these are rituals that have a long history within Tendai tradition, going back to its sixth-century Chinese founder, Zhiyi. For instance, *gyōja* engage in the the constantly walking meditation (*jōgyō zanmai*), one of the four types of meditation (*shishu zanmai*) practiced in Tendai, as they circumambulate the mountain. A *gyōja* also performs ritual practices, such as symbolic hand gestures (mudras) and chanting short efficacious ritual words and phrases (mantras), in order to gain the protection of Fudō myōō. The *gyōja* identifies with Fudō myōō, a deity who provides assistance and secures one's safety, destroys hindrances to spiritual practice, and conquers evil.

Arguably the most difficult, and certainly the most dangerous, ritual is *dōiri* ("hall-entering"), a nine-day (182-hour) confinement in which the *gyōja* may not eat, drink, sleep, or recline. This ritual occurs in the fifth year of the seven-year practice. The *gyōja* spends this time engaged in sutra and mantra recitation. During this period of sequestration, and especially in the later days, *gyōja* report experiencing a very heightened spiritual and sensory awareness. They are able, it is said, to be able to hear the ash from an incense stick fall on the floor and to smell food being cooked miles away.

The completion of the *sennichi kaihōgyō* marks a spiritual attainment that very few have ever achieved – according to Tendai literature, 48 *gyōja* have completed the seven-year ritual since 1585 and 11 of these are since 1945. One of the notions animating this difficult physical and mental practice is that pain and extreme asceticism contribute to spiritual transformation. A successful *gyōja* is understood to have realized the Buddha-nature (*busshō*) and thus attained enlightenment and is now considered and treated as a living Buddha. Japanese Tendai monks who have successfully completed *kaihōgyō* are treated with the kind of media attention usually directed at movie stars, pop singers, and politicians. Books and films about the *kaihōgyō* monks are extremely popular.

Pilgrimages to sacred sites have a long history in Japanese Buddhism. Once the activity of ascetic monks and nuns, they have, in contemporary Japan, become a very popular practice for lay Buddhists and for those just interested in the tourist aspects of such travel. We might wonder about the extent to which the pilgrims are also tourists and the tourists, whether they intend it or nor, are also pilgrims. There are elements of contemporary pilgrimage practice that made it sometimes difficult to distinguish between the two. Pilgrims and tourists often engage in the same kinds of rituals when at a pilgrimage site, and both are likely to visit the temple shop for souvenirs, both spiritual and otherwise. Reasons for undertaking a pilgrimage vary, but include this-worldly benefits, such as curing a disease or the attainment of wealth, as well as spiritual benefits.

Scholars working on Japanese pilgrimage often distinguish between two different kinds of ritual travel, linear and circular, that employ different terminology. (For a concise overview of the different terms used to describe Japanese pilgrimages, see Ambros 2006). A linear pilgrimage is religious travel to a sacred place (such as Mt. Hiei or Mt. Kōya) or a particular temple. In a circular pilgrimage one completes a circuit of multiple temples or sacred sites in a prescribed order. For instance, the Saikoku pilgrimage (Saikoku *junrei*) in western Honshū is a circular route to 33 sacred places connected with the bodhisattva Kannon (Skt. Avalokiteśvara; "Regarder of the Cries of the World"). Included among these 33 sacred sites, where the main object of veneration is usually Kannon, are some of Japan's oldest, best-known, and most visited temples, such as Hasedera, Kiyomizudera, Miidera (Onjōji), Rokuharamitsuji, and Ishiyamadera. The number of sites, 33, corresponds to the narrative in *Lotus Sūtra*, chapter 25, which explains that the bodhisattva Kannon takes on 33 different forms depending on the spiritual needs of the faithful. In addition to the Saikoku *junrei*, there are numerous other Kannon pilgrimage circuits throughout different parts of Japan.

The most famous circular pilgrimage route is the Pilgrimage to the Eighty-Eight Temples of Shikoku (Shikoku *henro*), which is connected with the ninth-century founder of Japanese Shingon, Kūkai (honorific name, Kōbō Daishi). The term *henro*, used to refer to the Shikoku pilgrimage, is also the word used for a pilgrim on this route. The 88 temples of the Shikoku pilgrimage are spread across a 750-mile circuit that goes around much of the island of Shikoku, one of Japan's four main islands. The circuit traverses a diverse topography, including seacoast, mountains, forests, and cities.

Pilgrims are easy to spot because they wear white robes. The white robe symbolizes a willingness to die along the spiritual journey and is similar in appearance to traditional funeral shrouds. In addition, pilgrims don a sedge hat and carry a pilgrim staff, begging bowl, and bell. At each temple, pilgrims climb 108 steps, which correspond to the number of sins delineated in Buddhist doctrine, as a way to acknowledge and expiate these sins. Pilgrims also typically burn incense, ring the temple bell, make an offering, and chant the *Heart Sūtra*. Pilgrims also carry a book for gathering the stamps of each temple visited.

Traditionally a pilgrim walked the route relying on alms (*settai*) from those living along the circuit for food and other necessities. Such a walk can take two or three months. Those with less time or physical stamina can take a tour bus or car, completing the full circuit in a week. Religious tourism of this kind is not difficult, but it is still considered to have spiritual merit. Others combine walking and riding, or only visit some of the temples, returning on multiple occasions until all temples have been visited. The order in which one follows the circuit is considered spiritually significant.

Although the Shikoku pilgrimage is Shingon-related because of the focus on Kūkai, it is nevertheless attractive to most Buddhists regardless of family lineage affiliation. Although each of the 88 temples has a hall that enshrines Kūkai (Daishidō), a characteristic of Shingon temples throughout Japan, the 88 temples represent several non-Shingon lineages and have main halls that enshrine a number of different Buddhas, bodhisattvas, and Buddhist protective deities.

Legend has it that Kūkai, who is said to have originated this pilgrimage, is traveling the circuit, also in pilgrim's garb, but going in the direction opposite from contemporary pilgrims, who are told they may pass Kūkai along the way. Related to this focus on Kūkai is the idea that the pilgrim and Kūkai are "walking together as a pair" (*dōgyō ninin*) – the pilgrim's staff represents Kūkai and has the characters for *dōgyō ninin* inked onto it.

Because the Shikoku pilgrimage is on the island of Shikoku, somewhat remote from Japan's main population centers, and because of the length of the circuit and the time it takes to complete, miniature versions of this popular pilgrimage have been created in some 40 locations throughout Japan. These smaller versions make it possible for pilgrims to gain the spiritual benefits of doing the actual Shikoku pilgrimage but without the time and financial expense. At some of these miniaturized sites, the possibility of gaining the same spiritual benefits is enhanced because soil from the actual Shikoku temple sites has been taken to the corresponding temple at the reproduced site (Reader 2005).

The term *mizuko kuyō* refers to a Buddhist ritual conducted for the well being and happy rebirth of miscarried or aborted fetuses. The word for fetus is *mizuko* (literally, "water child") and the word *kuyō* refers to a ritual memorial service. The *mizuko kuyō* practice became commonplace starting in the 1970s and continues to the present, though not without controversy. The controversy, however, is unlike debates in the United States over the morality of abortion. In Japan, where abortion is legal, the debates over *mizuko kuyō* are not usually about the morality of abortion, but rather whether distressed women are being preyed upon by the promotion of abortion rituals by some Buddhist temples.

For many temples that specialize in *mizuko kuyō*, these memorial services are their primary source of income. Some oppose the practice of *mizuko kuyō* because they see it as a crass way for *mizuko kuyō* temples to make money (fees for such rituals are typically quite high) from women and families in distress. Women, they assert, are manipulated by unscrupulous temples into extreme guilt about having an abortion and the need to set things right by spending money on *mizuko kuyō* rituals, memorial statues of Jizō – the bodhisattva who, among other things, is believed to protect children and the unborn – and other items in order to ameliorate the mother's potentially bad karmic consequence and to assure the aborted fetus a transition to a happy rebirth. These abortion rituals also sometimes involve the mother apologizing to the *mizuko* for putting it through such a horrendous ordeal and praying for its happy rebirth. This is often followed by a naming rite for the unborn child.

Making matters worse is the assertion – often made in temple advertising campaigns – that it is only through the practice of *mizuko kuyō* that the potential for retribution (*tatari*) by the angry spirits of spiritually unsettled fetuses can be ameliorated. Some argue that these practices are simply geared toward financial gain at the expense of women in distress. For these and other reasons, some Buddhist lineages are formally against the practice. For instance, Jōdo Shinshū opposes the practice of *mizuko kuyō* because it preys on the fear that the dead can take vengeance on the living; in this case the aborted fetus on the mother.

The debate, then, is not about the morality of abortion but about the morality of how certain temples push the necessity of *mizuko kuyō* rites. Is the practice of *mizuko kuyō* better understood as taking advantage of women in emotional distress for financial gain, or does this practice in fact play an important social role of ameliorating guilt and providing a positive therapeutic frame around an otherwise emotionally difficult experience? There are some who suggest that even if *mizuko kuyō* is a problematic ritual, it is, in the end, no different than spending money on funeral rituals for a deceased family member.

Buddhist scholars have debated the meaning of *mizuko kuyō* and why it is such a powerful symbolic rite. LaFleur (1992), in an important monograph on the history and meaning of *mizuko kuyō*, suggests that given the Buddhist context and the concept of rebirth, the notion of abortion can be seen in terms of postponing the birth of the fetus and not permanently ending life. Whether many women and families who have had abortions see the matter this way is unclear (Hardacre 1997).

Buddhism in Contemporary Japanese Culture

Films – including animated films (*anime*) – fiction, poetry, comics (*manga*), and various forms of new media have all been vehicles for expressing Buddhist thought in contemporary Japan. Sometimes these conceptualizations of Buddhist thought and practice are overt and other times they are simply implied or hinted at. The list of Buddhist-related media productions is long. Important examples include the very popular cartoon series by Tezuka Osamu (1928–1989), the highly regarded *manga* artist, entitled *Buddha* (now translated in an eight-volume English edition) that ran between 1972 and 1979; the *anime* series *Ikkyū-san*, which aired on Japanese television between 1975 and 1982, based on stories chronicling the Buddhist training of a young Ikkyū, an important fifteenth-century Zen monk; and, more subtly, some of the themes and images in the animated films of Miyazaki Hayao. Miyazaki's films are indicative of ways in which Buddhist ideas are blended with Shintō and other expressions of Japanese values. The sheer number and popularity of Buddhist-themed media underscores the extent to which Buddhist thought and practice continues to engage Japanese society. Not surprisingly, traditional Buddhist lineages and new and new new Buddhist movements all have a presence on the internet, using this medium as a way to present their doctrines to the public, offer services, announce events, and otherwise promote their activities (MacWilliams 2012).

Buddhist ideas and images are also found in contemporary art and architecture. Takaguchi Yoshiyuki (b. 1940) is an architect and an ordained Jōdo shū priest. His architectural designs are informed by his Buddhist sensibilities. As head priest at

Isshinji temple in Osaka from 1972 to 2005, he designed and built temple buildings for Isshinji. Temple buildings typically include Buddhist art, such as statues, paintings, and calligraphy. Takaguchi's temple buildings included art, but these were works he commissioned from secular contemporary artists, not from professional temple artists (Graham 2007: 238–241).

Another example of Buddhist imagery in contemporary Japanese art is the work of Mori Mariko (b. 1967; known more widely as Mariko Mori). Her creations include elements of performance, technology, video, fashion, and religious imagery. Examples of Buddhist imagery in her work include ideas and images related to the Pure Land of Amida Buddha and to the bodhisattva Kannon. She uses these Buddhist images to explore issues of personal identity, memory, and tradition. Her *Dream Temple* project (1998) was sparked by her interest in the Yumedono (Dream Hall) at Nara's Hōryūji temple. The object of worship at Yumedono is a Kannon image. Mori, in a discussion of this project, related that she wanted to express her own vision of what she felt was the transcendent beauty of the temple and statue of Kannon (Graham 2007: 268–269).

Prospects

This book has examined centuries of Japanese interactions with Buddhist thought and practice. In this historical process, we have seen ways that Japanese perspectives on the world have changed as a result of engagements with Buddhist traditions. We have also charted some of the ways that Buddhist thought and practice were transformed as a result of Japanese cultural sensibilities. The diversity of ideas, doctrines, rituals, and material culture that comprise the Japanese Buddhist historical record should make us mindful that Japanese Buddhism is better conceived of as multiple Buddhism(s) deployed in different times and places to meet a variety of needs and purposes. These multiple Buddhism(s) may share a family resemblance, but it is also important to understand the differences and disagreements between these many traditions.

It is, of course, impossible to know Japanese Buddhism's future prospects, but it is inevitable that these traditions will continue to change and adapt in relation to transformations in Japanese culture. Much as Mori has used Buddhist images and symbols in her art projects, such Buddhist representations are likely to appear in future Japanese cultural productions of all kinds. Regardless of whether one is a practicing Buddhist, Buddhist ideas and imagery permeate Japanese culture in a variety of ways, and in much the same way that ideas and images drawn from Christian and Jewish religious traditions are part of the American cultural vernacular. It is also probable that new forms of Buddhism will develop, much as Buddhist new religions were founded after the Meiji Restoration as responses to the spiritual, social, and other needs of new generations of Japanese disaffected by older forms of Buddhist thought and practice.

Finally, we would simply note that just as Japanese Buddhist traditions have transformed over time, so has Japanese Buddhist scholarship. The current generation of scholars of Japanese Buddhism has focused on issues such as the roles played by lay and monastic Buddhist women over the course of Japanese Buddhist history, and on nineteenth- and twentieth-century Buddhist thought and practice. Subsequent scholars will continue to fill in the gaps of our knowledge of Japanese Buddhist cultural history and will reframe historical narratives in new ways, utilizing new theories and methods. This volume is a modest attempt to chart the current state of a cultural history of Japanese Buddhism.

References

Ambros, Barbara. 2006. "Geography, Environment, Pilgrimage." In Paul L. Swanson and Clark Chilson (eds.), *Nanzan Guide to Japanese Religions*, 289–308. Honolulu: University of Hawai'i Press.

Graham, Patricia J. 2007. *Faith and Power in Japanese Buddhist Art, 1600–2005*. Honolulu, University of Hawai'i Press.

Hubbard, Jamie, and Paul L. Swanson, eds. 1997. *Pruning the Bodhi Tree: The Storm Over Critical Buddhism*. Honolulu, University of Hawai'i Press.

Itō Yuishin, and Fujii Masao, eds. 1997. *Sōsai Bukkyō: Sano rekishi to gendaiteki kadai*. Tokyo: Nonburu.

Kawahashi, Noriko. 1995. "Jizoku (Priests' Wives) in Sōtō Zen Buddhism: An Ambiguous Category." *Japanese Journal of Religious Studies* 22 (1–2): 161–183.

Kawahashi, Noriko. 2012. "Re-Imagining Buddhist Women in Contemporary Japan." In Inken Prohl and John Nelson (eds.), *Handbook of Contemporary Japanese Religions*, 197–212. Leiden and Boston: Brill.

Kawahashi, Noriko, and Masako Kuroki, eds. 2003. "Feminism and Religion in Contemporary Japan." Special issue of *Japanese Journal of Religious Studies* 30 (3–4).

Kawano, Satsuki. 2012. "From the 'Tradition' to a Choice: Recent Developments in Mortuary Practices." In Inken Prohl and John Nelson (eds.), *Handbook of Contemporary Japanese Religions*, 413–430. Leiden and Boston: Brill.

Kisala, Robert, and Mark R. Mullins, eds. 2001. *Religion and Social Crisis in Japan: Understanding Japanese Society Through the Aum Affair*. New York: Palgrave.

LaFleur, William R. 1992. *Liquid Life: Abortion and Buddhism in Japan*. Princeton, NJ: Princeton University Press.

MacWilliams, Mark. 2012. "Religion and Manga." In Inken Prohl and John Nelson (eds.), *Handbook of Contemporary Japanese Religions*, 595–628. Leiden and Boston: Brill.

Murakami Shigeyoshi. 1980. *Japanese Religion in the Modern Century*. Trans. H. Byron Earhart. Tokyo: University of Tokyo Press.

Reader, Ian. 1988. "The Rise of a Japanese 'New New Religion': Themes in the Development of Agonshū." *Japanese Journal of Religious Studies* 15 (4): 235–261.

Reader, Ian. 2000. *Religious Violence in Contemporary Japan: The Case of Aum Shinrikyō.* Honolulu: University of Hawai'i Press.

Reader, Ian. 2005. *Making Pilgrimages: Meaning and Practice in Shikoku.* Honolulu: University of Hawai'i Press.

Rowe, Mark Michael. 2011. *Bonds of the Dead: Temples, Burial, and the Transformation of Contemporary Japanese Buddhism.* Chicago: University of Chicago Press.

Shimazono Susumu. 1992. *Shin-shinshūkyō to shūkyō būmu.* Tokyo: Iwanami Shoten.

Shimazono, Susumu. 1995. "In the Wake of Aum." *Japanese Journal of Religious Studies* 22 (3–4): 381–415.

Shimazono Susumu. 1997. *Gendai shūkyō no kanōsei: Oumu Shinrkyō to bōryoku.* Tokyo: Iwanami Shoten.

Shimazono Susumu. 2003. "Shinshūkyō to Bukkyō." In Ōkubo Ryōshin *et al.* (eds.), *Nihon Bukkyō 34 no Kagi*, 290–298. Tokyo: Shunjusha.

Shimazono, Susumu. 2004. *From Salvation to Spirituality: Popular Religious Movements in Modern Japan.* Melbourne: Trans Pacific Press.

Stone, Jacqueline. 1999. "Some Reflections on Critical Buddhism." *Japanese Journal of Religious Studies* 26: 159–188.

Stone, Jacqueline I. 2006. "Buddhism." In Paul L. Swanson and Clark Chilson (eds.), *Nanzan Guide to Japanese Religions*, 38–64. Honolulu: University of Hawai'i Press.

Tamamuro Taijō. 1963. *Sōshiki bukkyō.* Tokyo: Daihōrinkaku.

Tamura, Yoshiro. 2000. *Japanese Buddhism: A Cultural History.* Trans. Jeffrey Hunter. Tokyo: Kōsei Shuppansha.

Tsushima Michihito, Nishiyama Shigeru, Shimazono Susumu, and Shiramizu Hiroko. 1979. "The Vitalistic Conception of Salvation in Japanese New Religions: An Aspect of Modern Religious Consciousness." *Japanese Journal of Religious Studies* 6 (1–2): 139–161.

Walter, Mariko N. 2008. "The Structure of Japanese Buddhist Funerals." In Jacqueline I. Stone and Mariko Namba Walter (eds.), *Death and the Afterlife in Japanese Buddhism*, 247–292. Honolulu: University of Hawai'i Press.

Watanabe Masako. 2002. "Shinshūkyō to josei." In Inoue Teruko, Ueno Chizuko, Ehara Yumiko, Ōsawa Mari, and Kanō Mikiyo (eds.), *Iwanami joseigaku jiten*, 259–260. Tokyo: Iwanami Shoten.

Woodard, William P. 1972. *The Allied Occupation of Japan 1945–1952 and Japanese Religions.* Leiden: E. J. Brill.

Further Reading

Ambros, Barbara R. 2012a. *Bones of Contention: Animals and Religion in Contemporary Japan.* Honolulu: University of Hawai'i Press.

Ambros, Barbara R. 2012b. "*Petto Kuyō*: Changing Views of Animal Spirits in Contemporary Japan." In Inken Prohl and John Nelson (eds.), *Handbook of Contemporary Japanese Religions*, 487–507. Leiden and Boston: Brill.

Bodiford, William. 1996. "Zen and the Art of Religious Prejudice: Efforts to Reform a Tradition of Social Discrimination." *Japanese Journal of Religious Studies* 23 (1–2): 1–27.

Constitution of Japan. http://japan.kantei.go.jp/constitution_and_government_of_japan/constitution_e.html.

Covell, Stephen G. 2004. "Learning to Persevere: The Popular Teachings of Tendai Ascetics." *Japanese Journal of Religious Studies* 31 (2): 255–287.

Covell, Stephen G. 2012. "Money and the Temple: Law, Taxes and the Image of Buddhism." In Inken Prohl and John Nelson (eds.), *Handbook of Contemporary Japanese Religions*,159–176. Leiden and Boston: Brill.

Covell, Stephen G., and Mark Rowe, eds. 2004. "Traditional Buddhism in Contemporary Japan." Special issue of *Japanese Journal of Religious Studies* 31 (2).

Hardacre, Helen. 1984. *Lay Buddhism in Contemporary Japan: Reiyūkai Kyōdan*. Princeton, NJ: Princeton University Press.

Heisig, James W., and John C. Maraldo, eds. 1995. *Rude Awakenings: Zen, the Kyoto School, and the Question of Nationalism*. Honolulu: University of Hawai'i Press.

Horii, Mitsutoshi. 2006. "Deprofessionalisation of Buddhist Priests in Contemporary Japan: A Socio-Industrial Study of a Religious Profession." *Electronic Journal of Contemporary Japanese Studies*. At www.japanesestudies.org.uk/articles/2006/Horii.html.

Hubbard, Jamie. 1998. "Embarrassing Superstition, Doctrine, and the Study of New Religious Movements." *Journal of the American Academy of Religion* 66 (1): 59–92.

Ikeda, Eishun. 1998. "Teaching Assemblies and Lay Societies in the Formation of Modern Sectarian Buddhism." *Japanese Journal of Religious Studies* 25 (1–2): 11–44.

Ikeda Eishun *et al.*, eds. 2000. *Gendai Nihon to Bukkyō*. 4 vols. Tokyo: Heibonsha.

Metraux, Daniel. 1988. *The History and Theology of Sōka Gakkai: A Japanese New Religion*. Lewiston, NY: Edwin Mellen Press.

Metraux, Daniel A. 1994. *The Sōka Gakkai Revolution*. Lanham, MD: University Press of America.

Metraux, Daniel A. 1996. "The Sōka Gakkai: Buddhism and the Creation of a Harmonious and Peaceful Society." In Christopher S. Queen and Sallie B. King (eds.), *Engaged Buddhism: Buddhist Liberation Movements in Asia*, 365–400. Albany: State University of New York Press.

Mitsunaga Kakudō. 1996. *Sennichi kaihōgyō*. Tokyo: Shunjūsha.

Murata, Kiyoaki. 1969. *Japan's New Buddhism: An Objective Account of the Soka Gakkai*. New York and Tokyo: Weatherhill.

Nelson, John K. 2012. "Japanese Secularities and the Decline of Temple Buddhism." *Journal of Religion in Japan* 1 (1): 37–60.

Nishiyama Shigeru. 1979. "Shinshūkyō no genkyō." *Rekishi kōron* 517: 33–37.

Prohl, Inken, and John Nelson, eds. *Handbook of Contemporary Japanese Religions*. Leiden and Boston: Brill.

Reader, Ian. 1991. *Religion in Contemporary Japan*. Honolulu: University of Hawai'i Press.

Reader, Ian, and Paul L. Swanson. 1997. "Editor's Introduction: Pilgrimage in the Japanese Religious Tradition." *Japanese Journal of Religious Studies* 24 (3–4): 225–270.

Reader, Ian, and George J. Tanabe, Jr. 1998. *Practically Religious: Worldly Benefits and the Common Religion of Japan*. Honolulu: University of Hawai'i Press.

Rhodes, Robert F. 1987. "The kaihōgyō Practice of Mt. Hiei." *Japanese Journal of Religious Studies* 14: 185–202.

Riggs, Diane E. 2004. *"Fukudenkai*: Sewing the Buddha's Robe in Contemporary Japanese Buddhist Practice." *Japanese Journal of Religious Studies* 31 (2): 311–356.

Rowe, Mark Michael 2004. "Where the Action Is: Sites of Contemporary Sōtō Buddhism."

Sharf, Robert H. 1995. "Sanbōkyōdan: Zen and the Way of the New Religions." *Japanese Journal of Religious Studies* 22 (3–4): 417–458.

Shimazono, Susumu. 1991. "The Expansion of Japan's New Religions into Foreign Cultures." *Japanese Journal of Religious Studies* 18 (2–3): 105–132.

Shimazono, Susumu. 1999. "Sōka Gakkai and the Modern Reformation of Buddhism." In Yosinori Takeuchi (ed.), *Buddhist Spirituality: Later China, Korea, Japan and the Modern World*, 435–454. New York: Crossroad Publishing Company.

Shimazono Susumu. 2006. "Contemporary Japanese Religions." In Paul L. Swanson and Clark Chilson (eds.), *Nanzan Guide to Japanese Religions*, 220–231. Honolulu: University of Hawai'i Press.

Stevens, John. 1988. *Marathon Monks of Mount Hiei*. Boston: Shambhala.

Sueki Fumihiko *et al.*, eds. 2011. *Gendai bukkyō no kanōsei* (Shin Ajia bukkyōshi 15, Nihon 5). Tokyo: Kōsei Shuppansha.

Swanson, Paul L. 1993. "'Zen is not Buddhism': Recent Japanese Critiques of Buddha-Nature." *Numen* 40: 115–149.

Swanson, Paul L., and Clark Chilson, eds. 2006. *Nanzan Guide to Japanese Religions*. Honolulu: University of Hawai'i Press.

Tsutsui, William M., ed. 2007. *A Companion to Japanese History*. Oxford: Blackwell.

Uchino, Kumiko. 1983. "The Status Elevation Process of Sōtō Sect Nuns in Modern Japan." *Japanese Journal of Religious Studies* 10/2–3: 177–194.

White, James. 1970. *The Sōka Gakkai and Mass Society*. Stanford, CA: Stanford University Press.

Character Glossary

The glossary lists characters for prominent Japanese terms, names, and phrases. Where appropriate, related (i.e., associated) terminology is also provided.

adashikuni no kami (alt. *tonarinokuni no kami, banshin*) 蕃神

Agon shū 阿含宗

Agui 安居院

ajari 阿闍梨

Ajaseō-kyō 阿闍世王経

akunin shōki 悪人正機

Amaterasu Ōmikami (alt. Tenshō Daijin) 天照大神

Amida 阿弥陀

Anyōji 安養寺

Asahara Shōkō 麻原彰晃

Asai Ryōi 浅井了意

Ashō 阿聖

Asuka 飛鳥

Asuka *bukkyō* 飛鳥仏教

Asukadera 飛鳥寺

Asukadera Daibutsu 飛鳥寺大仏

Atsuzōshi 厚造紙 (alt. 厚隻紙)

Aum Shinrikyō オウム真理教

Awa 安房

Ayahito no Yabo 漢人夜菩

Baisaō (alt. Maisaō) 売茶翁 (also, Gekkai Genshō 月海元昭)

baitoku 買得

bakufu 幕府

Bankai 鑁海

Basara ばさら (alt. 婆娑羅 etc.)

A Cultural History of Japanese Buddhism, First Edition. William E. Deal and Brian Ruppert.
© 2015 William E. Deal and Brian Ruppert. Published 2015 by John Wiley & Sons, Ltd.

Bekki 別記

bettō 別当 (rel. *bettōke* 別当家)

Bidatsu Tennō 敏達天皇

biku 比丘

bikuni 比丘尼

Birushana 毘盧遮那

Bishamonten 毘沙門天

biwa hōshi 琵琶法師

Biwako 琵琶湖

bodaiji 菩提寺

Bokkō-kutsu (Ch. Mogao-ku) 莫高窟

bōmori 坊守

Bongaku shinryō 梵学津梁

Bonmōkyō 梵網経

bonnō gusoku 煩悩具足

bosatsukai 菩薩戒

Bukkōji 仏光寺

Bukkyō katsu ron 仏教活論

Bukkyō Seito Dōshi Kai 仏教清徒同志会

Bukkyō tōitsu ron 仏教統一論

Bunchi 文智

burakumin 部落民

busshi 仏師

busshō 仏性

butsudō 仏堂

butsuji 仏事

byakugō (Skt. *ūrṇā*) 白毫

Byōdō'in 平等院

Chanoyu 茶の湯

Chigi (Ch. Zhiyi) 智顗

Chikotsu Dai'e 痴兀大慧 (also, Buttsū Zenji 仏通禅師)

Chikū 知空

Chinkai 珍海

Chinzei 鎮西

Chion'in 知恩院 (full name, Gachōzan Chionkyō'in Ōtanidera 華頂山知恩教院 大谷寺)

chishikiyui 知識結

Chōan (Ch. Chang'an) 長安

Chō'e 澄慧

Chōen 澄円

Chōfukuji 長福寺
Chōgen 重源
Chōken 澄憲
Chōnen 奝然
Chōsai 長西
Chōsen'in 長泉院
Chōzen 澄禅
Chūgūji 中宮寺
Chūhō Myōhon (Ch. Zhongfeng Mingben) 中峰明本
Chūron (Skt. *Mūlamadhyamaka-kārikā*) 中論
chūshakugaku 注釈学
chūshakusho 注釈書
Chūsonji 中尊寺

Dai-no-kawago 台皮子 (alt. 台皮籠)
Daianji 大安寺 (rel. Daikan Daiji 大官大寺)
Daibirushanakyō 大毘盧遮那経
daibutsu 大仏
Daifukuji 大福寺
Daigaku 大学
Daihannyakyō 大般若経
Daigo Tennō 醍醐天皇
Daigoji 醍醐寺 (rel. Kami Daigo 上醍醐)
daigongen 大権現
Daijō bussetsu ron hihan 大乗仏説論批判
daijōdaijin zenji (alt. *dajōdaijin zenji*) 太政大臣禅師 (rel. *daijin zenji* 大臣禅師)
Daijō'in 大乗院
Daikakuji 大覚寺
daikanjin-shiki 大勧進職
Daikokuten 大黒天
daimoku 題目
daimyō 大名
Dainichi 大日 (rel. Dainichi Nyorai 大日如来)
Dainichikyō 大日経
daiō 大王
daishi 大師 (rel. Kōbō Daishi 弘法大師, Ganzan Daishi 元三大師)
Daishi go-nyūjō kanketsu ki 大師御入定勘決記
Daishidō 大師堂
Daishōji 大聖寺
daisōjō 大僧正
Daitokuji 大徳寺

Daiyūzan 大雄山

dangi 談義 (rel. *dangi-bon* 談義本)

danna 檀那 (alt. 旦那)

danrin 談林

darani 陀羅尼 (rel. Daranisuke 陀羅尼助)

den 伝

dentō daihōshi 伝灯大法師

Dōgen 道元

dōgyō ninin 同行二人

dō'in sōbō 堂院僧坊

dōiri 堂入り

Dōja Chōgen (alt. Dōsha Chōgen, Ch. Daozhe Chaoyuan) 道者超元

Dōji 道慈

dōjō 道場

Dōkō 道興

Doku jinjakō bengi 読神社考弁疑

Dōkyō 道鏡

Dōryō Daigongen 道了大権現 (alt. Dōryō Gongen 道了権現)

Dōshin 導信

Dōshō 道昭

dōshu (alt. *dōju, dōshū*) 堂衆

Dōsōkaku (C. Daosengge) 道僧格

Dōtō 道登

e 会

e-maki 絵巻

e-toki 絵解き

Eben (alt. Ebin; K. Hyep'yon) 恵便

Echigo 越後

Edo 江戸

Eiga monogatari 栄華物語

Eihei shingi 永平清規 (full title: *Eihei Dōgen zenji shingi* 永平道元禅師清規)

Eiheiji 永平寺 (also called Kichijōzan 吉祥山)

Eison (alt. Eizon) 叡尊 (also called Kōshō bosatsu 興正菩薩)

eitai kuyōbo 永代供養墓

Emyō 恵妙 (alt. 慧妙)

En no gyōja 役行者 (also called En no ozunu / En no ozuno / En no otsuno 役小角)

Enchin 円珍 (also called Chishō Daishi 智証大師 / 智證大師)

Endon kanjin jūhokkai zu (Ch. *Yuandun guanxin shi fajie tu*) 円頓観心十法界図

Engakuji 円覚寺

engi 縁起

Enkō'in 円光院
ennen 延年
Enni Ben'en (alt. Enni Bennen, Enji Ben'en) 円爾弁円
Ennin 円仁 (rel. Jikaku Daishi 慈覚大師)
Enryakuji 延暦寺 (rel. *Enryakuji gokoku engi* 延暦寺護国縁起)
ensei 厭世
Enshō 円照 (also called Yūrenbō 遊蓮房)
Enshōji 円照寺
Erin 恵隣
Eryō 恵亮
Eshi 恵至
Eshin 恵心 (= Genshin 源信; rel. Eshin sōzu 恵心僧都, Eshin Sugiu-ryū 恵心椙生流)
Eun 恵雲
Ezenni 恵善尼

fubyōdō 不平等
fuda 札
Fudaraku Jōdo 補陀落浄土
Fudarakusen 補陀落山
Fudō 不動 (rel. Fudō myōō 不動明王)
Fujaku 普寂
Fuji-kō 富士講
Fujiwara 藤原 (rel. Fujiwara *hokke* 藤原北家)
Fujiwara no Atsumitsu 藤原敦光
Fujiwara no Kintō 藤原公任
Fujiwara no Michinaga 藤原道長
Fujiwara no Michinori 藤原通憲 (= Shinzei 信西)
Fujiwara no Moronaga 藤原師長
Fujiwara no Morosuke 藤原 師輔
Fujiwara Seika 藤原惺窩
Fujiwara no Tadahira 藤原忠平
Fujiwara Takamichi 藤原孝道
Fujiwara Tameaki 藤原為顕
Fujiwara no Teika (alt. Fujiwara Sadaie) 藤原定家
Fujiwara no Toshinari (alt. Shunzei) 藤原俊成
Fujiwara no Yorimichi 藤原頼通
Fujiwara no Yorinaga 藤原頼長
Fujiwarakyō 藤原京
fuju fuse 不受布施
fukaku 不覚
Fuke shū 普化宗 (also Fuke zenshū 普化禅宗, Komu shū 虚無宗)

Fukko Shintō　復古神道

Fukuda Gyōkai　福田行誠

Fukuryō　福亮

fumikura (alt. *fumigura, fugura,* mod. *bunko*)　文庫

Furukawa Rōsen　古河老川

Fusō ryakki (alt. *Fusō ryakuki*)　扶桑略記

gakuryo 学侶 (rel. *gakushō* 学生)

Gangōji　元興寺 (rel. Gangōji Gokurakubō 元興寺極楽坊)

Gangōji garan engi 元興寺伽藍縁起 (rel. *Gangōji garan engi narabi ni ruki shizai chō*
　元興寺伽藍縁起幷流記資財帳)

Ganjin (Ch. Jianzhen) 鑑真 (rel. Kakai Daishi 過海大師, Tōdai wajō 唐大和上)

ganmon (alt. *ganbumi*) 願文 (also called *hotsu ganmon* 発願文, *gansho* 願書)

garan 伽藍 (= *sanmen sōbō* 三面僧坊; abbreviation of *sōgaranma* 僧伽藍摩, also
　called *shūon* 衆園, *sōon* 僧園, *sōin* 僧院, *shōja* 精舎, *butsusatsu* 仏刹)

garan bukkyō 伽藍仏教

gasan 画賛 (= *san* 讃/賛)

Gedatsukai　解脱会

gegosha　外護者

gekokujō　下克上

Genji kuyō　源氏供養

Genji monogatari　源氏物語

Genkō shakusho　元亨釈書

Genmei Tennō　元明天皇

Genpi shō 玄秘鈔 (alt. 玄秘抄)

genpō　現報

Genrushō 源流章 (= *Jōdo hōmon genrushō* 浄土法門源流章)

Gensei 元政 (also called Fukakusa Shōnin 深草上人)

Genshin 源信 (*see* Eshin)

Genshō Tennō　元正天皇

genze riyaku (alt. *gense riyaku*) 現世利益 (also *genyaku* 現益, *genshōyaku* 現生益)

genzokusō　還俗僧

gesu 下衆 (rel. *geshi/gesu* 下司)

geten　外典

Gidarinji 祇陀林寺 (alt. Kōhan'in 広幡院)

Gien　義演

Gijō (Ch. Ijing) 義浄

Gikai　儀海

giki (Ch. *yigui*) 儀軌

Gion 祇園 (rel. Gionsha 祇園社, Gion shōja 祇園精舎)

Gishi-wajin-den　魏志倭人伝

gishiki sho 儀式書

gō (Skt. *karma*) 業

Go-Daigo 後醍醐

Go-Fukakusa'in Nijō 後深草院二条

Go-Mizuno'o 後水之尾

Go-ryū shōgyō 御流聖教

Go-Sanjō 後三条

Go-seibai shikimoku 御成敗式目 (also called *Jōei shikimoku* 貞永式目)

Go-shichinichi mishiho (alt. mishuhō) 後七日御修法

Go-toba 後鳥羽

godaiji 五大寺

goganji 御願寺 (also called *chokuganji* 勅願寺, *gogan* 御願)

Gogatsu tsuitachi kyō 五月一日経

gohō 後報

gohonzon ご本尊

gojisō 護持僧 (alt. 御持僧; also called *yoinosō* 夜居僧)

Gōke shidai 江家次第 (also called *Gōsochi shidai* 江帥次第, *Gō shidai* 江次第, *Masafusa shō* 匡房抄, *Gō shō* 江抄)

gokoku zuhō (alt. *gokoku shuhō/suhō*) 護国修法

Gokuraku Jōdo 極楽浄土 (rel. Gokurakuji 極楽寺)

gokuraku wa mui nehan no kai nari (alt. *gokuraku mui nehangai*) 極楽無為涅槃界

goma 護摩

Gongen-sama 権現様

gonjin (alt. gonshin) 権神

Gozan 五山 (rel. Gozan-ban 五山版)

Gufukuji 弘福寺

Gukan shō 愚管抄

Gushi 愚志

Guze Kannon (alt. Kuse Kannon) 救世観音

Gyōga 行雅

gyōja 行者

Gyōki (alt. Gyōgi) 行基 (also called Gyōki bosatsu 行基菩薩)

Gyōnen (alt. Gyōzen) 凝然 (also called Gyōnen daitoku 凝然大徳, Jikan kokushi 示観国師)

gyōnin 行人

Hachiman 八幡

Hachiman daibosatsu 八幡大菩薩

hafuribe 祝部

Hagaji (alt. Hagadera) 羽賀寺

Haguro 羽黒

haibutsu kishaku 廃仏毀釈

haja kenshō 破邪顕正 (also called *haken* 破顕)

Hakamaya Noriaki 袴谷憲昭

Haku Kyoi (Ch. Bai Juyi) 白居易 (also called Hakuraktuen [Ch. Bailetian] 白楽天)

Hakuhō 白鳳 (rel. Hakuhō bukkyō 白鳳仏教)

Hakuin Ekaku 白隠慧鶴 (also called Kōrin 鵠林, Shōjū kokushi 正宗国師)

Hamurogumi 葉室組

Hasedera (alt. Chōkokuji) 長谷寺 (alt. 初瀬寺, also called Hatsusedera 泊瀬寺, Buzanji 豊山寺)

hasshū 八宗

Hata 秦

hatto 法度

Hayashi Razan 林羅山 (also called Rafushi 羅孚子)

Heian 平安

Heiankyō 平安京

Heijō 平城 (rel. Heijōkyō 平城京 [alt. Heizeikyō])

Heijō 平壌 (K. Pyongyang)

Heike nōkyō 平家納経

Heizei Tennō 平城天皇

henro 遍路

henro ishi 遍路石

hibutsu 秘仏

Hie (alt. Hiyoshi) 日吉

Hiei (alt. Hie) 比叡 (rel. Hieizan 比叡山)

hihan bukkyō 批判仏教

hijiri 聖 (rel. *nenbutsu hijiri* 念仏聖, *ichi no hijiri* 市聖)

Hiko 英彦

Himiko (alt. Himeko, Pimiko) 卑弥呼

hinin 非人 (rel. *shukuhinin* 宿非人)

Hiraizumi 平泉

Hirata Atsutane 平田篤胤

Hitachi 常陸

Hizen 肥前

hō 法

hōben 方便 (rel. *hōben kedo* 方便化土)

hō'e 法会 (rel. *e* 会)

hōgen 法眼

hōi 法位

hōin 法印

hōjō-e 放生会

Hōjō ki 方丈記

Hōjō Sadatoki　北条貞時

Hōjō Tokimune　北条時宗

Hōjō Tokiyori　北条時頼

Hōjōji　法成寺

Hokekyō (Ch. *Fahuajing*)　法華経 (= *Myōhō renge kyō* 妙法蓮華経)

Hokekyō jikidan shō　法華経直談鈔

Hokke genki　法華驗記 (alt. *Honchō hokke genki* 本朝法華驗記, *Dai nihon hokke genki* 大日本国法華驗記)

Hokke hakkō'e　法華八講会 (more commonly, Hokke hakkō 法華八講)

hokke hijiri　法華聖

Hokke mandara　法華曼荼羅

Hokke metsuzai no tera　法華滅罪之寺

Hokke shū　法華宗 (rel. Hokke Shintō 法華神道)

Hokke zanmaidō　法華三昧堂

Hokkedō　法華堂

Hokkeji　法華寺

hokkyō (alt. *hōkyō*)　法橋

Hōkōji　方広寺 (also called Daibutsuden 大仏殿, Kyōto Daibutsu 京都大仏)

Hōkōji　法興寺 (also called Asukadera 飛鳥寺)

Hōkoku Daimyōjin　豊国大明神

hokōzen　歩行禅

Hokuriku　北陸

Hōkyōji　宝鏡寺 (also called Ningyōdera 人形寺, Dodonogosho 百々御所)

hon-matsu　本末 (rel. *matsuji* 末寺, *hon-matsu seido* 本末制度)

Honchō monzui　本朝文粋

Honchō shinsen den　本朝神仙伝

hondō　本堂

Hōnen　法然 (rel. *Hōnen shōnin denki* 法然上人伝記)

hongaku　本覚

Hongan　本願

Honganji　本願寺 (rel. Higashi Honganji 東本願寺, Nishi Honganji 西本願寺, Ishiyama Honganji 石山本願寺)

honji-suijaku　本地垂迹 (rel. *hon-jaku* 本迹)

honjōtan (alt. *honshōtan*; Skt. *jātaka*)　本生譚

Honkokuji　本圀寺 (also called Daikōzan 大光山)

Honnōji　本能寺

Honshū　本州

Honzan-ha　本山派 (also called Shōgo'in-ha 聖護院派, Shōgo'in-ryū 聖護院流)

honzon　本尊 (rel. *myōgō honzon* 名号本尊)

hōō　法王

hōō kyūshiki　法王宮職

Hōon'in 報恩院

Hōonkō 報恩講 (rel. Hōon'e 報恩会)

hōrin 法輪

Hōrin 宝林

hōryū 法流

Hōryūji 法隆寺

Hōshi 法師

hosshin 発心

Hosshin waka shū 発心和歌集

Hosshōji 法性寺 (temple of Northern Fujiwara House, distinct from Hosshōji below)

Hosshōji 法勝寺 (Sovereign Shirakawa's construction, distinct from Hosshōji above)

Hossō (Ch. Faxiang) 法相

hōtō (alt. *hōzu*) 法頭

hotsugan 発願

hōwa 法話

hōza 法座

Hyakuron (Ch. *Bailun*) 百論

hyōbyaku (alt. *hyōhyaku, hyōhaku*) 表白 (rel. *keibyaku* 啓白, *kaibyaku* 開白)

Ichigū Wo Terasu Undō 一隅を照らす運動

Ichijō'in 一乗院

Ie 家

igō 位号

igyō 異形

Ikarugadera 斑鳩寺

Ikeda Daisaku 池田大作

ikibotoke 生き仏

ikki 一揆 (rel. *gohō ikki* 護法一揆, *hokke ikki* 法華一揆, *ikkō ikki* 一向一揆)

Ikkō shū 一向宗

Ikkyū 一休 (rel. *Ikkyū-san* 一休さん)

Imitsu 意密

in 院

Inada 稲田

inga (Skt. *hetu-phala*) 因果

inge (alt. *inke*) 院家 (rel. *monzeki* 門跡)

ingei 印契

Ingen Ryūki (Ch. Yinyuan Longqi) 隠元隆琦

innen (Skt. *hetu-pratyaya*) 因縁

Inoue Enryō 井上円了

Inoue Tetsujirō 井上哲次郎

inzō (alt. *insō*; Skt. *mudrā*) 印相 (also called *in* 印, *ingei* 印契, *mitsu'in* 密印)

Ippen 一遍 (rel. *Ippen hijiri-e* 一遍聖絵)

Ise 伊勢 (rel. *Ise monogatari* 伊勢物語, Ise Anyōji 伊勢安養寺, Ise Jingū 伊勢神宮)

Ishime 石女 (alt. 伊志売)

Ishiwara Kanji 石原莞爾

Ishiyamadera 石山寺

Issaikyō (Ch. *Yijiejing*) 一切経 (rel. *Daizōkyō* 大蔵経)

Issan Ichinei (Ch. *Yishan Yining*) 一山一寧 (also called Issan kokushi 一山国師)

Isshi Bunshu 一糸文守

Isshinji 一心寺

Itō Shōshin 伊藤証信

Itsukushima 厳島

Iwashimizu Hachimangū 石清水八幡宮 (also called Otokoyama Hachimangū 男山八幡宮)

Izumi Shikibu 和泉式部

Jaku'un 寂運

ji (Ch. *shi*) 事

Jichihan (alt. Jippan, Jitsuhan) 実範

jidan seido 寺檀制度 (rel. *danka seido* 檀家制度)

Jien 慈円 (also called Jichin 慈鎮)

jikaku 自覚

jike 寺家

jikkoku 十穀

jikyōja (alt. *jikyōsha*) 持経者 (also called *jisha* 持者)

jimon 寺門 (= *jimonha* 寺門派)

Jingikan 神祇官

Jingoji 神護寺

jingūji 神宮寺

Jinjakyoku 神社局 (rel. Jinja shintō 神社神道)

Jinmu 神武 (= Jinmu Tennō 神武天皇)

Jinnō shōtō ki 神皇正統記

Jinshin no ran 壬申の乱

Jinson 尋尊

Jinzen 尋禅 (also called Jinin 慈忍, Iimuro wajō 飯室和尚, Myōkō'in 妙香院)

jisha bugyō 寺社奉行

jishu (alt. *teraju*, *teraji*, *terashi*) 寺主

Jishū 時衆 (also written 時宗, and called Yugyō-ha 遊行派)

jisshin 実神

Jitō Tennō 持統天皇

Jitsu'e 実慧 (alt. Jichi'e and 実恵)

Jiun Onkō 慈雲飲光 (also called Jiun Sonja 慈雲尊者, Hyakufuchi Dōji 百不知童子, Hyakufuku Dōsha 百福道者, Katsuragisanjin 葛城山人)

jiyū tōkyū 自由討究

Jizō 地蔵 (rel. *Jizō bosatsu reigen ki* 地蔵菩薩霊験記)

jizoku 寺族

Jōan 常安

Jōdo ritsu 浄土律

Jōdo Shinshū 浄土真宗 (rel. *Shinshū hōyō* 真宗法要)

Jōdo shū 浄土宗

Jōganji 貞観寺 (alt. Sumizomedera 墨染寺)

Jōgon 浄厳

Jōgū Shōtoku hōō teisetsu 上宮聖徳法王帝説

jōgyō zanmai 常行三昧 (also called *hanju zanmai* 般舟三昧, *butsuryūzanmai* 仏立三昧)

Jōgyōdō 常行堂

Jōjin 成尋

Jōjitsu 成実 (rel. *Jōjitsuron* 成実論)

Jōkai 定海 (also called Sanbō'in daisōjō 三宝院大僧正, Jōshō sōjō 上生僧正)

Jōkei 貞慶 (also called Gedatsu shōnin 解脱上人, Kasagi shōnin 笠置上人)

Jōkyū 承久

Jomei Tennō 舒明天皇

Jōmyō (Skt. Vimalakīrti) 浄名 (also called Jōmyō koji 浄名居士, Yuima 維摩)

joryū bungaku 女流文学

Jōshō 静照

Jōtōmon'in 上東門院 (Fujiwara no Shōshi 藤原彰子)

Jōyuishikiron (Skt. *Vijñaptimātratā siddhi*) 成唯識論

jōza 上座

jugonshi 呪禁師

jūhachidō 十八道

Juhō yōjin shū 受法用心集

Jūjūshinron 十住心論

Jūkaku 什覚

Jūnimon 十二門

Junnin Tennō 淳仁天皇

Jūshichijō kenpō 十七条憲法

jutō 寿塔

jūzenji 十禅師

Jūzen-kai 十善会

kabane 姓

kadan 歌壇

Kagerō nikki (alt. *Kagerō no nikki*) 蜻蛉日記

Kaichō 開帳 (also called *kaigan* 開龕, *keigan* 啓龕, *kaihi* 開扉)

kaidan 戒壇 (also called *kaijō* 戒場)

Kaidan'in 戒壇院

kaigen 開眼

kaihōgyō 回峰行

Kaiken 快賢

kaimyō 戒名

kaiso 開祖

Kaizenji 開善寺

Kakuban 覚鑁

Kakuju 覚樹

Kakunyo 覚如

Kakushin-ni 覚心尼

Kaku'un 覚運

Kamakura 鎌倉

Kamakura bukkyō 鎌倉仏教

kami (alt. *shin*) 神

Kamo 賀茂 (alt. 加茂・鴨)

Kamo no Chōmei 鴨長明

kanbun 漢文

kando 官度

Kan'eiji 寛永寺

Kangaku'e 勧学会

kange-bon 勧化本

kan'i jūnikai 冠位十二階

kanjin hijiri 勧進聖 (also called *kanjin sō* 勧進僧, *kanjin shōnin* 勧進上人, *kanjin bōzu, kange sō* 勧化僧)

Kanjin jikkai mandara 観心十界曼荼羅

kanjinsō 勧進僧

kanjō 灌頂

Kanjō'in 灌頂院

Kanmu Tennō 桓武天皇

kan'ni 官尼

Kannon (Skt. Avalokiteśvara) 観音

Kannongyō 観音経 (also called *Kanzeon bosatsu fumonbon* 観世音菩薩普門品)

Kannongyō hayayomi e shō 観音経早読絵抄

kanpaku 関白

Kansai 関西

kanshi 漢詩

kansō 官僧

Kantō 関東

Kantsū 関通

karamono (alt. *tōbutsu, tōmotsu*) 唐物

Karin'en 歌林苑

kasa 過差

Kasuga 春日 (rel. Kasuga-ban 春日版)

Katsuragi 葛城

Kawachi 河内

Kawaguchi Ekai 河口慧海

Kawakami Hajime 河上肇

Kawaradera 川原寺

Kazan'in 花山院

kebiishi (alt. *kenbiishi*) 検非違使

kechien kanjō 結縁灌頂

kechimyaku 血脈

Kegon'e 華厳会

Kegonkyō (Ch. *Huayanjing*) 華厳経 (rel. Kegon 華厳)

Keiaiji 景愛寺

Keii-kai 経緯会

Keiō Gijuku Daigaku (Keiō University) 慶応義塾大学

Keiran shūyō shū 渓嵐拾葉集

Keishū (K. Gyeongju) 慶州

Keizan 瑩山 (also called Keizan Jōkin 瑩山紹瑾, Butsuji zenji 仏慈禅師, Jōsai daishi 常済大師)

Keka 悔過 (rel. Keka'e 悔過会, Anan keka 阿難悔過)

Kenchi 顕智

Kenchōji 建長寺

kengyō 顕教

kenmitsu 顕密 (rel. Kenmitsu Bukkyō 顕密仏教, Kenmitsu Taisei 顕密体制)

kenmon 権門

Kenninji 建仁寺

Kenshin 顕真

kentō-sō 使唐僧

kenzuishi 遣隋使

kessha 結社

Ketsubonkyō (Ch. *Xuepenjing*) 血盆経

ketsujō ōjō 決定往生

Kichizō 吉蔵

Kii 紀伊

kikajin 帰化人

kike 記家

kikigaki 聞書

Kinmei Tennō 欽明天皇

kinsei 近世 (rel. *kinsei bukkyō daraku ron* 近世仏教堕落論)

kirigami (alt. *kirikami*) 切紙

Kiriyama Seiyū 桐山靖雄

kiroku 記録 (rel. *ki* 記)

kishōmon 起請文

Kitabatake Chikafusa 北畠親房

Kita'in 喜多院

Kitano 北野

kitō 祈祷

Kiyomizu-zaka 清水坂

Kiyomizudera 清水寺

Kiyozawa Manshi 清沢満之

kizoku bukkyō 貴族仏教

kō 講

kōan 公案

Kōbō Daishi 弘法大師 (also called Kūkai 空海)

Kōbō Daishi den 弘法大師伝

kodai 古代

kōdan 交談 (rel. *zōtan* 雑談)

Kōen 皇円

Kōfukuji 興福寺

kofun 古墳

kōhai 光背

koji 居士

Kojiki 古事記

Kojiki-den 古事記伝

kojitsusho 故実書

Kokan Shiren 虎関師錬

Kokawadera 粉河寺 (also called Fūmōzan 風猛山)

Kōkei (alt. Kōgei) 皇慶 (also called Tani ajari 谷阿闍梨)

Kōken Tennō 孝謙天皇

Kokin waka shū 古今和歌集 (=*Kokinshū* 古今集)

kokka bukkyō 国家仏教 (rel. *chingo kokka* 鎮護国家)

kokka shintō 国家神道

kokka no sōshi 国家の宗祀

Kōkōdō 浩々洞

Kokubunji 国分寺 (rel. Kokubunniji 国分尼寺, Kokubunsōji 国分僧寺)

Kokuchūkai 国柱会

kokudo shōgon 国土荘厳

Kokugaku 国学

kokumo 国母

Kokuri 高句麗 (K. Koguryŏ; rel. Kōrai 高麗)

kokushi 国師

kokutai 国体

Kōmeitō 公明党

komusō 虚無僧

Kōmyō 光明 (also called Kōmyō Kōgō 光明皇后)

Kōmyō Shingon 光明真言

Kōmyōji 光明寺

kondō 金堂

Kongōbuji 金剛峰寺

Kongōchōkyō 金剛頂経

kongōkai 金剛界

Kōnin Tennō 光仁天皇

Konjaku monogatari shū 今昔物語集

Konjikidō 金色堂

konjikisō 金色相

Konkōmyō-saishō-ō-kyō 金光明最勝王経

Konkōmyō shitennō gokoku no tera 金光明四天王護国之寺

Konkōmyōkyō 金光明経

Kōno 河野

Konpira 金毘羅 (alt. 金比羅)

Kōryūji 広隆寺

kosetsu 古拙

kōshiki 講式

Kōshin 弘真 (= Monkan 文観)

Kōshū (alt. Kōsō) 光宗

Kotani Kimi 小谷喜美

Kōtoku Tennō 孝徳天皇

Kōya 高野 (rel. Kōyasan 高野山, Kōya-ban 高野版, *Kōya hijiri* 高野聖)

Kōzanji (alt. Kōsanji) 高山寺

Kōzen (alt. Kōnen) 興然

kū 空

Kubo Kakutarō 久保角太郎

Kudara (K. Paekche) 百済

Kudara-dera 百済寺

Kudara Ōdera (alt. Kudara Daiji) 百済大寺

kuden 口伝 (rel. *kuketsu* 口決)

Kujō 九条

Kujō Kanezane 九条兼実

Kujō Michi'ie 九条道家

Kūkai 空海

Kumano 熊野 (rel. Kumano Sansho Gongen 熊野三所権現, *kumano bikuni* 熊野比丘尼)

kumitsu 口密

kuni tsu kami 国神

Kuratsukuri 鞍作

Kuratsukuri no Tasuna 鞍作多須奈

Kuratsukuri no Tori 鞍作止利

Kurodani 黒谷

kurōdo (alt. *kurando*) 蔵人

Kurozumi Munetada 黒住宗忠

Kurozumikyō 黒住教

Kusha 倶舎 (rel. *Kusharon* 倶舎論)

Kūya 空也

kuyō 供養

kyakusō (alt. *kakusō*) 客僧

kyōdan 教団

kyōgaku 教学

kyōgen kigo (alt. *kyōgen kigyo*) 狂言綺語

Kyōgyōshinshō 教行信証 (also *Ken jōdo shinjitsu kyōgyōshō monrui* 顕浄土真実教行証文類)

Kyōkai (or Keikai) 景戒

kyōkai 教会

kyōningyō 杏仁形

Kyōto 京都

Kyōto Teikoku Daigaku 京都帝国大学 (Kyōto Imperial University)

Kyūshū 九州

machishū (alt. *chōshū*) 町衆

mairi 参り (rel. *sankei* 参詣)

Maka shikan 摩訶止観

maki 巻

Makiguchi Tsunesaburō 牧口常三郎

mandara 曼荼羅

Manpukuji 萬福寺

mappō 末法

matsuji 末寺

Matsumoto Shirō 松本史朗

Matsuo Bashō 松尾芭蕉

Meiji 明治 (rel. Meiji *ishin* 明治維新)

Menzan Zuihō　面山瑞方

Mi-sai'e (alt. Go-sai'e)　御斎会

michi (alt. *dō*)　道

Midō kanpaku ki 御堂関白記 (also called *Nyūdō-dono onreki* 入道殿御暦, *Hōjōji sesshō ki* 法成寺摂政記, *Hōjōji nyūdō sadaijin ki* 法成寺入道左大臣記, *Nyūdō-dono on-nikki* 入道殿御日記)

Miidera　三井寺 (also called Onjōji 園城寺)

mikkyō 密教

miko (alt. *fujo*) 巫女 (also written 神子)

Mimasaka　美作 (also called Sakushū 作州)

Minamoto　源 (rel. Murakami Genji 村上源氏)

Minamoto no Tamenori　源為憲

Minobu　身延

minshū 民衆

mirai ki 未来記

Miroku (Skt. Maitreya)　弥勒 (= Miroku bosatsu 弥勒菩薩)

Miwa　三輪

Miyazaki Hayao　宮﨑駿

mizuko kuyō 水子供養

mōde 詣

mokkan 木簡

mokujiki shōnin 木食聖人

mondō 問答

Monju (Skt. Manjuśrī)　文殊 (= Monju bosatsu 文殊菩薩)

Monju'e　文殊会

Monmu Tennō　文武天皇

Mononobe　物部

Mononobe no Moriya　物部守屋

Mononobe no Okoshi　物部尾輿

monryū 門流

montei 門弟 (alt. *monteishi* 門弟子; rel. *monjin* 門人, *deshi* 弟子)

monto 門徒

monzeki 門跡

Mori Mariko　森 万里子

Motoori Norinaga　本居宣長

mu 無

muga no ai 無我の愛 (rel. *Muga-ai* 無我愛)

Mugaen　無我苑

Mugai Nyodai　無外如大

Mugaku Sogen (Ch. Wuxue Zuyuan)　無学祖玄

Mujaku Dōchū　無着道忠

Mukan Fumon 無関普門

Mukuhara 向原

Murakami Senshō 村上専精

Murasaki Shikibu 紫式部 (alt. Fuji Shikibu 藤式部)

Muromachi 室町

Muryōkō'in 無量光院

Muryōju'in 無量寿院 (rel. Muryōkōji 無量光寺)

Musō Soseki 夢想礎石 (also called Shōgaku kokushi 正覚国師, Shinshū kokushi
   心宗国師, Fusai kokushi 普済国師, Musō kokushi 夢想国師)

Myō'e 明恵 (also called Kōben 高弁)

myōgō (Skt. *nāma-dheya*) 名号 (also called *songō* 尊号, *tokugō* 徳号)

Myōhen 明遍 (also called Rengadani sōzu 蓮華谷僧都)

Myōhō-renge-kyō 妙法蓮華経 (same as *Hokekyō*)

Myōkenji 妙顕寺 (also called Gusokusan 具足山)

Myōkōji 妙光寺

Myōnin 明忍 (also called Shunshō 俊正)

Myōshinji 妙心寺 (also called Shōbōzan 正法山, Myōshinzenji 妙心禅寺)

Myōwakai 明和会

Myōzen 明全 (also called Butsujubō 仏樹房)

Nachi 那智

Naganuma Myōkō 長沼妙佼

Nagaoka 長岡

naigubu jūzenji 内供奉十禅師

naiten 内典

Naka no Ōe 中大兄 (= Tenji Tennō 天智天皇)

Nakatomi 中臣

Nakatomi-no-harae 中臣祓

Nakatomi harae kunge 中臣祓訓解

Nakatomi no Kamako 中臣鎌子

Nakatomi no Kamatari 中臣鎌足

Nakatomi no Katsumi 中臣勝海

Nakayama 中山

namu amida butsu 南無阿弥陀仏 (rel. *Namu amida butsu: ketsujō ōjō, rokujūmannin*
   南無阿弥陀仏:決定往生六十万人)

namu-myōhō-renge-kyō 南無妙法蓮華経

Nanbokuchō 南北朝

Naniwa 難波

Nanjō Bun'yū 南条文雄

Nanto rokushū 南都六宗

Nanto-shichi-daiji 南都七大寺

Nanzenji 南禅寺

Nara 奈良

Nara-zaka 奈良坂

Negoroji (alt. Negorodera) 根来寺

nenbundosha 年分度者

nenbutsu 念仏 (rel. *nenbutsu shū* 念仏衆, *odori nenbutsu* 踊念仏, *nenbutsu honzon* 念仏本尊)

nendai ki 年代記

nenjū gyōji (mod. *nenchū gyōji*) 年中行事 (rel. *nenjūgyōji sho* 年中行事書)

Nichiren 日蓮 (rel. Nichiren shū 日蓮宗, Nichiren-*shugi* 日蓮主義)

Nihon (alt. Nippon) 日本

Nihon kiryaku 日本紀略 (also called *Nihon kirui* 日本紀類, *Hennen kiryaku* 編年紀略)

Nihon ryōiki 日本霊異記 (= *Nihonkoku genpō zen'aku ryōiki* 日本国現報善悪霊異記)

Nihon sandai jitsuroku 日本三大実録

Nihon shoki 日本書紀 (alt. *Nihongi* 日本紀)

Nihonjin-ron 日本人論

Nijō 二条

Nijūgokajō goyuigō 二十五ヶ条御遺告

nikkei (Skt. *uṣṇīṣa*) 肉髻

Nikkō 日光

nikujiki saitai 肉食妻帯

Ninchō 忍澂 (also called Byakurensha Senyo Shin'a 白蓮社宣誉信阿)

Ningai 仁海 (also called Ono no sōjō 小野僧正, Ame no sōjō 雨僧正)

Ninnaji (alt. Niwaji) 仁和寺 (rel. Ninnaji O'muro 仁和寺御室, O'muro gosho 御室御所)

Ninnōkyō 仁王経

Ninshō 忍性 (also called Ryōkan 良観, Ninshō bosatsu 忍性菩薩)

Nipponzan Myōhōji 日本山妙法寺

Nishigori no Tsubu (alt. Nishikori no Tsufu) 錦織壺

Nishitani Keiji 西谷啓治

Nishiyama 西山

Nisshin 日親

Nisshō 日昭

Niwano Nikkyō 庭野日敬

Nō 能

Nōshin 能信

Nurishichikei (K. Norisach'igye) 怒唎斯致契

nyo'in (alt. *nyō'in*) 女院

Nyohō sonshō hō 如法尊勝法

Nyojō (Ch. Rujing) 如浄

nyonin kekkai 女人結界 (rel. *nyonin kinsei* 女人禁制)

nyūbu 入峰
nyūjō shinkō 入定信仰

Ōama no ōji 大海人皇子
Ōbaku 黄檗 (rel. *Ōbaku shingi* 黄檗清規)
ōbō buppō 王法仏法 (alt. *ōhō buppō*, also *buppō ōbō*)
obon お盆
ōchō 王朝
Oda Nobunaga 織田信長
Ōe no Masafusa 大江匡房
o'fumi (alt. *on-fumi*) 御文
Ogasawara Sadamune 小笠原貞宗
Ogawa Eiji 小川英爾
Ōhara 大原 (rel. *Ōhara mondō* 大原問答)
Ōjin 応神
ōjō 往生 (rel. *ōjōden* 往生伝, *Ōjōyōshū* 往生要集)
ōkimi 大王
Oku-no-in 奥の院
Ōmine 大峰
Ōmiwa 大神 (rel. Miwa 三輪)
O'mizutori お水取り
Ōmuraji Mononobe no Okoshi 大連物部尾輿
Ōnin 応仁
Onjōji 園城寺 (= Miidera 三井寺)
onmyōji (alt. *onyōji*) 陰陽師
Ōomi Soga no Iname 大臣蘇我稲田
orikami (alt. *origami*) 折紙
ōsei fukkō 王政復興
oshi (alt. *onshi*) 御師
Ōtani 大谷
Ōtomo 大友
Ōuchi Seiran 大内青巒
Owarida 小墾田
Ōyama 大山
Ōyama Seiichi 大山誠一

petto kuyō ペット供養

rahotsu 螺髪
raigō 来迎
Raiyu 頼瑜
Rankei Dōryū (Ch. Lanxi Daolong) 蘭渓道隆

Reiki kanjō 麗気灌頂

Reitan 靈潭

Reiunji 霊雲寺

Reiyūkai Kyōdan 霊友会教団

Reizei 冷泉

Renga 連歌

Rengeō'in 蓮華王院 (= Sanjūsangendō 三十三間堂)

Rennyo 蓮如

Rentai 蓮体

ri (Ch. *li*) 理

Rihō 理豊

Rihōō ki 吏部王記

rinjū gyōgi 臨終行儀

rinne 輪廻

Rinzai 臨済 (rel. Rinzai shū 臨済宗, Zen 禅)

risshi 律師

Risshō ankokuron 立正安国論

Risshō Kōsei-kai 立正佼成会 (rel. Dai Nippon Risshō Kōsei-kai 大日本立正佼成会)

Risshū 律宗 (rel. Shingon risshū 真言律宗)

ritsu 律 (rel. *ritsuryō* 律令, *ritsuryō teki kokka bukkyō* 律令的国家仏教)

riyaku 利益

rōei 朗詠

Rokkakudō 六角堂

rokudai 六大

rokudō (alt. *rikudō*) 六道 (also called *rokushu* 六趣, *rokkai* 六界)

Rokuharamitsuji 六波羅蜜寺

Rokuonji 鹿苑寺 (also called Kinkakuji 金閣寺)

rongi 論議

ryō 令

Ryōchū 良忠 (also called Nen'a 然阿, Kishu zenji 記主禅師)

Ryōgen (ca. 912–985; alt. Rōgen) 良源 (also called Ganzan daishi 元三大師, Tsuno daishi 角大師, Gobyō daishi 御廟大師.

Ryōgen (1295–1336) 了源 (also called Kūshō 空性)

ryōi 霊異

Ryōnin 良忍 (also called Shōō daishi 聖応大師)

Ryōun 霊雲

ryū 流 (rel. *ryūha* 流派, *hōryū* 法流)

ryūdōsei 流動性

Ryūkoku 龍谷

Ryūshō'in 龍松院

Ryūzai 隆済

sabetsu kaimyō 差別戒名

Saga Tennō 嵯峨天皇

Saichō 最澄 (also called Dengyō Daishi 伝教大師)

Saidaiji 西大寺 (also called Takanodera 高野寺, Shiō'in 四王院)

sai-e 斎会

Saigyō 西行 (also called Daihonbō 大本房, Daihōbō 大宝房・大法房)

Sai'in 西院 (alt. Junna'in 淳和院)

Sai'in Mi-eidō 西院御影堂 (also called Daishidō 大師堂)

Saiji 西寺 (alt. Udaiji 右大寺)

Saikoku *junrei* 西国巡礼

Saikoku sanjūsan reijō 西国三十三霊場

Saimei Tennō 斉明天皇

Saimyōji 西明寺

saisei itchi 祭政一致

Saisen 済暹

Saishōkō 最勝講

Saishōōkyō 最勝王経

Sakaino Kōyō 境野黄洋 (also called Sakaino Satoru 境野哲)

Sakamoto 坂本

Sakuden 策伝 (alt. 安楽庵策伝)

sanbō 三宝 (rel. *sanbō'e* 三宝会)

Sanbō'in (alt. Sanpō'in) 三宝院

Sanbōji 三宝寺

sangaku 三学

sangaku shinkō 山岳信仰

sangō 三綱

sangoku 三国

Sangyō gisho 三経義疏

Sanjō bōmon 三条坊門

Sanjūbanjin 三十番神

sanjūni sō 三十二相

sankei 参詣

sanmai hijiri 三昧聖 (also called *hakamori* 墓守, *onbō* 御坊・隠坊, *byōhijiri* 廟聖)

sanmitsu 三密 (rel. *sanmitsugyōbō* 三密行法)

sanmon 山門

Sanmonto 三門徒

Sannō 山王 (rel. Sannō Shintō 山王神道)

Sanron (Skt. Mādhyamaka) 三論

Sanzen'in 三千院 (originally called variously Entoku'in 円徳院, Enyū'in 円融院, Kajii monzeki 梶井門跡, Nashimotobō 梨本坊)

Sarugaku 猿楽

sazen 作善

Sei Shōnagon 清少納言

Seiganbō 誓願房

Seigantoji 青岸渡寺

Seigen (alt. Jōken, Jōgen) 成賢

Seimei-ō 聖明王 (K. Sŏng Myŏng Wang)

Seirei shū (alt. *Shōryō shū*) 性霊集

Seisetsu Shōchō (Ch. Qingzhuo Zhengcheng) 清拙正澄

seishin-shugi 精神主義

Seishinkai 精神界

Seisui shō 醒酔笑

Seizan 西山

sekkan 摂関 (rel. *sekkan seiji* 摂関政治)

semui-in 施無畏印 (Skt. *abhaya mudrā*)

Senba 仙波

senbō 懺法 (rel. Hokke *senbō* 法華懺法)

sencha 煎茶

sendatsu 先達

sengi 僉議

sengoku 戦国 (rel. Sengokuki 戦国期)

Senju 千手 (Kannon 観音)

Senjuji 専修寺

Senkyōji 泉橋寺

sennichi kaihōgyō 千日回峰行

Sennyūji 泉涌寺

Senshi 選子

Sensō'e 千僧会

Sesshō 摂政

setsuwa 説話

settai 接待

shabyō sōjō 潟瓶相承

shaji sankei 社寺参詣

Shaka *butsu* 釈迦仏

Shaka *sanzonzō* 釈迦三尊像

shakkyō 釈教

Shaku Sōen 釈宗演

Shaku Unshō 釈雲照

shakubuku 折伏

shakyōsho 写経所

shami 沙彌

shamini 沙彌尼

shanago 遮那業

shasei 捨世

Shiba Tachito 司馬達等 (alt. Shiba Tatto, Shiba Tatsuto)

shibunritsu 四分律

Shida 信太

shidai 次第 (rel. *shidai sho* 次第書)

shidaiji 四大寺

shido 私度 (rel. *shidosō* 私度僧, *shido sōni* 私度僧尼)

shidō 祠堂

Shihi 泗沘

shi'in 子院

Shijōkōhō 熾盛光法 (alt. Daishijōkōhō 大熾盛光法)

shikai 四海

shikaku 始覚

shikan taza 只管打坐

shikango 止観業

Shikoku 四国

Shikoku *henro* 四国遍路

Shima 嶋

Shimaji Mokurai 島地黙雷

Shimotsuke Yakushiji 下野薬師寺

shin (alt. *kami*) 神

shin bukkyō 新仏教

Shin Bukkyōto Dōshikai 新仏教徒同志会

shin shin shūkyō 新々宗教

shin shūkyō 新宗教

Shin-zenkōji 新善光寺

Shinano 信濃

shinbukkyō no jidai 新仏教の時代

shinbutsu 神仏

Shinbutsu 真仏

shinbutsu bunri 神仏分離 (rel. *shinbutsu bunri rei* 神仏分離令)

shinbutsu hanzen 神仏判然

Shingon 真言 (rel. Shingon shū 真言宗, Shingon *mikkyō* 真言密, 教 Kogi Shingon 古義真言, Shingi Shingon 新義真言)

Shingon Ritsu 真言律

shinjin datsuraku 心身脱落

shinjitsu hōdo 真実報土

Shinjō 心定

shinkoku 神国

shinmitsu 身密

Shinnen　真念

Shinnyoen　真如苑

Shinpukuji　真福寺

Shinran　親鸞 (also called Kenshin daishi 見真大師; rel. *Shinran shōnin go'innen* 親鸞聖人御因縁)

shinri kinshin　真理金針

Shinron　新論

shinsen (Ch. *shen-xian*)　神仙 (rel. *Honchō shinsen den* 本朝神仙伝)

shinshō　神聖

Shinshū hōyō　真宗法要

Shintō　神道 (rel. Ryōbu Shintō 両部神道)

Shinzoku kōdan ki　真俗交談記

shirabyōshi　白拍子

Shiragi　新羅 (K. Silla)

Shirakawa　白川 (alt. 白河)

Shirakawa　白河 (= sovereign, retired sovereign)

shishu zanmai　四種三昧

shitaku bukkyō　私宅仏教

ShiTennōji　四天王寺 (rel. *shitennō* 四天王)

shō　抄 (alt. 鈔)

Shōbō　聖宝

Shōbō　正法 (rel. *Shōbō genzō* 正法眼蔵, rel. *shōbōritsu* 正法律)

Shōchōju'in　勝長寿院

shōdō　唱導

shōen　荘園

Shōgei　聖冏 (also called Yūrenja Ryōyo 酉蓮社了誉)

Shōgo'in　聖護院

shōgyō　聖教 (alt. 正教)

shōhō　生報

shōjin　生身 (rel. *shōjin-no-hotoke* 生身仏)

Shōkai　聖戒 (also called Mia 弥阿)

Shōkaku　勝覚 (also called Sanbō'in gonsōjō 三宝院権僧正)

Shōken　勝賢 (alt. 勝憲; also called Jijū sōjō 侍従僧正, Kakutō'in gonsōjō 覚洞院権僧正)

Shōkō　聖光 (= Shōkōbō Benchō 聖光房弁長)

Shōkōmyō'in　勝光明院 (rel. Tobadono 鳥羽殿, Toba rikyū 鳥羽離宮)

Shōkū　証空 (also called Zen'ebo 善慧坊)

Shoku Nihongi　続日本紀

Shōman-gyō (Skt. *Śrīmālādevī siṃhanāda sūtra*)　勝鬘経

Shōmangyō gisho　勝鬘経義疏

shōmotsu　抄物

Shōmu Tennō 聖武天皇

shōmyō 声明

Shōmyōji 称名寺

shōnin 聖人 (alt. 上人)

shōō 聖王

Shōrai mokuroku 請来目録

Shōren'in 青蓮院

Shōrin'in 勝林院 (alt. Gyosan Taigenji 魚山大原寺)

Shōshin 証真

Shōshinge 正信偈 (alt. *Shōshin nenbutsuge* 正信念仏偈)

shoshū kengaku 諸宗兼学

shosonbō (alt. *shosonpō*) 諸尊法

Shōsōrin ryakushingi 小叢林略清規

Shōtoku 聖徳 (rel. Shōtoku Taishi 聖徳太子)

Shōtoku Tennō 称徳天皇

shū 宗 (rel. *shūha* 宗派)

shugenja 修験者 (rel. Shugendō 修験道)

shuhō (alt. *suhō*) 修法

Shūi kotokuden'e 拾遺古徳伝絵

Shūi ōjōden 拾遺往生伝

Shukaku (alt. Shūkaku) 守覚

shukke 出家

Shukongōjin (alt. Shūkongōjin, Shikkongōjin) 執金剛神

shukubō 宿坊

shūkyō hōjin rei 宗教法人令

shūkyō hōjin hō 宗教法人法

Shūkyōkyoku 宗教局

shūmon daigaku 宗門大学

Shun'e 俊恵

Shuni'e 修二会

Shunjō 俊芿

Shunpan 俊範

shuto 衆徒

sō ni arazu zoku ni arazu 非僧非俗 (= 僧に非ず俗に非ず)

sōbō 僧坊 (also 僧房)

Soga 蘇我

Soga no Iname 蘇我稲目

Soga no Iruka 蘇我入鹿

Soga no Umako 蘇我馬子

sōgakutō 総学頭

sōgisha 葬儀社

sōgiya 葬儀屋
sōgō 僧綱
sōjō 僧正
Sōka Gakkai 創価学会 (rel. Sōka Kyōiku Gakkai 創価教育学会)
Sōka Kyōikugaku Taikei 創価教育学大系
Sōkokubunji 総国分寺
sokui kanjō 即位灌頂
sokuichi 即一
sokushin jōbutsu 即身成仏 (rel. *Sokushin jōbutsu gi* 即身成仏義)
Sōmin (Ch. Sengmin) 僧旻
sōniryō 僧尼令
Sonnō Hōbutsu Daidōdan 尊皇奉仏大同団
Sonshi 尊子
Sonshō'in 尊勝院
Sonshun 尊舜
sōsai bukkyō 葬祭仏教
soshi 祖師 (rel. *soshi shinkō* 祖師信仰)
sōshiki bukkyō 葬式仏教
Sōshō 宗性
sōshokukyō 装飾経
Sōtō 曹洞 (= Sōtō shū 曹洞宗, Zen禅)
sōzu 僧都
Sūfukuji 崇福寺 (alt. Shigasanji 志賀山寺)
Sugawara no Takasue 菅原孝標 (rel. Sugawara no Takasue no musume 菅原孝標女)
suijaku 垂迹
Suiko Tennō 推古天皇
Sukehito 輔仁
Sumiyoshi 住吉
Suō 周防
Suzuki Daisetsu Teitarō 鈴木大拙貞太郎
Suzuki Shōsan 鈴木正三

Ta'amida-butsu Shinkyō 他阿弥陀仏真教
Tachibana no Aritsura 橘在列
Tachibana no Ōiratsume 橘大郎女
Tachikawa 立川 (rel. Tachikawa-ryū 立川流)
Taichū 袋中 (also called Ryōjō 良定, Benrenja nyūkan 弁蓮社入観)
Taigen no hō 太元帥法 (alt. 大元帥法)
Taihō *ritsuryō* 大宝律令
Taijō 胎乗
Taika 大化 (rel. Taika *kaishin* 大化改新)

Taimadera 当麻寺

Taimitsu 台密

Taira no Kiyomori 平清盛

Tairei 台嶺

Taizōkai 胎蔵界

Takada monto 高田門徒

Takaguchi Yoshiyuki 高口恭行

Takahatayama 高幡山 (=Takahatayama Fudō dō 高幡山不動堂)

Takaosanji 高雄山寺

Takashima Beihō 高嶋米峰

Takayama Chogyū 高山樗牛

Takuan Sōhō 沢庵宗彭

Takuga 託何

Tanabe Hajime 田辺元

Tanaka Chigaku 田中智學

Tani no ryū 谷流

tariki 他力

tassho 塔所

tatari 祟り

Tenbun no ran 天文の乱

Tendai 天台 (rel. Tendai shū 天台宗, Ch. Tiantai)

tengu 天狗

Tengu zōshi 天狗草子

Tenji (alt. Tenchi) *Tennō* 天智天皇

Tenjiku 天竺

Tenjukoku shūchō 天寿国繍帳

Tenkai 天海

Tenmu Tennō 天武天皇

Tennō 天皇

tentō (alt. *tendō*) 天道

Tetsugaku-dō 哲学堂

Tetsugakukan 哲学館

Tezuka Osamu 手塚治虫

Toda Jōsei 戸田城聖

Tōdaiji 東大寺

Tōdaiji yōroku 東大寺要録

Tōfukuji 東福寺

Togano'o 栂ノ尾

Tōji 東寺

Tōjiji 等持寺

tokudo 得度

Tokugawa Iemitsu　徳川家光
Tokugawa Ieyasu　徳川家康
Tokuitsu　徳一
Tominaga Nakamoto　富永仲基
Tōmitsu　東密
Tōnan'in　東南院
Tonkō (Ch. Dunhuang)　敦煌
Tōnomine　多武峰
toraijin　渡来人
Tori Busshi　止利仏師
Tosa　土佐
Tōshin (alt. Eastern Jin)　東晋 or 東晉
Tōshōdaiji　唐招提寺
Tōshōgū　東照宮 (rel. Tōshō Daigongen 東照大権現)
tosō　抖擻
Tosotsu　兜率 (alt. 都卒)
tōtai soku myōkaku　当体即妙覚
Towazugatari　とわずがたり
Toyome　乙嫁
Toyotomi Hideyoshi　豊臣秀吉
Toyouradera　豊浦寺
Tōzan-ha　当山派
Tsuchimikado Michichika　土御門通親 (alt. Minamoto Michichika 源通親, Koga
　　Michichika 久我通親)
tsuina　都維那
Tsurugaoka Hachimangū　鶴岡八幡宮 (Tsurugaoka Hachiman 鶴岡八幡)

Uchimura Kanzō　内村鑑三
Uda　宇多 (rel. Uda Tennō 宇多天皇)
Uji　宇治 (rel. Uji-no-hōzō 宇治宝蔵, Uji Hōjō'in 宇治放生院)
uji　氏
ujidera　氏寺
ujigami　氏神
ujiko shirabe　氏子調
ujizoku　氏族 (rel. *ujizoku bukkyō* 氏族仏教)
Umayado　厩戸皇子 (rel. Umayado no miko 厩戸皇子)
Ungo Kiyō　雲居希膺
Urabe Kanekuni　卜部兼邦
Urabonkyō (Ch. *Yulanpen jing*)　盂蘭盆経
Usa Hachimangū　宇佐八幡宮
ushirodo　後戸

Usuzōshi 薄隻紙 (alt. 薄草紙・薄造紙・薄草子)
Utsunomiya 宇都宮

waka 和歌
Wakan rōei shū 和漢朗詠集
wakō dōjin 和光同塵
wasan 和讃

yake nohara 焼け野原
Yakujō 薬上
Yakuō 薬王
Yakushi 薬師 (rel. Yakushi Nyorai 薬師如来, Yakushiji 薬師寺)
yamabushi 山伏
yamaguchi no shūron 山口宗論
Yamashinadera 山階寺 (alt. 山科寺)
Yamatai 耶馬台国
Yamato 倭 (alt. 大和)
Yōfukuji (alt. Eifukuji) 永福寺
yogan-in (Skt. *vara mudrā*) 与願印
yojō 余乗
Yōkan (alt. Eikan) 永観
Yōmei Tennō 用明天皇
Yomiuri Shinbun 読売新聞
yoriai 寄合
Yōrō ritsuryō 養老律令
Yōsai (alt. Eisai) 栄西
Yoshida Kanetomo 吉田兼倶
Yoshihito 栄仁
Yoshino 吉野 (= Kinpusen [alt. Kinbusen] 金峰山)
Yoshishige no Yasutane 慶滋保胤
Yōten ki 耀天記
yugyō 遊行 (rel. Yugyō-ha 遊行派)
Yuima'e 維摩会 (rel. *Yuimagyō* 維摩経)
Yumedono 夢殿 (rel. Yumedono Kannon 夢殿観音)
Yūshin 熊津
yūsō (alt. *yusō*) 遊僧
yūzū nenbutsu 融通念仏 (rel. *Yūzū nenbutsu e-maki* 融通念仏絵巻, rel. *Yūzū Nenbutsu shū* 融通念仏宗)

zaike 在家
zanmai 三昧
zasu 座主

Zeami　世阿弥

Zen (Ch. Chan)　禅 (rel. Zen shū 禅宗)

zenchishiki　善智識 (rel. *chishiki* 知識)

Zendō (Ch. Shandao)　善導

zenji　禅師

Zenkōji　善光寺

zenkon　善根

Zenrinji　禅林寺

Zenshin-ni　善信尼

zenshu (alt. *senshu, zenju*; distinct from Zen shū)　禅衆

Zentsūji　善通寺

Zenzai dōji　善財童子

Zenzō-ni　禅蔵尼

zettai mu　絶対無

Zōjōji　増上寺

Zoku honchō ōjōden　続本朝往生伝

Zoku kōsōden　続高僧伝

Zonkaku　存覚

Index

Note: Page numbers in *italics* refer to Figures; those in **bold** to Tables.

Abe Mika, 120
Abé, Ryuichi, 62, 70, 78, 79, 109, 122, 156
Abe Yasurō, 97, 126n22, 165n19
adashikuni no kami, 14, 22
Agon shū, 236–7
Agui, 113
ajari, 77, 78
Ajaseō-kyō, 58
akunin shōki, 118
amadera, 39n17
Amaterasu Ōmikami (alt. Tenshō Daijin),
    152, 219
Ambros, Barbara, 185, 192, 243, 245
Amida, 76, 78, 92–7, 99–102, 107, 112–14,
    117–20, 140–142, 179, 190, 221,
    244, 249
ancestral founders (*soshi, kaiso*), 115, 135,
    144, 151, 160
    ancestral-founder faith (*soshi shinkō*), 135
Anyōji, 147
Aryadeva, 57
Asahara Shōkō, 237
Asai Ryōi, 190
Ashō, 154
Aston, W.G., 25, 50, 51
Asuka, 24, 49, 53, 72
Asuka Buddhism (*bukkyō*), 24, 26, 28–36,
    39n17, 39n19, 39n20, 53, 72
    women and, 32

Asukadera (Hōkōji), 23, 31–2, 39n18, 39n19,
    39n21, 47, 49, 50, 64
Asukadera Daibutsu, 34
Atsuzōshi, 108
Aum Shinrikyō, 237
Ayahito no Yabo, 32

Baisaō, 189
baitoku, 174
bakufu, 124, 136, 210
Bankai, 155
Barnes, Gina, 37n1
basara, 164
Bauer, Mikael, 108
Best, Jonathan, 39n16
bettō, 107
Bidatsu Tennō, 23, 24
biku, 64
bikuni, 64
Birushana, 59
Bishamonten, 120
biwa hōshi, 180
Biwako, 68, 155
Blum, Mark, 139, 177
bodaiji, 176
Bodiford, William, 123, 145, 147–8, 159,
    176, 199
Bokkō-kutsu (Ch. Mogao-ku), 27
bōmori, 162–3

A Cultural History of Japanese Buddhism, First Edition. William E. Deal and Brian Ruppert.
© 2015 William E. Deal and Brian Ruppert. Published 2015 by John Wiley & Sons, Ltd.

Bongaku shinryō, 221
Bonmōkyō, 73
bonnō gusoku, 118
bosatsukai, 65, 72
Bowring, Richard, 62
Breen, John, 96, 127n30, 152, 211
Bukkōji, 140
Bukkyō katsu ron, 217
Bukkyō Seito Dōshi Kai, 214
Bukkyō tōitsu ron, 221
Bunchi, 200–201
burakumin, 239
busshi, 34, 36
busshō, 239, 245
butsudō, 21
byakugō, 36
Byōdō'in (Uji) 100, 106, 109, 112, *116*,
    126n24, *155*;
    Uji Hōjō'in, 158
    Uji-no-hōzō, 106

Chang'an *see* Chōan
Chanoyu, 189
Chigi (Ch. Zhiyi), 72, 73, 76, 124
Chikotsu Dai'e, 147, 156
Chikū, 200
China Sea interaction sphere, 14–15, 18, 54
chingo kokka, 55, 68
Chinkai, 117
Chinzei, 94, 137, 139
Chion'in, 138
chishikiyui, 59
Chōan (Ch. Chang'an), 19, 31, 55
Chō'e, 7, 181
Chōen, 139–40
Chōfukuji, *116*
Chōgen, 110, 112, 117, 153, 165n12
Chōken, 113, 127n28
Chōnen, 109
Chōsai, 139
Chōsen'in, 200
Chōzen, 193
Chūgūji, 162
Chūhō Myōhon (Ch. Zhongfeng Mingben),
    188

Chūron, 57
chūshakugaku, 197
Chūsonji, *116*
Cogan, Gina, 201
Collcutt, Martin, 144, 146–7
Como, Michael, 29, 38n10, 38n15

Dai-no-kawago, 108
Daianji (Daikan Daiji), 49, 56, 64, 81
Daibirushana-kyō, 73
daibutsu, 34, 59, 183
Daifukuji, 147
Daigaku, 76
Daigoji, 2, 7, 10, 79, 107, *116*, 135, 139,
    143, 155, 157, 173, 181, 182, 185, 197,
    202n8
Daigo Tennō, 79
daigongen, 183, 187, 196
Daihannyakyō, 93
daijin zenji, 65
Daijō bussetsu ron hihan, 221
daijōdaijin zenji, 65
Daijō'in, 140, 173
Daikakuji, *157*
Daikan Daiji *see* Daianji
daikanjin-shiki, 112, 191
Daikokuten, 191
daimoku, 107, 124, 164n1, 234
daimyō, 175, 180, 211
Dainichi, 59, 64, 78, 99, 156, 158, 244
Dainichikyō, 76
daiō see Great King(s)
daishi, 72, 75, 76, 95, 182, 191–2,
    202n12, 246
Daishidō, 246
Daishi go-nyūjō kanketsu ki, 95
Daishōji, 198
daisōjō, 64
Daitokuji, *116*, 146, 176, 187
Daiyūzan, 196
dangi, 154, 159, 190, 202n11
danka seido see jidan seido
Danna, 91, 176
danrin, 8, 197
darani (Daranisuke), 157, 197

Deal, William E., 13, 14, 22, 30, 35, 47, 50, 52, 91

den, 93–5, 126n25, 159, 166n20, 210

Denbō'e, **89**

Dharmaksema, 51

Dharmapala, 56

dharmas, 57, 101

Dobbins, James, 115, 118–19, 141

Dōgen, 8, 123, 139, 145, 148, 153, 165n6, 165n12, 198–9

   shikan taza and *shinjin datsuraku*, 123

   Shōbō genzō, 198

dōgyō ninin, 247

dōiri, 245

Dōja Chōgen (alt. Dōsha Chōgen, Ch. Daozhe Chaoyuan), 187

Dōji, 19, 24, 38n8, 62–3

dōjō, 119, 140, 163, 175

Dōkō, 180

Doku jinjakō bengi, 189

Dōkyō, 55, 65, 66, 68, 82, 84

Dolce, Lucia, 152, 160

Dōryō Daigongen, 196

Dōsen (Ch. Daoxuan), 63

Dōshin, 140

Dōshō, 63–4

dōshu, 121, 137, 180, 182

Dōsōkaku (C. Daosengge), 60

Dōtō, 47

Dunhuang *see* Tonkō

e, 142

Eben (K. Hyep'yon), 32, 39n22

Edo, 7–8, 143, 163, 171–2, 177, 183–201, 209–11

Eiga monogatari, 101

Eight *Lotus Sūtra* Lectures, **89**, 91, 93, 97, 174

Eihei shingi, 198

Eji, 27

Ekan, 30

Eison, 122–3, 145, 154, 162, 199

e-maki, 120–121, 126n18

Emptiness (J. *kū*), 57, 90, 100, 179, 238

Emyō, 47

En no gyōja, 180

Enchin, 75, 76

Endon kanjin jūhokkai zu (Ch. *Yuandun guanxin shi fajie tu*), 164

Engakuji, 145, 147, 220

engi, 19, 31, 34, 39n19, 66, 150, 162, 238

ennen, 100

Enni Ben'en, 112, 122, 144, 147–8, 153, 156

Ennin, 75, 76

Enryakuji, 5, 7, 72–76, 88, 93, 105, 108, 115, 117, 127n30

   Enryakuji gokoku engi, 105

ensei, 119

Enshōji, 200

Erin, 47

Eryō, 88

Eshi, 47

Eshin *see* Genshin

Esoteric Buddhism (*mikkyō*), 4, 6, 61, 62, 70, 71, 88, 92, 113, 115, 121, 124, 126n15, 136, 139, 141, 142, 144, 160, 164, 164n1

   Ennin, Enchin and, 75–6

   Kogi Shingon, 7, 185, 202n8

   Kūkai and, 75, 76–9

   Saichō and, 73, 74, 75

   Shingi Shingon, 7, 185, 202n8

   Shingon lineages (Shingon Mikkyō), 76–9, 92, 95, 98, 99, 105, 106–9, 154–7, 159, 236

   Shintō lineages and, 137, 151, 153, 194

   Tendai esoteric Buddhism (Taimitsu), 75, 92, 106, 160

   waka and, 149

   Zen lineages and, 144–5, 147, 149, 199, 201, 202n10

e-toki, 99, 163

Eubanks, Charlotte, 99

Eun, 47

Farris, William Wayne, 60, 68

Faure, Bernard, 80, 145, 148, 161, 163, 164

fuda, 120

Fudaraku Jōdo, 97

Fudō (Fudō myōō), 192, 245
Fujaku, 200
Fujieda Akira, 38n13
Fujiwara (Fujiwara hokke), 4, 45–6, 49, 56,
   62, 71, 76, 87, 88, 90, 91, 96, 100, 102,
   105, 106, 107, 108, 109, 111, 112, 114,
   127n27, 156
Fujiwarakyō, 49
Fujiwara no Atsumitsu, 114
Fujiwara no Michinaga, 95, 101, 106, 109
Fujiwara no Michinori, 108, 111, 113, 117
   see also Shinzei
Fujiwara no Moronaga, 105
Fujiwara no Morosuke, 90
Fujiwara no Tadahira, 90
Fujiwara no Takamichi, 105
Fujiwara no Tameaki, 149
Fujiwara no Teika, 149
Fujiwara no Toshinari, 105
Fujiwara no Yorimichi, 100, 109
Fujiwara no Yorinaga, 114
Fujiwara Seika, 187
fuju fuse, 178
fukaku, 151
Fuke shū, 186
Fukko Shintō 210
Fukuda Gyōkai, 213, 216
Fukuryō, 47
fumikura, 187
Furukawa Rōsen, 214
Fusō ryakki, 19, 21, 48, 125n7
Futaba Kenkō, 52, 63

gakuryo, 137
Gangōji, 31, 39n19, 49, 56, 57, 80
Gangōji garan engi (Gangōji garan engi narabi
   ni ruki shizai chō), 19, 31, 34, 39n19
Ganjin, 64, 99, 121
ganmon, 113
Ganto (K. Hwando), 31
garan, 103
garan bukkyō, 18
gasan, 99
Gedatsukai, 236
gekokujō, 164

Genji kuyō, 103
Genji monogatari, 103
Genkō shakusho, 144, 147
Genmei Tennō, 49, 55
Genpi shō, 182
genpō, 67
Genrushō (Jōdo hōmon genrushō), 139
Gensei, 199
Genshin (Eshin Sugiu-ryū), 91–2, 109, 139,
   160, 177
Genshō Tennō, 63
genze riyaku, 33, 39n23, 236
genzokusō, 39n22
gesu, 7, 180
Gien, 197
Gijō (Ch. Yijing), 19, 51, 63, 78
Gikai, 155
giki, 92 (Ch. _yigui_)
Gion, 158
Gishi-wajin-den (Ch. _Wei-zhi wo-ren-chuan_),
   38n6
gishiki sho, 88
_gō_ (Skt. _karma_), 66
Go-Fukakusa'in Nijō, 98
Go-Mizuno'o, 200
Go-seibai shikimoku, 172–3
go-shichinichi mishiho, 77, 96, 174
godaiji, 49
goganji, 79, 104
Gogatsu tsuitachi kyō, 58
gohō, 67
gohō ikki, 214
gohonzon, 234
Gōke shidai, 106
gokoku zuhō, 69
Gokuraku Jōdo, 92
Gokurakuji, 116, 122
Gongen-sama, 184
Gozan (Gozan-ban), 146–8, 177
Grapard, Allan, 96, 165n16
Groner, Paul, 70, 75, 82, 90, 123, 160
Gufukuji, 48, 49
Gukan shō, 105
Gushi, 63
Gyōga, 181

gyōja, 180, 244–5
Gyōki, 53–4, 55, 59, 63–4, 92, 99,
    112, 181, 192
Gyōnen, 139
gyōnin, 7, 180

Hachiman daibosatsu, 66, 96, 152
Hafuribe, 151
Hagaji, *182*
Haguro, 185
haibutsu kishaku, 213
haja kenshō, 216
Hakamaya Noriaki, 238–9
Haku Kyoi (Ch. Baijuyi), 102
Hakuhō, 45, 48, 50, 53, 54, 55, 72
Hakuin Ekaku, 188
Hamurogumi, 191
Harada Masatoshi, 144–6, 148, 149, 177
Hardacre, Helen, 211, 212, 223, 232, 248
Hasedera, **89**, *116*, *155*, 173, 246
Hasshū, 70, 177
Hata, 22, 28, 34, 38n10, 48
hatto, 8, 184, 197
Hayami Tasuku, 39n17, 52
Hayashi Makoto, 185, 186, 220
Hayashi Razan, 187, 189
Hayashi Yuzuru, 120, 121
Heiankyō, 68–9, 72, 73, 76, 77, 87–8, 92, 93,
    100, 101, 105, 106, 108, 113, 114, 161
Heijō (K. Pyongyang), 31
Heijōkyō, 45, 49, 55, 56, 57, 58, 65, 68, 69,
    76, 77
Heike nōkyō, 99
Heizei Tennō, 77
henro ishi, 193
hibutsu, 98
Hiei (mountain, monastery), 5, 7, 72–6, 88,
    89, 90, 92, 93, 99, 102, 103, 105, 108,
    114–18, 123–4, 125n7, 127n30, 139,
    147, 148, 150–152, **155**, 160, 161, 175,
    180, 187, 242, 244, 245
hihan bukkyō, 238–9
hijiri, 5, 91–3, 112, 119–21, 137, 140, 141,
    153, 158, 173, 181, 191, 197
Himiko, 38n6

hinin (shukuhinin), 122, 159
Hiraizumi, 100, 114
Hirata Atsutane, 194, 210
Hōben (hōben kedo), 73, 100, 118
hō'e (e), 48, 50, 99, 104, 126n15, 142
hōi, 145
Hōjō ki, 112–13
Hōjō Sadatoki, 141, 146
Hōjō Tokimune, 159
Hōjō Tokiyori, 147
Hōjōji, 100
Hokekyō see Lotus Sūtra
Hokekyō jikidan shō see Lotus Sūtra
Hokke genki, 91, 93
Hokke hakkō'e *see* Eight *Lotus Sūtra*
    Lectures
hokke hijiri, 91
Hokke mandara, 160
Hokke metsuzai no tera, 58
Hokke shū (Hokke Shintō), 141, 152, 164n2
Hokke zanmaidō, 99
Hokkeji, **89**, *116*, 161–2
Hōkōji (Kyoto), 183 *see also* Asukadera
Hōkoku Daimyōjin, 183
Hokuriku, 141, 175
Hōkyōji, 198
hon-matsu (hon-matsu seido), 176, 185
Honchō shinsen den, 95
Hōnen, 117–21, 124, 137–9, 141, 163, 165n6,
    179, 190, 197
    Hōnen shōnin denki, 139
hongaku, 92, 150–152, 239
Hongan, 191
Honganji, 119, 140, 175–80, 198, 200
Hongō Masatsugu, 80
honji-suijaku see Kami-Buddha relations
honjōtan, 179
Honkokuji, 178
Honnōji, 178
Honshū, 16, 37n4, 38n5, 100, 124, 158, 245
Honzan-ha, 180–181, 185
honzon (myōgō honzon), 119, 152, 175, 234
hōō kyūshiki, 65
Hōon'in, 7, 181, 185
Hōonkō, 141

Hōrin, 45
hōryū, 91, 106
Hōryūji, 28, 31, 35, 40, 56, 158, 232, 249
hōshi, 64
hosshin, 78
Hosshin waka shū, 101
Hosshōji, **89** (Temple of Northern
    Fujiwara House, distinct from
    Hosshōji below)
Hosshōji, 100 (Sovereign Shirakawa's
    construction, distinct from Hosshōji
    above)
Hossō, 10, 56, 57, 61, 63, 65, 70, 73, 74, 90,
    117, 197, 232
hōtō (alt. *hōzu*), 52, 60
hotsugan, 57
hōwa, 119
hōza, 224, 235
hōzu see hōtō
Hyakuron, 57
Hyeja *see* Eji
hyōbyaku, 113

Ichijō'in, 140
ie, 163
igyō, 154
Ikaruga Palace, 28
Ikarugadera, 28, 31
Ikeda Daisaku, 234, 235
ikki (*hokke ikki, ikkō ikki*), 175, 178
ikkō shū, 180
Ikkyū, 148, 164
    Ikkyū-san, 248
imitsu, 78
inga, 66
inge, 91, 103, 107
ingei see inzō
Ingen Ryūki (Ch. Yinyuan Longqi), 187–8
innen, 163, 190
Inoue Enryō, 217–18
Inoue Mitsusada, 30, 38n8, 46, 53
Inoue Tetsujirō, 217
inzō (Skt. *mudrā*) (*ingei*), 78, 153
Ippen, 105, 114, 119–21

Ippen hijiri-e, 120–121
Ise, 99, *116*, 125n12, 147, 151, 154, 155,
    156, 226
Ise monogatari, 149
Ise Anyōji, 155
Ishime, 32
Ishiwara Kanji, 225
Ishiyamadera, *155*, 246
Issaikyō, 51, 57–9, 184
Issan Ichinei (Ch. Yishan Yining), 145
Isshi Bunshu, 201
Itō Shōshin, 226
Iwashimizu Hachimangū, **89**, 151

Jaffe, Richard M., 200, 213, 216, 219
Jaku'un, 155
Jamentz, Michael, 111, 128n28
Jichihan, 121, 139
jidan seido (*danka seido, danka*), 7, 176,
    185, 191
Jien, 105, 118
jike, 91
jikyōja, 5, 91–2
jimon, 76
Jingoji, 77, **89**
jingūji, 96, 150
Jinmu Tennō, 197
Jinnō shōtō ki, 153
Jinshin no ran, 47
Jinson, 175
Jinzen, 90, 103, 114
jisha bugyō, 186
jishu (alt. *teraju, teraji, terashi*), 61
Jishū, 114, 141, 149, 164n4, 185, 202n12
jisshin, 150
Jitō Tennō, 21, 47, 49, 61, 70
Jitsu'e, 93
Jiun Onkō, 197, 199, 202n15, 220
jiyū tōkyū, 214
Jizō, 93, 94, 125n8, 190, 196, 247
    Jizō bosatsu reigen ki, 93
jizoku, 240
Jōan, 47
Jōdo ritsu, 199

Jōdo Shinshū (True Pure Land lineages), 6, 7, 119, 136, 140–141, 162, 166n20, 171, 174–6, 177, 178, 179–80, 183, 184, 188, 190–191, 197–8, 200, 213, 215, 217, 218, 219, 220, 221, 226, 242, 247
Jōdo shū (Pure Land lineages), 117, 137–8, 179, 185, 197, 199–200, 242, 248
Seizan line, 139
Jōgon, 197, 199
Jōgū shōtoku hōō teisetsu, 19, 26
Jōgyōdō, 118
jōgyō zanmai, 76, 139, 244
Jōjin, 109
Jōjitsu (*Jōjitsuron*), 57
Jōkai, 108
Jōkei, 117, 121, 124, 139
Jomei Tennō, 49
Jōmyō (Skt. Vimalakīrti), 90 *see also* Yuima
joryū bungaku, 103
Jōshō, 161
Jōtōmon'in (Fujiwara no Shōshi), 161
Jōyuishikiron, 56
jōza, 61
jugonshi, 30
Juhō yōjin shū, 154
Jūkaku, 154
Jūnimon, 57
Junnin Tennō, 65
Jūshichijō kenpō (Seventeen Article Constitution), 24, 26, 28
jutō, 176
jūzenji see naigubu jūzenji
Jūzen-kai, 216

kadan, 103
Kagerō nikki, 103
kaichō, 173, 190, 196, 201n2
kaidan, 57, 64, 72, 121
kaigen, 50
kaihōgyō, 244–5
Kaiken, 154
kaimyō, 194, 239
kaiso see ancestral founders
Kaizenji, 147

Kakuban, 79, 95, 135, 197, 202n8
Kakuju, 121
Kakunyo, 140–141
Kakushin-ni, 141
Kaku'un, 91
Kamakura (period, place, shogunate), 4, 5, 11, 70, 72, 87, 90, 91, 94, 104, 113, 115, 122, 124, 144–7, 153, 165n6, 172, 201n4, 220
Kamakura bukkyō ("Kamakura Buddhism" or "Kamakura Buddhisms"), 4, 6–7, 82, 87, 110, 113, 115–25, 135–42, 144–8, 159, 160, 174–80, 185
kami (alt. *shin*), 3, 4, 5, 8, 14, 19, 22, 24–5, 28, 47, 48, 54, 80, 88, 95–9, 105, 118, 120, 124, 125, 125n13, 126n14, n16, 136, 137, 149–53, 179–80, 183, 187, 191, 192, 197, 212–13, 226
Kami-Buddha relations, 5, 24, 96–9, 149–53, 179, 180, 192, 212–13
honji-suijaku, 88, 93, 98, 150–153, 197, 213
wakō dōjin, 151
Kamikawa Michio, 92, 104, 107, 109–10, 174
Kamo, 88
Kamo no Chōmei, 113
kando, 61
Kan'eiji, 185, 187
kange-bon, 190
kan'i jū nikai (twelve-rank court system), 26
kanjin hijiri, 64, 112, 173, 181, 186, 191–2, 201n5, n12
Kanjin jikkai mandara, 164
kanjinsō, 64
kanjō, 76, 77, 137
kechien kanjō, 88
sokui kanjō, 149, 153, 156
Kanmu Tennō, 61, 68, 69, 73
kan'ni, 32
Kannon (Skt. Avalokiteśvara), 34, 67, 93, 96, 97, 118, 163, 166n20, 181, 190, 191, 193–4, *195*, 196, 236–7, 245–6, 249
kanpaku, 71
Kansai, 39n17, 122, 136, 155, 175, 181, 191, 193, 194, 199

kanshi, 101–2, 110, 114
kansō, 61
Kantō, 7, 11, 119, 126n23, 136, 139–41, 154, 155, 160, 181, 190, 192, 193, 194, 196, 197
Kantsū, 200
karamono, 189
Karin'en, 105
kasa, 111
Kasahara Kazuo, 49, 140, 141, 160, 221
Kasuga (Kasuga-ban), 88, *116*, 126n16, 146, *155*
Katsuragi, 158
Katsuura Noriko, 82, 161
Kawachi, 45, 199
Kawaguchi Ekai, 221
Kawahashi Noriko, 240–241
Kawakami Hajime, 226
Kawaradera, 48, 49, 51
Kazan'in, 191
kebiishi, 159
kechien kanjō see kanjō
kechimyaku, 91, 159
Kegon'e, 100
Kegon lineages (Ch. Huayan), 56–7, 59, 61, 70, 77, 100, 109, 122, 200
Kegonkyō (Ch. *Huayanjing*, Skt. *Avatamsaka sūtra*), 56, 81, 99, 126n18, 165n18, 200
Keiaiji, 162
Keii-kai, 214
Keiō Gijuku Daigaku (Keiō University), 220
Keiran shūyō shū, 151–2, 160
Keishū (K. Gyeongju), 31
Keizan, 145, 202n10
Keka, **89**, 100
Kenchi, 140
Kenchōji, *116*, 145
kengyō ("exoteric" teachings), 71, 115
Kenmitsu Buddhism (Kenmitsu Bukkyō, eso-exoteric Buddhism), 7, 71, 87, 110, 113, 115, 117, 121, 124, 125, 138, 139, 140, 146, 148, 158, 175–6, 181, 185, 187, 201n3
Centrality of, in medieval era: 135–7

Kenmitsu system (Kenmitsu Taisei), 115, 158–9, 180
kenmon, 115, 156
Kenchōji, *116*, 145
Kenninji, 112, 123
Kenshin, 117
kentō-sō, 109
kenzuishi, 26
Ketelaar, James, 209, 212, 215
Ketsubonkyō (Ch. *Xuepenjing*), 163
ketsujō ōjō, 120
Kichizō (Ch. Jizang), 30
kikajin, 29, 38n15
kike, 150
kikigaki, 143
Kikuchi Hiroki, 92, 96, 144, 147
Kinmei Tennō, 21, 23, 24, 38n11
kinsei (kinsei bukkyō daraku ron), 171–2, 177–8
kirigami, 142, 159, 189
Kiriyama Seiyū, 236–7
Kiroku (*ki*), 159
kishōmon, 151, 179
Kitabatake Chikafusa, 153
Kitano, *155*
kitō, 158
Kiyomizudera, 191, 246
Kiyozawa Manshi, 215
kizoku bukkyō, 72, 85
kō, 73, **89**, 91, 93, 97, 102, 174, 175
kōan, 8, 123, 146–8, 188–9
Kōbō Daishi *see* Kūkai
Kōbō Daishi den, 95
kōdan (*zōtan*), 104
Kōfukuji, 49, 56, 64
Kogi Shingon *see* Esoteric Buddhism
Koguryŏ, 15, 16, 27, 30, 31, 32, 39n16
kōhai, 36
koji, 148
Kojiki, 210
Kojiki-den, 210
kojitsusho, 105
Kokan Shiren, 147
Kōkei, 91–2

Kōken Tennō, 57, 65
Kokin waka shū (=*Kokinshū*), 149
kokka bukkyō, 53, 55, 68, 72, 84
Kōkōdō, 215
Kokubunji (Kokubunniji, Kokubunsōji), 55,
    58, 59, 62, 65, 81
Kokuchūkai, 218
kokudo shōgon, 150
Kokugaku, 210–212
kokumo, 161
Kokuri (K. Koguryŏ; Kōrai) *see* Koguryŏ
kokutai, 211, 219
Kōmeitō, 235
komusō, 8, 186, 191
Kōmyō (Kōmyō Kōgō), 57–8, 80
Kōmyō Shingon, 190
Kōmyōji, *116*, 139
kondō, 35
Kongōbuji, 77, *196*
Kongōchōkyō, 76, 78
kongōkai, 79
Kōnin Tennō, 82
Konjaku monogatari shū, 125n8
Konjikidō, 100
konjikisō, 36
Konkōmyōkyō, 49, 51
Konkōmyō-saishō-ō-kyō, 19, 51, 58, 62
Konkōmyō shitennō gokoku no
    tera, 58
Konpira, 192, 194
Kōryūji, 173
kōshiki, 113
Kōshin (= Monkan), 154
Kōshū, 160
Kotani Kimi, 223
Kōtoku Tennō, 46
Kōya (mountain, monastery), 77, 95, 108,
    139, 144, 154, *155*, 160, 191, 192, 194,
    196, 199, 202n12
    Kōya-ban, 146, 194, 196
    Kōya hijiri, 197
Kōzanji, 10, 174, 199
Kōzen, 161
kū see Emptiness
Kubo Kakutarō, 223

Kudara (K. Paekche), 13–17, 23, 29–32, 39,
    52, 80
Kudara Ōdera (alt. Kudara Daiji), 49
Kudara-dera, 47
Kuden (*kuketsu*), 106, 142
Kujō Kanezane, 105, 117, 163
Kujō Michi'ie, 98–9, 144
Kūkai (Kōbō Daishi), 69–72, 75–9, 108, 109,
    135, 154, 156, 174, 191, 197, 246, 247
Kumano, **89**, 96–8, *104*, *116*, *155*, 191, 201n4
    Ippen and, 120
    Mountain ascetics and, 91, 96, 120,
        157–8, 180
    pilgrimage to, 93, 97, 192
    Kumano Sansho Gongen, 96
    kumano bikuni, 163–4
kumitsu, 78
kuni tsu kami, 14, 22
Kuratsukuri, 34
Kuratsukuri no Tasuna, 34
Kuratsukuri no Tori, 34
Kuroda Toshio, 24, 71, 103, 115, 122, 138,
    149, 150, 159, 165n11
kurōdo, 96
Kusha, 57, 70
Kusharon, 57
Kūya, 93, 105
Kuyō, 103, 142, 243
    mizuko kuyō, 244, 247–8
kyakusō, 5, 202n12
kyōgen kigo, 102
Kyōgyōshinshō, 118, 226
Kyōkai (or Keikai), 66
Kyōto Teikoku University (Kyōto Imperial
    University), 226
Kyūshū, 38n5, 66, 76, 96, 139, 158, 165n7

LaFleur, William R., 68, 148, 248
Lotus Sūtra (*Hōkekyō*), 27, 42, 43, 58, 63,
    67–68, 73–76, **89**, 91–3, 97, 98, 99, 100,
    102, 107, 111, 123, 124–5, 149, 152,
    153, 158, 160, 174, 193–4, 199, 219,
    222–4, 234–5, 246
    Hokekyō jikidan shō, 179
Luoyang, China, 31, 38

machishū, 178
MacWilliams, Mark, 248
Maka shikan, 72, 73
maki, 60
Makiguchi Tsunesaburō, 222, 226
mandara, 78
Manpukuji, 188, 198
mappō, 19, 24, 112, 117–18, 124, 182, 188, 216
matsuji, 123, 158, 176, 181, 185, 186
Matsumoto Shirō, 238–9
Matsuo Bashō, 189
Matsuo Kenji, 64, 82, 122, 158
Matsuo Kōichi, 100, 126n16, 137, 192
McCallum, Donald, 34, 36–7, 39n18; 39n19; 39n20; 39n21, 49
Meeks, Lori, 79–80, 161–3
Meiji (Meiji *ishin*), 184, 209, 210, 211–13, 215, 216, 218, 220–222, 240, 250
Menzan Zuihō, 198
michi (alt. *dō*), 174
Miidera *see* Onjōji
mikkyō see Esoteric Buddhism
miko (alt. *fujo*), 163, 179
Minamoto no Tamenori, 88–90, 110
Minobu, *116*, 141, *155*
mirai ki, 150
Miroku (Skt. Maitreya; = Miroku bosatsu), 34, 93
Mi-sai'e, 96, 126n15
Miwa, *116*, *155*, 197
mizuko kuyō see kuyō
Mizuno Seiichi, 35, 36, 40
Mogao Caves, China *see* Bokkō-kutsu
mokkan, 66
mokujiki shōnin, 191, 202n12
mondō, 95, 123, 148, 165n5, 190
Monju (Skt. Manjuśrī; = Monju bosatsu), Monju'e, 27, 89
Monmu Tennō, 60
Mononobe, 22, 24, 32
Mononobe no Moriya, 23
Mononobe no Okoshi, 14, 22
monryū, 103
montei, 91

monto, 119, 140, 166n20, 175, 176, 178
monzeki, 5, 90–91, 103, 107, 114, 177, 201n3
Mori Mariko, 249
Motoori Norinaga, 210
Mountain asceticism, 91, 95, 156–8, 180–181, 183, 191
mu, 179, 238
mudrā see inzō
muga no ai (Muga-ai), 226
Mugaen, 226
Mugai Nyodai, 162
Mugaku Sogen (Ch. Wuxue Zuyuan), 162
Mujaku Dōchū, 188
Mukuhara, 14
Mukan Fumon, 145
Murakami Senshō, 221
Murakami Shigeyoshi, 211, 213, 217, 232
Muryōju'in (Daigoji cloister and affiliate lineages), 7, 181, 201n5
Muryōju'in (hall in Hōjōji), 100
Musō Soseki, 146
Myō'e (Kōben), 118, 122, 139, 165n18
Myōhō-renge-kyō (*Hokekyō*) *see Lotus Sūtra*
myōgō, 119, 175
Myōhen, 117
Myōkenji, 178
Myōnin, 199
Myōshinji, 176, 187–8
Myōzen, 123

Nachi, 97, *104*, 191
Naganuma Myōkō, 233, 235
Nagamura Makoto, 91–2, 109, 143, 159, 198
Nagaoka, 68
naigubu jūzenji, 82
Naka no Ōe (= Tenji Tennō), 45
Nakatomi, 22, 32
Nakatomi no Kamako, 14, 22
Nakatomi no Kamatari, 45
Nakatomi no Katsumi, 23
Nakayama line (Hokke=Nichiren lineages), 178
namu amida butsu see nenbutsu
Naniwa, 22

Nanjō Bun'yū, 221
Nanto rokushū, 56
Nanto-shichi-daiji, 56
Nanzenji, *116*, 146, 147
Nara period, 31, 45, 48, 49, 51, 53–7, 59, 60, 66, 68, 82
Negoroji (Negorodera), *116*, 155, 181, 183, 197
nenbundosha, 61, 73, 75, 82
nenbutsu (namu amida butsu), **89**, 92, 105, 117–21, 125n8, 139, 140, 158, 164n1, 175, 180, 188, 199–200
   odori nenbutsu, 105, 121
   nenbutsu honzon, 175
nendai ki, 150
nenjū gyōji (nenjūgyōji sho), 88
Nichiren, 4, 124-5, 139, 152, 160, 219, 222, 223, 225, 226, 234, 235
   Nichiren lineages (Nichiren shū), 124, 141, 152, 159-60, 164n3, 164n4, 177, 184, 185, 197, 199, 213, 219, 222, 223, 226, 233, 235, 236, 242, 243
   Nichiren-*shugi*, 219
Nihon ryōiki (= *Nihonkoku genpō zen'aku ryōiki*), 66, 67, 80, 81
Nihon sandai jitsuroku, 88
Nihon shoki (alt. *Nihongi*), 13–14, 16–32, 34, 37, 38n8, 46, 47, 52
Nijūgokajō goyuigō, 95
nikkei (Skt. *uṣṇīṣa*), 36
Nikkō (Nichiren-lineage monk), 141
Nikkō (site, complex), 183, 187
nikujiki saitai, 213
Ninchō, 197, 199
Ningai, 10, 99
Ninnaji, 10, 79, 100, 103–5, 108, 111, *116*, 126n24, *155*
Ninnōkyō, 52
Ninshō, 122, 199
Nishida Kitarō, 237
Nishigori no Tsubu (alt. Nishikori no Tsufu), 32
Nishitani Keiji, 237–8
Nisshin, 178
Nisshō, 141

Niwano Nikkyō, 223, 235
Nō (Theater, or Noh) (Sarugaku), 100, 142, 149
Nōshin, 154–6, 165n14
Nurishichikei (K. Norisach'igye), 13
Nyohō sonshō hō, 92
Nyojō (Ch. Rujing), 123
nyonin kekkai, 160
nyūbu, 98
nyūjō shinkō, 95

Ōama, Prince, 47
Ōbaku (Zen) lineages, 187–8
ōbō buppō, 176
Obon, 243
ōchō, 96
Oda Nobunaga, 178, 180
Ōe no Masafusa, 94–5, 106, 114
o'fumi, 175
Ogasawara Sadamune, 147
Ogawa Eiji, 243
Ōhara (Ōhara mondō), 94, 108, 117, 190
Ōjin, 96
ōjō (Pure Land birth) (*ōjōden*, *Ōjōyōshū*), 92–5, 114, 117, 120
Ōkubo Ryōshun, 79, 83, 84
Ōmine (mountain range), 97, 108, *155*, 158, 181
Ōmiwa *see* Miwa
O'mizutori, 192
Ōmuraji Mononobe no Okoshi 大連物部 尾輿, 272
Ōnin war (Ōnin/Bunmei war), 2, 5, 6, 9, 171–4, 175–6, 178, 201n2, 201n5
Onjōji (= Miidera), 7, 76, 90, 93, 98, 157, 180–181, 185, 201n4, 246
onmyōji (Yin-Yang masters, practitioners), 8, 159, 179–80, 186, 192
ōsei fukkō, 209
oshi, 157, 192
Ōtomo, Prince, 47
Ōuchi Seiran, 218
Owarida, 14
Ōyama, 192
Ōyama Seiichi, 28, 38n14, 62, 63, 83

Paekche *see* Kudara
petto kuyō, 243
Piggott, Joan, 14–16, 38n5, 38n9, 39n19, 46,
　52, 83, 85
pilgrimage, 4, 93, 95–8, 101, 109–10, 140,
　154, 162, 165n12, 192, 194, 200, 244,
　245
　confraternities (*kō*), 196
　Kumano pilgrimage, 97–8
　Shikoku pilgrimage, 192–3, 246–7
　Saikoku pilgrimage, 191, 193, *193*, 245–6
Pop (King), 31
preaching (*shōdō, sekkyō, e-toki*), 6, 8 51, 63,
　99, 112, 113–14, 140, 154, 161, 179,
　184, 190–191, 194
Pure Land, 36, 67, 70, 75
Pure Land lineages *see* Jōdo shū

rahotsu 36
raigō, 94
Raiyu, 155
Rambelli, Fabio, 137, 142–3, 151, 197
Rankei Dōryū (Ch. Lanxi Daolong), 162
Reader, Ian, 39n23, 192, 193, 237, 247
Reiki kanjō, 137
Reitan, 200
Reiunji, 199
Reiyūkai Kyōdan, 222, 223, 224, 226, 235
Reizei (poetic house), 149
renga, 142
Rengeō'in (= Sanjūsangendō), 106
Rennyo, 6, 7, 119, 174–6, 177, 178, 179–80,
　191
Rentai, 190
Rihō, 198
rinjū gyōgi, 94
rinne, 67
Rinzai Zen lineages; (Ch. Linji Chan), 10,
　98, 110, 115, 136, 144, 145–8, 159,
　165n8, 187–9, 198, 201, 202n10,
　219–20
risshi, 30
Risshō ankokuron, 124, 141
Risshō Kōsei-kai (Dai Nippon Risshō
　Kōsei-kai), 222–4, 226, 234, 235–6

Risshū (alt. Ritsu; Precepts lineages), 57, 61,
　64, 70, 121, 158, 162–3
　Jōdo Precepts (Jōdo ritsu) movement,
　199
　Shingon risshū (Shingon Ritsu), 122, 123,
　159, 162, 190, 199, 202n15
ritsu (= *ritsuryō*, distinct from Risshū/Ritsu
　above), 46, 53, 60–63, 64–5, 70, 81, 85
riyaku, 54
rōei, 102, 110
rokudai, 78
rokudō (alt. *rikudō*) (also called *rokushu*,
　rokkai), 67
Rokuonji (= Kinkakuji), *116*
rongi, 126n16, 165n5, 174
Ruppert, Brian, 96, 147, 158, 161
ryō, 46
Ryōchū, 139
Ryōgen (912–985), 90, 91, 135, 182
Ryōgen (1295–1336), 140
ryōi, 66
Ryōnin, 120
Ryōun, 47
ryū (sub-lineage = *ryūha*), 10, 106, 136
　hōryū (Dharma lineage), 91, 92, 106,
　126n23, 149
　monryū, 103
ryūdōsei (fluidity), 96
Ryūkoku University, 198
Ryūzai, 181

sabetsu kaimyō, 9, 239
sacred works (*shōgyō*), 6, 103, 106–8, 110
Saga Tennō, 77
Saichō (also called Dengyō Daishi), 61,
　69–77, 83, 84
Saidaiji, 10, 56, 123, 146, 158–9, 163
sai-e, 51
Saigyō, 111, 148, 153, 165n12, 192
Sai'in Mi-eidō, 191
Saikoku pilgrimage *see* pilgrimage
Saimei Tennō, 49
Saimyōji, 199
saisei itchi, 210, 211
Saisen, 95, 114

Saishōkō, 113
Saishōōkyō, 63
Sakaino Kōyō, 214
Sakuden, 189–90
Śākyamuni (J. Shaka), 3, 13, 52, 89, 95, 125, 151, 179, 199, 213, 221, 236
  Shaka Triad, 33–7
Sanbō'e, 88–90, 91, 93, 97, 101–2, 110
Sanbō'in (cloister, lineage), 107–8, 144, 155, 157, 181–2
sangaku, 142
Sangō, 61, 107
Sangyō gisho, 27
Sanjūbanjin, 152
sanjūni sō, 36
sanmitsu (sanmitsugyōbō), 78
sanmon, 76
Sanmonto, 140
Sannō, 150–152, 153
Sanron, 10, 30, 39n19, 57, 61, 62, 70, 79, 117
Sanzen'in, 94, 108, *155*
Sarugaku *see* Nō
sazen, 93
Sei Shōnagon, 90
Seigen, 108
Seimei-ō (K. Sŏng Myŏng Wang), 13, 16, 19, 29
Seirei shū, 114
Seisetsu Shōchō (Ch. Qingzhuo Zhengcheng), 146–7
Seishin-shugi movement, 215
Seishinkai (journal), 215
Seisui shō, 190
Seizan line *see* Jōdo shū
sekkan, 71, 87
semui-in, 36
sendatsu, 97, 157
sengi, 137, 192
sengoku (warring states), *sengokuki*, 171, 177, 180
Senjuji, *116*, 140, *155*
Senkyōji, 158
sennichi kaihōgyō, 244–5
Sennyūji, 146, 158

Senshi, 101–2
Sensō'e, 185
sesshō, 71
setsuwa, 66, 80
settai, 246
shabyō sōjō, 156
Shaka butsu *see* Śākyamuni
Shaka Triad *see* Śākyamuni
Shaku Sōen, 219–20
Shaku Unshō, 213, 216
shakubuku, 234
shakyōsho, 57, 59–60
shami, 64
shamini, 64
shanago, 73
shasei, 199
Shiba Tachito (alt. Shiba Tatto, Shiba Tatsuto), 18, 32, 34
shibunritsu, 74, 199
shidai (shidai sho), 92, 106
shidaiji, 49
shido (shidosō, shido sōni), 61, 76
shidō, 196
Shihi (K. Sabi), 31
shi'in, 103
shikai, 153
shikaku, 151
shikan taza see Dōgen
shikango, 73
Shikoku pilgrimage *see* pilgrimage
Shima, 32
Shimaji Mokurai, 218
Shimotsuke Yakushiji, 155
shin bukkyō (journal), 72, 214
Shin Bukkyōto Dōshikai, 214
shin shin shūkyō, 236
Shinbutsu (monk), 140
shinbutsu bunri (shinbutsu bunri rei), 212
shinbutsu hanzen, 212
shinbukkyō no jidai, 171
Shingi Shingon *see* Esoteric Buddhism
shingon (Skt. *mantra*), 78
Shingon (Shingon Mikkyō) *see* Esoteric Buddhism
Shingon Ritsu *see* Risshū

shinjin datsuraku see Dōgen
shinjitsu hōdo, 118
Shinjō, 154
shinkoku, 125, 150
shinmitsugyō, 78
Shinnen, 193
Shinnyoen, 236
Shinpukuji, *116,* 145, 147, 154–6, 165n13
Shinran (also called Kenshin daishi; Rel.
    Shinran shōnin go'innen), 117–19, 120,
    135, 140–141, 162–3, 175, 184, 191,
    198, 215, 226
Shinri kinshin, 217
shinshō, 153
Shintō, 1, 4, 24, 98, 165n11, 179, 182, 194,
    201n6, 209–10, 212
    Buddhist Shintō, 137, 150–153, 182, 192
    Fukkō (Restoration) Shintō, 210–211
    Separation of Buddhism and, 210,
    212–13
shinsen (Ch. *shen-xian*), 95
Shinzei, 108, 111, 127n28
shirabyōshi, 100
Shiragi (K. Silla), 15, 16
shishu zanmai, 244
shitaku bukkyō, 18
shitennō, 51
Shitennōji, *116, 155*
shō (shōmotsu), 92, 105, 142, 159, 179, *182,*
    190, 193–5
Shōbō (monk), 79, 135, 182–3
Shōbō genzō see Dōgen
shōbōritsu, 199
Shōchōju'in, *116,* 136
shōdō see preaching
shōen, 111
Shōgei, 137, 197
Shōgo'in, 98, 181
shogunate, 2, 5, 7, 120, 136, 137, 139, 141,
    144, 146–7, 149, 153, 158, 171–7, 184,
    185–7, 192, 196–8, 209, 211
shōgyō see sacred works
shōhō, 67
shōjin, 98

Shōkai, 120
Shōkaku, 107–8
Shōken, 108
Shōkō, 139
Shōkōmyō'in, 106
Shōkū, 119, 139
Shoku Nihongi, 49, 50, 63, 66
Shōman-gyō (Skt. *Śrīmālādevī sihanāda*
    sūtra), 27
Shōmangyō gisho, 27
Shōmu Tennō, 49, 57, 58, 59, 64, 65, 80, 81
shōmyō, 102
Shōmyōji, 10, *155*
shōnin, 92, 191
shōō, 187
Shōrai mokuroku, 174
Shōren'in, 108, 138, 140
Shōshin, 117
Shōshinge (= *Shōshin nenbutsuge*), 175, 184
shoshū kengaku, 115, 153, 178
shosonbō, 156
Shōsōrin ryakushingi, 188
Shōtoku, (Shōtoku Taishi, Umayado no
    miko, Senior Prince Shōtoku) 20, 24,
    25–30, 33, 35, 37, 62
Shōtoku Tennō, 65, 66, 80, 82
shū (= *shūha*), 10, 11, 56–7, 70, 77, 107, 115,
    117, 119, 121, 124, 136–42, 179–81,
    184–91, 194–6
    Buddhist academic scholarship and, 221
    Early modern precept movements and,
    198–201, 213
    Temple Buddhism and, 241–8
    Tokugawa-era Buddhist scholasticism
    and, 197–8
Shugendō *see* Mountain asceticism
shugenja see Mountain asceticism
shuhō, 77, 113, 142
Shūi kotokuden'e, 140
Shukaku, 103–5, 126n23
Shukongōjin, 98, 100
shukubō, 157
shūmon daigaku, 144
Shun'e, 104–5

Shuni'e, 192
Shunjō, 121
Shunpan, 160
shuto, 100, 173
Silla *see* Shiragi
Smits, Ivo, 105
Snodgrass, Judith, 220
sōbō, 103–5, 126n21, 154, 156
Soga, 21, 23–5, 28, 29, 30, 31, 32, 33, 34, 45, 46
Soga no Iname, 14, 22
Soga no Iruka, 45
Soga no Umako, 23–5, 31–2
sōgakutō, 160
sōgisha, 243
sōgiya, 243
sōgō, 60
sōjō, 30, 52, 60
Sōka Gakkai (Sōka Kyōiku Gakkai), 210, 222–3, 226, 233–5
Sōka Kyōikugaku Taikei, 222
Sōkokubunji, 58
sokui kanjō, 149, 153, 156
sokuichi 120
sokushin jōbutsu (*Sokushin jōbutsu gi*), 78, 154
Sōmin (Ch. Sengmin), 47
Sone Masato, 71–2
sōniryō, 53, 60, 61, 63, 81
Sonnō Hōbutsu Daidōdan, 218
Sonoda Kōyū, 25, 46, 48, 49, 52
Sonshi, 88
Sonshō'in (Tōdaiji) 100
Sonshun, 152
sōsai bukkyō, 171
soshi see ancestral founders
sōshiki bukkyō, 233, 242
Sōshō, 139
sōshokukyō, 99
Sōtō lineages (Sōtō shū, Sōtō Zen), 123, 139, 145, 159, 171, 177, 184, 189, 194, 196, 198, 199, 213, 218, 238–9
sōzu, 52, 60
Staggs, Kathleen M., 227, 228
state temples, 48–50

state-sponsored Buddhist rituals, 46, 48, 50–52
Stavros, Matthew, 148
Stone, Jacqueline I., 72, 90, 92, 94, 115, 123, 124, 142, 144, 145, 152, 156, 159, 160, 178, 239, 241
Sueki Fumihiko, 105, 119, 145, 150, 172, 176, 178, 179, 183, 215, 218, 219, 221, 224, 225,
Suiko Tennō, 24–7, 30, 35, 39n19, 47
Sukehito, 111
Suzuki Daisetsu Teitarō (D. T. Suzuki), 146–7, 220
Suzuki Shōsan, 184, 187, 188

Ta'amida-butsu Shinkyō, 141
Tachikawa (Tachikawa-ryū), 149, 154
Taichū, 190
Taihō *ritsuryō*, 53
Taika (Taika *kaishin*), 46, 48, 52, 53
Taimadera, 190
Taimitsu *see* '"Tendai esoteric Buddhism" under Esoteric Buddhism
Taira Masayuki, 115, 119, 138, 159, 161
taizōkai, 78
Taizong, Emperor (Tang dynasty), 49
Takada monto, 140, 175
Takahashi Shin'ichirō, 103, 139
Takahatayama (Takahatayama Fudō dō), 155, *155*
Takaosanji, 77
Takashima Beihō, 214
Takayama Chogyū, 219
Takuan Sōhō, 187
Takuga, 141–2
Tamamuro Fumio, 183
Tamamuro Taijō, 53, 233, 242
Tamura Enchō, 18, 31, 38n16, 53
Tamura Yoshirō, 36, 50, 79
Tanabe, George J., Jr., 39n23
Tanabe Hajime, 237, 238
Tanaka Chigaku, 218–19, 225
Tang dynasty, 45, 46, 53, 55, 81
Tani no ryū, 92

tariki, 118, 188, 215, 238
tassho, 176
tatari, 247
Tea culture, 189
Teeuwen, Mark, 96, 127n30, 151–2, 156
Tenbun no ran, 171, 178
Tendai lineages (Ch. Tiantai), 4, 7, 61,
       69–71, 72–6, 79, 88, 90–94, 98, 99, 102,
       105–6, 108, 109, 113, 115, 117–18, 120,
       124, 138, 139, 140–141, 144–5, 151–4,
       159–60, 177, 179, 180, 183, 185, 187,
       197, 213, 241–2, 244–5
Tengu zōshi, 148
   tengu, 192, 196
Tenji (alt. Tenchi) Tennō, 45, 47, 50
Tenjiku, 13
Tenkai, 183–4
Tenmu Tennō, 45, 47–52, 59
Tennō, 14, 20, 37n3, 47, 54, 57, 60–61, 66, 69,
       71, 77, 88
tentō, 179
Tetsugaku-dō, 218
Tetsugakukan, 217
Tezuka Osamu, 248
Toby, Ronald P., 47, 69
Toda Jōsei, 222, 234
Tōdaiji, 4, 10, 49, 55, 56–60, 65, 72, 74, 77,
       79, **89**, 98, 100, 109, 112, 114, 117, 121,
       139, 146, 158, 191, 192
   Tōdaiji yōroku, 96
Tōfukuji, 10, 98–99, 122–3, 144, 147, 156,
       173
Tōji, 77, **89**, 108, 158, 191, 202n12
Tōjiji, 148
tokudo, 61
Tokugawa Iemitsu, 173
Tokugawa Ieyasu, 183
Tokuitsu, 74
Tominaga Nakamoto, 200
Tōmitsu *see* "Shingon Mikkyō" under
       Esoteric Buddhism
Tonkō (Ch. Dunhuang), 27, 38n6
Tōnan'in, 79
Tori Busshi, 18, 34, 36, 40

Tōshōdaiji, 56, 57, 64
Tōshōgū (Tōshō Daigongen), 183, 187
tosō, 98, 157
Towazugatari, 163
Toyotomi Hideyoshi, 172, 183
Toyome, 32
Toyouradera (alt. Gangōji), 80
Tōzan-ha, 181–2, 185
True Pure Land lineages *see* Jōdo Shinshū
Tsuchimikado Michichika, 139
tsuina, 61
Tsuda Sōkichi, 28
Tsuji Zennosuke, 171–2, 197
Tsurugaoka Hachimangū, 136

Uchimura Kanzō, 217
Uda Tennō, 79
Uejima Susumu, 4, 100, 109, 125n10,
       126n15, 126n24,
uji, 15, 16, 37n2
ujidera, 23, 31
ujigami, 54
ujiko shirabe, 212
ujizoku (*ujizoku bukkyō*), 29, 30, 39n17, 45,
       53, 72
Uji (site) *see* Byōdō'in
Umayado (Umayado no miko) *see*
       Shōtoku
Ungo Kiyō, 188
Urabe Kanekuni, 182
Urabonkyō (Ch. *Yulanpen jing*), 163
Usa Hachimangū, 96
ushirodo, 98
Ushiyama Yoshiyuki, 81, 82

Vinaya *see* Risshū

waka, 101–3, 105, 126n19, 148–9, 190, 198
Wakabayashi, Haruko, 148
Wakan rōei shū, 102, 110
wakō dōjin see Kami-Buddha relations
wasan, 119, 175
Washizuka Hiromitsu, 36, 39n16
Williams, Duncan, 144, 183, 194, 197

yake nohara, 173
Yakujō (Bodhisattva Superior Medicine), 36
Yakuō (Bodhisattva Medicine King), 36
Yakushi (Yakushi Nyorai), 34, 35, 96, 196
Yakushiji, 49, 51, 56, 64, 66, 89, 155
yamaguchi no shūron, 179
Yamashinadera, 49 *see also* Kōfukuji
Yamatai, 38n6
Yamato, 13, 15, 16, 18, 19, 20, 21, 22, 23, 25,
    29–34, 37n2, 37n3, 37n4, 38n5, 39n17,
    39n19, 45, 46, 47, 54, 68, 80
Yamato Great King(s), 16, 20, 25, 31, 54
Yijing *see* Gijō
yogan-in (Skt. *vara mudrā*), 36
yojō, 198
Yōfukuji, 116, 136
Yōkan, 117, 139
Yōmei Tennō, 24, 26, 35
Yomiuri Shinbun, 226
yoriai, 175
Yōrō *ritsuryō*, 63, 61
Yōsai, 110, 112, 123, 125n8, 144, 145, 148,
    153, 165n12, 202n10
Yoshida Kanetomo, 152
Yoshida Kazuhiko, 24, 38n8, 38n12, 39n17,
    45, 49, 50, 53, 54, 62, 68, 82, 136, 161,
    171
Yoshihito, 159
Yoshino (=Kinpusen), 28, 97, 116, 155,
    157–8, 181, 185
Yoshishige no Yasutane, 102
Yōten ki, 151

yugyō, 120
    Yugyō-ha, 141–2
Yuima, 27, 90
Yuima'e, 90
Yuimagyō (Skt. *Vimalakīrti sūtra*), 27, 90
Yumedono (Yumedono Kannon), 34, 249
Yūshin (K. Ungjin), 31
yūsō, 100
yūzū nenbutsu, 112, 120
    Yūzū nenbutsu e-maki, 120, 121

zaike, 152
zasu, 75, 76, 107
Zeami, 149
Zen (Ch. Chan) (Zen shū) *see* Rinzai Zen
    lineages; Sōtō Zen lineages
zenchishiki (*chishiki*), 93, 142
Zendō (Ch. Shandao), 117, 197
zenji, 30, 65
Zenkōji, 119, 140
zenkon, 95
Zenrinji, 189
Zenshin'ni, 80
zenshu (temple assistants), 7, 180
Zentsūji, 116, 155
Zenzai dōji (Skt. Sudhana), 101
Zenzō-ni, 32
Zhiyi *see* Chigi
Zhung-feng Ming-ben *see* Chūhō Myōhon
Zōjōji, 197, 200
Zoku kōsōden, 63
Zonkaku, 198